THE BORDERS OF ISLAM

The Borders of Islam

Exploring Huntington's Faultlines, from Al-Andalus to the Virtual Ummah

Edited by

Stig Jarle Hansen, Atle Mesøy, Tuncay Kardas

Columbia University Press
New York

Columbia University Press
Publishers Since 1893
New York   Chichester, West Sussex
Copyright © 2009 Stig Jarle Hansen, Atle Mesøy, Tuncay Kardas and the Contributors
All rights reserved

Library of Congress Cataloging-in-Publication Data

The borders of Islam : exploring Huntington's faultlines, from Al-Andalus
to the virtual ummah / edited by Stig Jarle Hansen, Atle Mesøy, Tuncay Kardas.
    p. cm.
Includes bibliographical references.
ISBN 978-0-231-15422-2 (alk. paper)
    1. Huntington, Samuel P. 2. East and West. 3. Civilization, Islamic. 4. Islam—Relations.
I. Hansen, Stig Jarle. II. Mesøy, Atle. III. Kardas, Tuncay. IV. Title.

CB251.B67 2009
909'.1—dc22

2009003311

∞

Columbia University Press books are printed on permanent and durable acid-free paper.
This book is printed on paper with recycled content.
Printed in India

c 10 9 8 7 6 5 4 3 2 1

References to Internet Web sites (URLs) were accurate at the time of writing. Neither
the author nor Columbia University Press is responsible for URLs that may have expired
or changed since the manuscript was prepared.

Contents

CONTENTS

Preface and Acknowledgements

This volume seeks to offer the reader a systematic, critical, in-depth investigation of some of the most important states that are situated on what Samuel P. Huntington defined as "Islam's bloody borders". There is a great need to go beyond the media headlines in order to understand the political, cultural, ideological, and religious factors that influence political dynamics on the so-called borders of Islam. *The Borders of Islam* explores how religion influences conflicts, insurgency and politics in the twenty countries that have been chosen for in-depth studies.

The book is the product of a large collective effort by all the contributors, as well as commentators from all around the world. We would like to convey our deepest thanks to all the researchers who have given their valuable input and comments, as well as the Norwegian Research Council that supported the copy-editing process. We would also like to thank the many interviewees who discussed with our contributors the themes addressed. Last but not least, we would like to thank our publisher, Michael Dwyer—you have been incredibly patient.

Stig Jarle Hansen *Oslo, October 2008*
Atle Mesøy
Tuncay Kardas

INTRODUCTION

Huntington and "Islam's bloody borders"

Stig Jarle Hansen, Atle Mesøy, Tuncay Kardas

What is the clash?

In recent years the expression/theory "clash of civilizations" has been used frequently in the media, often referring to conflicts involving Islam.[1] The examples of incidents interpreted as signs of a clash of civilizations are many. Theo van Gogh, the Dutch film maker, was for example killed by a radical violent Islamist because he produced a movie with a critical perspective on gender equality and Islam.[2] The killer, Moroccan-born Mohammed Bouyeri, declared the murder to be part of a holy war, a war of religions.[3] The expression "clash of civilizations" was first used to describe the relationship between a supposedly western civilization and Islamic civilization in Bernard Lewis' 1990 article "The Roots of Muslim Rage".[4] However, it became most associated with Samuel P. Huntington who employed the term in an article published in 1993 in *Foreign Affairs*.[5] According to Huntington, future conflicts will increasingly be ignited by cultural and religious issues.[6] Huntington followed this in 1996 with the book *The Clash of Civilizations and the Remaking of World Order*. He described Islam as being the most conflict-prone civilization. Moreover, Huntington claimed that the borders of Islamic civilization and the rest of the world, "Islam's bloody borders", were filled with war and conflict that supposedly proved his point.[7]

1

While there have been several quantitative research projects examining his thesis, systematic in-depth case studies of the various border zones of the civilizations have been lacking. This book systematically examines the border zones of Islamic civilization by investigating whether events and local dynamics in these border zones contribute to a global confrontation between Islamic and surrounding civilizations.[8] Studying cases from a wide range of countries such as Afghanistan, Bosnia, Bangladesh, Chechnya, Ethiopia, Indonesia, Pakistan, Philippines, Nigeria, Somalia, Sudan, Spain, and Turkey, the book goes beyond solely examining the dynamics of confrontation in the areas physically bordering Islamic civilization, by also studying the new border areas created by patterns of emigration. Islamic enclaves in traditional Christian or secular societies such as the United Kingdom, France, Scandinavia and the United States are explored. Lastly, it studies the new global border, the Internet, as Huntington focused on increased communication contributing to a civilizational discourse, by making civilizational communication easier as geographical distance becomes a less important barrier to communication.

The thesis

Huntington's thesis is, in short, that future conflicts will increasingly be between what he calls "civilizations".[9] Civilizations are according to him "defined both by objective elements, such as language, history, religion, institutions and by the subjective self-identification of people". Although religion is only one out of many defining criteria of a Huntingtonian civilization, and although the borders of what he defines as civilizational entities and the world religions at times are different, he names three civilizations according to world religions, the Orthodox, Hindu and Islamic civilizations.[10] In 1993 and 1996, when he wrote his major articles, Huntington claimed that religion and religious identity are becoming more prominent as political factors.[11] Huntington suggested that the importance of religious cleavages will rise because of the increased contacts and interaction between the different parts of the world.[12] Through the information technology revolution, religious and political groups have increased their ability to disseminate information and communicate across borders. For Huntington, this communication in turn weakens local identities and traditions; in consequence, broader identities, such as religious identities, will become strengthened.[13] Old values and beliefs are constantly being challenged by new impulses, what were previously believed to be sacred values are desecrated, and relativism is spreading. To Huntington this may be one of the reasons why people are searching for religious answers with the comfort and foundational beliefs these environments can promise.[14] Samuel Huntington, supported by notable scholars commenting upon Islam in particular, such as Gilles Kepel, claims that religion gives a sense of belonging in the modern world, filled with people moving between classes, countries, and even families.[15] Huntington's "clash" is thus not only a result of differences between ancient civilizations and religions; it is equally a result of the factors that dominate the modern world, and of modernity itself. Some of the most important ideologies and belief systems, that act as alternatives to religion, are also in decline. Capitalism has its problems, and many fail to believe in the solution offered by the free market. Nationalism, the worship of the state and the nation, was undermined not least by critical scholarship attacking the perception of some kind of primordial foundation of the state, and even the justification of the state itself.[16] Communism was discredited because of the fall of the Soviet Union. On the other hand, the collapse of the Soviet empire led to the rise of the local ally of the United States in the Middle East, Saudi Arabia. It crucially removed the many obstacles, such as Soviet support for Baathist/Marxist regimes in the Middle East, and a possible ideological counterbalance that hindered Saudi Arabia from spreading radical texts and missionaries around the world. Additionally, the collapse of the Soviet Union was used by extremists to demonstrate that a superpower could be destroyed by militant Islamic networks, focusing on the role the war in Afghanistan had supposedly played in this collapse.[17] Secular Pan-Arabism/Baathism had been severely discredited by the failure of Nasser's Egyptian regime to fight wars with Israel efficiently, after the huge losses in the 1967 war, which sparked a revival of religiously-based militant movements.[18] Last, the weakening of the state might accelerate developments leading to a clash of civilizations, as loyalty towards the state weakens, and the state becomes less able to govern its citizens, there is ideological space for civilisational loyalties.

Huntington points to the borders of one specific civilization, defined by religion, namely the Islamic, as particularly problematic. Building on Ted Gurr's quantitative studies of ethnopolitical conflicts, he draws the conclusion that Muslims in the early 1990's were engaged in more inter-group violence than non-Muslims.[19] Although Huntington argues that Islam was spread with the sword and that it glorifies militaristic virtues,[20] he does not claim that these values of Islam created most of the conflicts in the past, but rather that the values, in combination with the effects of modernity and of

3

demographics, will spark conflict in the future. He also emphasises that the vast demographic growth of Muslims[21] and the fact that many Muslims are young and unemployed as having the potential to spark conflicts. The combination of the above factors will, according to Huntington, create conflicts between Muslims and non-Muslims. Huntington employed the expression "Islam's bloody borders" to illustrate the effect.[22]

To Huntington there are three types of civilizational conflicts: those between states that are dominant in each civilization (core states), international fault line conflicts, (those between two states on the fault line of a civilizational border), and finally, domestic fault line conflicts, taking place within a single state. This book will analyse the second and third versions of supposedly civilizational conflicts on the borders of Islam; it seeks to explore the political and conflict dynamics of what Huntington defines as "Islam's bloody borders", to examine the role of religion, and of Islam in particular.

Several newer, quantitative (statistical) studies have seemingly underlined the increased centrality of Islam in conflict. Monica Duffy Toft demonstrates how rebel groups who identified with Islam were far more involved in religious civil wars, and that religious wars were longer and more intense.[23] Andrej Tusicisny claims that: "the Islamic civilization remains the most conflict-prone".[24] Tanya Ellingsen suggests that the importance of religion has grown after the Cold War, and that increased religiosity makes intra-state conflict more probable. Ellingsen underlines that the economic conditions and the regime type of the country in question are key elements.[25] Fox maintains that after 2002, following the Iranian Revolution, religion has been an element in the majority of all domestic conflicts that meet the definition of state failure.[26] He also shows however, that Muslims are statistically more likely to fight with other Muslims than with members of other religions, thus that religion and civilization are not always overlapping. Furthermore he illustrates the crudeness of the term "civilization", which is used to join together several religious sub-groups, for civilizational entities that Huntington emphasized were strongly influenced by religion (the Islamic); and entities in which religion played a minor part (the African).

Cleavages and flexibility

Religious differences within Islam have been the theme of another group of Huntington's critics. Halliday, Beedham, Yamazaki, Walt, Gurr, Sen, Kader,

Heilbrunner, Rocecrance, and Tipson, all argue that civilizations, including the Islamic, are divided by internal cleavages.[27] They are supported by statistical analyses conducted by Fox and Sandler.[28]

Islam is divided, as are all world religions. The conflict between the respective belligerents in a leadership struggle within Islam that resulted in two different interpretations of Islam, Sunni and Shia, has continued up to this day, and has played a major role in later wars. It was a factor in driving Iran into becoming a *de facto* ally of the US when the latter intervened in Afghanistan in 2001. The American-led Northern Alliance received support as well as military advisors from Iran, partly because of the Afghan Taliban regime's persecution of Shias.[29] Moreover, the Sunni/Shia divide has fuelled civil wars in Lebanon, Yemen, Syria, and Iraq. The Sunnis too are divided: different legal schools, based on the works of Muhammed al-Shafi, Malik ibn Annas, Abu Hanfa and Ahmad ibn Hanbal, were established in the seventh and eighth centuries. Sufism, another, often quietist, strand of Islam, also developed.[30] The divisions between the various Sunni law schools, Shafi'i, Maliki, Hanafi and Hanbali are on their own not major: traditionally all of the law schools accept the legitimacy of their rivals. Sufism was also in general accepted as a part of Islam. This was to change within the Hanafi school of thought when Muhammad ibn Abd al-Wahhab (1703–1792) reformed the works of Ahmad ibn Hanbal. Ibn Abd al-Wahhab's book, *Kitab al-Tawhid* ("Book of Monotheism"), condemned the worship of ancestors, explicitly targeting the Sufi practice of invoking a Sufi saint in prayer. He also condemned Shiism and several of the customs within other law schools, creating deep fissures within Islam.

However, it is again necessary to underline the importance of modernity and modernization in Huntington's thesis. He sees the clash of civilizations as a product of a process in which local identities are weakened, in a world that is experiencing a renewed focus on religion partly because of this weakening. A paradox of the previously described resurgence in religion is that it is actually a process of weakening religion as well as its strengthening. Old institutions are weakened, the law schools are increasingly confused with each other, and the rich philosophical tradition of Islam is fading. Somalia could serve as an example: Salafists and war put pressure on the traditional Islamic traditions of that country. The growth of new and poorly educated but nevertheless religiously active strata contributed to a weakening of the traditional Somali religious institutions, and a growth of a new generation of self-appointed religious leaders with little formal religious education.[31] This is not only a Somali phenomenon, for those Oliver Roy refers to as "new intellectuals" have emerged globally. Intellectuals not trained in the religious orthodoxy, who nevertheless claim to be religious leaders, seem to fill an ideological vacuum in the whole Islamic world.[32] Several of these new scholars are seemingly, at times, able to span old cleavages within the religion, often also gathering supporters for extremist organizations. The case of Abu Hamza al-Misri, a former bouncer at strip clubs in Soho, London, who ended up as an extremist Sheik and a leader of the militant extremists in the Finsbury Park Mosque in London before he was imprisoned, is perhaps one of the most notable examples.

Weakened religious structures and the lack of traditional anchorage might paradoxically lead to cooperation between members of previously hostile religious groups and clashes of civilizations even in the midst of what Huntington defines as "Western Civilization". This volume will also examine developments such as new structures of information and the Internet, and explore how the latter might build bridges spanning old cleavages within Islam by breaking down old religious entities and by allowing "new intellectuals" to emerge.

National interest and small group action

Some of the bloodiest wars in the history of mankind have been between states of supposedly similar civilizations and/or religions, a fact perhaps explained by the many ideological, cultural and theological divisions within civilizations.[33] Indeed, Huntington has been criticized because he supposedly fails to see the cleavages and fissures within civilizational entities. The policies of the various states within a civilization are seen as following state interests rather than being based on an abstract idea of civilization, or some form of religious solidarity.[34] States within so-called Islamic civilization have often been split and have seldom managed to act in concert, at times supporting non-Muslim countries, even supposedly enemies, against members of their own civilization. There are many examples of this: in 1976 supposedly Muslim Syria even supported the Christian Lebanese militia against other Muslims because of national interest. The Christian Maronite militia was also supported by Israel, which technically put Syria on the same side as Israel. Muslim countries have also often engaged in civil wars and covert actions in other Muslim countries, sometimes to the detriment of their war efforts against "enemies outside their civilization". According to Anwar al-Sadat, former president of Egypt, in 1967 Egypt for example deployed 30 per cent of its infantry, 16 per cent of its armour, and 10 per cent of its artillery in Yemen to support its allies in the Yemeni civil war (1962–1970).[35] Sadat claims that this seriously weakened Egypt in its 1967 war against Israel. Despite knowing that Israel was a potent non-Muslim enemy, Egypt chose to contribute heavily to fighting fellow Muslims rather than use these resources to fight non-Muslims.

Notably, Huntington acknowledges the fact that state interests remain essential, but he also claims that the states are losing power and will lose even more power in the future. To Huntington, the "clash of civilizations" is becoming more essential because of the recent global trends weakening the power of states. States are losing control over money flows, the flow of ideas, technology and people.[36] People move from place to place, global news networks such as Al-Jazeera and CNN spread news and ideas across borders, as does the Internet. Also, new global actors have emerged: al-Qaeda, a non-state actor, created a watershed in international politics when it launched attacks against the World Trade Center, the Pentagon and possibly Capitol Hill on 11 September 2001. Polls in the United Kingdom suggested an increase in hostile attitudes towards Islam after September 11 and the various terrorist attacks in Europe, indicating that actions of relatively small groups can change public opinion in a country.[37] Indeed, in the case of al-Qaeda and the 9/11 terrorist attacks, actions of a single non-state organization indirectly triggered, and/or legitimized, two large wars, in Afghanistan and Iraq, as well as new alliances, and new bureaucratic structures, which drastically changed state structures and politics around the world. Huntington sees the state as weakened and national interests as becoming less important and/or having to take different forms, converging with the interest of the civilization in question, and making transnational religions more significant. In short, individuals and organizations are increasing their power compared to states, with individual interests often defined by a civilizational sense of belonging.[38] Huntington also sees regional entities such as the European Union creating new identities, which again have the potential to create new conflicts as civilizations united by such arrangements engage in competition.[39] Additionally, leaders might become more dependent on social sentiments, their weakened state apparatus putting them in need of popular support that civilizational rhetoric might conveniently create.

Grievances

On 30 June 2006, fifty-four civilians, thirty-four of them children, died during an Israeli attack on the Lebanese city of Qana.[40] The conflict between

Hezbollah and Israel lasted from 4 June until the ceasefire on 14 August 2006, and was broadcast around the world.[41] One of the authors saw how the campaign enraged Muslims in the relatively secular country of Turkey, and there were demonstrations in places as far away as in Mogadishu, Somalia.[42] In a sense this was the effect of modernity described by Huntington; that is, global news networks such as Al-Jazeera and CNN spreading the news around the world with consequent effects on civilizations. However, it also illustrates several points raised by the critics of Huntington who focus on how such grievances as the suffering and poverty of the Muslim world have fuelled the conflicts explored by his books.[43] Some critics go so far as claiming that Huntington was right when he claimed that there were conflicts along civilizational fault lines, but that he failed to understand why these conflicts occurred. Notably, scholars such as Thomas and Sayyid see the weakening of western hegemony, western ideology and western discourse as leading to an increasing relevance of religion and culture, but without sharing Huntington's other assumptions. For Thomas this is because of a search for non-western authenticity.[44] For Sayyid, who has a totally different epistemological approach to Huntington, the conflicts between non-western and western cultures and religion are a form of anti-western resistance.[45] Mohammed Ayoob follows this line of argument, while highlighting many of the mechanisms described by Huntington, most importantly western support for autocracies in the Middle East based on western secular ideologies, autocracies that failed to establish legitimacy and thus de-legitimized the supposedly western ideology they were based on. However, Ayoob adds that injustice could make Islamism the voice of the global poor.[46]

Political grievances may in a direct way contribute to hate and conflict. For instance, western states, the Soviet Union, China, and Cuba have supported highly repressive regimes in the Middle East. Egypt, a major receiver of American military aid, has actively used torture and systematic censorship of the press.[47] Iraq, having benefited from American, Soviet and Cuban military support, was equally repressive.[48] Repression and torture of religious activists have been an essential part of the policies of the allies of the great powers, to the extent that Esposito and Tamimi use the expression "militant secular fundamentalism" to describe their actions.[49] There are real reasons for these grievances, and they are prominent in the rhetoric of organizations for example al-Qaeda, such that Osama bin Laden could ask "How many acts of oppression, tyranny and injustice [have] you carried out, O callers to freedom?"[50] According to Fawaz A. Gerges, western support for local repressive regimes was a fundamental factor for several jihadist organizations in the change of focus from aiming at the removal of local regimes to targeting non-Islamic targets in the West.[51]

Significantly, the frontline fighters of al-Qaeda seem to be from relatively rich (middle class) families, and usually from families remote from the various conflicts, lending credibility to claims that personal grievances are not creating such extremism.[52] Nonetheless, in a world under the constant gaze of global news-networks, these frontline fighters will inevitably have been exposed to pictures from Lebanon and Palestine. After the Iraq invasion, images and stories from Iraq have seemingly been the main rallying symbol for the recruitment of jihadists.[53] Pictures from these conflicts are effectively used for recruitment and motivation sessions hosted by extremist organizations.[54] The messages on jihadist web sites exploring these conflicts are numerous, especially for the Iraq war. Names such as Faluja and Abu Ghraib have entered into the discourse of the jihadists, and pictures of prisoners tortured by American guards are extensively used. Indeed, of the twelve statements released by Osama bin Laden and Ayman al-Zawahiri in 2004, only one failed to mention Iraq.[55] The screening and distribution of gory videos from conflicts in the border zones of Islam was a vital recruitment strategy for London Imam Abu Hamza al-Misri, whose recruits were in turn involved in the 7 July 2005 attacks against the underground system in London.[56]

Repressive regimes, often supported by the West, can also play a "blame game" in which all ills can be blamed upon sources outside the control of the regime in question, namely western powers. Such regimes might encourage the media to print such hyped-up conspiracy theories as the obviously fake "Protocols of Zion the Wise" employed in the propaganda of Adolf Hitler, in order to distract attention from abysmal internal conditions.[57] As suggested by Edward Said, long-time critic of United States policies in the Middle East, this might even lead to a stereotyping of non-Muslims, including entities such as the United States, reinforcing the possibilities of a clash of civilizations.[58]

Of "clash" theories

Until quite recently, the study of "religion and politics" had been a rather neglected topic; it was not seen as an important factor in itself but rather as a mere instrument that could be manipulated by the existence of other dominating factors.[59] As argued by Philpott, the dominating approaches to international relations to a certain extent neglected religion, or claimed that at best it was an instrument that could be used to fool the masses into obedience. Classical Marxism saw religion as "opium for the people".[60] Realism, a theoretical approach to international relations that focuses on state interest and international anarchy as the main determining factors of international politics, left little room for religion in shaping national interests, and failed to examine the way religions can create supra-national loyalties.[61] The general realist claim was that states should place their own security and survival over compliance with any absolute moral obligation, even when such obligation is rooted in a rationally discernible common morality; as a result religious morality could and should not influence policy.[62] Liberalists neglected the topic; moreover, they predicted that religion was being replaced by rational calculations. During the 1960s and 1970s philosophers and social scientists such as Peter Berger pronounced that religion was dying and that rationalism was taking over.[63] As Scott Thomas claimed, what the world witnessed was rather a resurgence of religion.[64] Regimes such as Iran and the Soviet Union, which had tried to secularize their own populations, often with violence, collapsed. Indeed, religious issues now constitute a significant parcel of the international agenda.

Broadly speaking, there are three different approaches to the role of religion in politics.[65] The first view is that of the "primordialists", who point to the "autonomous conflict-generating power of religious difference" and claim that irreconcilable understandings of religious similarities and differences are and will be the primary causes of contemporary and future conflicts.[66] They hold that because the Cold War is over, the impact of religion will be increasingly felt on the foreign policy behaviour of states of relevant civilizations. Alliances between states of similar religious traditions and backgrounds against other states of cosmologies/civilizations that are built upon (rival) religious traditions will become increasingly common. The primordialist approach marshals a pragmatic and simplistic construction of religiosity as a self-contained practice in which certain subjects are forever locked. Variations in the interpretation of the values of a specific religion over time, for example why Christians have stopped burning witches, are neglected.

The second and perhaps biggest group is called "instrumentalists". They believe that the causes of clashes or political violence do not stem from differences in religious cosmologies but from "growing economic, social and political inequalities in and between nations".[67] They hold that political entrepreneurs often try to cloak existing cleavages in religious terms in such a way that their ability to mobilize their constituency is through instrumentalizing "old myths and sacred traditions for their own aggrandizement".[68] In some instances this is done to cover global structural problems that benefits specific individuals, in some cases by rulers/political leaders, who employ religion to create support and further their own ambitions. However, this approach often neglects the limits the tenets of religion put on political entrepreneurs: you have to maintain a religious reputation to be perceived as religious, and cannot act publicly in ways that disturb that image, and there are social rules that must be kept. Moreover, such an approach neglects the way in which religion reshapes actors as well as being reshaped by social interaction.

The third group consists of the "constructivists". The latter hold that political or religious conflicts are the products of cognitive structures such as ideology and religion, which provide shared understandings for the public and the elites. In this view religions are intersubjective structures, which equip actors with "value-laden conceptions of the self and others and consequently affect their strategic choices". That is, an actor's identity is significantly shaped by a religious doctrine, which affects the behaviour of actors according to the dictates of that doctrine. Like the instrumentalists, the constructivists locate the political entrepreneurs at a centre stage because of their power and ability to "muster mass support for their plans and to try to invoke the religious traditions of their societies in order to legitimize their choices". However, unlike the instrumentalists, the constructivists hold that the ability of the leaders to manipulate religion is limited.[69] The leader has to follow at least a minimum of requirements stipulated in the religion to be believed. Some constructivists even claim that individual identity and perception will be formed by the general beliefs held within an organization, or groups.[70] Leaders, as well as followers, might fully believe in the religion, despite the religion being socially constructed, its contents varying over time, and the religion being far from primordial.

Within the last approach, religion becomes something changing; religious regulations and the meaning of a religious identity might change over time.[71] The norms and social rules within religions tend to change as time goes by. Secondly, identities and interests are *not* given or unchanging but contingent and formed through discourse. It is not a given that a particular issue should create religious hatred. The way Jews were treated by priests in Spain during the Spanish inquisition, compared with the way Jews are treated by Catholic clergy nowadays illustrates the point: what initially was a violent relationship has changed into a peaceful one, although the clergy continues to be Christian. Thirdly, if the sources and traditions of great religions are multifaceted and subject to systematic reinterpretations and rearrangements by the political and social authorities, then clearly the contemporary call to arms of the militants against the infidels or lukewarm believers is one privileged interpretation over others and is unavoidably historical and contingent. The situation in Iraq could for example be interpreted as a clash between Islam and the West; indeed many jihadists interpret it like this. However, it is not the only interpretation: the war can also be seen as a clash between Shias and Sunnis, and it can be seen as a clash between criminal elements and an Iraqi state, between a specific American administration and Iraq, or a situation in which initially peaceful groups fail to communicate and this creates problems. Conflicts are not inevitable, because there is a dynamic of *escalating* the status of cultural and religious differences (existing within and between religious communities).

Cultural and religious discourse might define perception for many individuals, and many individuals will act upon their beliefs, and even have the potential to influence global relations. Organizations such as al-Qaeda can also be seen as forms of a belief system, in which individuals join up, not because they are recruited actively by the organization—they might never meet other members of the organization at all—but because they believe in the organization's credo.[72] Indeed, the argument of "clash of civilizations" itself may serve as a belief system at the service of a wide range of opportunists from political to religious fields. The insights from instrumentalist and constructivist approaches can help us delineate how, once political and religious actors really believe in the "clash" thesis, then the "clash", supported by strategies of actors that want to use the clash thesis instrumentally, can indeed come true.

The choice of cases

The border zone of Islamic civilization, with the inclusion of the new borders, numbers more than fifty countries; not all of them can be studied in detail in one volume. Rather than touching vaguely upon all cases, this book will present selected cases in more detail. The cases are chosen on the basis of the size of the various countries as well as their prominence in the media (the latter potentially enhances the global impact of the case, as it can be used by various political and religious groups to argue for popular mobilization). Each of the cases is studied by experienced area experts. The cases are tied together by regional introductions that examine the regional dynamic of that specific border zone, identifying similarities and differences within the zone. The book will be divided into five parts, the first analysing Islam's Asian borders (Israel/ Palestine, Lebanon, Afghanistan, Pakistan, Indonesia, Philippines), the second analysing its African borders (Nigeria, Sudan, Ethiopia, Somalia), the third its European borders (Chechnya, Turkey, Bosnia, and Spain) the fourth the new Islamic borders created by emigration and technology (UK, Spain, United States, France, Scandinavia, and the Internet).

Region I

Asia and the Middle East: Borders at the Centre of Islam?[1]

Stig Jarle Hansen

Asia is both numerically and culturally central for Islam. Asia contains the numerically largest Muslim states in the world.[2] Islam originated in a particular sub-region of Asia, the Middle East, and the most important shrines of Islam are located in this sub-region. The role of the Islamic teaching institutions of the Middle East gives the area a special position. Famous Islamic universities located in the Middle East, such as the Al-Azhar in Cairo, influence the contents of Islam itself, their religious scholars tutor students from all over the world and their interpretations of the *Qur'ān* are spread globally. Scholars based in the region also issue *fatwās*, religious rulings that provide guidelines on how a Muslim ought to behave in various situations. Moreover, several of the conflicts in the region are popular with the media, they gain global attention, provide supposed examples of the clash of civilizations, and are actively used in propaganda efforts by organizations such as al-Qaeda.[3]

The impact of the ideas developed and events taking place in the Middle East deserve special attention; many of the events and ideas continue to have impact across the Islamic world. The growth of the philosophies of revivalist Islam, the growth of the financial power of Saudi Arabia, as well as the growth of pan-Islamic networks, as a consequence of the wars in Afghanistan, have had impacts from Scandinavia in the North, to Nigeria in the South, from the United States in the West to the Philippines in the East. At the start of the twentieth century an ideological revival of Islamism (the revival that today still inspires many militant jihadist organizations), emerged in the region; this renewal was also to have a global impact. Islamic philosophers such as Jamal al-Din al-Afghani (1838–1897), Muhammad Abduh (1849–1905), Rashid Rida (1865–1935), Hasan Al-Banna (1906–1949), Abul Ala Maududi (1903–1979), Muhammad ibn Abd-al-Wahhab (1703–1792) and Sayyid Qutb (1906–1966) are some of the theorists that formed the basis for the modern Islamist tradition as well as forming a loose ideological basis for many of the current day Salafi-jihadist organizations, including al-Qaeda.[4]

The teachings of the above philosophers were inspired by the expansion of European power during the late nineteenth and early twentieth century.[5] The foundation for unity, the formula to ensure strength when facing the West, was to be a re-authenticated Islam from a time that pre-dated any foreign influence. "Salafism" is often used to describe the followers of such a "back to the roots" approach to Islam, since the Islamic states were seen as having strayed from proper Islam.[6] In many ways the early reformers adopted western ideas, western techniques of production and organization, as long as this was not seen as contradicting Islam.[7] The reformers also emphasized the use of reason, *ahl al-ray*, and distanced them selves from many of the interpretations of the previous traditions of what the Prophet supposedly had said and done, which they perceived to be false.[8] Several of the early reform philosophers wanted to reintroduce *ijtihad* (the process of making a legitimate and moral decision by independent interpretation of the legal sources: the *Qur'ān* and the Sunnah), and thus re-examine the prevailing legal "truths" of Islamic society. The focus on *ijtihad* created division amongst Muslims, the traditional Islamic clergy often wanted to follow age old traditional interpretations rather than re-examining original sources. The teaching of the early reform philosophers thus divided rather than unified the Islamic world.

The combination of an emphasis on renewal and a deeply anti-colonial rhetoric attracted followers from an emerging middle class.[9] Inspired by the works of Rashid Rida, Muhammad Abduh and al-Afghani, but driven by Egyptian workers' complaints against British discrimination, Hasan Al-Banna launched the Society of Muslim Brothers in Egypt in March 1928.[10] By the late 1930s, it had established branches in every Egyptian province. A decade later, it had 500,000 active members and as many more sympathizers in Egypt alone, while its appeal was felt in several other countries. One of the brotherhood's major philosophers, Sayyid Qutb, defined most regimes of the world including supposedly Islamic ones as *jahiliyya*. The term *jahiliyya* was taken from the *Qur'ān*, where it was used to describe supposedly barbaric conditions of the pre-Islamic world. The definition of regimes in the Arab world as *jahiliyya de facto* meant that the Muslims participating in and actively working for these regimes were defined as infidels, and exempted from the protection that Islam gives to other Muslims. Although there are discussions of how to interpret Qutb, his *jahiliyya* discussion can and has been used to justify violence against other Muslims.[11] In the end, Sayyid Qutb served as an inspiration for groups such as al-Qaeda, by providing them with a theoretical justification for their struggle.[12]

Ideational "factories"

In many ways Saudi Arabia functioned as a centre for the dissemination of ideas with many similarities to Sayyid Qutb's teachings. The Saudi monarchy in itself had a religious foundation, a result of the 1745 alliance between Muhammad ibn Saud and the previously mentioned puritan reformer, Muhammad ibn Abd-al-Wahhab (1703–1792). Abd-al-Wahhab shared many views with conservatives within the Muslim Brotherhood, one such view was a focus on returning to the roots of Islam, the practices of the Prophet Muhammad and the four righteous Caliphs. The Saudis used the term "Salafism" to define their own ideology. However, there were large differences between the Brotherhood-based version of Salafism and the Saudi based: the former's emphasis on renewal and reform and its use of rationalism in the interpretation of the *Qur'ān* was in large part rejected by the Saudi version of Salafism. The Wahhabi-inspired Saudi version of Salafism was more conservative than the Brotherhood's; it also tended more strongly to condemn fellow Muslims holding different opinions regarding interpretations of the *Qur'ān*.[13]

During the 1960s Saudi Arabia engaged in a cold war with Egypt, which fervently attacked the conservatism of the kingdom. The popularity of Nasserism in the Middle East meant that Saudi Arabia faced a struggle that, because of the defeats of monarchs around the Middle East in the face of Nasserites, as well as Egyptian presence in Yemen, Saudi Arabia's neighbour, must have been seen as a matter of survival. American support for Saudi Arabia made the situation seem brighter, but was offset by massive support to Egypt from the Soviet Union. Saudi Arabia was more than ready to support Nasser's enemies. Many Brotherhood members and other religious scholars from around the Islamic world fled to Saudi Arabia from prosecutions and torture by nationalist and secularist regimes. Some of them, including Sayyid Qutb's brother Muhammad Qutb, were to gain prominent positions within the Saudi Arabian university sector, an ideal position to spread their own world view.

Egypt's defeat in the 1967 war with Israel, as well as the increasing oil wealth of Saudi Arabia, was to change the balance between the two countries drastically, as well as empower religious activists based in Saudi Arabia. Firstly, Islamism became legitimized while Egyptian-style pan-Arabic nationalism was weakened. Egypt in 1967 was ruled by Gamal Abdel Nasser's predominantly secularist/nationalist regime, and the ideology of this regime was viewed as having been defeated in the 1967 war. Economic prosperity enabled Saudi Arabia to spread its ideological literature and ideology more efficiently across the Islamic world. The United States saw Saudi Arabia as an ally in the struggle against the Soviet Union—the secularism of the latter had alienated religious scholars in the Middle East—and Saudi Arabia served as a buffer against the expansion of the regional allies of the Soviet Union.[14]

Saudi and US support for the Pakistani efforts to prevent a Soviet victory in Afghanistan were to have global consequences. Three million Afghanis fled to Pakistan, and had to be provided for partly by Islamic charities, many of them Saudi supported.[15] The rise to power of General Zia ul-Haq's regime, a regime which actively employed Islam to establish legitimacy and to mobilize against Pakistan's traditional enemy India and granted tax relief to charities, also contributed to a focus on religion amongst the refugees, as did the charity and education-focused activities of numerous Pakistani religious schools. Volunteers started to arrive, actively encouraged by *fatwas* issued by religious scholars in their home countries. Many Camps and Schools in Northern Pakistan and Afghanistan were turned into ideational factories, in which national borders were broken down; volunteers were from all over the Islamic world and new pan-Islamic organizations were created. In these factories the deeper understanding of Islamic philosophy weakened as recruits for the jihad in Afghanistan, with little in-depth understanding of Islam, were trained.[16] However, a more simplistic interpretation of Islamic history and philosophy, in many ways very similar to Huntington's clash thesis, was disseminated. The sheer number of volunteers coming to the training camps of Afghanistan ensured that this ideology was dispersed and connections were made between individuals from various nations.[17] The charities and organizations developed to handle the refugees meant that a pan-Islamic (with the exception of Shia activists, Shiism being defined by many Salafists as non-Muslim) organization boom followed. In this sense Afghanistan was a motor for the transnationalization of Islam.

The victory over the Soviet Union was viewed by many of the Muslim fighters that came to fight in Afghanistan as the major confirmation of the ideology of the organizations that emerged in Afghanistan, despite the role played by Mikhail Gorbachev in withdrawing the Soviet forces, and the massive American aid for the resistance. The ideological factory in Afghanistan was closed after the Soviet withdrawal, but some of the fighters returned home, and became members of global or local jihadist organizations.[18] International connections were kept.

The establishment of the Taliban regime in 1996 meant that the "ideational factories" opened again; possibly more than 20,000 passed in and out of these "factories".[19] The factories spread the ideology of al-Qaeda, and broke down the barriers for students against the use of violence.[20] Ironically, the rhetoric now became focused on one of the major sponsors of the resistance towards the Soviet Union, as well as the major helper of Bosnian Muslims, the United States, partly because of the latter's involvement in the Israel-Palestinian conflict, and the ongoing US presence in Saudi Arabia after the 1990–1991 Gulf War. Versions of the "clash of civilizations thesis" played a major part in the indoctrination taking place in these camps, several conflicts, many of them treated in this book (the North and South conflict in Sudan, Israel-Palestine, Chechnya-Russia, Bosnia (Serbs, Croats and Muslims), Nigeria (Christians and Muslims), and Kashmir (Pakistan-India)) were presented in simplified ways and stereotyped in order to prove an eternal enmity between the supposedly Christian West and the Islamic world.[21] As will be shown later in the book, the interpretations of al-Qaeda drastically overlooked the role inter-Islamic strife and alliances between Muslims and Christians played in many of these conflicts.

The American invasion of Afghanistan as a consequence of the September 11 attacks removed the ideational hub; the al-Qaeda bases were simply destroyed and ideological cohesion within al-Qaeda was weakened.[22] The Iraqi debacle created an alternative. Firstly the conflict was easy to stereotype. By using a "pick-and-choose" approach to history, overlooking the general conflict between Sunnis and Shias in that country, as well as the conflict between different clans, a "clash of civilizations" was constructed, pictures of American atrocities in the Abu Ghraib prison definitively helping this effort. The Iraq conflict spurred discussions on the internet that are likely to have improved recruitment to extremist organizations. However, a stronger American presence prevented training facilities of the scale that had existed in Pakistan and Afghanistan. Currently, the lack of control in Pakistani borderlands with Afghanistan might enable the "ideational factories" to open again, ironically in the territory of one of the allies of the US

International belief systems facing local context

The above history of the global spread of a specific interpretation within the Islamic philosophical tradition suggests a civilizational dynamic in many ways similar to the one suggested by Huntington. But the spread of the jihadist ideology was hampered by several local factors: it was harder to preach Islamic unity when local animosities, conflicts and interests intervened in local conflicts; it was easier to see local conflicts as a "clash of civilizations" in training camps in Afghanistan than in the rice fields of the Philippines. For example in Iraq, the attacks against Shias discredited al-Qaeda, and the latter was trapped by the local context.[23] The existence of strong Sufi movements also inhibited the spread of Salafist-inspired jihadism which, despite public attempts to embrace all forms of Islam, was caught up by its own *takfir*-inspired ideological past. In many of the cases where extremist organizations such as al-Qaeda gained a foothold, local factors such as the legacy of colonialism, the part played by religion in processes of national identity-building, as well as widespread poverty (which allowed radical charities to gain foothold), played a large part.

Religious differences *did* play a part in the local dynamics of the conflicts on the borders of Islam. As argued by Rigby and Johansen in chapter one, exploring the Israeli-Palestinian conflict, extremist religious groups have to be dealt with on their own terms.

In chapter two, Nassif explores the Lebanese conflict, and points to the importance in this conflict of religious cleavages, but he also demonstrates how marriages of convenience often transcend religion. Chapter three explores similar dynamics in Afghanistan. Written by Giustozzi, this chapter explores the interaction between religion and other factors in Afghanistan. Chapter four, written by Khory, explores Pakistan, including its relationship with India. Chapter five, written by Schulze, demonstrates how jihadist rhetoric has local importance, much of it because of socio-economic differences. Chapter five is in a way about a case not in the centre of the Islamic world, but a case that nevertheless belongs to Asia, illustrating the dynamics of a smaller eastern Asian state with a religiously divided population, the Philippines. Here, Reid explores the case of jihadism, and also illustrates how a divide and rule tactic employed by the former colonial overlord lingers on and influences the dynamics of a supposedly religious conflict.

1

Israel/Palestine—Multiple Agendas and Division Lines

Andrew Rigby and Jørgen Johansen

Wherever you travel around the world people have heard of the Israeli-Palestinian conflict. What is it about it that makes it so special? There is no single answer to this question. In many parts of Europe and North America there is a sense of guilt over the historic persecution of the Jews within "Christendom", persecution that culminated in the Holocaust. Secondly, the core of the conflict zone is a location that is special to the three Abrahamic faiths; it is a region that is commonly referred to as "The Holy Land". As the birthplace of three of the world's major religions the region has been susceptible to repeated interference by religiously-minded outsiders. Third, this region was also the site of almost two hundred years of violent conflict in the twelfth and thirteenth centuries between Christian Crusaders and the Muslim rulers of the Holy Land, with Jerusalem at its centre. Fourth, there is a Jewish, as well as a Palestinian, diaspora spread around many parts of the world. Agencies within both these networks seek to raise the profile of the conflict within their countries of domicile and they are effective. Fifth, the conflict has proven extremely intractable—there have been violent confrontations between Jews seeking to secure their own state in the region and Arabs who have opposed them since the 1930s, and despite occasional periods of optimism regarding a settlement, the divisions between the two sides remain as deep as ever.

23

The thesis of this chapter is that the Israeli-Palestinian conflict in essence is a straightforward, if prolonged, struggle between rival nationalisms, two peoples competing for control of the same piece of territory. However, this conflict has been rendered more and more complex due to the number of actors and agencies who have used it in pursuance of their own interests. Each of them portrays the conflict in a particular light, naming and defining it according to their own interpretive schema. Each defining agent frames the conflict in such a manner that it becomes an issue which resonates with constituencies and communities within the region and around the globe. The result is that a range of different groupings, networks and organizations claim a degree of ownership of the conflict insofar as they make a connection between their own interests and the outcome of the conflict. As a result, the conflict has been transformed into some kind of hydra-like phenomenon—it takes on a different face according to who is doing the defining. It adds to the complexity that not all of the actors will benefit from a peaceful settlement of the core issues. One consequence of this has been that the conflict has been rendered relatively invulnerable to peace-making efforts because there are too many agents with a vested interest in its outcome. Particularly significant in this context are those agencies that have adopted a "religio-civilizational" paradigm as a means of interpretation and guide to action.

For "true believers" of whatever faith or political creed, life is generally seen in Manichean terms of good and evil, black and white, us and them. Conflict is readily represented as some kind of essentialist clash between adherents of fundamentally opposed "missions". Such simplifications and dichotomies tend to mask the diversity and pluralism that exists within any particular global faith community—for them the complexities of the world are reduced to a basic bipolar paradigm. With regard to the Israeli-Palestinian conflict their reductionism has had the effect of prolonging the suffering and the violence, insofar as they have used their influence to oppose any form of compromise that most observers acknowledge to be necessary if a sustainable peace process is to begin. As "true believers" they know that ultimate reality conforms to their world-view, whatever surface events may take place. Whatever others might claim, they can invoke spiritual/cosmic truths to legitimize their position and their actions.

This makes them intransigent and destructive in any conflict situation in which they are involved. To the extent that they view the conflict through their religious lens of civilizational conflict between true believers and satanic forces, they thereby create a pressure on other parties to the conflict to react in terms of a similarly-grounded paradigm—indeed through such processes what is essentially a conflict about rival nationalisms can come to be drawn with a civilizational brush, taking on the very hue that was at first only imagined.[1]

In this chapter we shall use the term "fundamentalism" in a manner similar to Schenker's use of the term, to refer to those adherents of any faith that share certain core ideal-typical characteristics: 1) an active intolerance of all faiths and interpretations of religion other than their own; 2) an unshakeable conviction that their interpretation of particular sacred texts is the literal truth; 3) a passionate commitment to their belief system and an eagerness to promote it—particularly by mobilizing their own community in opposition to others, and 4) unquestioning adherence to a set of values that overrides other moralities and laws. The aim of this chapter is to review those "fundamentalist" actors and agents that have sought to impose their own religio-civilizational definition on the conflict and who have thereby rendered the Israeli-Palestinian conflict uniquely intractable.

Jewish fundamentalism

Parties to the conflict are complex communities, characterized by a range of ideologies and belief systems, driven by their own fractures and internal tensions that impact directly and indirectly upon the core conflict. Thus, within the Jewish diaspora and the Israeli Jewish population there has emerged what we might call Jewish fundamentalists, whose beliefs and practices are anathema to those Jews who seek a just settlement with their neighbours. They have impacted upon the conflict in a number of ways.

For such people the confiscation of Palestinian territory is a process of rightful reclamation of land that was promised to the Jews by their God. The 1967 conquest seemed proof to significant numbers of followers of the spiritual leader Rabbi Avraham Kook that they were living in a messianic age. His teachings were developed by his son, Rabbi Svi Yehuda, for whose followers the conquest of East Jerusalem and Judea and Samaria in 1967 was further evidence of their involvement in the unfolding of a divinely ordained historical process. They were part of a great chain beginning with the first Zionist Congress through the establishment of the state of Israel up to the acquisition of the new territories. As such they have constituted the backbone behind the settler movement outside of the Greater Jerusalem conurbation and those settlements immediately adjacent to the old "Green Line" (the pre-1967 border between Israel and the West Bank). The subsequent spread of illegal settlements has become one of the main obstacles to a peace settlement.

As early as 1968 one of their number, Rabbi Moshe Levinger, founded the Jewish settlement of Kiryat Arba, adjacent to Hebron. Then in the mid-1970s some of his contemporaries constituted a movement called *Gush Emunim* (Bloc of the Faithful) fired by the determination to settle in all parts of Eretz Israel, and founded the settlement of Elon Moreh outside of Nablus. In 1977 there was the Likud election victory and Menachem Begin took office with the promise that "...there will be many more Elon Morehs".[2]

Gush Emunim never had a formal membership list or anything like that, but the late Ehud Sprinzak portrayed the movement as the visible tip of a large iceberg, which embraced the social and political base of more mainstream political parties in Israel such as the National Religious Party.[3] Through such links *Gush Emunim* could exercise an influence over the Israeli government, as Sprinzak observed:

"The *Gush* today is not merely a movement deeply rooted in present-day Israeli political culture but it has also created a new reality for thousands of people who now live in Judea and Samaria, ready to protect it at virtually any price. For tactical reasons they may not affiliate themselves with the extremist *Gush Emunim*, but rather claim to be ordinary members of the legitimate settlements of Judea and Samaria. Intellectually, spiritually, and ideologically, however, they will always remain *Gush* people. ... Any Israeli government that tries to sever the link between these people and their settlements will find itself fiercely opposed, not only by *Gush Emunim* but also by the iceberg of its many supporters."[4]

Given the nature of Israeli political life, the "veto power" of such groupings should never be underestimated. The Israeli electoral system makes any attempt to move towards a peace process susceptible to "spoilers". The whole country is treated as a single electoral constituency, and any party receiving more than one per cent of the national vote gains representation in the Knesset in direct proportion to their percentage of the overall vote. This means that there is virtually no possibility of having a single-party government in Israel, the government is always composed of a coalition of parties. As a consequence quite small parties can exercise a disproportionate influence over policy during the horse-trading that precedes the formation of any government, and can exercise a veto power over issues during the life of a government by threatening to withdraw from the governing coalition.

Messianic Jews, like their counterparts in other faiths, occupy a radically different world from that of their more mainstream co-religionists and the secular members of their society. They believe there was a Covenant (Genesis 15) between God and the Jewish people, and that Judea and Samaria (the West Bank) is at the very heart of the Promised Land of Israel. Consequently they have an absolute conviction that whatever apparent set-backs their cause might suffer their ultimate success is guaranteed because it is God's will.

In the following of God's will there is no room for compromise, and it is beholden upon the faithful to resist any measures to undermine what has already been achieved. Furthermore, it follows from this type of belief that those Jews who are committed to territorial compromise and a two-state solution can be defined as traitors to their land and to their people. Moreover in the collective body of Jewish law, customs and traditions (*Halakah*) they can find the necessary theological support for such a view. It was this kind of thinking that led to the assassination of Yitzak Rabin on 4 November 1995 by Yigal Amir, who believed he was following God's will in killing someone who had committed the ultimate act of betrayal by signing an agreement ceding territory to the Palestinians. Amir was born in Israel, but he and those who share his beliefs have found ready support amongst sections of the Jewish diaspora, particularly in the USA. Indeed, some of the most extreme Jewish figures in Israel emigrated from the US, amongst the most infamous being Meir Kahane, the founder of the Jewish Defence League, and Baruch Goldstein, who murdered twenty-nine Palestinians and wounded fifty others at the Cave of the Patriarchs in Hebron on 25 February 1994. Speaking a few months prior to Rabin's murder, the president of the Rabbinical Alliance of America, a national organization of 540 Orthodox rabbis, claimed that:

"According to Jewish law, any one person—you can apply it to who you want—any one person who wilfully, consciously, intentionally hands over human bodies or human property or the human wealth of the Jewish people to an alien people is guilty of the sin for which the penalty is death. And according to Maimonides—you can quote me—it says very clearly, if a man kills him, he has done a good deed."[5]

Amos Oz claimed that Rabin's murder made him realise that "the real battle in the Middle East is no longer between Arabs and Jews but between fanatics of both faiths and the rest of the people in the Middle East who want to find some reasonable compromise."[6] If only it were so simple. He omitted to mention the "fanatics" of the third of the Abrahamic faiths: the evangelical Christian Zionists.

Christian fundamentalists

Since Rabin's assassination over twenty years ago by a Jewish fundamentalist zealot, another fundamentalist religious network has laid claim to the conflict between Israel and Palestine. Christian Zionism is a movement within Protestant fundamentalism and conservative evangelism that is based on the belief that Christ will return to earth to establish the millennial kingdom under his rule, and that the modern state of Israel is a necessary precondition for this "second coming". Consequently Christian Zionists support the maximalist claims of political Zionism to Israeli sovereignty over all of historical Palestine, including Jerusalem. According to their prophetic timetable the victory of Israel in the 1967 war was evidence of the accuracy of their literal interpretation of certain biblical texts. They supported the subsequent expansion of settlements under Menachem Begin's Likud coalition government, endorsing the theological claims made by settlers that God had promised the biblical lands of Judea and Samaria to the Jews. However, it was not until President Jimmy Carter revealed his belief that the Palestinians had a right to a homeland of their own that they began to mobilize politically on any significant scale. They paid for full-page notices in major North American newspapers stating:

"The time has come for evangelical Christians to affirm their belief in biblical prophecy and Israel's divine right to the land. ... We affirm as evangelicals our belief in the Promised Land to the Jewish people ... We would view with grave concern any effort to carve out of the Jewish homeland another nation or political entity."[7]

In the subsequent 1980 presidential elections Carter was defeated by his Republican rival Ronald Reagan. One of the reasons was that an estimated 20 million fundamentalist and evangelical Christians voted for Reagan and against Carter.

Whilst the influence of the Christian Zionists waned somewhat during the Clinton years at the White House, they became increasingly significant players during the presidency of George W. Bush. Their influence grew after the terrible events of 11 September 2001, and they have grown to become the most significant element within the broad pro-Israeli lobby in the USA, carrying far more weight than the older America-Israel Public Affairs Committee (AIPAC). AIPAC is in itself quite significant, as one of its leading figures, Pastor John Hagee, observed to the BBC: "When a congressman sees someone from AIPAC coming through the door, he knows he represents six million people. We represent 40 million people."[8] According to their web-site AIPAC now has 100,000 members.[9] In addition to regular meetings with members of the Congress they closely follow how the US federal representatives and senators vote on issues that touch upon Israel's interests. And in interpreting Israel's interests AIPAC has aligned itself with the far right in both the USA and Israel who are opposed to territorial compromise. The biggest sanction wielded by AIPAC is the capacity to vilify as anti-Semitic any public figure, academic or journalist who presumes to criticize Israel for its repression of the Palestinians living under occupation. One of the most recent American figures to be targeted was former President Jimmy Carter who, in his book *Palestine: Peace Not Apartheid*, criticized successive Israeli governments for their abuse of Palestinian human rights. Democratic politicians in the USA rushed to distance themselves from Carter, funding for the Carter Center was cut, and one of the Center's senior fellows resigned.[10]

Whilst AIPAC is driven by its commitment to furthering the interests of Israel in this world, the Christian Zionists (like their Jewish fundamentalist counterparts) believe they are players in a cosmic script and have no time for the exigencies of state politics. When Prime Minister Sharon insisted on seeing through his decision to withdraw Israeli forces unilaterally from the Gaza Strip, there was a massive outcry from both Jewish and Christian fundamentalists. Sharon's subsequent stroke was perceived by many as Divine judgement. The American evangelical broadcaster Pat Robertson warned:

"He was dividing God's land and I would say woe unto any prime minister of Israel who takes a similar course to appease the EU, the United Nations, or the United States of America, ... God says 'this land belongs to me. You better leave it alone.'"[11]

For both fundamentalist Christians and Jews, the Biblical description of Armageddon is connected to a transcendent imperative that justifies actions others see as dangerous, confrontational and aggressive. The "Promised Land" must be ready to receive the Son of God when he comes. This "end-of-time theology" binds hawkish Jewish groups to right-wing Christians. The question of whether or not the Messiah they await has been here before is a detail of disagreement both camps can live with for the time being.

Palestinian Muslim fundamentalism—the rise of Hamas

Hamas originated as the underground military wing of the Muslim Brotherhood (MB) in the occupied territories during the period of the first intifada that commenced in 1987. The MB had been founded in Egypt in 1928. It always emphasized the importance of non-violent work to guide and encourage people to become good Muslims as a necessary pre-requisite for the creation of a truly Islamic society and state. Although banned between 1949 and 1952 in Gaza its influence grew, and even after the 1967 occupation it continued to emphasize non-violence—organizing openly and convening meetings that were more concerned with aspects of Islam than resistance to the occupation. With the outbreak of the first intifada, however, some of the younger members of the MB began to criticize this political quietism. They were concerned about the emergence of *Islamic Jihad* as an active element within the Palestinian nationalist movement. The MB therefore decided to adopt a more activist stance against the occupation and created the Islamic Resistance Movement (Hamas) as its "fighting arm" early in 1988.[12] It grew to become the strongest Islamic resistance force in the West Bank and Gaza Strip, and in the process constituted the first significant challenge to the hegemony of the mainstream secular nationalist movement, a challenge which continued to grow, as evidenced by their electoral victory in January 2006.

The founding charter or covenant of Hamas was published in August 1988. In it, opposition was expressed towards the Palestine Liberation Organization's preparedness to settle for a two-state solution. Such initiatives, it was claimed, "run counter to the principles of the Islamic Resistance Movement, since giving up part of Palestine is like giving up part of our religion."[13] Hamas, it claimed, was a "link in a long chain of jihad against the Zionist occupation", that worked "towards raising the banner of Allah on every inch of Palestine."[14] Since the land of Palestine was considered to be Islamic *waqf* dedicated for future generations of Muslims, then jihad or Holy War was inevitable. According to the covenant:

"There is no solution to the Palestine question except by Jihad. The initiatives, options and international conferences are a waste of time ... When an enemy occupies some of the Muslim lands; Jihad becomes obligatory for every Muslim. In the struggle against the Jewish occupation of Palestine, the banner of Jihad must be raised."[15]

In a nutshell, Hamas was calling for a holy war against the "Zionist entity" and the establishment of an Islamic state throughout historic Palestine. They were not seeking the establishment of a democratic Palestinian state but a theocracy, and whilst Hamas stressed that "it is possible for all followers of different religions to live in peace and with security", it claimed that this could only happen "in the shadow of Islam".[16] Within this framework there is no place for peace negotiations with Israel, insofar as the aim is to raise "the banner of Allah on every inch of Palestine".[17] Moreover, this rejectionist stance was extended to the US and the West because the "imperialistic powers in the capitalist West ... support the enemy with all their might—material and human."[18]

From this perspective it is clear that Hamas should be ranked alongside the other agents of "fundamentalism" that have been reviewed in this chapter.

Like their Jewish and Christian counterparts they interpret the conflict through a religio-civilizational lens, like them they view any deviation from the path sanctioned by their faith as apostasy, and like them they contribute to the conflict's intractability.

The increased popularity of Hamas has been due to a deepening disillusionment with the policies and the performance of the Palestinian Authority (PA) dominated by *Fatah*. The PA proved itself to be inept, corrupt and autocratic during a period when the occupation broadened and deepened and the suffering of the population increased accordingly. People grew increasingly frustrated at the lack of any manifest "peace dividend". Between 1992 and 2002 the percentage of the Palestinian population living below the poverty line trebled from 20 to 59 per cent. By 2005 some 75 per cent of the Gazan population was living in poverty with a 50 per cent male unemployment rate. Characterized by corruption and cronyism, the PA failed to deliver adequate services to meet the basic needs of the population. This gap in service provision was filled to some degree by the welfare activities of Hamas organized through the mosques and its charitable organizations. Hamas has gained popularity for its effective and uncorrupted work within social services. They won the elections for their support to fulfil people's basic needs. All these factors help explain the growth of Hamas. It should also be acknowledged that for a population whose living conditions and quality of life was in free-fall, the occasional pain inflicted on the enemy by Hamas-organized violence also generated support.[19]

In other words, the increasing support for Hamas that resulted in their electoral victory in 2006 reflected not so much a sudden spread of some kind of fundamentalist religio-civilizational sentiment amongst the Palestinians living under occupation, but was evidence of a deepening disillusionment with the policies and the performance of the dominant secular Palestinian political class. At the same time there is little doubt that the influence of Islam has grown alongside the rise of Hamas in contemporary Palestinian society. But once again the causality is complex. In the absence of functioning state structures people have turned to civil society to meet basic needs, and the mosques are one of the few pillars of Palestinian civil society that have not been undermined by the Palestinian Authority. Thus, in a situation where there is no functioning state judiciary and legal system, people turn to the Islamic courts (as well as tribal leaders and the heads of the large families and clans) to settle their claims.[20] In the increasingly anomic conditions that have characterized Palestinian society since the outbreak of the Al Aqsa intifada in 2000, where nothing is certain or predictable anymore, religion provides a structure and a meaning to life. This is particularly so for the majority of the Palestinian population who are socially conservative and for whom Islam is their religion.[21] In a situation where Palestinians have begun to lose hope and confidence in the future, where their status as Palestinians is becoming weaker and weaker regionally and globally, then their identity as Muslims becomes all the more attractive. Islam exerts a heightened appeal as a source of identity because it seems to be a growing force in the world. By identifying with this strong global community Palestinians can gain a sense of empowerment.[22]

Hamas started life as an armed resistance movement driven by a mix of nationalism and faith. As we have seen, however, its growth in popularity was not so much due to its proclamations of faith but rather the belief that it was a better vehicle for achieving the Palestinian nationalist vision of a state than the discredited old guard of Fatah. The political leadership of Hamas has been fully aware of this and realised some years ago that if they were to become the dominant political force then the resistance movement would have to transform itself into a political party, and this in turn would require some form of accommodation with the "Zionist entity". Hence, in June 2003 a Hamas spokesman said that Hamas could settle for an agreement with Israel based on the 1967 borders and would leave the "next generation" to decide on a permanent agreement.[23]

However, the transformation from a resistance movement to a political party is not an easy process, and it was unfortunate for Hamas that the 2006 elections resulted in them becoming the majority party in the Palestinian legislature. They were not ready for this outcome. In some ways the transformation of Hamas is reminiscent of the changes that took place within the PLO during the 1970s when the maximalist dream of establishing a secular democratic state in the whole of Palestine was relinquished in favour of an acceptance of a two state solution. The same process is going on within Hamas except they have to recognise the need to relinquish the vision of an Islamic theocratic state in the whole of Palestine. As with the PLO there is the same playing with words to camouflage the fundamental changes taking place. So with Hamas in 2007: instead of renouncing violence, they implemented a truce; instead of formally recognising Israel they acknowledged the reality of the state on its borders; instead of accepting all previous agreements they agreed to "respect" them. Furthermore, as with the old secular nationalist movement there is a division within Hamas between the internal and the external leadership, with the insiders far more attuned to the realities of the occupation and the alternatives facing the Palestinians. At the time of writing it remains unclear how this process will unfold.

The war on terror: increasing the problems?

Networks like al-Qaeda with its figure-head Osama bin Laden need Palestine, alongside the invasion of Afghanistan and of Iraq, to justify their attacks on the "West" and to substantiate their claims that the Muslim world and its holiest places are under constant threat from the infidels. For this reason they have no interest in a constructive outcome to the Israeli-Palestinian conflict, it would be seriously damaging to their cause. In subsequent statements by al-Qaeda, Palestine has always been the central symbol of the injustices suffered by Muslims throughout the world.[24] In April 2006 bin Laden used the sanctions against the Hamas government in Palestine as evidence that "the blockade which the West is imposing on the government of Hamas proves that there is a Zionist-crusaders war on Islam."[25] By such means bin Laden and al-Qaeda lay claim to the conflict in Palestine, seeking to project it as the embodiment of the clash between two religio-civilizational forces. By presenting the conflict within such a framework, they render the Palestinians' own struggle vulnerable to the charge of terrorism by those who view the world through the lens of the war on terror. Furthermore, by presenting the struggle as a zero-sum conflict around which no compromise is possible, they feed the deep fears of Israelis that the very existence of their state is at stake, whilst also reinforcing the misplaced confidence of the "rejectionists" within the Palestinian political community who refuse to recognise the existence of the Jewish state. In this fashion the likes of al-Qaeda and its spokesmen (they are invariably men) repeatedly reinforce the most radical irredentists within both the Israeli and the Palestinian camps, stoking the fires of violence and undermining the possibilities of a sustainable peace.

Conclusion

Some of the most powerful "spoilers" of any peace process based on a compromise between the rival national claims of the Israeli Jews and the Palestinians are those who are driven by a religio-civilizational outlook that locates the conflict within a broader global framework of good against evil, the godly against the satanic.

Collectively the impact of these faith-driven parties has been to prolong the conflict. They have proven themselves capable of weakening any peace process to which they have been opposed. Prime Minister Rabin was assassinated by a Jewish fundamentalist in 1995 because he was betraying the Jewish people and their covenant with God. The Christian Zionists, especially in the USA, have mobilized to pressure the US government to endorse the most provocative acts of the Israeli government. Certain Islamist political groups around the world have used the plight of the Palestinians to generate support and justify their condemnation of the West, and by association have facilitated the labelling of the Palestinian resistance as 'terrorist', thereby reinforcing a significant obstacle to peace by de-legitimising the Palestinian national struggle. At the same time Hamas succeeded in reinforcing such a label by their sponsorship of suicide bombings that targeted Israeli civilians as part of their successful undermining of the Oslo peace process to which they were opposed.

Of course the intractability of the Israeli-Palestinian conflict cannot be attributed solely to the malign influence of 'true believers' with a vested interest in its perpetuation. The failures of leadership amongst Palestinians, Israelis, the United States, and the European Union in particular must also be factored in. And here, perhaps. lies a seed of hope for the future. Within hours of taking office in January 2009 the new United States President Obama pledged a new approach to the Muslim world and committed to working for peace in the Middle East, thereby signalling a clear break with the catastrophic legacy of his predecessor at a time when publics around the world were reeling from the shock of Israel's armed response to Hamas provocation which resulted in the deaths of over 1200 Palestinian civilians. This most recent slaughter confirms the need to dialogue with all the main actors and underlines how the failure to engage with Hamas has resulted in lethal damage to the Palestinian project.

2

Lebanon—Between "Clash" and Coexistence

Hicham Bou Nassif

Lebanon is, *par excellence*, the land of encounter between Islam and Christianity in the Arab world. The country is divided between mainly Maronites, Greek Orthodox, Greek Catholics, Sunnis, Shias, Druze and Alawis. Lebanese religiously-defined groups have cooperated as the Maronites and the Druzes did in the sixteenth century when they were united in a close alliance under the leadership of the great feudal prince Fakhreddin the second. But often, they have adopted antagonist approaches, notably in their attitudes *vis-à-vis* interferences by external players. Recently in 2005, Maronites, Sunnis and Druze rose in rebellion against the Syrian occupation of Lebanon whereas the Shias remained faithful allies of the Syrian regime. But immediately after the Syrian withdrawal, swathes of the Maronite community became disenchanted with what they identified as "Sunni hegemony" over Lebanon which led them to a previously unimaginable alliance with the Shias of the pro-Iranian and pro-Syrian fundamentalist Hezbollah. The swiftness in which an intra-communitarian alliance can turn into rivalry, indeed sometimes open warfare, attests to the fact that even in the heydays of communitarian harmony, communities do not lose their consciousness of distinctiveness *vis-à-vis* the others.

Christian-Islamic relations in modern Lebanon: a historical perspective

The creation of modern Lebanon in 1920 under the auspices of the French mandate was built on an inherent contradiction. Almost half of its inhabitants were Muslims, whereas the new emerging republic was supposed to be a Christian homeland (*foyer national Chrétien*). In fact, the history of the Christians of Lebanon at the time was that of a unique success story for a non-Muslim minority in the Arab world.[1] This is particularly true concerning the evolution of the Lebanese Christians all through the nineteenth century until the beginning of the twentieth century. Indeed, their European predisposition enabled them to be the local partners of western enterprises thriving to dominate eastern markets in the decaying Ottoman Empire, and also to welcome the dissemination of foreign missionaries amidst their towns and villages. The contact with European capital assured them economic prosperity: a new Christian bourgeois elite flourished in Beirut where it virtually controlled the bulk of the foreign trade of the city, while the Christian peasantry in the rural areas benefited from the mulberry tree cultivation vital to the expanding silk trade with Europe. Also, the activity of the missionaries—Jesuits, Capuchins, Lazarists, Franciscans and Benedictines to name only the Catholic orders—gave the Lebanese Christians a notable cultural advance on the Muslims.[2] The growing disparity between the communities was bound to affect the vision each group had of itself and of the others. Thus, it confirmed in the Christians their sense of superiority *vis-à-vis* the Muslims, but it also entrenched in the Muslims a sense of suspicion towards the Christian, protégés, of the West. Mutual notions of the Muslims as culturally inferior and of the Christians as an enthusiastic kind of fifth column working for the benefit of the West were bound to have severe implications on the relations between the different Christian and Muslim communities. The Druze and Sunni resentment of the new-found Christian wealth and feeling of self-importance generated an atmosphere of communitarian tension that culminated in the massacres of 1860 mainly in Mount Lebanon and Damascus, still vivid in the collective memory of the Christians until today. In a few weeks, thousands of them were slaughtered.[3]

The bloody events of 1860 enhanced the Christian sense of insecurity. Large parts of the Christian elite and, more importantly, the powerful Maronite church, adhered to the idea of the necessity of creating some kind of autonomous or even independent entity, separate from the Muslim hinterland, and under Christian authority. But when the occasion to do so did finally present itself after the fall of the Ottoman Empire in 1918 and the institution of the French mandate on swathes of the former Ottoman provinces in the Levant, the Lebanese republic that emerged was hardly largely Christian in its demographical composition.[4] The necessity of ensuring the economic survival of the fledgling state compelled its architects to add, to its Christian dominated mountainous core, the essentially Sunni cities on the coast and the mainly Shia regions in the east and the south. The Maronites enjoyed a simple, but not an absolute majority in the new state. They were the largest single religious group, and they regarded Lebanon as essentially, if not exclusively, theirs.[5]

The National Pact (*al mithaq al watani*) of 1943 allowed Lebanon to gain independence from a France weakened by its defeat in the Second World War and the subsequent rise of the British influence in the Middle East. In its essence, the pact was an understanding between Christian and Sunni leaders who agreed that the former would stop asking for the protection of France and join the struggle against its mandate over Lebanon whereas the latter would relinquish their quest of Arab unity and accept an independent Lebanon as their final homeland.[6] The logic of this pact was later described as the "No East, neither West" formula. the Republic of the notables that emerged afterwards was sometimes depicted as allowing a Christian hegemony over the Lebanese Muslims. In fact, it was built on a meticulous equilibrium between the various communities, leaning it is true, in favour of the Christians. Thus, the latter were to have an exclusive hold on the presidency, the most powerful position in the political regime, but also over the command of the army and the governorship of the central bank. The distribution of seats in the parliament was to be on a six Christians for five Muslims basis. On the other hand the Muslims got the post of prime minister, exclusively held by the Sunnis, and the clearly less significant post of speaker, held by the Shias. Rather than being dominated by the Christians, the Muslims were engaged in a kind of asymmetric relation with them. Clearly the liberal orientation of the country and the westernization of its culture were as much a sign as a product of Christian prominence. But the logic of the inter-communitarian equilibrium prevented the Christians from pushing their advantage too far. Thus, when President Camille Chamoun (1952–1958) adopted a staunchly pro-western and anti-Nasserite stand in the fifties at a time when president Gamal abd el Nasser of Egypt, the idol of the Arab masses, was engaged in a bitter power struggle with the western camp in the region, the upheaval that ensued on the

Lebanese scene between pro-Chamoun forces, mainly Christians, and pro-Nasser forces, mainly Muslims, ignited the first Lebanese civil war in 1958. The confrontation ended when president Chamoun was replaced at the end of his term by President Fouad Chehab who distanced himself from the western camp while maintaining close ties with President Nasser, an orientation not readily endorsed by large parts of the Christian constituencies. The 1958 crisis and its consequences was a clear sign of the limits to the political clout of the Christians in Lebanon. Most of all, it showed that the Muslims had a *de facto* veto over the major decisions that affected the future of the country.

Seventeen years later Lebanon was again engaged in a protracted internecine conflict that ravaged its people from 1975 until 1990. "Lebanonization" entered the political lexicon as a synonym to "Balkanization", a state of continued civil strife caused by irremediable atavistic communal hatred leading to partition. Indeed the turbulent history of the "shattered country" could be seen as corroborating the theory that differences between the tenets of Islamic civilization and those of their neighbours led inevitably to confrontation. However, a closer look at the Lebanese conflicts may reveal a complicated picture with some of its aspects not easily compatible with the "clash of civilizations" world-view. Revisiting contemporary Lebanese conflicts will not sap the basis of the clash theory, for at each one of them, the cleavage was unmistakably drawn on fault line communitarian frontiers. Although Huntington is not oblivious to the possibility of manipulating religious identities for political purposes this factor is completely absent in his approach to contemporary conflicts in Lebanon, which he mentions several places in his book. If one thing is clear in complicated Lebanese politics and history, it is the ever present readiness of local leaders to surf on the dangerous tides of sectarian fear and the zeal of easily manipulated constituencies, in order to build popular power bases and to accumulate political clout.

Lebanon and the clash

Starting in May 1958, Lebanon witnessed three months of bloody events that culminated with the landing of 15,000 US soldiers on its shores in order to quell the conflict. From the outset, the confrontation was clearly based on sectarian lines, for the fight pitted Islamic rebels against Christian loyalists to the Maronite president Camille Chamoun. It has already been mentioned that the Lebanese Christians, historically fostered a strong feeling of identification with the West. Practically speaking, that means they looked to western countries—mostly France—for inspiration in their social habits and cultural orientation. Muslims less easily share Christian admiration for the West, seen as pro-Israeli and imperialist. During the forties, the regional political system was still mainly pro-western in its outlook, which rendered Lebanese inter-communitarian cooperation easier. However, the failure of the liberal regimes in the face of Israel in 1948 discredited them and opened the Pandora's Box of the military populism of the Arab putchist generals. Syria lost its civilian rule in 1949 followed by Iraq in 1958. But the most influential coup with long lasting implications for the Middle East was that of Gamal Abd el Nasser's "free officers" in Egypt in 1952. Nasser adopted Arab unionism as an official ideology for his regime. When he emerged victorious in the 1956 Suez crisis, effectively challenging the imperial powers of Britain and France, he became the idol of the Arab masses and, among others, the Lebanese Muslims. With the rift between the western camp and the dominant force of the Arab world widening, the relations between Christians and Muslims in Lebanon were being more and more strained as the "Nor East, neither West" formula intimately associated with the national pact was subject to extreme pressure.[7]

The 1958 standoff was a confrontation between two clearly identified religious groups, the Christians on one side, and the Muslims on the other.[8] On both sides the *leitmotiv* for popular mobilization was sectarian tension and zeal. The Christians identified the Nasserite tide as a vital danger for "their Lebanon", and thus, for their continuity in it. If Arab unionism was to prevail, they were bound to be once more a non-Muslim minority living under Muslim rule with the status of second-class citizens that had been theirs for centuries under the Ottomans. From the Muslim point of view, however, Nasser was a historical chance as an avenger of Arab pride in the face of the arrogant West, as a driving force towards the achievement of the old dream of unity, and as an ally whose support could shift the internal balance of force on the Lebanese scene on their favour.[9] Religious identity was thus the major demarcation line that moulded the divergent reactions of the Lebanese groups. The external intervention was also divided. Indeed, the rebels received active support in arms and men from all along the porous Lebanese border. They could count on ardent popular sympathy mainly in Egypt and Syria, united at the time under Nasser leadership in the United Arab Republic. At first the Americans were reluctant to intervene directly but when a coup toppled the pro-American regime of the Hashemite dynasty in Iraq, and the region was seemingly falling in the hands of the pro-Soviet Nasser, they sent troops to Lebanon in response to an urgent request from President Chamoun.

Seen retrospectively the 1958 conflict was not between left and right, conservatives and liberals. It was a sectarian confrontation between religious groups with core states of the respective civilizations concerned intervening each on the side of the protagonist that belonged to its culture. However, although both the Al Saud dynasty regime in Saudi Arabia and the Hashemite family regime in Jordan base their legitimacy on religious grounds, the first as the guardians of Islam's holiest cities in Mecca and Medina, and the second as the descendants of the Prophet Mohammed, they were actually during the 1958 crisis on the side of President Chamoun and his Christian followers. Indeed, in the context of the cold war, the al-Sauds and the Hashemites were in the western camp, as was Chamoun himself, while Nasser and his followers were leaning to the Soviets. Thus, the fact that they belonged to the same "civilization" as the Lebanese Muslims, did not stop Saudi Arabia and Jordan from supporting their Christian foes.

Moreover, just like president Chamoun, the leaders of the Muslim rebels were actually part of the same oligarchy of notables that ruled Lebanon. Their vision of the president was that he was supposed to be *primus inter pares*, the first among the notables not a ruler over them. When Chamoun grew too powerful a president, he became a danger to the established elite. In the parliamentarian elections of 1957, many of the *Zaims* (the communitarian leaders) lost their seats to the benefit of pro-Chamoun elements. The *Zaims* accused the Lebanese president of manipulating the elections to ensure that his supporters would win a first step towards ensuring a second mandate—not allowed by the Constitution—in the presidency. And when the political system, more and more dominated by Chamoun, failed to offer a way for them to satisfy their grievances, they took their action to the streets. In its essence, their opposition to Chamoun was completely political. In its essence, their opposition to Chamoun was completely political. In fact, when Chamoun's successor in Office, President Fuad Chehab, allied himself with Pierre Gemayyel, the leader of the Phalange party and Chamoun's greatest competitor for Sunni leadership, Chamoun and Salam tacitly coordinated their efforts against Chehab. Chamoun's successor in office, President Fuad Chehab, allied himself with Pierre Gemayyel, the leader of the Phalange party and Chamoun's greatest competitor for Christian leadership and with Rachid Karame, Saeb Salam's own competitor for Sunni leadership.

The fact that their respective partisans had been engaged in bitter fighting just a few years previously and that Lebanese died by the hundreds in the conflict was in no way an obstacle towards what came to be an effective collaboration between the two men. This example is only one among many others showing how easy it is for the communitarian *Zaims* of Lebanon to lead their streets to war in the name of the defence of the "endangered community" when they fail to negotiate a way for their competition over the spoils, and then go back to ally themselves with the same foes they violently opposed in the—often very near—past, this time in the name of "national unity" with changing political circumstances. In its essence, the war of the leaders was a quarrel over political clout and influence. But it was a conflict that pitted pro-Nasser Muslim leaders against a pro-western Christian president and it was easy for both sides of it to enlist support on a communitarian basis. Difference between Muslims and non-Muslims generated tension, but then again, this tension could have been confined to accepted limits if the political elite had negotiated a peaceful way to resolve differences between its members. The conflict that broke out was the result of a deliberate choice of the leaders to utilize the mounting sectarian tension in their bickering.

In 1975, the Lebanese communities were once again divided over the way to deal with an external factor, the Palestinian national movement. Starting in 1967, Palestinian elements had begun using south Lebanon as a base to launch guerrilla warfare against Israel. Their activity proved to be a formidable challenge to the Lebanese state which, on one hand, was unable to confront the destructive retaliatory actions launched by Israel, and on the other, to prevent the Palestinians from challenging the authorities, establishing a *de facto* rule over swathes of Lebanese territories, notably in the South. The conflict was this time over the freedom of movement that should be given to the Palestinian resistance in Lebanon (*Hourriat al Amal al fida'i*). Rhetorically, both groups had non-sectarian justifications for their respective positions. Thus, the Christians stood against the freedom given to the Palestinian movement in the name of Lebanese sovereignty. The Muslims defended it in the name of the sacred value of the Palestinian cause. But in fact, the real stake was once again sectarian. From the Christian perspective, the Palestinian presence grew to transform itself into a lethal threat, demographically and militarily. As Muslims, the growing clout of the Palestinians couldn't but heavily transform the delicate internal equilibrium to their disadvantage. From the Muslim perspective however, the Palestinians were a historical chance to reshape the Lebanese system that gave the better part to the Christians. The Mufti Hassan Khaled declared in 1976 that the Palestinians were in fact "the army of the Muslims", just as the Lebanese army was "the army of the Christians". The alliance between the two groups was both identitarian (the Lebanese Muslims

leaning to the side of their Palestinian brethren in their fight against the Jewish state, and the Palestinian Muslims leaning to the side of the Lebanese
Muslims against the Lebanese Christians), and utilitarian (the Palestinian
Liberation Organization (PLO) was eager not to alienate the whole Lebanese
establishment against it and thus needed a cover for its activity that could only
be provided by the Muslims. They, on the other side, needed the power of the
Palestinians in order to extort concessions from their Christian foes).

With the war erupting in 1975, the violence of the communal antagonism
could be seen through the radical attitudes of the protagonists. The director
of the *Dar-el-Fatwa*—the supreme religious body of the Sunni community—
thus wrote: "there is a clear stance in Islam that forbids the Muslim from being
indifferent towards the State, and thus, his stance *vis-à-vis* the rules of governance and the ruler can not accept half measures. Thus, the ruler is either Muslim and the rule Islamic, or the ruler is not Muslim and the rule is not Islamic;
the latter case makes the Muslim compelled to refuse the system and to strive
to obliterate it, by means of persuasion or by force, secretly or openly."[10] A few
years later, the Christian protagonists clustered in the Lebanese front produced what is probably the most important document explaining their grievances and hopes in which they warned, for their part, that "Christianity in
Lebanon does not want for itself more than it wants for others but will not
accept less than what others want for themselves", asserting that "The Lebanon
we want must keep Christianity in it free and secure, enjoying control over its
values and destiny."[11] With each community considering the conflict as a war
of survival, it is hardly surprising that a logic of communitarian cleansing came
to be a driving force for some of its particularly cruel chapters, notably in its
incipient years. A detailed record of that period of the Lebanese conflict has
been provided elsewhere and we will not expatiate on the atrocities committed by the protagonists.[12] However, it is important to note that the effort of
the warring factions clearly concentrated on building "pure" communitarian
zones free of any presence of outsiders. Both sides resorted to the brutal tactic
of "identity card slaughtering" in which civilians abducted by armed factions
were immediately shot if their identity cards happened to indicate that they
belonged to the opposing group.

Though many western media were lured into applying Marxist schemes on
the interpretation of the war—the proletarian and underprivileged Muslims
vs the rich Christians clinging to their "privileges"—the conflict had in fact
little to do with class struggle.[13] The essential nature of its dynamics, notably
on the popular mobilization level, was sectarian. The great internal actors were

the communitarian leaders and parties who, notably in the first years of the conflict, could count on genuine and massive popular support from their respective communities.

Nevertheless, when applied to the Lebanese case, the clash theory reveals some conspicuous weaknesses. First of all, though Huntington mentions Sunni-Shia fighting in his book, "the clash" leaves little room for analysis of this phenomenon, perhaps just as important as Islamic quarrelling with non-Muslims. Writing about Lebanon, Huntington mentions the "Maronite Christians" fighting a losing battle against "the Shias and other Muslims".[14] The picture that is presented is one of a conflict between Muslims and non-Muslims while an important aspect of the Lebanese war was in fact that of different Muslim sects engaging in some of the bloodiest clashes of the crisis. Thus, the Sunni Mourabitoun militia was eradicated by the Shia Amal in 1984. The Mourabitoun had previously clashed with the Druze Progressive Socialist Party commonly known by its acronym of PSP, which, in its turn, was engaged in a bitter conflict with Amal starting in 1985 after initially allying itself with Amal against the Mourabitoun. The Shia militia also launched a protracted war against the Palestinian camps in western Beirut that lasted from 1985 to 1988, which added to the Sunni-Shia tension in the country. In brief, the years 1984–1988 had witnessed an alliance between a Shia force (Amal) and a Druze force (PSP) in a fight against the sole Sunni militia in Beirut (The Mourabitoun), and then an alliance between the Druze (PSP) and the Sunni backed Palestinians against the Shia Amal. If we add to this picture the bloody fights of 1985 in the city of Tripoli pitting the Sunni fundamentalists of the *Tawheed* Movement against Alawi militiamen—allied with some leftist elements and backed by the Syrian army—we conclude that the inter-Islamic bickering was, at least during that period of the war, as strong if not stronger than Christian-Islamic tension. Even though all Muslim sects had their opposition to the Christians in common, it is important to note that there had never been an encompassing multi-sectarian "Islamic" militia in Lebanon, but "Sunni" or "Shia" or "Druze" or "Alawi" forces. Basically focusing on the Muslims vs non-Muslims side of the fault line conflicts, the clash theory says little about the important cracks inside "Islamic civilization" and thus contributes to conveying a static vision of Islam that ignores some of its major internal and deeply conflictual dynamics.

Furthermore, the Lebanese crisis is identified by Huntington himself as a "fault line war". The characteristic of this kind of confrontation, according to his theory, is that each group engaged in it will strive to "mobilize support from civilization kin groups."[15] Some aspects of the communitarian strategies relevant to their external alliances do corroborate this approach. Thus, the Sunnis were able to rely heavily on the fighting force of their Palestinian kin in Lebanon. When the Palestinian Liberation Organization (PLO) was evacuated from Beirut after the Israeli invasion of 1982, they received active political support from Saudi Arabia. At first glance, the alliance between Iran and the Shias buttresses the theory too. But in fact, Iran began to be engaged on the side of the Shias only after the Islamic Revolution had succeeded in toppling the Shah in 1979. The Lebanese war actually started four years earlier in 1975 during which the Shah regime showed little sympathy for the cause of the Shias in Lebanon. This means that identifying with kin is not as automatic as Huntington would suggest. Rather than being some expression of cultural solidarity, it is more of a political act inevitably linked to calculations of national interest that a country can choose to take or not to take. Noticeable was the fact that the West showed an almost complete lack of interest in the fate of Lebanese Christians. In his influential book relevant to the "life and death" of oriental Christians Jean Pierre Valognes explains the apathetic stance of the West to the ordeal of its Lebanese co-religionists by the fact that no western country wishes to alienate Islam for the sake of Christian minorities in a gesture that can generate no real benefits.[16] In fact, when the Christians were engaged in a bitter fight with the Palestinians in the 70s, they turned to the Syrians for help. When they were essentially at war with the Syrians in the 80s, they received active support from Iraq. In civilizational terms, the Iraqis and the Syrians, all part of the world of Islam, are alien to the Lebanese Christians. But in their struggle against Lebanese Muslims, the Christians were able nonetheless to build cross-cultural alliances with them at different times of "the fault line war" they were engaged in, a fact that fits uneasily with the analysis presented by Huntington's theory.

Lebanese communities and the post-Syrian order

After thirty years of occupation (1976–2005) and fifteen years of complete hegemony (1990–2005) Syrian troops were forced to withdraw from Lebanon in April 2005, under both external and internal pressure. During the long Syrian overlordship the communal balance of power, that was before the Lebanese civil war (1975–1990) in favour of the Christians—mainly—and the Sunnis, shifted in favour of the Shia allies of Damascus. With a new phase of Lebanese history beginning after the departure of the Syrians, the balance of power will shift, once again, into a new equilibrium that is yet to be determined. The uncertainties of the post-Syrian era and the bitter legacy of the past three decades of both internal violence and foreign occupation as well as different aspirations towards the future of the country and its positioning in the great game of power currently taking place in the Middle East have put the inter-communitarian relations of the different Lebanese groups, already strained, under renewed pressure. Each community will try to adapt to the new scene in a way that enhances its capability to hold the maximal degree of power in the political structure of what could be called the "third Lebanese Republic".[17] That is particularly true of the Maronites, the Sunnis and the Shias, three communities who aspire to play the central role in Lebanese politics.

The Maronites had great expectations about the post-Syrian era; they aspired to regain their once central position in the Lebanese system, lost during the period of Syrian hegemony, after the withdrawal of the Syrians. However, in a pluralistic society based on consociational democracy, the demographic weight of a community is crucial to its political clout. For decades, the demographic weight of all Christian Lebanese communities, including the Maronites, was in decline, whereas that of the Sunnis and the Shias was booming. This is due mainly to the fact that backward regions in the country—like Sunni Akkar or the Shia south—are mainly Muslim. The peasant culture and traditions of these areas still takes pride in extended families. The Maronites, on the other hand, have undergone and completed decades ago a process of rapid and full urbanization. Most Maronites live in typical middle class families with both parents professionally active. Also, while no official figure exists concerning the waves of emigrants that fled the country during the last three turbulent decades, it is usually admitted that the numbers of the Christian emigrants outnumber the number of Muslims. Furthermore, while the Shias managed to build a "sacred alliance" with Iran and Syria which has given them powerful financial, political and military backing, and while the Sunnis cultivate the benefits of their kinship with Saudi Arabia, the Maronites have no regional sponsor. Western countries like the US and France tend to deal with the powerful Hariri Sunni dynasty, which they have clearly chosen to be the cornerstone of both their Lebanese politics and the new Lebanese order. The Maronite and Christian masses in general currently feel threatened and marginalized in Lebanon. After a brief rejoicing that followed the departure of the Syrians, their mood is bleak. The thirty-three days of violence between Hezbollah and Israel in the summer of 2006 were a war they did not choose to fight. The heavy blow to the Lebanese economy that ensued from the Israeli raids further undermined the confidence of the Maronites in their country and in their future in it. And once again, the waves of emigrants leaving Lebanon are stuffed with Christians, depriving the community of its most socially mobile and educated elements. For decades the Maronites, who where finally defeated by the Syrians at the end of the Lebanese war in 1990 and witnessed, as a consequence, a severe setback in the influence they previously enjoyed in Lebanese politics, hoped the post-Syrian era would be for them an occasion of a "re-emergence of the vanquished". So far, that has not been the case.

As for the Sunnis, it is important to remember that the new era in Lebanese history and the withdrawal of Syrian troops actually began with the assassination of prime minister Rafic Hariri, one of their most prominent leaders in modern times, on 14 February 2005. Months before his assassination, Hariri and his Druze feudal lord ally Walid Jumblatt—both former Syrian allies—began to dissociate themselves from Damascus and move to an alliance with the staunchly anti-Syrian Christians. This important shift in internal Lebanese politics set the scene for what it was hoped would be a quiet revolution. History seemed to be moving fast after the adoption by the Security Council of the 1559 Resolution that called for Syrian withdrawal and Hezbollah disarmament in September 2004. The dramatic assassination of Rafic Hariri in what was immediately assumed, by large sectors of Lebanese public opinion, to be a Syrian act, triggered massive anti-Syrian rallies and renewed international pressure on Syria, which had to withdraw its last soldier from Lebanon by 26 April 2005.

The assassination of Hariri unified the community under the leadership of his son and political heir, Saad Hariri. In the legislative elections that followed in May/June 2005, Hariri's "Future Movement" swept the majority of the seats consecrated to the Sunni community along with many other non-Sunni seats. Rafic Hariri's lifetime friend and former minister of finance Fouad Seniora holds the position of prime minister, while Hariri supporters maintain key portfolios in the government as ministers of Finance, Interior and Education. Via Hariri's clout, the Sunnis could emerge as the most powerful community of post-Syrian Lebanon. And, while the *bras-de-fer* with the Syrian regime continues and the tension with Shia Hezbollah is extremely high, many Sunnis feel that their hour has come in Lebanese politics.

This power shift in favour of the Sunnis was accompanied with a profound change in the ideological discourse of the community. Historically, the Sunnis of Lebanon adopted flamboyant national Arabic rhetoric and orientation. The Maronites who defended Lebanese sovereignty used to be accused of "isolationism" by the Sunni masses (and by the Lebanese left). But the popular anger of the Sunnis against the Syrians after the assassination of Hariri was expressed in purely Lebanese nationalist rhetoric. While Sunni figures occasionally continue paying lip service to Arab nationalist ideals, the main goal of the community evolved into what was historically seen as a Maronite one, the defence of the independence and sovereignty of Lebanon against neighbouring Syria. The fact that the Syrian regime borrowed heavily on Arab nationalist slogans contributed in discrediting these same slogans in the eyes of the Lebanese Sunnis. But the shift from Arabism to Lebanese nationalism could also be seen as the logical consequence of the transformation in the internal balance of power between the Lebanese communities, with the Sunnis gradually moving to the central position which was once that of the Maronites. The less Sunnis had reasons to complain about their lot in Lebanon, the more they were prepared to show loyalty to it. In that sense, it becomes understandable that, since the period that followed Rafic Hariri's death revealed to the Sunnis that they could lose the position as Lebanon's most powerful community, they reacted to the new internal equilibrium by unprecedented signs on both the popular and the elite level of Lebanese patriotism.

While the Maronites fought the Syrian occupation of Lebanon during the war years and the Sunnis resented it, the Shias were the most trusted allies of Damascus since it sent its troops to Lebanon in 1976. As the war ended in 1990, Shias found themselves on the side of the victorious Syrians. They were rewarded. The amendment of the Taef agreement in 1989 had bolstered the prerogatives of the Shia speaker and Nabih Berri, the leader of Amal militia, was elected to this post in 1992. Amal was absorbed by the Lebanese army, which is believed to have had, since then, a largely Shia majority. But the main beneficiary of the Syrian control over Lebanon was Hezbollah. The fundamentalist organization was the only militia that was allowed to keep its arms in order to continue its warfare against Israel. The Syrian President Hafez el Assad knew he had to face tough negotiations in the peace process in the Middle East, and Hezbollah was a winning card he could skilfully use against the Jewish state. Transformed into an emblematic "national resistance", Hezbollah, that was until then seen by many Lebanese as a terrorist diehard outsider group, shrewdly benefited from the continued struggle in the south and its role in it to bolster its position in the Shia community, and that of the Shia community in Lebanon. Indeed, the military prowess of the organization allowed it to present itself as the protector of the Shia region in the south, and to present the Shias themselves as the "shield" of Lebanon against Israeli military might. But the role of Hezbollah was far from confined to military action. Using an uninterrupted flow of millions of dollars streaming from Iran, it organized efficient social service networks including schools, hospitals, mosques, libraries and research centres. Hezbollah helped young Shia couples getting married by arranging for them to build houses or even organizing collective marriage ceremonies. Paying particular attention to its propaganda strategy, the organization built a media empire including the notorious "*Al Manar*" broadcasting corporation. Through its powerful media, Hezbollah disseminated and popularized its cult of martyrdom, radical version of Shia Islam, and hatred of Israel and the West. A charismatic leader, the secretary general of the organization Hassan Nasrallah, excelled in using the deaths of Hezbollah militants on the front—including that of his own son—as occasions to bolster Shia sense of importance and mission. The result of years of tense proselytism and iron-disciplined militancy was a success in transforming the biggest community of Lebanon into a well-organized machine that Nassrallah could use against all enemies, internal and external, and to establish Hezbollah itself not only as a state in the state, but also as a state *in place* of the state.

With Amal dominating large sectors of the public services and Hezbollah rising in might, politically as well as militarily, the "Pax Syriana" era were the golden years for the Shias of Lebanon. The withdrawal of the Syrian army could not have been an occasion of rejoicing for them, and the new phase was seen as potentially full of danger. The refusal of Hezbollah to disarm should be analysed, not only through the calculations of Iran concerning its nuclear weapon programme or its struggle with Israel, but also through the ambitions and fears of the Shia community and its assessment of the eternal balance of power game in Lebanese multicultural society in the post-Syrian era. As Nassrallah knows, by refusing to disarm, he is sabotaging any chance for a strong state to be established in Lebanon. But if such a state would be that of the ever more powerful Lebanese Sunnis, he is in no hurry to see it established. Nassrallah will only disarm under a status quo that will ensure the Shias maintain the privileged share that was theirs during Syrian rule. Ironically, the rhetoric of the Lebanese Shia leadership is all about fighting the "Zionist enemy" and the "American hegemony". But its *Realpolitik* could very well be essentially preoccupied by the ambitions of the Sunni Lebanese brethren. In that sense, the refusal of Hezbollah to disarm and its dramatic consequences for Lebanon and the region could be seen as yet another aspect—the Lebanese part—of the great revival of the Sunni/Shia cleavage that is boiling dangerously in the Middle East.

Conclusion

The Lebanese political system is based on "political confessionalism" guaranteeing for each religious group a quota in the parliament, the council of ministers and the state's administration. The Lebanese constitution promulgated in 1926 asserted that the communitarian structure of the regime was to be only transient. It was hoped that the feeling of belonging to the nascent republic would sap the basis of communitarian identification, and Lebanon would thus be able to pass from the consociational form of democracy to a simple majoritarian one. Eight decades later, communitarian zeal and loyalty are stronger than ever in the country. Religious affiliation has successfully resisted the assaults of modernity and secularism. Furthermore, the great wave of the Islamic revival buttressed even more the role of religion as a conveyor of identity as much as a political actor. No significant political force in Lebanon can claim to represent a solid multi-communitarian constituency. However, it is impossible to reduce the complexity of Lebanese history simply to a communitarian division in the name of an encompassing "civilizational" theory. Islam in Lebanon has many internal fractional divisions. Furthermore, while religious diversity can by itself generate tension between the believers in "different Gods", it is also true that the political ambitions of both internal elites and external factors can often stimulate religious fanaticism as a tool of political action, rendering confessional harmony a much harder goal to achieve.

3

Afghanistan: "Friction" Between Civilizations

Antonio Giustozzi

In *The Clash of Civilizations* Huntington characterized the Soviet "defeat" in Afghanistan as the result of the confluence of three factors: American technology, Saudi money and Muslim demography and zeal.[1] There is some truth in this characterization, although American technology was not so important (the role of Stinger missiles has been overestimated), American money was at least as important as the Saudis' and the role of Pakistan and of Afghanistan's rugged geography should also be highlighted. Moreover, with regard to Muslim "zeal" and the participation of other Islamic countries in the conflict, some important qualifications have to be made. This chapter will review the rise of political Islam in Afghanistan in its interaction with foreign presence and influence. It will try to determine to what extent the factors driving its growth were internal or external ones and whether they can be described as 'civilizational' in character. The chapter will start from the very early days of the politicization of Islam in Afghanistan in the nineteenth century and continue through the repeated turmoil of the twentieth century, with a particular focus on the anti-Soviet jihad of the 1980s. Finally, the chapter will deal with the Taliban regime of the 1990s and the post-2001 Taliban insurgency, as well as with the role of international jihadist groups within it.

51

From the early days to the 1980s "jihad"

The politicization of Islam in Afghanistan is a long-term process which started with the First Anglo-Afghan war in 1839–1842 and continued with the second Anglo-Afghan war in 1878–1880.[2] Throughout the first half of the twentieth century, occasional clashes between Pashtun tribal groups and the British in what is nowadays the North-West Frontier Province of Pakistan, which was lost by Kabul following an agreement with the Afghan monarch, contributed to fuel a feeling of victimization at the hands of the British Empire. During the first half of the twentieth century the influx of refugees from Central Asia also contributed to fuelling a sense of enmity at the popular level between Afghanistan and its non-Islamic neighbours. The main carrier of this sense of Islamic identity in opposition to non-Islamic neighbours was the clergy, whose limited capacity for long-term mobilization prevented the political crystallization of these feelings. Although more than 80 per cent of Afghans are Hanafi Sunni Muslims (almost all the remaining ones are Shias), the clergy was always fragmented in a number of independent and often rival networks, centred around respected *ulama* or Sufis.[3] The Afghan clergy did not enjoy a very high social status, particularly among the Pashtun tribes; they were only able to emerge as key players when acting as bridges among different communities that had their own grudges against the government or foreign powers. This contributed to giving an Islamic colouring to confrontations between Afghanistan and Russia or Britain. The clergy failed to mobilize on a large scale against the skilful tactics of King Abdur Rahman in 1880–1900, who reduced their power and status to benefit the central government, while claiming for himself a leading role in waging jihad against internal unbelievers or heretics.

Defeated and partially co-opted by King Abdur Rahman in 1880–1900, the clergy again played an important role in the 1928–1929 mobilization against King Amanullah, whose weakly-conceived and implemented reform efforts left him exposed to the reaction of the clergy and local leaders.[4] Nonetheless, religious networks remained quite fragmented and never national in nature; the strongest of them, like the Qadiriyya and Naqshbandi *tariqas*, still had their influence mainly limited to specific regions. Some figures, like the Mujaddidi family (Naqshbandi leaders), became the main pole of the conservative opposition to the state. However, their ability to mobilize support in the absence of explicit challenges from Kabul was modest.

When in the 1960s organized Islamist parties made their first appearance in Afghanistan, their influence was limited. Indeed, until 1978–1979, there was little sign in Afghanistan that Islamist and Islamic fundamentalist groups had a bright future ahead. The arrival to power of the leftists of *Hizb-i Demokratik-i Khalq* (People's Democratic Party) in April 1978 was however a turning point. The leftists awakened the dormant clergy by antagonising it and presented it with an easy target for counter-mobilization, and created the conditions for the Islamists, until then isolated, to gain a wider support both within and without Afghanistan. Their appeal expanded much further once the Soviet army entered into Afghanistan with the aim of consolidating the pro-Soviet regime in Afghanistan. External support between 1979 and 1992 eventually ran into the billions of US dollars, with about \$3–3.5 billion coming from the US alone and possibly even more from government and private sources in the Muslim world (chiefly Saudi Arabia). The Saudi Arabians were lobbied by the Americans to contribute large resources to the anti-Soviet effort, but private contributors were likely motivated by personal feelings of solidarity and ideological sympathy with Afghan Islamists and fundamentalists.[5] That level of support allowed a number of Islamist, fundamentalist and religious parties to fund their expansion inside the country, arming hundreds of thousands of followers. Much of the private funding went not into the purchase of weapons and ammunition, but in the creation of a framework of support inside Pakistan: some of these parties tried to expand their core constituencies by educating/indoctrinating a new generation of prospective members. Schools were established in the refugee camps in Pakistan and sometimes even inside Afghanistan. Some groups and tendencies within the so-called "mujahedin" also benefited indirectly by funding coming to Pakistani religious establishments in the wake of the Soviet invasion. Conservative Muslim organizations invested heavily in the creation of Islamic *madrasas*, which in turn started raising hundreds of thousands of young Pakistanis and Afghans according to fundamentalist precepts.[6] More general religious appeal and the support of the clergy decisively helped the religious parties. It is difficult to discern any element of "civilizational" conflict from sheer xenophobia, external patronage and the self-interest of the clergy, but it can plausibly be argued that the religious worldview of many Afghans contributed to mobilize them against the leftist regime and even more so against Soviet presence. Nonetheless, there is evidence that the religious parties also decisively benefited from the exclusive channelling of external support by the Pakistanis. Although the clergy was an important component of the revolt from the beginning, many other components of Afghan society were also involved: local leaders, community and tribal elders, urban intellectuals, students, many of whom did not interpret the struggle as a religious one, but in nationalistic or parochial terms. However, by the mid-1980s, the non-religious opposition had been starved out of support and thoroughly marginalized.[7]

Throughout the 1980s, there was little sign that any Afghan Islamist or fundamentalist groups had any objection to receiving supplies paid for by the Americans or any inclination to rely on exclusive support by fellow Muslims. Since the distribution of supplies was handled by the Pakistanis, there was little direct contact between the Afghan mujahedin and the Americans; only a handful of agents, mostly CIA, were regularly meeting Afghans. Some of the leaders of the mujahedin, like Gulbuddin Hekmatyar, did not hide their contempt for the Americans and in general for the 'West', but nonetheless continued happily to receive their help; it was only in 1991 Hekmatyar broke his relations with the US following his opposition to the American attack against Iraq and was cut off from their help.[8] However, he was also cut off from official Saudi help. To various degrees during the 1980s and later, most religious parties in the resistance movement accepted young Muslim volunteers from around the world to fight among their men against the leftists and the Soviet army, as private Arab funding often came with this string attached. Even Rabbani, who among the Islamist leaders maintained the friendliest relations with the US, had no objection to jihadist volunteers joining the ranks of his commanders. Only Sufi leaders like Mujaddidi and Gailani did not take jihadists in, which is not surprising given that they often had a Wahhabi, Salafi or Islamist background and were therefore largely hostile to the brotherhoods anyway. However, jihadist volunteers were not particularly popular among the Afghan population and there were violent incidents with locals reported.[9]

An indication of the mostly opportunistic exploitation of "brotherly" Islamic help to the resistance movement is given by the fact that during the 1980s and 1990s expressions of hostility to America or the West seem to have been limited mainly to sections of the clergy and to a few activists. There is little indication that the fundamentalist constituency, which gradually expanded thanks to the work of the ever-growing number of madrasas, harboured any particularly strong hostility towards America at this stage. There was little talk of issues such as Palestine and Americans were mostly not considered an enemy insofar as they stayed away and did not interfere. The civil wars of 1993–2001, which pitted Islamic factions against each other, sometimes with the support of non-Islamic countries (such as Russia) or of a Shia regime such as Iran's, show eloquently the limits of Islamic solidarity when not supported by hard-core interests. Another indication of scant interest in jihad-ist solidarity was an agreement signed by the Rabbani government to deport Egyptian "terrorists" who were living in Afghanistan after having taken part in the war.[10]

The Taliban from 1994 to 2008

The Movement of the Taliban, which emerged in 1994, mobilized support inside Afghanistan mainly by relying on the support of clergy and on the war-weariness of the population; mobilization behind them was always quite limited. Although the Taliban's leadership initially bore a strong Pashtun Ghilzai character, due to its origins in Ghilzai areas, it was never a Pashtun tribal movement and it tried with some success gradually to incorporate cleri-cal networks throughout the country. Foreign jihadist groups were allowed to stay, as they had been allowed by the old mujahedin factions, possibly because of a feeling of solidarity among movements which shared at least some basic principles,[11] but probably also because they were sponsored by wealthy patrons in the Muslim world. The main external source of support of the Taliban was initially from Pakistan's PPP-led and secular government, even if jihadist ele-ments present in Afghanistan at that time, like Osama bin Laden himself, also contributed to the coffers of the Taliban once they took Kabul.[12] The agenda of the Taliban, as well as their views, were at that time entirely focused on Afghanistan itself. Sources of diplomatic support, such as Pakistan, Saudi Arabia and Qatar advocated a stabilization of the regime and diplomatic cau-tion. Their concerns were strategic ones, not unqualified Islamic solidarity. Although the Taliban always resisted external pressure to expel suspected ter-rorists, at one point in 1998 they seem to have come close to expelling one of the guest jihadist groups (al-Qaeda) and might only have been prevented from doing so by the August 1998 Cruise missile attacks on training camps.[13] Moreover, within the Movement of the Taliban several elements were clearly in favour of working for the recognition of major external powers, first and foremost the US. The Taliban's efforts at reducing the production of opium and derivatives in 1999–2000, clearly motivated by the desire to please Wash-ington, might have been the temporary Taliban inclination towards US com-pany in the negotiations with Turkmenistan concerning the possibility of building a pipeline across Afghan territory. External confrontation until 2001 occurred mostly with Shia Iran, not with any western power or even Russia. The Taliban's relations with the various jihadist groups based in Afghanistan were far from always good. Indeed most of the Arab volunteers had a very low opinion of the Taliban and in some cases their camps were closed and their arms taken away, or brought under the control of the Taliban government.[14] At the same time it is true that one of these jihadist groups (bin Laden's) showed strong determination in the face of opposition by fellow jihadists in allying with the Taliban. It gradually expanded its influence over the leadership of the Taliban after 1998 on the strength not only of its funding but also of the Arab origins of its leaders.[15] Afghan clerics and particularly the more conservative ones remained easily impressed by pious Arabs with a proven curriculum of selfless commitment to Muslim causes.[16] Tensions between bin Laden and the Taliban did not cease in 1998 and various incidents, including the suspension of his military activities, occurred between 1991 and 2001, but ultimately bin Laden succeeded in his embrace of the Islamic Emirate of Afghanistan. Moreover, the need to enlist motivated fighters against the Taliban's internal enemies led to the re-opening of all the camps that had had been closed in 2000.[17]

It is far from clear whether the refusal by the leadership of the Taliban to hand over Osama bin Laden to the Americans was the result of his own influence, of Islamic solidarity or any other factors. It is worth noting that bin Laden had been violating the rules of conduct set out by the Taliban for their jihadist guests.[18] Pakistani diplomacy seems to have lobbied actively for the surrender of bin Laden, without success. It has even been argued that the Taliban's decision to protect bin Laden was a consequence of Pashtun traditions of hospitality.[19] All in all the most credible explanation is that the diplomatic inexperience and incompetence of the Taliban misled them into thinking that they could negotiate an advantageous deal with the Americans by procrastinating in the handing over of bin Laden; their formation also seems to have led them to approach the issue in terms of judicial resolution, demanding proofs of his alleged crimes, rather than in terms of diplomatic realism. They failed to understand that Washington was not going to accept any procrastination.

By and large the Movement of the Taliban seems to have been in a state of disarray in late 2001-early 2002.[20] The Taliban seems to have believed that the Afghan population would support them against the external intervention of a non-Muslim power, but war-weariness proved more important than any sense of hostility to foreigners. Indeed, foreign troops were initially welcomed by many Afghans in 2001. Temporarily deprived of funding, scattered and humiliated, the leadership must have been particularly susceptible to the approaches of the jihadists, both bin Laden's group and any other attracted to Afghanistan by the presence of the Americans. Despite being on the run, bin Laden seems to have maintained access to funding; indeed his ability to gather private contributions must have increased in the wake of the 9/11 attacks, as he was propped up to celebrity status. During the years of the jihad against the Soviets, bin Laden alone was receiving an average US$20 million of funds annually from sympathisers; an unknown amount of private contributions was at the same time being channelled to other jihadists and Afghan armed groups.[21] After 2001, networks of jihadist sympathisers around the Muslim world were re-activated to support anti-American activities in Afghanistan. Initially, however, the state of disarray of both the Taliban and al-Qaeda must have made it difficult to find credible interlocutors who could guarantee that contributions would be put to good use. Then, in 2003, the American invasion of Iraq distracted the attention of jihadist networks, drawing funding (as well as volunteers) away from Afghanistan. Therefore, until at least 2006–7 the amount of funding channelled to the Taliban through jihadist networks is likely to have been well below what had been channelled in the 1980s. In any case, some money was still coming through and in the summer of 2002 the Movement of the Taliban, having in part reorganized its ranks, started insurgent activities along the border of Pakistan.[22]

Jihadist funding seems to have had varying impacts on the Taliban. In the south-eastern region (Khost, Paktika, Paktya), jihadist volunteers and Afghan Taliban seemed to be cooperating closely and fighting together. The jihadist volunteers were a large percentage of the fighters. In eastern Afghanistan the presence of the Taliban was modest and jihadist volunteers developed their own autonomous networks. In southern Afghanistan, the area under the direct responsibility of the Quetta Shura, the presence of jihadist volunteers was always much lower than in the south-east, a fact which casts some doubts on its willingness to open the doors fully to the jihadist groups which supported it with money.[23] If the intervention of the jihadists and their acceptance by the Taliban are to be interpreted as a manifestation of Islamic or civilizational solidarity, it is clear that their importance should not be overstated.

Undoubtedly by 2005 the propaganda apparatus of the Taliban was entering an altogether new dimension, not only in terms of the technology being displayed (CDs, video-CDs and DVDs, as well as web-sites and print publications), but also in terms of its contents. The typical themes of worldwide jihadist propaganda were now featuring fighting in Afghanistan, Palestine,

Iraq and elsewhere. It is not clear however who produced these media products, as they were signed by some private companies and did not bear any official "Taliban" logo, even if Taliban commanders often featured in them. It is not clear therefore whether they were fully endorsed by the leadership of the Taliban or whether they originated among groups of sympathisers who were relatively marginal to the leadership. Therefore, they cannot be taken as the conclusive proof of a shift of the Taliban towards international jihadism. During 2007–2008 there were reports of rifts within the leadership, between elements closer to the jihadists and others keener to keep some distance. In particular, the leading military commander in the south, Mullah Dadullah, seems to have incarnated the jihadist tendency, while Mullah Omar would have led the more cautious majority. Contrasts between Mullah Dadullah and other southern commanders on political issues seem indeed to have existed, although Mullah Omar's reproaches to Dadullah appear to have been mainly motivated by his disregard of the rules established by the leadership. It is quite possible that the leadership of the movement might have tried to play on both sides, letting some leaders pay homage to the jihadist cause in order to keep the funds coming while at the same time trying to limit the actual influence of the jihadists in order not to alienate the Afghan population with the often extremist attitudes of the latter, to avoid worrying neighbouring countries too much (Central Asia and Iran) and to maintain autonomy. Mullah Omar himself repeatedly stated that the aim of the Movement was the expulsion of foreign troops from Afghan soil, implying his lack of interest in a worldwide jihadist campaign.[24]

In order to support the thesis of the clash of civilizations, there should be evidence that the fighters were mainly motivated by hostility to foreign presence in the country, or to foreign-inspired reform such as the secularization of the legislation, the conduct of competitive elections, and some measure of female emancipation. If we examine the different sources of support for the Taliban, we see that only some of them can be described as motivated by a hatred of foreigners that can be described at least in part as deriving from cultural or religious differences. This is the case of the core Taliban fighters, the students of religion recruited mainly in the Pakistani *madrasas* and indoctrinated by Deobandi clerics. Since they are the product of an educational system fostered by political groups and tendencies with specific views about relations with western powers, their existence can hardly be taken as a proof of a natural tendency of Muslims to drift towards confrontation with the "West".[25]

The extensive support or sympathy for the Taliban within the clergy can instead be described as a more genuine indicator of cultural and religious hostility. It is impossible to measure with any degree of precision the extent to which clerics stood by the Taliban's side, but whatever little research has been done on the attitudes of the clergy in Afghanistan points out that hostility towards foreign presence is very deeply rooted within their ranks. As pointed out earlier in this chapter, the clergy in Afghanistan have been the main carrier of religious hostility and xenophobic feelings since the First Anglo-Afghan war, but were only able to mobilize for collective action when some major challenge unified their disparate networks against a common enemy. Since the 1980s a growing percentage of Afghan mullahs and *ulama* were trained in radical or conservative Pakistani *madrasas*, presumably strengthening any existing linkages with wider religious networks. The latter factor seems to be of some importance since pro-Taliban feelings among the clergy seem stronger among relatively younger, Deobandi-influenced clerics. Sufi orders and non-Deobandi conservatives (such as the *Tablighis*) do not appear to support or sympathise with the Taliban. It is also possible however, to point out other factors that may have contributed to the hostile attitude of the clergy towards reforms sponsored by external powers.

Some of the reforms begun after 2001 and supported by the "international community" must have been seen as threatening by the mullahs, who had been greatly favoured by the Taliban regime. The re-introduction of state education, for example clearly weakened the opportunity for the mullahs to make a living by offering Qur'ānic school education to village children. The prospect of a re-professionalization of the judiciary, coming after its clericalization under the Taliban, also meant declining employment opportunities for clerics. The arrival of new media like television and home entertainment, rapidly popular throughout Afghanistan, must also have been seen as threatening to the cultural hegemony of the mullahs. They had already opposed innovations like cinemas before the start of the conflict in 1978, but after 2001 the pace of innovation was much faster, even breathtaking.[26]

A second source of Taliban recruits after 2001 has been the disgruntled youth, in particular poor villagers who have no prospect of serious employment and at the same time own no land. In a country where most people marry by the age of 20, all marriage prospects are on hold until they can show their ability to support a family. This situation confines them to the bottom of the social ladder, particularly in the rural areas. Their social marginality makes them privileged targets for recruitment by movements that challenge the status quo, such as the Neo-Taliban after 2001, but does not imply per se a "cultural" rejection of western values. It is usually once recruited into the Taliban that these marginal youth are socialized into a specific way of thinking and their cultural profile altered.

In contrast to Pakistan, where there is abundant evidence of jihadist recruitment among educated people, the Afghan Taliban has never been able to attract members of the intelligentsia in significant numbers.[27] Disgruntled local communities, particularly common in southern Afghanistan, are the third and last major source of recruitment for the Taliban. The higher strata of rural society however, such as elders, have always maintained an uneasy relationship with the Taliban. Under pressure from local communities, they have sometimes sided with the Taliban, but have then ended up being marginalized by them.[28] Following the fall of the Taliban regime at the end of 2001, a number of local players aligned with the Americans were empowered as provincial and district authorities. The majority had grudges against those who had supported the Taliban in power and started pursuing their private vendettas, without distinguishing between individuals and their communities. The reaction of local communities, which in some cases tried to fight back under the leadership of their elders, created a vicious cycle of conflict. Gradually whole communities in provinces like Kandahar, Uruzgan and Helmand were pushed into the arms of the Taliban, with the consent of the elders who viewed this as a way to gain access to weapons and ammunition as well military support against their local enemies.[29] In these cases, the rationale for joining the insurgency was clearly not a cultural factor, but a response to harassment by government authorities. The Taliban also gained sympathy due to the dysfunctional status of Afghanistan's judiciary. From 2005 they started establishing their own parallel judiciary, which seems to have been welcomed, although it is unlikely that this was a major recruitment factor.[30]

In other cases many communities were pushed towards supporting the Taliban insurgents as a reaction to the growing presence of foreign troops in their home areas. This was the case of most of Helmand, which rose against the British contingent deployed there from the spring of 2006. Was this the reaction of Muslim villagers to the arrival of a foreign army, which carried cultural values incompatible with theirs? Available evidence suggests that a number of factors contributed to the revolt in Helmand. Tension pre-existed to the deployment of the British, as would have harassment and discrimination by the local authorities existed in Helmand too, even if the local governor had been more effective at forming alliances and distributing patronage in order to contain opposition to low levels of violence. In the absence of major measures to rectify the past abuses, the removal of the governor under the insistence of the British in 2006 liberated the compressed grievances as his patronage network was weakened. Moreover, the British were certainly not a welcome presence in Helmand, where folk traditions passed on stories about the excesses of the Anglo-Afghan wars. Even the state educational system, whose reach to rural Helmand had always been rather limited, had for many years propagated hostile views of Britain as a historical enemy of Afghanistan. Such hatred was therefore a result of a historical past and of indoctrination by a secular state, rather than a result of cultural hostility per se. Another factor was the aggressive behaviour of the first British units to be deployed in Helmand, a regiment of paratroopers that actively sought a fight with the initially limited groups of Taliban present in the province. The British were perceived to behave arrogantly and disrespectfully of local traditions. Later deployments adopted a more cautious and respectful approach, although not always consistently, but the damage had already been done. Probably the most important factor in determining widespread opposition to British presence was the perception by locals that such a large deployment would alter the balance of forces and eventually lead to the eradication of poppy cultures, which are very common in Helmand. Although the British stated publicly that they did not want to become directly involved in eradication, their message rarely reached out to the villages and to the extent that it did, it did not appear credible given Britain's previous role in the eradication effort in Afghanistan.[31]

In sum, the sources of opposition were mixed. While cultural ("civilizational") hostility might have played a role, many other factors were also at play. There is evidence that the presence of foreign troops, foreign assistance missions and a "liberal" government established with outside support did cause significant reactions throughout Afghanistan. This occurred in a number of ways. The behaviour of foreign troops and private security companies (PSCs) was an issue. While the former were themselves relatively well behaved towards civilians, the latter's arrogant attitude was often attributed by the Afghan "men in the street" to foreigners as a whole. Many Afghans were unable to distinguish between PSCs and regular troops. Even if foreign regular troops on the whole were not particularly abusive by any historical standard, some 'background friction' and a number of major incidents still occurred. Whenever foreign troops were setting up road blocks, searching civilians and their homes, preventing local drivers from overtaking slow-moving military convoys, interrogating Afghans or excluding Afghans from specific locations for security reasons, this friction occurred.[32]

Major incidents had mostly to do with the tendency of Americans and some other foreign contingents to rely on firepower when feeling threatened. Particularly from 2006, both ISAF and Enduring Freedom escalated the use of air raids in fighting the insurgency. Although the targeting was probably as accurate as ever in the history of air bombardment, significant civilian casualties still occurred. While confirmed civilian casualties have run in the hundreds each year, it has been difficult to estimate the actual numbers. Both ISAF and US sources claim that many local reports of civilian casualties were exaggerated either because of a misinformation campaign by the Taliban, or because of the villagers' hope that they would get financial compensation. While this is probably true, such claims still had an impact on Afghan public opinion because there was a substantial amount of evidence to support the idea that American firepower was being used indiscriminately. One extreme case was an incident in Nangarhar province in June 2007, where eight policemen were killed in a friendly fire incident which lasted hours. The credibility of ISAF/US claims about the accuracy of their air raids was called into question by their failure to identify even uniformed police. Air power aside, several extreme incidents were confirmed involving ground troops suggesting a siege mentality among US troops in particular and a high degree of 'trigger-happiness'.[33]

These incidents and the "background friction" however cannot be described as "civilizational" in nature; they could have happened with any army in any country; indeed they resemble similar incidents involving ill-disciplined or trigger-happy Afghan government forces. If we are looking for friction that is specifically civilizational in nature, a number of issues can be identified. The presence of women among the foreign troops, for example, was seen as challenging culturally; often elders and Afghan men in general resented having a foreign woman as interlocutor whether military or not.[34] Foreign sponsorship of female emancipation was also resented, particularly when it led to positive discrimination in employment.[35] The already-mentioned support for the professionalization of the judiciary was also controversial, as well as the attempt to insert "international" human rights standards in the legislation and "secularize" it, although they both moved very slowly up to 2008 at least. Finally, pressure on the executive and judiciary to avoid the implementation of aspects of the legislation that were seen as particularly controversial from a "western" point of view were also resented.[36]

Conclusion

Huntington's idea of a "clash of civilizations" captures some aspects of the dynamics of Afghanistan's politics. The rivalries among Islamist and fundamentalist groups, including the fact that quite a few of them aligned with foreign intervention in 2001 and later, point out how the substratum of "civilizational" hostility to foreign presence had a limited impact. Sympathy for non-Afghan jihadist groups was limited mostly to the elites of the political parties, with little grassroots support. Foreign presence in Afghanistan during the 1980s, but also after 2001, was undoubtedly resented as challenging by many Afghans of conservative views; indeed in some cases the outrage was almost universal in Afghanistan. Similarly, some of the reforms which the Soviets or the international community tried to push through were perceived as confrontational by specific (and sometimes wide) sectors of Afghan society. Distinguishing between specific aspects of Afghan culture and more general Islamic traits is not always easy in these cases however for example the role of women in society is even more controversial in Pashtunwali than it is in Shariah. Since large sectors of the clergy often volunteered to lead the protest against these aspects of foreign intervention in Afghanistan, it could still be argued that the challenging of aspects of Islamic "civilization" played a role in the genesis of conflict in Afghanistan in the 1980s and after 2001. However, within the larger context of the series of Afghan conflicts that started in 1978, such "civilizational" clashes appear to have been on the whole quite marginal compared to other causes of conflict. Although foreign intervention exacerbated the conflict, it started primarily as a fight for power among Afghans; mobilization was primarily driven by local concerns and local conflicts. In this sense it could be argued that rather than a "clash of civilizations", what initially occurred in Afghanistan was a more modest "friction of civilizations". This friction was exploited for mobilization purposes by Islamist and fundamentalist political groups that shared a vision of the war as a conflict of civilizations. These groups invested major resources in the indoctrination of the new generation along these lines. From their perspective the "clash of civilizations" was a self-fulfilling prophecy: they campaigned for it to occur and in doing so they, to some extent, made it happen. The "clash of civilizations" was therefore primarily a political project of specific groups and factions, not an inevitable collision of cultures and religions.

4

Pakistan—Have the Chickens Come Home to Roost?

Kavita Khory

The idea of a "clash of civilizations," largely discredited since its formulation in the early 1990s, was resurrected in the aftermath of 9/11 and gained powerful currency among policymakers and scholars in Europe, North America, and South Asia. Attractive in its conceptual and rhetorical simplicity, the "clash of civilizations" thesis obscured more political phenomena than it sought to explain. Nowhere was this more apparent than in the case of Pakistan, where complex South Asian and colonial histories and cultures were reduced to sound bites. A "clash of civilizations" was invoked within and outside of Pakistan to serve the strategic and tactical interests of a variety of state and non-state actors that had little to do with millenarian conflicts of the sort identified by Huntington.[1] Shaped by particular historical and social conditions, political Islam's appeal in Pakistan, like other post-colonial societies, is best studied in relation to ongoing nation- and state-building processes occurring within an international system that is defined by asymmetric power relations and pervasive economic inequality. The evolution of political Islam in Pakistan, I argue, is rooted largely in historical contingencies, domestic politics, and the quest for state security within and outside of its territorial boundaries.

Political Islam is neither a new phenomenon in Pakistan's history and society, nor is it undifferentiated and static in its ideology, organization and practice. In the waning years of the British Empire, Mohammed Ali Jinnah and the All India Muslim League's quest for a separate state for Muslims in India assured Islam's centrality, at least symbolically, in the newly-created state's ideology. Locating the demand for Pakistan in a distinctive religious identity, however, precluded Islam from being relegated to the private sphere, despite Jinnah's vision of Pakistan as a secular state. Simultaneously, powerful local and provincial identities and interests in the newly-constituted state convinced its leaders that only a highly centralized state and a singular conception of national identity, based on the Urdu language and Islam, could weaken competing identities and claims, for example, in the North West Frontier Province (NWFP) and Sindh, where support for the Muslim League was lukewarm at best.

Pakistan's strategic objectives, exemplified by the conflicts with India, are intimately linked with its national identity and ideology. The long-standing nexus between Pakistan's domestic politics and foreign policies, specifically the war in Afghanistan and the insurgency in Kashmir, produced optimum conditions for extremist ideologies and political violence to flourish under state sponsorship. As a proximate cause, the US's global war on terror, manifested most dramatically in Afghanistan and Iraq, has also become a powerful mobilizing force for Islamists in Pakistan, who have fully capitalized on anti-US sentiment, which, until recently, did not register strongly in Pakistan's politics. Compelled to support the US's war in Afghanistan in October 2001, General Musharraf broke off ties with the Taliban regime in Kabul, which owed its existence to Pakistan's military and its intelligence services. The Pakistan government, in reversing long-standing policy, was perceived as having abandoned its allies in Afghanistan and their supporters in the NWFP and Baluchistan. Ironically, the United States' endorsement, in the first place, of an "internationalized jihad" in Afghanistan during the 1980s set a precedent for justifying organized violence along religious lines.

Local and regional grievances, as perceived by Islamist organizations and supporters, are filtered through "grand narratives", which connect the "local and the global" by drawing upon the Muslim *Ummah's* collective grievances and an acute sense of humiliation, which can be derived from the Israeli occupation of Palestine, the conflict over Kashmir or the wars in Bosnia, Chechnya, Afghanistan, and Iraq.

The rich, complex and dynamic history of political Islam and its appeal in Pakistan cannot be summarized easily in a single chapter. I will, therefore, limit my analysis to addressing four key questions: first, given the plurality of

Islamic beliefs, practices and lived experience, what is the discursive function of Islam in Pakistan's politics? Why do state and non-state actors privilege Islamic idioms and symbols over others to define group boundaries and mobilize socio-economically diverse constituencies? Second, what factors explain the rise and decline at various times of the relative power of Islamist parties in Pakistan? Third, what strategies have state elites employed to negotiate the claims and agenda of Islamist organizations and parties? Lastly, what accounts for the rise of extremist organizations and armed militancy associated with radical forms of Islam in Pakistan?

In order to address these questions, I will focus on each of the following: nation- and state-building endeavours in Pakistan, with specific reference to the selection and use of Islam as a key signifier of political identity; the powerful nexus between domestic politics and foreign policy, as defined by the threat perceptions and security objectives of civil-military elites; and the consequences, unintended or otherwise, of Pakistan's policies, specifically in relation to Afghanistan, Kashmir and the global war on terror.

Nation, state, and Islam

In the aftermath of partition and the massive carnage that followed, Jinnah, Pakistan's first leader, offered a secular, liberal vision for Pakistan and equal rights for its citizens. In keeping with his conception of Muslims in India as essentially a "political force", dedicated to self-rule in a confederation or as a separate state, Jinnah saw no contradiction in reverting to a secular form of politics once Pakistan was established.[2] But consigning religion, specifically Islam, to the private sphere was improbable in light of the rationale for creating a separate state for the Muslims in India. At the same time, forging a consensus on the precise role and status of Islam in the polity was highly unlikely given the different interpretations of Islam and its diverse practices formed through local cultures and traditions in South Asia and beyond. While invoking religion as the ideological basis of Pakistan, the ambivalence and anxiety of elites about the role of Islam in Pakistan's society and the public arena, however, gave organizations like the *Jama'at-i-Islami* (JI), the self-proclaimed "vanguard of the Islamic revolution," an opportunity and the political space to agitate for an Islamic constitution and the enforcement of Shariah law.[3] Believing that nationalism symbolized western, not Islamic values, the JI's leader Maulana Syed Abul'l-ala-Maududi, in fact, had opposed the Pakistan movement prior to 1947. In a newly independent Pakistan, however, Maududi quickly became one of the strongest proponents of using state power to enforce an Islamic system of law governing all aspects of Pakistan's politics and society.[4]

Maududi's vision of a polity governed by Islamic laws was seen at the time as a challenge to the legitimacy of the state itself. Between 1949 and 1951, several of JI's leaders, including Maududi, were imprisoned and forced to moderate their demands for an Islamic state. As Ayesha Jalal points out, any legislation or policies likely to enhance the power of the *ulama* was "unacceptable" to the leaders of the Muslim League prior to partition and the western-educated and relatively secular bureaucrats and military officers afterwards.[5] Though hostile to Maududi's call for an Islamic state, civilian and military leaders from Liaqat Ali Khan to General Ayub Khan continued to believe that a Pakistani nationalism, privileging Islam and the Urdu language, could successfully counter multiple identities rooted in regional and linguistic cultures, urban and rural economies, income and class status, and feudal and tribal structures of authority and patronage.

Despite invoking Islam as a unifying force in Pakistan, the relationship between Islamist parties and the state remained complicated and contentious under the rule of both General Ayub Khan and Zulfiqar Ali Bhutto, who alternated between cracking down on Islamist parties on the one hand, and appeasing, co-opting or appropriating their agenda on the other. *Jama'at-i-Islami*'s leader, Maulana Maududi, for example, opposed Ayub Khan's efforts to reform Muslim family law so as to give more protection to women in divorce and inheritance proceedings, and criticized Ayub's move to remove the word "Islamic" from the country's official name. Refusing to compromise on the family law issue, Ayub Khan, who had little sympathy for Islamists and even banned the JI and imprisoned Maududi at one time, amended the constitution in 1962 to rename the country as the Islamic Republic of Pakistan.[6]

Bhutto's populist election manifesto in 1970 proposed far-reaching economic reforms under the title of "Islamic socialism," partly to diffuse opposition from the *ulama*, who believed that socialism was antithetical to Islamic values. Motivated more by the interests of their middle-class constituents in cities like Karachi than religious fervour per se, the Islamist parties' opposition to Bhutto's economic policies nonetheless was framed in religious rather than economic terms.[7] In a more consequential example of pandering to Islamist parties, Bhutto conceded to the long-standing demand of Islamists to declare Ahmadis a religious minority, despite the community's support for the PPP in the 1970 elections. In the 1973 constitution, Bhutto designated Islam as the state religion.[8] As Bhutto learned, at immense political and personal cost, invoking Islam and conceding to Islamists' demands could not compensate for deeply flawed economic policies and political ineptitude.

Both Ayub Khan and Bhutto, who in a last desperate attempt to hold on to power banned alcohol and gambling and declared Friday as a weekly holiday, used Islamic symbols and idioms selectively to integrate a diverse polity, legitimate state authority and limit the *ulama's* political influence. Even though Islamist parties at the time did not command popular support at the provincial or national levels for several reasons including sectarian divisions, poor organizational structures, narrowly focused agendas, and a lack of "charismatic leadership,"[9] they were courted by civilian and military leaders alike. Aside from their legitimizing function, Islamist parties had the capacity to mobilize core party cadres for demonstrations of "street power," for example, the anti-Ahmadi riots in Lahore in 1953, which could challenge state authority or depose governments, as shown by the protests and riots that led to the ouster of Prime Minister Zulfiqar Ali Bhutto in 1977.

Predictably, a singular, highly coercive national identity aimed at preserving the power of the Punjabi-dominated state exacerbated conflicts over resource allocation and political power among Pakistan's provinces and led to the secession of East Pakistan and the creation of Bangladesh in 1971. In an early example of the mosque-military nexus, the JI collaborated with the Pakistani military in 1971 against the *Mukti Bahini* fighting in East Pakistan. Rather than modifying state policies to address ethno-linguistic grievances, the secession of East Pakistan heightened fears about ethnic claims among the ruling elite, who brutally suppressed nationalist movements seeking greater autonomy within the federation, and in extreme cases, the creation of a separate state. Zulfiqar Ali Bhutto deployed the military against Baluch nationalists to quell an insurgency that lasted from 1973–1977. Sindhi nationalists, in turn, bore the brunt of military force in the 1980s under General Zia ul-Haq's rule. The break-up of Pakistan demonstrated that a common religious identity could not easily displace ethnic and linguistic identities or mitigate genuine grievances against the state. Yet, civilian and military leaders after 1971 could not resist the trappings of Islam or the lure of Islamist parties to do their bidding.

Islamizing politics and society: Zia and his successors

General Zia ul-Haq, in a significant departure from past policy, initiated not only an extensive restructuring of Pakistan's society and politics in accordance with Islamic values and laws, but actively sought the counsel of *ulama* and gave them unprecedented political power, which they could not attain through the ballot box. Advancing the military-mosque nexus, Islamist parties—*Jama'at-i-Islami, Jamiat-ul-Ulema-i-Pakistan*, and *Jamiat-ul-Ulema-i-Islam*—which played a leading role in ousting Bhutto's government through massive protests in 1977, benefited greatly from General Zia's own proclivities toward a stricter, essentialist interpretation of Islam.

Drawn selectively from Sunni interpretations of Islamic law and practice, General Zia's Islamization policies were opposed by Shias. Constituting between 15 per cent and 25 per cent of Pakistan's population, Shias, first of all, rejected the official interpretation of the *zakat* law, governing the taxation of Muslims, and staged mass protests against the martial law regime. While the government granted Shias an exemption, the clash over the *zakat* law only heightened Shia anxieties about their status in Pakistan, without resolving doctrinal disputes, which had now become heavily politicized with the state at the epicentre of the conflict. The government's ill-conceived *zakat* ordinance, in fact, encouraged the formation of militant groups among Shias, such as the *Tehrik-i-Nifaz-i-Fiqh-i-Jaffria* (the Front for Defence of the Shariah) and *Sipha-i Mohammed* (Mohammed's Army). Sunnis countered by forming their own militant organizations[10]

Sectarian militias, though largely independent of organized political forces, often colluded with mainstream Islamist parties, especially during the war in Afghanistan. The *Jamiat-ul-Ulema-i-Islam* (JUI), for example, was closely allied with the *Sipah-Sahaba Pakistan* and the *Lashkar-e-Jhangvi*, two extremist groups who targeted Pakistani Shias and allegedly tried to assassinate Nawaz Sharif when he was prime minister. Despite its religious overtones, sectarian militancy was rarely about theological differences. Rather, the coercive and unrepresentative nature of the state and local politics broadened the appeal of sectarian militancy among rural and urban populations, especially in the Punjab.

The scope of Zia's Islamization policies, though vast, did not alter either the traditional sources of political power represented by feudal elites in the rural areas of Punjab and Sindh, or the tribal structures in Baluchistan and the NWFP. The traders and industrialists in Pakistan's cities, meanwhile, focused principally on recovering their economic power lost under Bhutto's nationalization policies, and remained largely indifferent toward the growing Islamization of the state and its institutions. Women and religious minorities, who, as the most vulnerable members of society, could be targeted easily to appease the *ulama* and retain their support, felt the impact of Zia's policies most acutely. Although there was some resistance to the state's systematic attack on women's rights, it was confined largely to urban centres like Lahore and Karachi.[11]

In the long run, General Zia's narrow conception of Islam and its precepts proved to be divisive to heighten ethnic tensions, and to precipitate the rise of sectarian clashes, the foremost of which was, armed conflict between radical Sunni and Shia organizations. Although sectarian conflict was not unheard of in Pakistan, the scale and intensity of the violence in the 1980s was significantly different from earlier episodes, such as the anti-Ahmadi agitation in 1953.[12] In fact, General Zia's Islamization measures and political machinations aggravated not only Sunni-Shia differences, but also deepened the schisms among Sunnis themselves.

Contrary to her public pronouncements and the PPP's election manifestos, Benazir Bhutto, who was prime minister from 1988–1990 and 1993–1997, did little to reverse General Zia's Islamization policies, or address sectarian violence, growing ethnic polarization and armed conflict, specifically in Karachi. Women and religious minorities, who had borne the brunt of Zia's Islamization measures, were the most disappointed by Benazir Bhutto's inability, or unwillingness, to tackle the highly discriminatory *hudood* ordinances, the law of evidence and blasphemy laws, which had bred and legitimized a culture of coercion and violence particularly against women and religious minorities. Benazir Bhutto's successor, Nawaz Sharif, who also served two terms as prime minister, was more inclined toward religiosity in the public sphere, and lobbied for the imposition of Shariah law. This was principally to solidify his party's majority in parliament, consolidate his executive powers and pre-empt any opposition from Islamist parties. "The greatest assistance Benazir and Nawaz offered the Islamists," Stephen Cohen suggests, "lay in what they did *not* do": specifically rebuilding Pakistan's public school system as a way of undercutting the appeal of *madrasahs* set up during Zia's administration.[13]

Therefore many respects, General Musharraf's collaboration with Islamist parties and organizations to advance Pakistan's domestic and foreign policy goals, is hardly an anomaly in the state's history and politics. Despite his public platform of "enlightened moderation" and attempts to rein in militant organizations before and after 9/11, General Musharraf caved in to the demands of Islamist parties when challenged on major policy initiatives. Examples include: an attempt to overturn the blasphemy law, which is frequently used against religious minorities and even Muslims; the proposal to eliminate religious identification in passports; and efforts to reform the curriculum of *madrasahs* and limit the flow of foreign funds and students after 9/11. In each case, Musharraf, though well intentioned, backed off in the face of threats by Islamist parties to withdraw their support from his fragile parliamentary coalition led by a faction of the Pakistan Muslim League (PML-Q).

Foreign Policy and Islam

Pakistan's foreign policy from 1947 and onwards was centred on the violence of partition and its conflicts with India, principally over the disputed state of Kashmir. Three wars between India and Pakistan in 1948, 1965 and 1971 heightened Pakistan's fears of India and its quest for regional dominance. After the creation of Bangladesh in 1971, which essentially negated Jinnah and the Muslim League's rationale for establishing a single state for Muslims in South Asia, Zulfiqar Ali Bhutto asserted and reoriented Pakistan's Islamic identity in a bid to counter India's regional hegemony. By casting Pakistan as a leader among developing states and a champion of Islamic causes, whether in Palestine or Kashmir, Bhutto hoped to restore the national pride of his compatriots, develop economic and strategic links with oil-rich Persian Gulf states, and shift Pakistan's foreign policy away from its Indo-centric focus in South Asia.

Bhutto's critique of western military and economic power, specifically that of the US, reflected his ambition to be a leader of the third world, particularly Muslim countries. For Bhutto, a common Muslim identity and collective action were strategic choices, rather than reflections of cultural conflict or religious animus. By acquiring nuclear technology, strengthening the Organization of the Islamic Conference, and cooperating with Muslim states in the region, Bhutto hoped to advance Pakistan's strategic objectives *vis-à-vis* India. By welcoming both Saudi investments into Pakistan's economy and Iran's military assistance for quelling an insurgency from 1973–1977 in Baluchistan, Bhutto, perhaps unwittingly, drew both states into Pakistan's politics. Their competing visions of Islam clashed against the backdrop of the Iranian Revolution in 1979, sectarian violence in Pakistan, and the war in Afghanistan.[14]

Although state policies are largely responsible for sectarian militancy from 1979 onwards, regional developments, namely the Iranian Revolution and the Soviet war in Afghanistan, exacerbated ethnic and sectarian violence, and strengthened links between Islamist parties and organizations and external benefactors, principally Saudi Arabia and Iran. Coinciding with the Iranian Revolution, sectarian differences in Pakistan were exploited by Iran and Saudi Arabia, as each sought to advance its own distinctive interpretation of Islamic doctrine through moral and material assistance. Concerned chiefly with asserting their power and influence in the region, the Iranians and Saudis found both a strategic entry point in Pakistan's escalating sectarian conflicts and willing proxies to serve their interests. While Shia organizations increasingly relied on Iran for support, Sunni groups turned to Saudi Arabia, which was intent on limiting Iran's revolutionary ambitions by strengthening Sunni regimes in neighbouring states.[15]

From 1980, Saudi-funded *madrasahs* proliferated throughout Pakistan, propagating their message of a rigid Wahhabi form of Islam and related ideologies of violence. Though only a small number of *madrasahs* were actively involved in recruiting foot soldiers for the war in Afghanistan and later Kashmir, the growing presence of *madrasahs*, reinforced more conservative social and political mores in Pakistan, which made it easier to attract recruits and justify jihadi causes in South Asia and beyond.[16] Although *madrasahs* did not conduct military training or directly arm their students, a network of seminaries, located in the proximity of Pakistan's border with Afghanistan, became the linchpin for the US's covert war against Soviet forces in Afghanistan.

For General Zia and his civilian and military successors—Benazir Bhutto, Nawaz Sharif and General Musharraf—providing diplomatic, material and military support to the Afghan mujahedin at first, and later, the Taliban, served vital strategic interests. The key sources of enduring tension between Pakistan and Afghanistan are: first, the border dispute over the Durand Line; second, Afghan support of Pushtun nationalism and separatist movements in Pakistan; and third, India's long-standing good relations with Afghanistan, which stir fears of encirclement among Pakistani policy-makers. The war in Afghanistan offered Pakistan an unprecedented opportunity to counter Indian influence in Afghanistan, install a friendly government in Kabul, and bolster a weak and unpopular military regime through massive infusions of foreign military and economic assistance.

The Soviet invasion of Afghanistan drew widespread regional and international opprobrium, with the exception of India, which supported Soviet actions and strongly opposed the mujahedin based in the NWFP. Willing to serve as proxies for the US war in Afghanistan, Pakistan's military and intelligence agencies, including the Inter-Services Intelligence (ISI), seized the opportunity to burnish their Islamic credentials by forging a jihad against Soviet forces, while building a highly profitable network for recruiting, training and arming the mujahedin. By doing so, General Zia accomplished two things at the outset: one, he got the international community to restore foreign aid to Pakistan, which had been reduced significantly because of the military's ouster of Zulfiqar Ali Bhutto in 1977 and his subsequent execution, despite international appeals to commute his sentence. Two, he used the war in Afghanistan to gain the support of a group of religious parties, thereby weakening opposition to his tenuous rule and embarking on a new phase in the military's relationship with Islamists.[17]

Husain Haqqani, Ahmed Rashid and Steve Coll, among others, have chronicled how the CIA, working with the ISI, funded, armed and trained the predominantly Afghan mujahedin after the Soviet invasion.[18] While the US was the mujahedin's principal backer, it was matched in its financial contributions by Saudi Arabia, and supported by China, a coalition of European states, and Muslim countries like Egypt, Turkey and the United Arab Emirates. This transnational coalition essentially fought the last battle of the Cold War. However, the US war in Afghanistan, became Pakistan's war after the Soviet Union withdrew and the US lost interest in its mujahedin and Pakistani clients who, with the collapse of the Soviet Union, no longer served a strategic purpose. Disengaging quickly from its covert operations in Afghanistan, the US further destabilized the region by trusting feuding mujahedin factions, and their eager sponsors in Pakistan's intelligence agencies, to bring about a military solution to a devastating decade-long war.

Pakistan's support of the mujahedin and their Taliban successors was formed in part by the long-standing ties of the "mosque and the military". The military and its Islamist allies agreed on the broad strategic goals of the war, largely determined by regional security considerations, rather than an abstract idea of a global jihad, which characterized much of the Islamists' public discourse surrounding the war against the Soviet Union. While the military and its intelligence agencies, in collusion with the CIA, developed the strategies and tactics for conducting covert operations in Afghanistan, Islamist parties and *madrasah* networks laid the ideological groundwork for the war and supplied the recruits to fight it.

Several journalists and scholars have carefully documented the scope and complexity of the connections between the military and the intelligence services, on the one hand, and the Islamist parties and militant organizations, on the other. Analysing the myriad and murky links between the military and

Islamists, not to mention an array of affiliated and independent militant organizations, would take up far more space than this volume allows. A few anecdotal examples, however, give us a sense of the role Islamist parties played in recruiting and training mujahedin forces, the Afghan Taliban, and their recent offshoot, the Pakistani Taliban.

The *Jama'at-i-Islami* (JI), Zahid Hussein notes, was the "original face of jihad" in Afghanistan.[19] Though lacking in broad-based national support, the JI's leadership gave political cover and legitimacy to General Zia's regime. The party, in return, gained substantial leverage and resources to advance its domestic agenda, while serving the interests of its military sympathizers. The ISI, according to some accounts, was influenced by the JI's long-standing ideological and political connections with dissident Afghan groups such as the Afghan Brotherhood, and individuals like Gulbuddin Hekmatyar and Burhanuddin Rabbani, who were the chief recipients of the intelligence services' monetary and military support from 1979–1992.

When mujahedin leaders like Hekmatyar and Rabbani failed to stabilize Afghanistan after the Soviet withdrawal, the ISI turned to other Pakistani militant groups such as *Harkat-ul-Ansar*, which was affiliated with the JUI, and owed its power to the emerging Taliban forces.[20] Until 1993, the JUI was largely excluded from the political mainstream and had very little influence over the military's tactical support and training of various mujahedin factions operating throughout the Soviet occupation. This did not prevent it, however, from expanding its organizational structure and procuring financial resources from the Saudis, among others, to set up its own network of *madrasahs* in the NWFP and the predominantly Pushtun areas of Baluchistan. The JUI, as a result, was well prepared on the ground when Prime Minister Benazir Bhutto invited the party to join her ruling coalition in 1993 and appointed JUI's chief, Maulana Fazlur Rehman, as chairman of the National Assembly's Standing Committee for Foreign Affairs—a position that gave the JUI access to state resources and institutions, including the military, and allowed it to lobby for the Taliban in Pakistan and the Middle East.[21]

The JUI's network of *madrasahs*, like many others, was openly used to raise funds and provide a ready supply of recruits, Pakistani and foreign, for the ongoing jihad led by the Taliban.[22] Support for the Taliban was also channelled through two extremist groups associated with the JUI, the *Sipah-Sahaba Pakistan* and *Lashkar-e-Jhangvi*. Both groups were implicated in the killings of hundreds of Shias in Pakistan, as well as two assassination attempts on Prime Minister Nawaz Sharif. Leaders of both organizations sought refuge with the Taliban in Afghanistan when Sharif's government tried to curtail their operations in the Punjab.[23] Products of the same Deobandi *madrasahs*, the Taliban propagated their own unique brand of radical Islam that had little do with Pushtun culture or traditions, let alone Islamic law and practice. The Taliban's model of a militant Islam, Zahid Hussein points out, was largely at odds with local beliefs and traditions.[24] The ideological symbiosis between the Taliban and local leaders, for example, in North and South Waziristan, is a relatively recent development that occurred after the US ousted the Taliban from Kabul in 2001.

Despite the extensive involvement of Islamist parties and militant sectarian organizations, Pakistan's support of the Taliban was driven largely by its national interests and security concerns, and not religious ideology or an abstract notion of a pan-Islamic identity. Believing that Pakistan had "earned the right to stay as a dominant player, in Afghanistan,[25] civilian and military leaders had four key objectives: one, to end the civil war in Afghanistan; two, to create a stable security environment that would allow over three million Afghan refugees to return home; three, to gain strategic access to Central Asian states for trade and energy resources, and finally, to limit Indian influence in the region. The Taliban, Rasul Rais argues, were the only organized force at the time that could control the violence in Afghanistan and establish a semblance of authority. Whether the Taliban would have succeeded without Pakistan's diplomatic, financial and military support for recruiting, training and arming Taliban fighters is not entirely clear, though Pakistan's continued support of the Taliban's regressive rule was deeply unpopular among its neighbours, including Iran, and the larger international community.[26]

As the war in Afghanistan was winding down, the ISI began to siphon militants to Kashmir in order to bolster the insurgency against the Indian government. Partly in retaliation for India's involvement in the creation of Bangladesh, the military's training and arming of pro-Pakistan insurgents in Kashmir from 1987 onwards was intended to mire India in a low-intensity conflict, without risking a full-scale war. As the Kargil conflict of 1999 demonstrates, however, nuclear weapons in the arsenals of both India and Pakistan did not prevent the two states from going to war in the disputed area of Kashmir, although the threat of nuclear weapons prevented the conflict from escalating further. By promoting Islamist factions like *Hizbul Mujahideen* in Kashmir, the ISI weakened the leadership of the Jammu and Kashmir Liberation Front, which drew its inspiration from a deep-rooted, culturally oriented Kashmiri identity, rather than an Islamic one.[27]

The war on terror: reversing course?

Pakistan's support of the US war on terror, launched after 9/11, implied a radical shift in the country's foreign and security policies. Leaving aside the US Deputy Secretary of State Richard Armitage's now infamous remark that Pakistan should be prepared to be "bombed back to the Stone Age," if it did not cooperate with the United States, General Musharraf, in his memoir, *In the Line of Fire*, identifies a combination of strategic imperatives and security compulsions that led him to support the US intervention in Afghanistan. But doing so meant repudiating Pakistan's support for the Taliban regime, as well as cracking down on sources of Islamic extremism and violence in Pakistan, including the *madrasahs* from where the Taliban emerged in 1994, and, finally, cutting off aid and assistance to Kashmiri insurgents.[28] Though threats of American reprisals against Pakistan partially explain Musharraf's acquiescence to US demands, aligning once again with the US meant the end of Pakistan's international isolation and a resumption of aid and assistance to the military, which had been cut off because of Pakistan's "transgressions": nuclear tests in 1998, the Kargil incursion in 1999, and Musharraf's coup against Nawaz Sharif in October 1999.

Rather than fully dismantling a complex and shadowy network of extremist organizations, sustained by the military and its agencies for over two decades, General Musharraf's counter-terrorism operations, Ashley Tellis argues, were "segmented" and "discriminative," conforming to Pakistan's national interests.[29] After seven years, Pakistan's support for the Taliban remained largely undiminished, *madrasah* reforms appeared half-hearted and ineffectual, and proscribed organizations like the *Lashkar-e-Tayyaba* resurfaced under new names.[30] In Quetta and Peshawar, the Taliban operate freely with the support of Musharraf's allies in the *Muttahida Majlis-e-Amal* (MMA), a six-party Islamist coalition, which controlled the provincial governments in the NWFP and Baluchistan from 2002–2007.[31]

The military, by supporting the US war on terror on the one hand, and allowing the Taliban and al-Qaeda to regroup on the other, has tried to preserve its strategic options in Afghanistan.[32] Islamabad's "double game" in the war on terror, Stephen Cohen contends, is driven by the military's dislike of Karzai and his close relationship with India, which is still seen as a major threat to Pakistan's security and interests, particularly if and when US and NATO forces leave Afghanistan.[33] Pakistan's "double game," combined with flawed US policies, however, has turned the border region between Afghanistan and Pakistan into the "command and control center for leadership of al-Qaeda, the Afghan Taliban and groups from Central Asia."[34] Although Pakistan's military and law enforcement agencies apprehended some "foreigners" in the area linked to al-Qaeda, they rarely interfered with the Taliban's cross-border operations, thus undermining the US-led NATO forces' mission in Afghanistan.[35] Aside from the local and regional security threats emanating from Pakistan's northwest border areas, militant camps, flourishing in the NWFP and Baluchistan, serve as sanctuaries and training camps for militants from Central Asia, the Middle East and Europe, who, in turn, are implicated in terrorist attacks in Europe and elsewhere.

The Afghan Taliban's Pakistani offshoot, which emerged in the Federally Administered Tribal Areas (FATA) between 2002 and 2004, poses a far more serious threat to the state, not only in the border region, but also in settled areas like the Swat valley. Here, the indigenous Taliban's growing power and indiscriminate violence has systematically undermined traditional Pushtun tribal structures and political authority, and threatened the interests of long-established Islamist parties like the JUI, which sees itself in the political "mainstream."[36] Consisting of a network of small independent groups, the Taliban, under the leadership Baitullah Mehsud, whom the Musharraf government implicated in Benazir Bhutto's assassination, announced the formation of an umbrella organization *Tehrik-i-Taliban Pakistan* (TTP) in December 2007.

Although the extent of cooperation among the different local Taliban groups and other militant organizations, such as the *Tehreek-e-Nafz-e-Shariat-e-Mohammed* (TNSM)[37] is unclear, the Taliban's principal aim is to control territory along the border between Pakistan and Afghanistan in order to fight NATO forces in Afghanistan and launch a "defensive jihad against the Pakistan army."[38] US policies in the Middle East and South Asia reinforce the belief among militants that the wars in Afghanistan and Iraq are being fought against Islam, thus justifying calls for a global jihad to liberate Muslim lands. The Pakistani Taliban, observers claim, are providing al-Qaeda with "liberated areas" for recruitment and training.[39] As Stephen Cohen put it, "the militants are not interested in ministerial bungalows in Islamabad, they want to turn Pakistan into a base from which they can attack other soft Muslim and eastern states (and India)."[40] Military operations against militants and their supporters have resulted in a growing number of casualties, including women and children, which reinforces animosity toward Musharraf and his US allies, while building support for the Taliban, who, in the absence of government authority, offer a semblance of security for the local population.

The military's ill-conceived peace deals with militants in North and South Waziristan in 2006 did little to curb Taliban incursions into Afghanistan or forestall attacks on Pakistan's military, which has become a key target for Taliban militia.[41] The declining authority of the state and its lack of political will, combined with divisions within the military itself, have left the rank and file of the military demoralized and unwilling to fight against the myriad Islamist factions operating in the NWFP and Baluchistan, where a low-level insurgency, unrelated to the conflict with the Taliban, is going on.[42]

Afghanistan and Kashmir: the "blowback" effect

Pakistan's involvement in Afghanistan and Kashmir, and its support of US military and strategic goals in the region, have proven to be catastrophic for state and societal security. First, the long-term human and environmental costs of the wars in Afghanistan are incalculable. Hosting three million Afghan refugees in the NWFP and Baluchistan created its own set of tensions over scarce resources, sometimes manifested along ethnic lines. In an environment where few employment opportunities existed outside of a burgeoning war economy based on narcotics and weapons, conflicts between citizens and refugees over resources were inevitable. Rather than sites of temporary refuge, many Afghan camps turned into semi-permanent settlements, where a second-generation of Afghan refugees, including the Taliban, has grown up in desperate and violent conditions. As many refugees moved into the urban areas of Baluchistan, NWFP, and eventually further south to Karachi, they put even more pressure on an already strained supply of jobs, housing and civic services and intensified local conflicts and violence.

Second, the wars in Afghanistan and the insurgency in Kashmir, more consequentially, militarized Islamic activists in Pakistan. By using Islamist parties and organizations as instruments of foreign policy, the military gave them enormous power and resources, which were routinely diverted from the wars at hand to domestic conflicts and enemies, who became surrogates for the foreign wars. Largely dependent on the goodwill and support of their civil service and military patrons at first, Islamist militants and organizations have become more self-sufficient and autonomous as a result of the protracted conflicts, thus making it much harder for the military to control its clients, despite the external and domestic pressure after 9/11 to do so.

Third, Pakistan's role as a "front-line ally" of the US, first against the Soviet Union, and later, in the war on terror, enhanced the power and influence of the ISI Directorate to manipulate both foreign and domestic allies and enemies. Penetrating deeply into all sectors of Pakistan's society and economy, the military's defence-industrial complex has attained monumental proportions at the expense of genuine political and economic development, making it even more difficult to imagine a political dispensation where the military would voluntarily disengage from the public sphere and accept civilian authority and control over its organization.[43]

Finally, institutional efforts to redefine the military's cultural and social norms along Islamic lines were already underway when Pakistan extended its support to the mujahedin in 1979. The war in Afghanistan and the insurgency in Kashmir intensified public expressions of piety by military officers and encouraged strict adherence to Islamic rituals and practices among its rank and file, who worked closely with various Islamic groups and organizations to execute the military's covert operations in the two theatres of war. Although it is difficult to gauge precisely the level of sympathy among military personnel for hard-line Islamist groups and causes, the enduring collaboration between the military and Islamists has "produced men at arms who consider themselves soldiers of Islam." In a stark reminder of the long-lasting and lethal consequences of the "mosque-military" connection, lower-ranking military officials, in collusion with extremist organizations, were implicated in an assassination attempt on General Musharraf in December 2003.[44]

Conclusion

Though contentious at times, the relationship between state elites, civilian and military, and Islamists in Pakistan has been politically contingent and mutually beneficial. The state has accommodated and co-opted Islamists to retain power and legitimize unpopular civilian and military regimes, often at the expense of secular and ethno-nationalist parties as seen in the 2002 elections. Islamist parties have a long tradition of functioning within established state structures, competing in elections, and forming coalitions with other political parties, including the Pakistan People's Party (PPP).[45] Rarely unified, Islamists engage in what passes for "normal" politics in Pakistan without resorting to armed violence. Yet, at times, Islamists, along with other state and non-state actors, have encouraged, enabled and participated in extremist movements and armed violence.

Armed militancy in Pakistan is a product of deliberate state policies, culminating in the failure of the state to fulfil its obligations to its citizens for ensuring their welfare and security, irrespective of religion, gender or ethnicity. The Ghazi brothers' six-month long occupation in 2007 of Islamabad's Lal Masjid and their attempts to impose Shariah law in the capital, along the lines of the Taliban, suggest that the state is willing to endure a degree of militancy and violence if it serves its strategic interests, even when extremists defy the writ of the state and its armed forces in the capital itself.[46] Tolerating and encouraging the growth of radical Islam and its functionaries in a much more fluid regional and global security environment than seen during the Cold War, however, has raised levels of violence in Pakistan far beyond the imagination and control of the military and intelligence services. This is shown by the retaliatory killings of military and police personnel and a record number of suicide bombings undertaken by the Taliban and al-Qaeda after the army finally launched an operation against the Ghazi brothers in July 2007.[47] A vocal critic of Pakistan's support of the Taliban and their al-Qaeda affiliates, Benazir Bhutto's assassination on 27 December 2007 is by far the most powerful reminder that Pakistan's proxy wars have come home with a vengeance.

A recent survey conducted in Pakistan's urban areas, though limited, reveals the complexity of public opinion about Islam and its role in politics and society. Posing a "paradox for the American mind," a large majority of Pakistanis, according to Steve Kull, wants a greater role for Islam and the Shariah in Pakistan. A preference for giving Islam more prominence in the public sphere, however, is accompanied by a strong desire for democratic reforms and representative institutions.[48] Contrary to popular assumptions, most Pakistanis reject the Taliban form of Islam, support *madrasah* reforms, and hold negative views of militant organizations such as al-Qaeda and the local Taliban.[49] But plans to fund and train members of the paramilitary Frontier Corps and place US troops on the ground in Pakistan, have further fuelled anti-American sentiments throughout Pakistan. A majority of Pakistanis believe that continued US military presence in the region is the most critical threat facing the country.[50] Many Pakistanis, especially middle class professionals and members of civil society, deeply distrust the US for its support of General Musharraf as a matter of political expediency and operational convenience, and its profound failure to live up to its democratic ideals at home and abroad. Under the threat of impeachment, pressured by civil society and media, and more or less abandoned by the military, President Musharraf resigned from office on August 18, 2008. Although the results of the February 2008 elections have yielded a new, albeit weak, democratic dispensation, and a fairly peaceful political transition by Pakistan's standards, the human and military security challenges facing Pakistan, within and beyond its borders, are unlikely to dissipate, especially in light of US government reports suggesting that al-Qaeda had succeeded in establishing a "safe haven" in Pakistan's Federally Administered Tribal Areas, one of the poorest regions in the country.[51]

5

Indonesia—The Radicalization of Islam

Kirsten Schulze

Indonesia is the largest Muslim country in the world with a population of 240 million of which 88 per cent are Muslim. It is also one of the most moderate Muslim countries with a history of pluralism and tolerance. Since the 1998 fall of President Suharto, Islam in all its variations has seen a cultural and political revival. Muslim political parties proliferated as a result of the democ- ratization process itself, which provided the political space, but also as a result of the 1997 economic crisis and the slow recovery that allowed Muslim social, welfare, and educational organizations to provide essential services to the community where the state was failing. While the vast majority of Indonesian Muslims are moderate and tolerant, Indonesia has not escaped radicalization. At a political level this radicalization has manifested itself in repeated demands for Islamic Law or Shariah and the reopening the 1950s debate over the nature of the Indonesian state. At a "military" level, a number of jihadist organizations have emerged in the context of communal conflicts and trans- national jihadists, notably *Jemaah Islamiyya* (JI), have been actively targeting western interests in Indonesia.

This chapter looks at the radicalization of Islam in Indonesia. It will focus on five key areas: First, the radicalization of mainstream organizations; sec- ond, radicalization in the context of communal conflicts; third, the rise of

Shariah in conflict and post-conflict areas; fourth, the implementation of Shariah-like by-laws at district and regency level, and fifth, the emergence of JI. It will be argued here that while JI might pose the more immediate and violent threat, the greater, albeit long-term challenge to the nature of the Indonesian state is coming from the non-violent Islamist political parties and pressure groups. They have been unravelling the "secular" state at grassroots level by getting Shariah and Shariah-like by-laws adopted at district and regency level against majority wishes and without so much as a response from the central government in Jakarta.

Radicalization of the mainstream

Islam came to Indonesia via trade routes as early as the eleventh century. It was first embraced by traders and then by some of the kingdoms such as Mataram in Central Java and the sultanates of Ternate and Tidore in North Maluku. By the sixteenth century it had spread across the archipelago to the west. It was adopted by large parts of the population, absorbed into the local culture, and mixed with local customs and beliefs. In the early twentieth century, modernist Islam rose to prominence with the establishment of *Muhammadiya* in 1912. Since then mainstream Islam in Indonesia has been divided into modernists and traditionalists represented by the social organizations *Muhammadiya* and *Nahdatul Ulama* (NU). Where modernists focused on *ijtihad*, Shariah, purism, scripturalism, universalism, urbanism and "high culture", traditionalists looked toward *taqlid, adat* or custom, syncretism, mysticism, local custom and popular culture.[1] *Muhammadiya* chairman Din Syamsudin explained *Muhammadiya's* philosophy and differences with traditionalist Islam as follows:

"Our philosophy is based on the *Qur'ān*, hadith, *ijtihad* and reason. We don't follow the classical school like NU. In fact we don't follow any of the *madhab* but we are not a Salafi movement. We are against *bid'a*, superstition and ancestor worship—which NU practices. In the areas of *akida* and *ibadah* we are puritanical, Salafi, but in education and social programmes we follow Muhammed Abduh."[2]

Muhammadiya has 35 million followers and is affiliated with the National Mandate Party or *Partai Amanat Nasional* (PAN). In line with its modernist philosophy *Muhammadiya* has a built up broad network of educational institutions ranging from kindergartens to universities. NU has 40 million mainly Javanese members and is affiliated with the National Awakening Party or *Partai Kebangkitan Bangsa* (PKB). They run the majority of rural Muslim boarding schools or *pesantren*.

Both NU and *Muhammadiya* were purely social organizations during Suharto's New Order. Their affiliated political parties only emerged post-Suharto. As institutions, neither NU and *Muhammadiya*, nor PKB and PAN pursue a radical agenda. Yet all four have become radicalized as a result of being targeted by non-violent radical organizations, most notably the Prosperous Justice Party or *Partai Keadilan Sejahtera* (PKS) and *Hizb-ut Tahrir* (HT), as well as by the personal political ambitions of their top leadership.

One area targeted has been the education system. NU runs an estimated 6,000 *pesantren* and according to Zuhairi Misrawi, NU programme coordinator for *pesantren* and community development, many schools have been radicalized.

"The radicals approach the *pesantren* through opening dialogue with the *kyai* [religious leader], they talk to the *kyai* about struggling for Islam and the *kyai* also want to struggle for Islam. And then the radicals talk about implementing Shariah and the *kyai* think this is a good idea. We have not found a way to prevent this. The *kyai* get approached by PKS, *Hizb-ut Tahrir*; MMI [*Majelis Mujahedin Indonesia*—the Indonesian Mujahedin Council] and DDII [*Dewan Dakwah Islam Indonesia*—the Indonesian Islamic Preaching Council]. In my estimate we have lost 2,000 *pesantren* to the radicals within the last three years."[3]

Muhammadiya schools have faced similar challenges. *Muhammadiya* chairman Din Syamsudin claims that "of our *pesantren* we have lost maybe 1 per cent to the radicals."[4] Another target has been the mosques. As Zuhairi explained:

"The radicals want to take over our mosques. They make speeches to get the sympathy of the people and to influence them to vote for PKS. The mosques are becoming the centre of the radicals. Every Friday now there are sermons saying that the Christians are infidels and that liberal Muslims are infidels. This is happening in the mosques of NU and *Muhammadiya*. PKS is very successful in their strategy through the mosque."[5]

Hizb-ut Tahrir has pursued a similar approach but it targets areas where NU is not strong such as Aceh and Central and East Kalimantan. "*Hizb-ut Tahrir* talks about an Islamic state and now the people want an Islamic state."[6]

NU and *Muhammadiya* have also lost some of their younger generation. As Din Syamsudin explained:

"FPI [*Front Pembela Islam* or the Islamic Defenders Front] gets its members from disaffected NU and they are generally based in NU areas. In *Laskar Jihad* there are *Muhammadiya* children."[7]

Syamsudin sees the radicalization of the youth "linked to students who go to the Middle East. They bring back ideas and these ideas are transmitted through their sermons."[8] Zuhairi explained that the problem is not just the appeal of radical solutions to the youth or being targeted by the radicals, but also that the political elites of both NU and *Muhammadiya* have been flirting with radicalism because they think it will make them more popular or get them elected.

"The NU elites and the people are different. The elites just think about politics, for example Hasyim Muzadi [NU chairman]. Our problem is the political elite in NU within the context of the struggle for democracy. Pluralism and human rights are still a problem. While we [the grassroots] are struggling for pluralism MUI [the Indonesian Muslim Ulama council] issues a *fatwa* against pluralism and the deputy chairman of MUI is NU! [The chairman is *Muhammadiya*]."[9]

There is no doubt that MUI has radicalized. During Suharto's New Order regime MUI was a bland organization whose primary function was to issue *halal* certificates and to announce the sighting of the moon at the beginning of *Ramadan*. MUI never made any pronouncements that could even vaguely have been considered political never mind radical. This changed post-Suharto, partially because MUI was trying to distance itself from its regime-co-opted status. In the search for legitimacy it adopted a more conservative interpretation of Islam. In 2005, this conservatism took on radical tones when MUI issued a number of highly contentious *fatwas*. These *fatwas* prohibited interfaith prayer, mixed marriages, interfaith inheritance, religious pluralism, liberalism, and secularism. In 2006, MUI called upon all provincial governments to pass anti-sin laws, especially against prostitution. MUI supported the draft anti-pornography legislation during the same year but spoke out against the draft anti-discrimination legislation, which would have protected religious minorities.

The popular discourse has also radicalized, especially when looking at issues such as Iraq, Afghanistan, Palestine, US foreign policy and the "war on terror". This has not translated into popular support for Shariah and an Islamic state, however. Islamists in the first post-Suharto elections believed they would obtain over 50 per cent of the vote; they only achieved 38 per cent, roughly what Islamists had polled in the last democratic elections in 1955.[10] Subsequently, concerted efforts were made to mobilize public opinion on Shariah. This effort was led by *Partai Keadilan* later renamed PKS and HT and supported by militant organizations such as *Laskar Jihad* and FPI. Depending on whether it was perceived as politically expedient at the time it also received backing from the Star and Crescent Party or *Partai Bulan Bintang* (PBB),

PAN, and the Development Unity Party or *Partai Persatuan Pembangunan* (PPP). It started with reopening the debate on whether Indonesia should be an Islamic state. This had been a heated debate when the constitution was drafted in 1945 with Muslim parties such as *Masyumi* preferring an Islamic state and pushing for the inclusion in the preamble of the so-called Jakarta Charter, which made Shariah obligatory for Muslims. The Charter was never adopted as non-Muslim eastern Indonesia threatened to leave the newly formed republic. Post-Suharto, the Islamists succeeded in reopening this debate at parliamentary level, only to find that their mobilization efforts had not been successful. There was no parliamentary support for changing the constitution. In 2002, the People's Consultative Assembly or *Majelis Permusyawaratan Rakyat* (MPR) rejected their proposal to implement Shariah. This rejection was backed by both NU and *Muhammadiya*.[11]

More recently, the Shariah debate has re-emerged in the guise of anti-pornography legislation with demonstrations in favour of the laws, which would require women to cover their bodies totally, forbid kissing or handholding in public, and outlaw revealing films, art, publications. While the majority of Muslims did not agree with this legislation they remained a silent or rather silenced majority as critics were immediately labelled as anti-Muslim. Similar dynamics were evident in the national parliament.[12] Looking at the radicalization of NU, PKB, *Muhammadiya*, PAN, MUI and the general public discourse it becomes clear that this has not been a random phenomenon but the result of well-thought-out strategy by PKS. This strategy has five components. First, to reopen the debate on the nature of the Indonesian state at parliamentary level. Second, to get headmasters, teachers, and *kyai* to embrace the idea of the Islamic state and to disseminate it through the schools. Third, to use the mosques to spread their message. Fourth, to change legislation at grassroots level by getting district and regional legislatures to adopt Shariah-like by-laws. And fifth, to influence public opinion and the popular Muslim discourse through issues like immorality, pornography, and "anti-Muslim" western foreign policy. PKS is playing a long game. Its ultimate aim is to turn Indonesia into an Islamic state not through the use of force, which it sees as counterproductive, but through elections and legislation change. For both it has targeted the grassroots. It has been successful, as PKS, unlike other Indonesian political parties, has a clear platform and is willing to put in the footwork rather than just showing up at election time. And last but certainly not least, PKS has a reputation of not being corrupt.

Conflict and jihad: the case of Ambon and *Laskar Jihad*

In the wake of the fall of Suharto communal conflict erupted in parts of the Indonesian archipelago. In the areas of Maluku and Central Sulawesi these conflicts quickly became labelled religious conflicts between Muslims and Christians. And not surprisingly, these conflicts produced local jihadists and attracted jihadists from other parts of Indonesia and abroad. While the former were primarily involved in defending their neighbourhoods, family and friends, the latter also brought with them radical ideologies. Both the fighting and the influx of new ideologies transformed what essentially were socioeconomic conflicts into jihads and radicalized the local Muslim population. Muslims in other parts of Indonesia, most notably Java, were also radicalized and drawn into the jihad, mainly as a result of the lack of adequate response from the central government, which "forced" Muslims to take the protection of their brethren into their own hands.

Ambon is a good example of how a socio-economically-driven communal conflict became a jihad and how both local Muslims and Muslims in Java were radicalized. The conflict in Ambon erupted on 19 January 1999 from a seemingly innocuous argument between a Christian bus driver and a Muslim passenger.[13] This exploded into widespread Muslim-Christian violence and the conflict spread throughout Maluku. Over the next three years between 5,000 and 9,000 people were killed and some 400,000–750,000 internally displaced in what became viewed as a religious conflict. Closer analysis of the underlying causes of the violence, however, reveals that Ambon was a social conflict with roots in the social engineering undertaken by the Dutch when they set foot on the Spice Islands some 350 years ago. Under the Dutch the Christians became the local partners of the Dutch East Indies spice traders and the colonial administrators, who saw to it that the Christians received the more fertile lands, better education, employment in the civil service, and positions in the colonial army. Indeed, the relations between Ambon's Protestants and the Dutch colonial administration were so good that many Ambonese fought on the Dutch side in Indonesia's war of independence and attempted—albeit unsuccessfully—to establish their own republic, the Republic of South Maluku (RMS), at the end of this war.[14]

When Maluku became part of Indonesia the Christians of Ambon maintained their social hegemony despite the fact that they were never fully trusted after the RMS uprising.[15] Their educational advantage allowed them to dominate the local civil service, the education system, and the media. Indeed, it was only in the 1980s and 1990s that their position and with it their unencumbered access to resources was being eroded. The Muslim challenge was the result of a number of factors. First, the educational gap was beginning to narrow. Ambonese Muslims started entering university and eventually started competing for the civil service, education and media jobs, which the Christians had for so long considered theirs. Second, on the back of President Suharto's transmigration programme, a significant number of Muslim spontaneous migrants from neighbouring Sulawesi arrived in Ambon and found their niche in the informal sector. These migrants together with the local Muslims became a demographic threat. And third, from the late 1980s Suharto actively started courting Muslim support, creating the perception that the government was pursuing an Islamization policy. In 1992, the first Muslim, Akip Latuconsina, was appointed governor of Ambon. He started to bring Muslims into his administration. By 1996 all regents were Muslim, even in Christian majority areas, and "regional heads of national departments, previously almost all Christian, were replaced by Muslims."[16] Not surprisingly, Ambon's Christians started to feel squeezed from all directions while Muslims saw a change in status quo within their reach. Tensions between the two communities ran high but were kept under control by the security forces. Only after the fall of Suharto's military regime was the lid lifted off the simmering pot and violence openly erupted.[17]

During the first two waves of violence the Christians maintained the upper hand. Muslim sections of Ambon city, especially the migrant areas, were burnt. Muslims were displaced and mixed neighbourhoods cleansed. The local Muslim population was radicalized almost over night. Neighbourhood defence organizations known as *laskar lokal* emerged armed with spears, bows and arrows, knives, machetes and eventually home-made guns and bombs. Muslim clergy adopted the rhetoric of jihad and preached anti-Christian sermons. Conspiracy theories abounded. Muslims believed the Christians had planned the conflict and that they had outside Christian support from Europe, Australia and America.[18]

When the images of burnt buildings and refugees hit the national media, Muslims across Indonesia were incensed and asked what the government was doing to stop the conflict. President Gus Dur veered between indecisiveness and apathy. After a year of government inaction Muslim politicians such as Amien Rais called for a jihad to support their Muslim brethren. Answering this call a stream of jihadists set off for Ambon. The most prominent group to arrive there was *Laskar Jihad*, which had been established in January 2000 to "save Ambon". But it was not until four months later that an estimated 3,000 mujahedin departed for Ambon. They were joined by jihadists from *Laskar Mujahedin, Kompak Mujahedin* and *Jemaah Islamiyya* who brought with them automatic weapons. Local and non-local jihadists combined forces and changed tactics from the *ad hoc* defence of Muslim areas to actively targeting Christian enclaves. Having successfully shifted the military balance in favour of the Muslims, some groups such as *Laskar Jihad* proceeded with spreading their Salafi ideology, including imposing Shariah in March 2001.[19] *Laskar Jihad*'s ultimate ambition was to transform all of Indonesia into an Islamic state.[20] The conflict in Ambon was thus only a starting point and a test-case to assess the strength of the non-Muslim opposition as well as the reaction of the central government and the Indonesian Muslim population.

When the conflict in Ambon finally ended with the 2002 Malino Agreement, which called for non-local combatants to leave Ambon, Muslim Ambon had changed. Muslims were no longer embracing joint holiday celebrations with Christians—not because of an understandable distrust so shortly after the conflict, but because of the fear of being contaminated by non-*halal* food. In some areas dress had changed. For instance, in the area of Kebun Cengkeh, which had been a *Laskar Jihad* stronghold, many men now wore Pakistani style *shalwar kamis* and women were covered head to toe in black *abayas*.

Conflict and Shariah: the case of Aceh

Conflict has not only given rise to jihadists but also to demands for Shariah. While such demands were not surprisingly voiced in the Poso and Maluku conflicts, which were seen as Christian-Muslim conflicts, and indeed, a form of Shariah has been implemented in North Maluku since the end of the conflict, Shariah also came up in the context of the Aceh conflict. What makes Aceh interesting is that Shariah was not a grassroots demand by the people but was lobbied for by the Acehnese elites and *ulama* and perceived by Jakarta as some sort of conflict resolution mechanism and as something the Acehnese wanted. As a result Aceh became the only part of Indonesia in which Shariah has been legislated for by the national government in Jakarta in contradiction with Indonesia's "secular" constitution. Aceh was seen as an exception because of the separatist struggle, which was waged in this province between 1976 and 2005. Aceh was granted special treatment under Law 44/1999 which was passed under the Habibie government and then subsequently taken up by President Gus Dur during whose term the autonomy legislation was drafted,

debated and redrafted. Law 18/2001 then provided Aceh with special autonomy status which not only included the devolution of political powers and
the right to keep 80 per cent of the province's resources but also the recognition of Acehnese culture and heritage by granting Aceh Shariah. Special
autonomy came into effect on 1 January 2002 and Shariah was partially implemented from March 2002 onwards.

This partial implementation focused on Islamic dress. Women in urban
areas had to be covered except for the face, hands and feet. This was followed
by some additional regulations such as the prohibition of alcoholic drinks and
the flogging of Ramadan violators. However, as the separatist conflict continued neither autonomy nor Shariah were ever fully implemented. Shariah was
again included in the post-conflict 2006 Law on the Governance of Aceh
(LoGA). The LoGA contains sixteen articles on Shariah and its application.
It covers religious observance, family law, civil law, criminal law, justice, education, proselytising, and defence of the faith.[21] It further provides for additional
stipulations to be regulated by Aceh's by-laws or *qanun*. According to these
sixteen articles "every individual living in or visiting Aceh shall respect
Shariah."[22] Many of the *qanun* focus on morality and women. The *qanun* on
"proximity" or *khalwat* and intimacy or *ikhtilath* defines *khalwat* as "the act
of being alone committed by a man and woman who are not legally married."[23]
Khalwat carries a punishment of being caned ten times. *Ikhtilath* is defined
as "the act of adultery between a man and a woman not legally married" and
includes "holding hands, kissing, hugging."[24] It carries a punishment of
being caned twenty times. *Zina* is defined as the sexual act between a man and
a woman not legally married and carries a punishment of being caned a hundred times.

Since the Aceh conflict was not about Islam but about dissatisfactory centre-periphery relations, political over-centralization, economic exploitation,
and human rights abuses by the security forces, the question arises why Aceh
ended up with Shariah? The explanation can be partially found in Aceh's history and the image promoted by both Acehnese and non-Acehnese—namely
that the Acehnese are more religious than anyone else in Indonesia. Shariah
was the norm in Aceh intermittently throughout history. Indeed, before it
became part of Indonesia Aceh was an Islamic Sultanate. Since Indonesian
independence Aceh had some form of Shariah on at least four occasions. First
from 1949 to 1951 when Aceh had special status; second, from 1953 to 1959
when Aceh was part of the *Darul Islam* rebellions; third, from 1959 to around
1967 when Aceh was *Daerah Istimewa* or special territory, and fourth from

2002 onwards when Shariah was implemented as part of the autonomy package. During these periods different aspects of Shariah were highlighted, mainly focusing on family law and dress code. With the 2006 LoGA the province for the first time received the permission to apply Shariah criminal legislation and with it corporal *hudud* punishments. Indeed, Shariah effectively replaced the national criminal code and a new Shariah police or *Wilayatul Hisbah* patrolled the streets to counter moral transgressions.

Aceh's history and self-portrayal made national parliamentarians and the central government in Jakarta believe that the Acehnese wanted Shariah and that granting Shariah would help resolve the separatist conflict. This belief was at best misguided. The Free Aceh Movement or *Gerakan Aceh Merdeka* (GAM) never demanded Shariah in thirty years of conflict. Its aim was an independent Acehnese state. The exiled leadership articulated the struggle in the language of self-determination, the illegal transfer of sovereignty, and an unfinished decolonization process.[25] When Shariah was included in the special autonomy package in 2001 GAM saw this as a sinister game by Jakarta—as the Indonesian government's attempt to portray GAM as militant Islamists in order to undermine international support and also as an attempt to turn a vertical, separatist conflict into a horizontal one. As one of the GAM negotiators explained before the implementation of Shariah, "the Indonesian government overseas says the Acehnese are Islamic fundamentalists. They think we can be quelled with Shariah and they use it to portray us as fanatics."[26] After Shariah started to be implemented the same negotiator commented that: "they are trying to turn the conflict about sovereignty into a conflict about religion."[27]

Yet GAM's position was not unambiguous. While it was primarily focused on freeing Aceh from what it saw as Javanese neo-colonialism, the movement emerged and recruited from a population for whom Islam was an integral part of their identity. Not surprisingly, until July 2002 GAM advocated the return to the historic Islamic Sultanate. It has since advocated democratic elections as a way to decide the nature of a future independent Aceh. Moreover, individual GAM commanders sometimes resorted to enforcing a form of Shariah in their fiefdoms and at grassroots level the struggle was sometimes expressed in Islamist terms. A press release by GAM's Central Bureau of Information in March 2002 exemplified GAM's difficult position. It rejected Shariah as the gift from Jakarta but it did not reject it as such or indeed rule it out for any future Acehnese state.[28] While GAM never demanded Shariah, Acehnese politicians and *ulama* lobbied quietly but persistently for it. One of the key lobbyists was Abdullah Puteh, Aceh Governor from 1999 until 2006. Puteh believed that Shariah could function as a mechanism of conflict resolution in Aceh. Shariah could be a way of returning GAM into the fold. His reasoning was that if everyone followed Shariah, GAM as good Muslims would not wage war on the Indonesian government, which is a Muslim government.

While the local politicians constituted one group who actively lobbied Jakarta for Shariah, Acehnese *ulama*—mainly those who were urban and modernist—constituted the other. They supported the implementation of Shariah for a number of reasons: first, and most obviously, the *ulama* as clergy saw religious law being the product of divine revelation as superior to man-made secular law. Second, Shariah was a way of regaining the status and arguably the power they lost as a result of their co-optation by Suharto. In Aceh many *ulama* were used to support the government party Golkar's election campaign, in return for money, positions and funding for Muslim boarding schools.[29] As a result of this co-option by a regime responsible for a wide range of human rights abuses in Aceh, the population lost their faith in the religious establishment.[30] Third, the *ulama* saw Shariah as a way of dealing with the shortcomings of the politicians. Their ultimate aim was for Shariah to produce clean governance, social justice, economic equality and ultimately prosperity for all the people of Aceh. By introducing a higher level of morality, they hoped to free Aceh from corruption, extortion, crime, drug abuse, and prostitution. And forth, they also saw Shariah as more in line with the traditional forms of governance as represented by Acehnese customs or *adat*. Thus Shariah for them is a way of reforming the politicians and the system.[31]

This lobbying by both the *ulama* and Acehnese political elite, combined with Aceh's history and Acehnese self-portrayal as being more devout than anyone else as well as misperceptions held by national parliamentarians and the central government ensured that the Acehnese population received Shariah although they never asked for it.

Shariah through by-law

While the Indonesian government always considered Aceh to be a special case, Islamist political parties, movements, and local leaders in other parts of Indonesia saw Aceh as a precedent and as an inspiration. When it started to implement Shariah in 2002 in the context of special autonomy some regencies and districts in other parts of Indonesia decided to push ahead with Shariah-like by-laws of their own, following the logic of "if Aceh can have Shariah so can we" and claiming that they were responding to grassroots demands.

Aceh being officially granted Shariah reinforced already existing Shariah projects. At the heart of these was South Sulawesi. Here efforts to implement Shariah date back to the 1999 Islamic *Ummah* Congress in Makassar, which established a Preparatory Committee for the Upholding of Shariah. This committee decided that the best way to achieve the implementation of Shariah would be through the regional autonomy laws. They then set up a pilot project in Bulukumba. Once Bulukumba had passed these new by-laws, which focused on morality issues such as dress, prostitution, gambling, and drinking, district heads and regents from other parts of Sulawesi were invited to view the pilot project and encouraged to make similar changes in their own areas. The Sulawesi district heads and regents were followed by others from Java and beyond. And many of them indeed pushed for similar changes back home.[32]

For instance in Maros regency in South Sulawesi the local government issued a regulation on 12 October 2002 that all male civil servants had to wear the traditional Muslim *koko* shirts and black *peci* on Fridays and women must wear the headscarf or *jilbab* every day. Shariah was also introduced in Sinjaj regency in South Sulawesi. The focus was again on female Muslim dress code. In West Java, in November 2002, the regent of the Indramayu regency declared the partial implementation of Shariah at a plenary meeting of the regional House of Representatives. Female civil servants now had to wear the *jilbab* and men the *koko*. Activities had to stop for 20 minutes for the noon *subuh* prayer and *asar* afternoon prayer. More recently Tangerang, an industrial commuter town on the outskirts of Jakarta, imposed a curfew on women. Women were not permitted outside after darkness as that encouraged prostitution. This had a detrimental impact on the local economy. Not only was there the "famous" case of the teacher arrested while waiting for the bus home, but also women who had worked nightshifts were now unemployed. To make things worse, one of the main home industry products of the area, embroidered *kebaya* blouses, was stopped because the *kebayas* were deemed to be too sexy. In West Sumatra, in Padang regency, a Shariah-like by-law was passed which made the *jilbab* part of girls' school uniforms, irrespective of religion. The new regulations further stipulated that in order to obtain a high-school degree all students, irrespective of religion, had to pass an exam on the *Qur'ān*.

These are few examples of the success of the Bulukumba pilot project and the Islamists strategy of implementing Shariah at the district and regency level. And it all boiled down to electoral politics. Eva Kusuma Sundari, PDI-P national parliamentarian, was watching these developments as part of a group of concerned parliamentarians from secular, nationalist, and minority backgrounds. She explained that:

"The Islamists are about 'elite-capture.' They steal the stage at the local level and use Islam to get into parliament. Most of the areas where they are now implementing Shariah were won by secular parties. The Islamists strike a deal, a 'contract', with candidates running for elections. They will approach the candidate from any party and will promise to mobilize the Muslims in their support. In turn, if the candidate gets elected he has to support Shariah. The candidate usually agrees because he needs the votes."[33]

In July 2006 this group of parliamentarians claimed that some forty districts and regencies had already adopted Shariah.[34] They also pointed to PKS as "the initiator of these changes through by-law" through its "broad network of people who infiltrated all political parties and the government at all levels from 2002 onwards."[35] They believed that these changes gained momentum under President Susilo Bambang Yudhoyono since September 2004,[36] whom they perceived as weak and "backed into a corner by [vice president] Jusuf Kalla and PKS."[37] These parliamentarians and their constituencies were not only disturbed by the unravelling of Indonesia's "secular", pluralistic state at grassroots level, the infringement upon minority rights, and the unconstitutionality of these by-laws, but also by the fact that no one in the central government was either taking this seriously enough or was willing to take this issue on for fear that it might damage their own political career. This lack of central government response resulted in discussions in non-Muslim areas about secession from Indonesia should it become an Islamic state. In 2006, the local parliaments in (Protestant) North Sulawesi and (Catholic) East Nusa Tenggara endorsed such a move with similar positions emerging in (Hindu) Bali, (Protestant) Papua, (Protestant) North Sumatra, and (Catholic) West Kalimantan.

Militant Islam: *Jemaah Islamiyya*

The most obvious evidence of the radicalization in Indonesian Islam came in the form of *Jemaah Islamiyya* (JI) and the October 2002 Bali bombings. JI was founded in 1995 in Malaysia by Indonesian clerics Abdullah Sungkar and Abu Bakar Ba'asyir. Sungkar and Ba'asyir had fled Indonesia in 1985 and returned to Indonesia in 1999 following the revoking of the subversion law.

Sungkar died in November 1999 and was succeeded by Ba'asyir, who ran a religious school in Solo, as the organization's emir. JI traces its roots to the 1940s and 1950s *Darul Islam* rebellion which sought to transform Indonesia into an Islamic state. Its ideology is Salafi and jihadist. Its aim is to establish a South-East Asian Islamic state encompassing Thailand, Indonesia, Malaysia, Singapore, Brunei, and the Philippines. It also seeks to purify Islam within those countries and to reduce non-Muslim influences. As Ba'asyir explained with respect to Indonesia, "the majority of Indonesians are Muslims therefore you should have Islamic law. We have to fight for that."[38] JI has a distinctly anti-Christian and anti-western orientation. Ba'asyir believed that the conflict in Ambon was "started by the Christians and Jews."[39] Muslims had no option but to respond with force and this was clearly a case of self-defence. He portrayed the Bali bombings in a similar way. Bali bomber Amrozi "is not a terrorist. He was defending himself."[40] JI's "self-defence" included the 2002 Bali bombings, the 2003 Marriot Hotel bombing, the 2004 Australian Embassy bombing and the 2005 Bali bombings as well as the so-called Christmas Eve bombings in which eleven churches across the country were hit simultaneously in 2000. It was also alleged to have perpetrated the bomb attacks on the Jakarta Stock Exchange in 2000, on the Atrium Mall in Jakarta in 2001, on a McDonald's restaurant in Sulawesi in 2002, and on a karaoke café in Sulawesi in 2004.

JI is believed to have a membership of several hundred throughout South-East Asia. It has a rigidly hierarchical structure headed by an *emir*. Below the *emir* are four councils—a governing council, a religious council, a *fatwa* council, and a disciplinary council. The governing council is headed by a central command, which makes operational decisions and exerts authority over four regions or *mantiqis*. *Mantiqi* I covers Singapore and Malaysia. Its main function is economic. *Mantiqi* II covers Indonesia except Sulawesi. This is the arena of jihad. *Mantiqi* III covers Mindanao, Sabah, and Sulawesi. Its purpose is training. And *Mantiqi* IV covers Papua and Australia. Its function is fundraising. The *mantiqis* are divided into *wakalah* or districts and *fiqh* or cells. JI is further organized into brigades, battalions, squads and has a special operations unit.[41]

JI has not been immune to splits and factionalization. The main split was caused by Ba'asyir's succession to *emir*. This split is generational as well as over the means to achieve an Islamic state.[42] It is between the ageing Ba'asyir and a younger group of militants who included Riduan Isamudin "Hanbali", Abdul Aziz "Imam Samudra", Ali Gufron "Mukhlas" and Abdullah Anshori "Abu

Fatih". Ba'asyir wanted to open up the movement through the establishment of the *Majles Mujahedin Indonesia* (MMI) and to take advantage of the new openness of post-Suharto Indonesia to struggle politically for an Islamic state. The young militants saw this as anathema to Sungkar's strategy of an underground, primarily military struggle. It was this younger faction that resorted to bombings and car suicide bombings with high or military grade explosives such as C4 and RDX under the guidance of top bomb-making experts Reading University-trained Malaysian engineer and university lecturer, Azhari Husin, and Nurdin Mohamed Top.[43]

The split became more pronounced with the repeated arrest, trial and imprisonment of Ba'asyir, which in the eyes of the young militants just confirmed that an Islamic state could not be achieved peacefully and that Ba'asyir was too "soft" to lead.[44]

Fragmentation of JI has also been the result from the pressure of Indonesia's counter-terrorism operations, which has destroyed much of JI's financial, command, and decision-making structure.[45] This has left JI functioning at cell level only. JI's popular support base was also reduced as ordinary Indonesians grew increasingly angry at the indiscriminate nature of JI's campaign. While many Indonesian Muslims had little sympathy with the US or Australia whom they regarded as arrogant, interventionist, imperialist, and anti-Muslim, they had no sympathy for the killing of innocent Muslims.

Conclusion

Indonesian Islam has retained its pluralist and tolerant image beyond the fall of Suharto and has proved that Islam and democracy can co-exist. Indeed, there has only been a marginal rise in the electoral support for Islamist parties, most notably PKS, and more often than not this has been motivated by issues such as clean governance and accountability rather than Shariah. At the same time, however, there has been an undercurrent of radicalization, expressed both violently and peacefully. It has affected mainstream institutions like NU, *Muhammadiya* and MUI; non-Islamist Muslim political parties like PAN, PKB, PBB and PPP; and the general public discourse. At the foreign policy level, this radicalization is grounded in solidarity with Muslims in Iraq, Afghanistan and Palestine. Domestically it was born out of successive Indonesian governments' ineffective responses to poverty and corruption as well as the communal conflicts in Ambon and Poso. While, at first glance, militant Islamism such as practiced by JI seems to be the greater threat, it is in fact non-violent Islamism that is the greater challenge—for three key reasons. First, JI has already alienated large parts of its support base and its capacity has been significantly reduced by a highly effective counter-terrorism policy. Second, the non-violent radical Islamist agenda is being successfully implemented slowly, step by step through a carefully planned multi-level strategy, which ranges from electoral politics, to targeting the education system and mosques, to influencing the public debates, and, most crucially, implementing Shariah-like by-laws. And third, this unravelling of the "secular" state from below has not met with strong opposition at either popular or government level despite the fact that neither endorse these views.

There is an ongoing radicalization in Indonesia. However, the ongoing radicalization, as has been shown in this chapter, is a result of complex political processes, local poverty and corruption. Labelling them a "clash of civilizations" becomes simplistic.

6

Philippines—"Civilizational" or Colonial Border?

Ben Reid

The Philippines occupies an important place in both the contemporary "war on terror" and in Huntington's *Clash of Civilizations*. For Huntington, the bi-polar world of Cold War conflict has given way to a multi-polar world of civilizations. Fluid and somewhat difficult to define, crucial sources of conflict in the contemporary world are clashes between these civilizations. Most recently, considerable attention has been placed on Huntington's identification of an Islamic civilization (amongst the nine he identifies), given the emergence of jihadism and conflict with the West. Each civilization is in a process of negotiation with forms of modernization and the impact of globalization.[1]

Huntington gives some attention to the Philippines as a border region in his model. It is a "torn country" divided between Muslim and western "civilizations".[2] If Huntington's model is applied to the case of the Philippines, it could be argued that the majority population inherited western values and forms of government from Spanish and later US colonization. Mindanao in the south, however, is divided between this culture and Islamic civilization. Huntington notes, therefore, that conflict has and will continue to occur as a "fault-line" between civilizations and in part due to the low "ingestability" of Islamic populations in non-Islamic majority states.[3]

Indeed, the south of the Philippines, including the largest island Mindanao, has been the location of a long-running secessionist conflict between the insurgencies based amongst the predominantly-Muslim Bangsamoro national-minority population and the Philippine state. The Bangsamoro tend to identify themselves as a separate nation to the rest of the mainly Malay-Christian (although ethnically and linguistically diverse) population of the Philippines. The Bangsamoro's absorption into Islamic culture and society meant that it was generally better able to resist the impacts of Spanish colonization. It was only in the twentieth century, after US annexation in 1898, that the Bangsamoro were "pacified" and later allocated as part of the newly independent Philippine state in 1946.[4]

More recently, an al-Qaeda linked organization—the *Abu Sayaaf* (ASG)—emerged and engaged in several high-profile bombings and kidnappings. Factions of the Philippine military and state, aided by US forces, used this as a pretext for intensification (for a time) of its counter-insurgency war against the mainstream Moro-Islamic Liberation Front (MILF). Subsequent negotiations have led to a ceasefire, although the spectre of al-Qaeda involvement is regularly used by military and some foreign commentators to motivate increased militarization and US intervention in the Philippines.[5]

Does the recurrent conflict between Muslim secessionists and the Philippine state confirm the validity of Huntington's claims? This chapter argues that this is not the case. The conflict in the Philippines has different origins and causes. Instead the conflict must be understood through examining the shared legacies of colonialism and the dynamics of poverty and political exclusion, the military dependence of the Philippine elite on the US and how both of these actors desire territorial integrity and access to Mindanao's resources.

The Bangsamoro conflict: background and context

The history of multi-religious interaction in the Philippines goes far back in time. Islamic influence had been gradually expanding in the Philippine archipelago when the Spanish colonists arrived in the fifteenth century. However, the majority population remained organized according to tribal affiliations. Village "*datu*" chiefs tended to more readily accept Spanish authority and American administration in return for privileges. Much of the population assumed the status of sharecropper agriculturalists, while a Philippine and Mestizo-based elite emerged in control of a *hacienda*-based economy and society.[6] Mindanao remained a relative exception as the Sultanates were more readily able to resist Spanish colonialism and Christianization. While the Islamic population was concentrated in the west of Mindanao, much of the remainder of the island remained sparsely settled until well into the twentieth century.[7]

US colonial control from 1898 and formal independence in 1946 both contributed to important changes in Mindanao. First, the US colonial authorities were much more effective in integrating the Islamic population into colonial control. The sultans were progressively brought under control by military and political means by the 1920s.[8] Second, greater attention was given to exploiting the resources of the island. Parity rights, guaranteed by post-war treaties, ensured American firms could continue to own large tracts of land developing large-scale rubber, copra and pineapple export plantations. Third, legislation was enacted in the post-war period, modelled on the US Homestead Act, which allowed settlers access to freehold land. The latter point resulted in surge of Malay Christian settlers to Mindanao. The mostly landowning-based elite in the more densely populated regions of Luzon and the Visayas continually frustrated attempts to implement comprehensive land reform, granting ownership to the now predominantly tenant farmers.[9] One way to ease the resulting social tension and growing landlessness was to encourage internal migration to Mindanao. While urban populations grew, industrial employment tapered off in the mid-1960s with the dismantling of exchange and import controls. The previously sparsely populated island began to experience change and new social pressures.

On the other hand, independence for the Philippines was accompanied by the introduction of a range of treaties that—as well as the parity ownership rights mentioned above—ensured the Philippines remained largely dependent on the US for defence. The Philippine elite, by and large, acted as comfortable clients of the former colonial power. The presence of the US military helped maintain their security in a political context that blended the formal operation of republican democracy with a highly unequal social and economic system and episodes of political repression.[10]

Mindanao constituted a considerable "gift" to the economic and political elite, as a resource rich island and outlet for displaced rural populations. Throughout the colonial and post-colonial period, the elite encouraged some level of "othering" between the Christian majority and the Islamic minority in the Philippines. Although there was formal acceptance of the minority, attitudes of mistrust and discrimination were encouraged towards Islam. This facilitated a process of incorporation and loyalty to the predominantly Christian elites. Discrimination against and forming of antagonistic attitudes towards Islam therefore acted as a hegemonic device of incorporating marginal Christian populations into the Philippine state. Negative attitudes towards Islam and the Muslim minority have existed and continue to predominate amongst different sectors of the Philippine population. Underpinning this was the use of Mindanao as a settler frontier for displaced rural Christian populations in place of comprehensive and redistributive land reform.[11] The "othering" of the Islamic population justified its displacement and encroachment of Christian settlers (as it did in Tribal Lumad areas also). By the late 1960s, however, economic growth had further declined and poverty began to increase for much of the population. The Mindanao frontier was already exhausted as a site for large-scale settlement. The political system lapsed increasingly into authoritarianism that culminated in President Ferdinand Marcos' declaration of martial law and dictatorship in 1972. Backed by the US and World Bank finance, Marcos launched a seemingly ambitious New Society economic and social development programme focused on the resource exploitation of "virgin areas".[12]

The emergence of a fully-fledged secessionist movement and accompanying national identity was in direct response to these changes. While tension had long existed between the Bangsamoro population in the south and the majority population, the former had become a minority in their own homeland regions by the late 1960s. A pro-independence Muslim (Mindanao) minority movement emerged in 1968. Nur Misuari later established the Moro National Liberation Front (MNLF) and an associated armed wing.[13]

During the Marcos years the MNLF became one of the largest threats to the dictatorship and US military support was repeatedly needed by the Philippine military to fight insurgency. For the MNLF, while Islam was considered central to the Bangsamoro identity, their ultimate goal was the formation of a separate secular state. This was embodied in the very notion of the Bangsamoro national identity. The term Moro was originally a Spanish term of abuse for the Islamic population. The MNLF appropriated this slur into the formulation Bangsamoro as an inclusive term for peoples of the south of the Philippines. Special measures were repeatedly made to reassure Lumad tribal and Christian populations that their rights would be respected and that they could indeed identify as Bangsamoros.[14] Ideologically, the MNLF advanced a hybrid vision that combined aspects of non-Marxian socialism with nationalism. Through the 1970s it developed strong relations with Gaddafi's Socialist People's Libyan Arab Jamahiriya. Libya remained a key supporter of the movement through the Organization of the Islamic Conference.[15] As a low-intensity conflict, it has been estimated that some tens of thousands of casualties occurred, with displaced and wounded numbering in the hundreds of thousands.[16] After 1986 a series of negotiations between the newly returned democratic government of Corazon Aquino and the MNLF was initiated. In the meantime popular sentiment and other factors combined to end direct US military presence in the Philippines. The Philippine military, however, remained dependent on US support and a visiting Forces Agreement was eventually agreed in 1998. It appeared though that the Mindanao conflict was being de-militarized as in 1996 the South Philippines Council for Peace and Development was established to oversee a peace agreement in the already established Autonomous Region of Muslim Mindanao. This incorporated many MNLF personnel into local administration, with Misuri as Governor. By 1999 there was widespread disillusion with the outcome of the negotiations, which resulted in renewed secessionist sentiment.[17]

Since 1999 the Philippine state and military's main policy has been towards combating the influence of the principle beneficiaries of the renewed sentiment of the rival secessionist Moro Islamic Liberation Front (MILF). The MILF had now become a much larger group than the MNLF with considerable popular support. Originating as a more identifiably "Islamist" splinter from the more secular and nationalist MNLF in 1985, its leaders had established contact with and been trained by the mujahedin rebels in Afghanistan. Here there is some evidence of a more explicitly Islamist politics. McKenna does note that there are three different symbolic components to Bangsamoro secessionism.[18] The first is the territorial component that is emphasized by the MNLF with its goal of separate state. The second is a desire to recapture certain lost spiritual goals and values, as is common with various movements inspired by what Scott refers to as the nostalgic "remembered village".[19] The most recent is the influence of Middle-Eastern trained clerics with various political and cultural approaches to Islam. The MILF's principle goal is a programme of Islamization (including the formation of an Islamic state) there is little agreement amongst leaders about the precise meaning of this.[20] The MILF retain an emphasis on the notion of Bangsamoro nation, although they are less inclusive of Christian and Lumad populations. It is debatable to the extent that their self-identification as the Bangsamoro amongst secessionist rank and file. They often regard themselves as simply Moros (Islamic). Yet, there are a range of ideological influences and positions and none which can discernibly be linked to a global jihadist programme.

Both the Estrada and Arroyo governments and the Armed Forces of the Philippines have periodically used operations against the third much smaller and directly al-Qaeda linked group—the *Abu Sayyaf* (ASG)—as a cover for more extensive military activity against the MILF.[21] The Philippine military and government elite regularly refer to all groups as "Southern Philippine Terrorists". The ASG is, however, quite separate from either the MILF or MNLF. It was formed in 1991 under the leadership of Abdurajik Janjalani who, as with the main leaders of the MILF, was a veteran of the Afghan wars. By 1995 the ASG had been active in large-scale bombings and attacks in the Philippines. Unlike the MILF, the ASG openly admits affiliation and sympathy with al-Qaeda, although al-Qaeda does not repay this sympathy and has distanced itself from ASG because of the latter's ransom activities. ASG has no more than few hundred armed troops and is opposed by the MNLF and MILF. The ASG is also listed as a Designated Foreign Terrorist Organization by the US State Department, unlike the other two.[22] The ASG is very much outside the mainstream of the secessionist groups, which most recently have engaged in more collaboration over electoral and other matters. There is, therefore, a considerable history of divergence between the Banagsamoro minority and the majority Christian Malay population. Two main organizations exist with differing conceptions of the relationship between Islam and the Bangsamoro national identity. Their attitudes and relationships to jihadist groups also differ. The third group—the ASG—is more marginal and is directly linked to global jihadist networks.

Islam and the Philippines: clash of civilizations?

Is the conflict then a reflection of the clash of civilizations being played out in a torn nation? The conflict is better understood as a reflection of colonial history, the endemic problems that confront the Philippine state and the legitimate aspirations of the Bangsamoro for national self-determination. As elsewhere in the world, jihadists have sometimes tried to incorporate these demands and adapt their political programmes.

First and most importantly, the separateness of the Bangsamoro is only partially connected to Islam. They are best understood as a distinct population that was only colonized after much of the rest of the Philippines. With this colonization they were subjected to numerous processes of predatory exploitation both directly by the colonial power and subsequently by the client regime and elite of the Philippines. The growing sense of alienation and eventual revolt by the Bangsamoro could easily have eventuated, regardless of whether they were Muslims or another minority identity.[23] It is notable that indigenous minorities in Mindanao and the Cordillera in Luzon, while not demanding full independence, share historical parallels with the Bangsamoro and their alienation from the Philippine state.[24] The emergence of the national Bangsamoro identity is therefore strongly connected with the character of colonization and the post-colonial forces that shaped the emergence of the Philippine state. These incorporated the Bangsamoro population into the highly-centralized Philippine state, hence the MNLF leader's creation of an inclusive southern Philippine national identity.

Second, Bangsamoro sentiments in favour of self-determination have important continuities with the values of national self-determination that emerged within the majority Philippine culture. The emergence of an independence movement in the Philippines during the late-nineteenth century amongst the *Ilustrados* was initially closely linked to emergence of ideas, liberty and social justice.[25] In particular, the *Katipunan* independence movement had a substantial membership based amongst the rural and urban plebeian population in Luzon and the Visayas, especially in the densely-settled Tagalog-speaking areas. While the status of the Bangsamoro in the independence movement was ambiguous, there are two implications that flow from subsequent historical events. The original project of an independent Philippine republic was never fully realised. The movement was instead taken over by a faction led by Emilio Aguinaldo (which was based largely amongst the owners of large landholdings and *hacienda* estates) that accepted United States intervention and control in 1898. As noted above, the landowning classes of the territory acted as a base of support for colonial authorities. These same groups dominated Philippine politics and society after formal independence in 1946.[26] Mindanao, incorporated by the US colonisers, became the focus of widespread settlement and resource exploitation.

Third, the first wave of secessionism that was led by the MNLF in the 1970s was not really explicitly Islamist. As noted above, while Islam was recognized as a component of the Bangsamoro national identity, the MNLF emphasized its role as a secular nationalist movement, with non-Marxian socialist values.[27] Secessionism emerged largely as a result of growing disenchantment with the impacts of the Manila-based political elite's policies and aspirations for national self-determination. Both groups have historically received support from the Organization of the Islamic Conference (OIC). Yet the OIC has for the most part supported a solution of negotiated settlement, with Malaysia most recently playing a role of brokering talks between the Philippine government and the MILF. As with the MNLF, however, the MILF situates itself as part of a legacy of anti-colonial struggle.[28] The Philippine elite are castigated as "neo-colonialist" masters.

Far from being a reflection of Islamism, there is a shared culture between the majority Philippines and the Bangsamoro. The difficulty arises from the form of colonial incorporation that occurred. The Bangsamoro secessionists are, therefore, best understood as an outcome of reaction to their form of colonial incorporation and rule by the colonial Philippine state and elite. Far from representing values of liberty and self-determination, the Philippine state has acted as an expression of colonialist ambitions in Mindanao. The conflict is thus not between Islam and Christianity/westernism, but over attempts to end the historical legacies and consequences of the formation of the colonial Philippine state. The Philippine state and its governing elite continue to violate principles of self-determination for an important minority population in the Philippines. Again this is not exclusively a grievance of the south, as recent attempts at constitutional reform have foreshadowed further devolution to regions and federalism.

Fourth, the persistent claims that have recently emerged linking the secessionists with various expressions of militarist and Islamic fundamentalism do not stand up to scrutiny. While it is true that the ASG does have extensive links to al-Qaeda, it is very much a minority group amongst the Bangsamoro. The ASG is mainly involved in various kidnapping and extortion activities and the exact boundaries of its operations blend with those of criminal gangs in Mindanao. It even rejects the support of Islamic states and organizations, such as the OIC, that have been sympathetic to the MNLF and the MILF.[29] The MILF has an explicit goal of implementing Islamic law, yet it has frequently pointed out that it aims to respect the rights of non-Islamic and tribal populations in a potentially independent state. While MILF leaders trained and fought with mujahedin guerrillas in Afghanistan, there is no definitive evidence linking them to ongoing relationships with jihadist groups. Some researchers have claimed that such links exists. Often the sources are the Philippine media and military, including curious claims about the presence of men with beards and turbans at the MILF base camp when it was overrun in 2000.[30] Organisations like the International Crisis Group once made similar claims about links with *Jemaah Islamiyah*, adding that tendency to fragmentation with the MILF may contribute to the future emergence of a more Jihadist faction. They have recently admitted that counter-terrorist action against the

ASG risks accelerating conflicts with the MILF and MNLF.[31] More of a case has been made that some collaboration did exist between the MILF and the International Islamic Relief Organization, although these linkages appeared to have ended by 2000. Yet, the MILF has consistently condemned the ASG and it denies any links with al-Qaeda or more recently the *Jemaah Islamiyah*. The United States government has not formally considered the MILF a foreign terrorist organization since 2002.[32] While Islamism is regarded as an aspect of Bangsamoro identity, most of the politics and inspiration for the group stems from perceived injustices that they have experienced from the Philippine state. Even some authors of these claims concerning links with al-Qaeda admit that the MILF "may have legitimate national liberation aspirations."[33]

There is a demarcation in Philippine culture and politics between an expansionist and chauvinist tendency and a republican-democratic sentiment, just as there are in other political cultures. The relationship between Christianity and Islam is secondary at best, as the locus of conflict revolves around national issues of power and the manipulation of ethno-religious differences and identities. There is arguably, therefore, a form of fundamentalism that is implicit in the ideology of the Manila-based elites that justify their control over Mindanao. Accordingly, there are persistent and various attempts to promote the notion that the Philippines is a Christian nation containing the threat of Islamism in the South. In actuality though, it is the Manila-based elites who are mobilising religious chauvinism to justify the continued forced control over the Bangsamoro population that ignores their strong historical case for self-determination. The emergence of purported al-Qaeda links amongst the Bangsamoro secessionists has been used at times as justification for more direct involvement by the United States military in the conflict. Again, far from being a reflection of an inherent conflict between Christianity and Islam, the prospect of intervention is best explained as a reflection of the ongoing colonial inheritances of the Philippines.[34] As indicated above, the elite that controls much of Philippine politics and society collaborated with the colonial occupiers. Various aspects of this collaboration continued after independence in 1946, especially around defence. The Philippine elite gained, through the permanent presence of US military, a means of securing its control over much of the population. Any internal threat to their rule could be counteracted with the US support that was crucial to defeating the threat posed by the leftist *Hukbalahap* insurgency in late 1940s and early 1950s. As indicated above though, one of the consequences of the mass democratic struggle that ousted Ferdinand Marcos in 1986 was the eventual removal of US forces and non-renewal of the agreement allowing the presence of US bases. Marcos was widely perceived as being strongly supported by and even acting as an agent of US interests. A motivation for the acceleration of conflict in Mindanao, by the Philippine state, has been to opportunistically provide the justification of foreign military support in an attempt to roll back some of the growth of pro-independence and republican sentiment that flowed out of the anti-dictatorship period. While the immediate rationale is clearly the secessionist threat, there is a wider motivation of encouraging a direct US presence as a deterrent against other challenges from within the majority Philippine population itself.[35]

Bangsamoro secessionism is not really a reflection of an intrinsic clash between Islamic and Christian cultures. On the contrary, the Bangsamoro nationalists share a legacy of anti-colonialism and demands for self-determination with the early Philippine revolutionaries. Unfortunately the latter's aims were never realised and the result was the construction of colonial Philippine state and elite that forcibly incorporated the population in Mindanao. There is no evidence of deep-rooted support for jihadist fundamentalism amongst the Bangsamoro and such claims seem opportunistically oriented to obtaining more military support from the US. At time of writing, the Philippine military was again engaging in military attacks on MNLF positions in Jolo. Again there were claims made that the military was in pursuit of *Jemaah Islamiyah* operatives.[36]

Bangsamoro nationalism and self-determination

In conclusion, Huntington's notion of the "torn nation" has little value as a framework for explaining the conflict in Mindanao. Bangsamoro nationalism has strong continuities with and is an expression of demands for self-determination and anti-colonialism. These values are not the monopoly of the West and attempts to portray the conflict as a clash of cultures are strongly connected to attempts to obscure the colonial origins and nature of the problems in Mindanao. The issue of the Islamic identity of the Bangsamoro and their location in an apparent "border region" between civilizations is largely a secondary aspect of the conflict.

On the contrary, the Bangsamoro conflict is best understood as a reflection of the divergent interests of at least three different actors. The first actor is the hegemonic Philippine elite with its historical and contemporary alliances with colonial US power; its power was largely obtained through collaboration with US colonization after 1898 and the maintenance of their large landholdings. These landowning elites acted as a base of support for US colonial and post-colonial influence throughout much of the twentieth century. In return the colonial authorities provided security and declined to implement any policies that would undermine the power of these groups. The Malay (and Mestizo) Christian identity of these elites were largely a reflection of the colonial experience and mechanism used for the promotion of a common identity between the elite and other sections of the majority Philippine population. Anti-Bangsamoro sentiments were promoted amongst the majority population to facilitate identification with elite goals and divert attention away from deep-seated problems such as the absence of substantive agrarian reform. Mindanao and its later colonized populations played a two-fold historical role as a resource-rich region open to exploitation and as an outlet for surplus rural populations that would otherwise have been accommodated through employment in urban industrial sector or allocated land through redistributive reform. On the other hand, there is the Bangsamoro population with its more intact pre-colonial identity and Islamic social organization. Its experience of later colonization and exploitation by Manila-based elites has meant that a separate national-identity emerged. While Islam is a factor in this, the separate identity has more to do with the ongoing legacies of colonial construction of the Philippine state. The Bangsamoro could arguably identify with another set of faith-based or ideological set of values and there would still be secessionist issues. While Islamism is a component in the politics of both the MNLF and the MILF they are much more imbued with a sense of secular nationalism. Global jihadist Islam has little basis of support outside what the Philippine government itself regards as the marginal and declining ASG.[37] At time of press negotiations are continuing between the MILF and the government of the Philippines. The outcome will almost certainly be the recognition of the need for some form of genuine autonomy for the West of Mindanao and the Bangsamoro, as was first attempted in 1996–97. Arguably though, a final resolution of the conflict can only come with the international and Philippine recognition of a separate nation-state.

Unfortunately colonization and the consolidation of historical elite control in Manila established a Philippine state where much of the population remains excluded from real self-determination. The colonial state entrenched a set of relationships based on social and political exclusion of the majority of the population and resulted in ongoing poverty for much of the population.

Region II

Africa, the Crescent of Islam[1]

Stig Jarle Hansen

Africa is central in the Islamic world. Islam in Africa is widespread and the continent contains several of the numerically largest Muslim states in the world; indeed, the number of Muslims in Nigeria is larger than in any Middle Eastern country.[2] Islam in Africa is almost as old as the religion itself, North Africa being conquered by the first generation of Muslims. On the east coast of Africa, Arabs founded permanent Islamic colonies and spread Islam in the process. In the middle of Africa the spread of Islam stopped after north Africa was conquered, while Islam progressed southwards in the west of Africa. Ali Mazrui calls the geographic form of African Islam a "crescent".[3] Islam was spread in the wake of trade; local leaders often found it tempting to have Arab traders as business partners, and held their culture in high regards. However, war was also used to expand Islamic states. There were active attempts on behalf of Islamic empires to expand and conquer larger parts of Africa.[4] The attempts that the Islamic empires made to expand were in the end dwarfed by the expansion of the European powers. By the start of the twentieth century, all of the Islamic states south of Sahara were controlled by the European powers. There were major conflicts between the western colonial powers and Islamic revivalist movements as the *Derwishes* of the "Mad Mullah" rising in Somalia or the Mahdist rising in Sudan. However, Muslim clergy often cooperated with the colonial authorities.

During the period from 1956 until 1978 the European powers gradually withdrew from Africa. Despite the initial nationalist fervours amongst the African elite the new African states were plagued by war, indeed Africa became the most conflict-ridden continent on the globe.[5] In most of these wars, such as the various Congolese civil wars, the wars in Namibia, Angola and Mozambique, the Katanga war, the war in South Africa, the Eritrean insurgency, the war in Liberia, the war in Sierra Leone and in Rwanda, religion played a small role; although religious leaders supported various sides in public, the various religions were divided. Indeed, in many cases, such as the Eritrean-Ethiopian conflicts, the Somali civil war, the Sierra Leonian wars, as well as the wars in Rwanda, Mozambique, Angola and Namibia, and the recent Darfur crisis, members supposedly of the same religious groups killed each other.[6] In several cases religion played a minor role: in Uganda, the regime of Idi Amin Dada was widely seen as drawing upon the Islamic groups of the country. In the Biafra war, Christian Igbos argued that they were exposed to an Islamic onslaught; however, the conflict can equally be seen as a conflict between tribes, the Christians amongst the western Yoruba tribe in the end sided with the Muslims of the northern tribes against the Igbos.[7]

Africa was, and is, also plagued by widespread poverty. As a result of the poor social conditions, religion may provide alternative meaning to life that secular institutions are incapable of, and in some instances even fill institutional vacuums by providing services that the state has failed to provide. Indeed, there are many examples where Islamic institutions have provided justice (for example through Shariah courts), social services (through Islamic charities), as well as schooling (also through Islamic charities). The pan-Islamic organization boom spurred by the economic growth of the Gulf countries drew the external world closer to African Islam. Islamic charities contributed to the welfare of millions of Africans, in this sense that they addressed very real needs in Africa. Countries such as Saudi Arabia increasingly sponsored mosques, *madrasahs*, and charities across Africa. Several of the new and often Gulf State/Saudi Arabian-sponsored religious institutions have been known for their extreme political views, and have been observed closely by local authorities.[8] Given the problems of the African states it is not surprising that the Africans put more trust in the political opinions of their religious leaders than respondents outside Africa, and that BBC polls shows that the most trusted group in African society is the religious clergy.[9]

There have been active jihadist organizations in Africa. Moreover, several African countries have sponsored militant religious organizations. During a period where radicalism was prevailing, Sudan played host to Osama bin Laden, and functioned as a financial channel for him.[10] Sudan was accused of supporting an assassination attempt against Egyptian president Hosni Mubarak in 1995, and it supported Eritrean Islamic Jihad as well as the Ugandan Allied Democratic Forces.[11] Nevertheless, Sudan was internally divided and Sudanese president Bashir in the end actively attempted to remove the most extreme elements in order to stop Sudan from being an international pariah.[12] Another centre for Islamist/jihadist groups was oddly enough Eritrea. Eritrea, ruled by a secular elite, dominated by its Christian highlanders, and troubled with its own jihadist organizations, sponsored the Islamic courts of Somalia, illustrating how national interests create marriages of convenience. The Isaias Afewerki regime in Eritrea was desperately searching for allies in the region after alienating the neighbouring regimes in the whole of the Horn of Africa.[13]

Poverty, state vacuum and the quest for foreign support

Africa is plagued by poverty and ill-functioning government institutions. The chapter written by Sakah Mahmud as well as the one by Stig Jarle Hansen, show how charities and religious institutions move in to fill this vacuum. The case of Somalia explores how a desire for justice enabled Islamists in Somalia to gain control, and how adherence to Islamic norms gave them grassroots support. The chapter also illustrates how local popular support created conditions in a local movement, which enabled more global jihadist elements to gain access to power. Chapter nine, written by Terje Østebø, illustrates how Islamic reformism can fill another form of vacuum, in the case of Ethiopia, that of alienation from the state. Chapter ten, exploring Sudan, written by Gérard Prunier, illustrates how a central power might depict a conflict using religious terminology to get foreign support, despite the facts on the ground being different.

7

Nigeria—Islamist Activism and Religious Conflicts

Sakah Mahmud

Although religious conflicts in Nigeria have intensified since the late 1970s and early 1980s, it was the re-introduction of full Shariah in 1999–2000 by twelve states in northern Nigeria that gave the country its current image of Islamic fundamentalism in sub-Saharan Africa. While the events were peaceful in most of the twelve states they caused sectarian violence and tension in some states as well as political tension between the states and the federal government. The situation remained unsettled when religious violence erupted again in late November 2002 in the northern city of Kaduna over the Miss World beauty pageant being held in the capital city of Abuja.[1] These two religious conflicts concerning Muslims and Islam, occurring within range of the terrorist attacks on the United States on 11 September 2001, helped to refocus global attention on sectarian issues in Nigeria.[2]

In view of the on-going interest on the global resurgence of Islam in public affairs, Islamist activism and religious conflicts in Nigeria raise two important questions. First, what is the nature of religious conflicts in Nigeria and why is Islam often involved in the conflicts? And second, how do these conflicts relate to the "clash of civilizations" debate? This chapter addresses the questions by arguing that religious activisms and the conflicts they generate must be understood in their historical context as well as the multi-ethnic/religious structure of Nigerian society. Thus, the conflicts are determined essentially by local factors—competition between groups for resources and influence. However, external influences cannot be ignored as forces of contemporary globalization influence religious activisms consequently relating them to the debate on "clash of civilizations."[3] The nature of the "weak state" in Nigeria and its inability to mediate and manage conflicts enables the above factors to have an effect.[4]

The nature and variety of religious conflicts in post-independent Nigeria

Understanding the nature of religious conflicts in Nigeria since independence requires a conceptual categorization of the variety of conflicts. Combining these categories into one monolithic term of "religious conflicts" obscures a clear understanding of the nature of this complex phenomenon. The categories are not mutually exclusive and they take different forms that are interwoven. Each category may require a different theoretical approach for explanation.[5] For this purpose, three broad categories can be identified as follows: 1) intra-religious conflicts (Muslim versus Muslim); 2) the inter-religious conflicts (Muslim versus Christian); and 3) state versus religious activists. Because of the multiplicity of these conflicts only the prime examples in each category will be highlighted.

The first category—intra-Islamic—was earliest the form of religious conflicts in northern Nigeria emerging from the competition between the dominant traditional Sufi brotherhoods of *Qadiriya* and *Tijaniya*. This conflict derived from the public role that Islam played in the region and the prominent socio-political and religious roles that the brotherhoods assumed. These factors explain the intensity of confrontations between the brotherhoods as they competed for followers, positions and access to public goods and services. It did not help matters that earlier on, the colonial administration sided with the *Qadiriya* (to which the founder of the Caliphate and his descendants belonged) while the *Tijaniya* was considered as a threat to stability in the region.[6]

At the same time the rivalry between the brotherhoods took a territorial pattern with the *Qadiriya* dominant in Sokoto and *Tijaniya* in Kano. Religious rivalry was also being transformed into a political one as the period coincided with the emergence of secular (nationalist) politics. Sir Ahmadu Bello, the Premier of Northern Nigeria, as well as a prince of the Caliphate, inherited the volatile religio-political situation. The rivalry manifested itself in the power struggle between the Premier and the Emir of Kano, Muhammad Sanusi from the mid 1950s to the early 1960s ending with the supremacy of the Premier.[7] Yet, the polarization in the north caused by the rivalry was more than personal. There was a political interest at stake since the Premier required a common front in the region in competition with the leaders of the south. Thus the Premier attempted to unify the north using both religious and political means to do so.

The unification process included the creation of a new "transbrotherhood religious community" the *Usmaniya*, whose overall function was "designed to consolidate a Northern Muslim community."[8] He also founded a modern Islamic organization—the *Jama'atu Nasril Islam* (JNI) to promote the teaching of proper Islam.[9] In his dealing with the non-Muslim populations of the region, the Premier accepted the watered-down Shariah recommended by the departing colonial administration.[10] These efforts were on-going when the Premier was assassinated during the first military coup in January 1966.

From 1966 to 1999 (excluding 1979–1983), military regimes dominated Nigerian politics and had to deal with more intra-Islamic and Muslim-Christian conflicts. The late 1970s and the 1980s witnessed the emergence of the *Izala* (from its Arabic name *Jama'atu Izalat al-Bid'a wa-Iqamat al-Sunna*, translated as Society for the Eradication of Evil Innovation and the Establishment of the Sunna). Its spiritual leader was Sheikh Abubakar Gumi, a confidant of the late Premier Sir Ahmadu Bello. *Izala* was founded as an Islamic reformist movement opposed to the practices of the Sufi orders which it considered as "innovations" (*bida'a*) and thus anti-Islamic.[11] Attacks on the brotherhoods coupled with *Izala's* growing popularity led to violent clashes in many cities especially in Kaduna, Kano and Sokoto states. The challenge of the *turuq* by the *Izala* made the two previously opposed brotherhoods to unite against their common enemy, the *Izala*.[12] In a broader sense *Izala* should also be seen as reacting against the socio-political status-quo which was usually seen by reformers as "un-Islamic". The confrontations between the *Izala* and the *turuq* did not cease until emergence of another violent religious movement—the *Maitatsine*—in Kano in December 1980 led by Muhammad Marwa. The movement criticized what it considered as un-Islamic practices of Muslims including materialism.[13] Its activities resulted in violent confrontations with other Muslims and with the state in many cities of northern Nigeria beginning with Kano in December 1980 where over 4,000 people were killed including the leader and many of his followers.[14] While the uprising did not seem to have any foreign connections, the influence of the Iranian Islamic revolution in 1979 could not be ruled out. The movement also attracted many immigrants to Kano including those from other African countries.[15] For explanations of the uprising, references were made to the economic conditions and fanaticism. Those who saw a millennial explanation noticed the approach of the year 1400 of the Muslim calendar. However, the economic and fanatic explanations seem more plausible.[16]

The last case of the intra-Islamic conflicts during the military era was the small Muslim Brotherhood (a Shia group). Its leader, El Zak-Zaky (a former leader of the radical Muslims Student Society of Nigeria), was imprisoned several times in the 1980s for his activism by the late Military ruler General Sani Abacha. The group drew its inspiration from the Islamic Revolution, which had a lot of influence on El Zak-Zaky's activism. Conflicts involving the group have been reported in parts of Sokoto (seat of the Caliphate) which is prominently Sunni and not sympathetic with the Muslim Brotherhood's Shia preaching and activism.

Finally and more recently (2000 to the present) there have been the activities of so-called Taliban in parts of northern Nigeria. A prime example of these groups is the "Taliban of Nigeria" (also known as the *Hijra* Group), which emerged in northeastern Nigeria in 2004. The group's stated goal is to create an Islamic state in Nigeria. The group's activities so far have been limited to attacking police stations and hauling the arms left behind by the fleeing police. Up to now the police seemed to have been able to contain their activities even though they remain a security risk and challenge for the federal government.

Religious conflicts between Christians and Muslims stemmed mainly from the social structure of Nigeria that emerged out of colonialism. Different religious and ethnic groups still see themselves differently. Admittedly, some of the violence might have been caused by adherents who are intolerant or fanatical. One form of such conflicts involved cases where the religious sensitivities of adherents (usually between Christians and Muslims) were provoked either consciously or unconsciously. The violence over the 2002 Miss World beauty pageant was triggered by an offensive article written by a Christian journalist, Isioma Daniel, who probably did not anticipate the Muslims' reaction because of her ignorance of Islam. The case is complex because of its connection to the existing Shariah controversy in Kaduna. Some of the contestants had already condemned the pending death sentence (by stoning) passed on a Muslim woman, Amina Lawal, for adultery.[17] In the five days of

Muslim-Christian violence that followed, over 200 people were killed. In another case a Muslim protest over the Danish newspaper caricatures of the Prophet in February 2006 killed about fifteen Christians in the northern city of Maiduguri, followed by revenge killings of Muslims in the southern city of Onitsha. In the end, as a newspaper reported, "The cycle of tit-for-tat sectarian violence has put the death toll beyond 100, making Nigeria the hardest-hit country so far in the caricature controversy."[18] There have also been conflicts over accusations of Christians desecrating symbols of Islam. In December 2001, an Igbo Christian truck driver in Kano, Uche Ochukpue, was beaten to death by Muslims after driving his truck over a copy of the *Qur'ān*.[19] A similar violent clash occurred in March 2007, in the northeastern city of Gombe, where a Christian teacher Mrs Olusesan was beaten to death by Muslim students for seizing an Islamic booklet from a student in an examination hall.[20]

The second form of conflict in this category originates from economic, political or ethnic inequalities and grievances between groups who happen to be clearly divided along ethnic and religious lines. This was characteristic of conflicts in Kaduna, Plateau, and Benue States—the non-Muslim Middle Belt section of Nigeria that has been part of the northern region since the colonial period. These areas came under Muslim hegemony during the colonial period in the 1950s and have resented the policy. Violence of this type broke out in Kafanchan, in Kaduna state, in March 1987 between the Christian Kataf of the town against the ruling Muslim Hausa-Fulani. The conflict started on the campus of the College of Education, Kafanchan, during a Christian annual crusade for converts. The preaching of a recent Muslim convert to Christianity, Bello Abubakar, aroused the anger of the Muslim students. A confrontation between the two camps ensued and spread outside the town, pitting Christians against Muslims. Meanwhile, in the state capital of Kaduna (300 kilometres away) radio broadcasts reported that Muslims were being killed and mosques burnt. The reports mobilized other Muslims as the violence (which lasted for six days) spread across the state. Although the style of preaching by a Muslim convert and the fact that there were Christian posters claiming "Welcome to Jesus Campus" were cited as the immediate causes of the conflict, there has been a long-standing resentment of the Muslim *emirs* ruling the predominantly Christian Kataf.[21]

Similar clashes in the central Plateau state of Nigeria have also pitted nomadic Muslim Fulani against indigenous Christian peasants. In May 2004, Christian militia in Yelwa in Plateau state killed over 200 Muslims before the federal government declared a state of emergency in the state. Revenge attacks on Christians by Muslim youth followed in Kano. In this conflict the Christians of Yelwa consider themselves the indigenous people and the Muslim Hausa-Fulani as the "foreigners."

At this point, it is worth mentioning the urban dimension of many ethno-religious conflicts. They have occurred in cities like Kano, Kaduna, Lagos, Maiduguri, Sokoto, Ibadan, and Port Harcourt. As for the northern cities, they have experienced Christian evangelical activism the most. The social conditions in the cities necessitate religions groups being active and providing their members (usually immigrants) with social services that are not often provided by the state. However, increasing Christian activism in the north has been considered as insensitive to Muslim feelings and as an "invasion" of Muslim territory. In 1980, there was sectarian violence in Kano protesting the visit of a European evangelist, and another incident to protest against the building of a church near a main mosque in the city. Each of these two episodes led to violent confrontations between Muslims and Christians.[22]

In response to Muslim activism in the north and what Nigerian Christians see as attempts by Muslims to dominate Nigerian politics, the Christian Association of Nigeria (formed in 1976) has since become very vocal on issues of Nigerian politics. Its leaders have openly vowed to meet Muslim activism with whatever means necessary (even violence). Such a response has heightened the religious rivalry between the two groups.

Islamist activism has caused further conflicts between Muslims and the Nigerian state during the long period of military rule. The military's attempt to reverse the "weak state" problem by breaking up the old regions and creating new states did not help to overcome the regional, ethnic and religious allegiances. Besides, the policy was considered by some Muslims as a reduction of their influence on national politics. In that situation the state responded to religious activism in three ways: 1) "manipulation" of religious sentiments, 2) outright repression and intimidation, and 3) ignoring the demands and wishing them to wither away. In any case, none of the approaches has worked satisfactorily. While "manipulation" led to more political intrigues and frustration by those who felt left out, repression especially of the Muslim radicals tended to provoke further activism. The third approach only made issues recede just to resurface with greater force.

In dealing with the *Izala* the state arrested some ranking members only after violent confrontations. That did not silence them until other prominent Muslims (in government and private life) brought the different sides in 1988 to a reconciliation that only partially succeeded. What actually made *Izala* tone down its activism was the fear that they would be associated with the *Maitatsine*. As mentioned earlier, the leader of the Muslim Brotherhood and many of its members were imprisoned by General Abacha for their activism. In the case of the *Maitatsine* the state seemed to have little choice but to engage in violence, which was actually started by the movement against the police. A similar approach was taken against the current "Nigerian Taliban." In the two instances, state authorities had the support of the traditional Muslim leaders in Kano. Since the use of force has been mostly against Muslim activists, a perception of the military state as "anti-Islamic" permeated among Muslims during military rule. The military in turn increased its repression rendering the situation into a vicious cycle of protest and violence. The military's strategy often backfired since many religious leaders felt that activism (public preaching, denunciation of corruption and injustices) were their religious obligations.[23]

When the state offered jobs to persons on the basis of their religious affiliations (as Muslims or Christians) in an attempt to gain the support of their groups, the state might be seen to adopt a *manipulation approach*.[24] In most cases however, some of the appointees were not considered representatives of the religious groups. The strategy also produced counter-demands from groups that felt left out from the share of such public goods. A parallel case to this strategy was Nigeria's "secret" attempt to join the Organization of the Islamic Conference (OIC) in January 1986—a move thought to favour Muslims. The attempt backfired as Christians protested until the government withdrew its membership. On other various occasions, the state embarked on building mosques and churches in public places for worshippers even though the federal constitutions have been clear in their statements that "No government shall overtly give preferential treatment to any particular religion." Apparently the federal government and the Shariah states have found ways to interpret the clause to support their religious roles.

The third approach has been for the state to ignore conflicts of religious nature hoping that the issues would wither away. This approach was demonstrated in the state's responses to demands for Shariah courts at the federal level. In the constitutional debates of 1977–1978 and 1988–1989, the two military regimes of Generals Obasanjo and Babangida respectively considered the issue too sensitive to debate publicly since members of the Constituent Assembly showed signs of a split along sectarian lines. Instead the governments intervened each time and came up with compromise positions that did not fully satisfy either of the two positions: that Shariah could exist at the state level for those states that wished but not at the Federal level. For the proponents, their chance came finally during the early years of the new democratic government in 1999–2000 when the Zamfara state governor, Sani Yerima, announced on 27 October 1999 that the state was adopting full Shariah. Eleven other states followed the Zamfara example in quick succession, invoking a constitutional provision of state rights in a federal structure to implement Shariah law. Instead of accepting the challenge to debate the issue publicly in the National Assembly or take the case to the courts to clarify as some legal personnel suggested, the President of the Republic initially ignored the issue. Four months elapsed and the Shariah controversy had already claimed many lives in the sectarian violence in Kaduna before the President made his first national broadcast on the issue calling for caution. This approach clearly illustrated the "weak state" effect on the government in which it felt helpless to confront national issues head on.

Islamist activism, religious conflicts in Nigeria and the "clash of civilizations"

How does religious activism and its attendant conflicts relate to the clash of civilizations debate? The discussion reflects the essentially local focus of religious conflicts in Northern Nigeria. The "others" or adversaries in each of these conflicts were either members of different sects of the same religion, adherents of other religions, or the secular state. Also the social conditions and religious values to which these activists address or respond were often local. Yet these "others" could be regarded as representing external forces or interests. And globalization (often equated with westernization by these groups) was also seen as a factor responsible for many local conditions. At the same time globalization provides the tools for interconnections and cross-fertilization of ideas across national borders. This opens up opportunities for groups to seek alliances as well as to identify potential enemies. It is in this regards that one can relate local religious conflicts to the international arena and to Huntington's clash of civilizations thesis. To start with, Huntington is correct to acknowledge the importance of religion in the lives of adherents. This is more so in the less developed countries where the failure of secular institutions to satisfy the physical and psychological needs of the people often leads most to seek spiritual alternatives. Problems with nation building by "weak states" compel people to seek solace and security in those with whom they share a common identity.[25] It is partly on this basis that religious activism and conflicts in Nigeria should be understood.

There are cases of Muslim activism that point to a clash of civilizations. One is evident in the Muslim demonstrations against the United States war in Iraq where Muslims took sides with the Arab cause. What binds Nigerian Muslims and the Middle East is the Islamic religion. Symbolically, flags of the United States and other western powers were burnt publicly during the demonstrations, but such expressions of sympathy for the Arab cause have not led to direct attacks on western interests in Nigeria.[26] Muslim leaders have also used the war in Iraq to create the perception that they may be a party to the war even though the reasons do not seem plausible. They refused the World Health Organization's vaccination programme against polio in 2003, because they suspected a "western conspiracy to wipe out Muslim children." However, the WHO is an agency of the United Nations, which was actually against the war. The case shows the complexity of the thesis and how misperceptions can generate ideas to signify a "clash" between the West and Muslim populations.

As for the fringe groups involved in Islamist activisms and their potential for the clash of civilizations, there is an on-going case between the Federal Government and a 40-year-old Nigerian accused of being an agent of al-Qaeda with plans to attack Americans in Nigeria. He, however, has pleaded not guilty.[27] If the case against him is proven it would be the first direct link between a Nigerian Muslim and the terrorist organization. Even then, would this singular act constitute the clash of civilizations? It would vindicate those who fear that poverty in Sub-Saharan Africa could lead to security problems. The man was alleged to have received US$1,500 for his participation in the terrorist plot. This is a large sum of money by Nigerian standards and is enough to make a poor Muslim take the risk, but should this act be considered a commitment to religious injunctions (which relates to the idea of a clash of civilizations) or an act for material gain? Still it is instructive that of the millions of Muslims in northern Nigeria this has been the only case of its type. It therefore questions the extent to which a commitment to a civilizational clash exists among Muslims in Northern Nigeria.

Religious identities could lead to sympathies. The "global war on terror", when extended to other predominantly Muslim countries, tends to produce sympathetic feeling for the "little guy" seen as the "victim". The more states like Nigeria refer to the term in their confrontation with Muslim extremists, the more likely it is that the idea of a "clash" will become internalized among the local population who already view the conflict as a war targeting Muslims.[28] By referring to Muslim groups suspected of security breaches as "terrorists" or "jihadists" the Nigerian government unintentionally helps to fuel the activism of fringe groups wishing to brand their activities as Islamic.[29]

The argument has been made so far for a *potential* "clash of civilizations" emerging from Islamist activism and conflicts in Nigeria. However, stronger evidence emerged from the analysis to show that the objective conditions existing in Nigerian social formation would make it difficult to translate these conflicts into a real "clash of civilizations" with the West. The major confrontation between Africans (including Muslims) and the West was over independence from colonialism, which was also different from the Middle Eastern experience. In Nigeria, even though colonialism compromised Shariah law in northern Nigeria, it also empowered many Muslim leaders in the region.[30] As Clapham observed, "Whereas for African states, anti-colonialism most prominently took the form of a demand for political independence, Arab ones were more concerned with the cultural threat which imperialism presented to their language and religion."[31]

Another factor that could limit the clash concerns the political economy of development in Nigeria. The level of development (or underdevelopment) renders many groups dependent on state resources, foreign investments, and foreign sources of industrialization. Nigeria's two leading trading partners have been the UK and the United States in that order. When the Muslim (and other) leaders talk about development they are essentially thinking about their relations with the western world. Imports from the western world provide the bulk of consumable items for their populations. These leaders know that a real "clash of civilizations" originating from them would negatively affect the prospects of societal development of their communities.[32] Most of these leaders' budgets are paid for by the federal government, which in turn depends on the global economy. Thus the practical requirements for "development" push these leaders into leaning towards the West rather than towards a clash of civilizations on religious grounds.

Finally, there is a problem with the identity question in relation to the clash of civilizations. Do Muslims in Northern Nigeria identify with "African civilization" or with "Islamic civilization?" They could belong to both in which case their identity becomes a situational variable. The choice makes it not inevitable that they engage in a clash with the West. Perhaps nowhere is this flexibility manifested more than in the conspicuous absence of Islamic political parties among the Muslim politicians in Northern Nigeria such as are found in the Middle East and North Africa. Instead the Shariah state governors belong to secular political parties. The Shariah implementation therefore seems to be a policy matter rather than a socially, transforming movement.[33] The case for a clash of civilizations involving the fringe groups of so-called "Nigerian Taliban" is even less promising. While these groups' resort to violence makes news headlines, they lack the public legitimacy and the resources to sustain a struggle with the state much less sustain a clash with the West. So far, their strategy of attacking police stations and stealing arms to protect themselves poses limitations to their agenda. Looking to the future, however, these groups could become more dangerous and a serious threat to national security if they are able to acquire the financial resources to purchase arms in substantial quantities. The possibility of this happening exists with easy illegal financial transfers and the global arms trade made possible by globalization. This prospect coupled with the "weak state" in Nigeria could turn these groups into a formidable security threat that could have a major impact on the continent.

Conclusion: between the immediate and future clash

This chapter has focused on the nature of Islamist activism and its attendant conflicts in relation to the clash of civilizations debate. Huntington's important insight into the causes of the global resurgence of religion (especially Islam) into public affairs is seen to apply to the role of Islam in public affairs in northern Nigeria. As a result of poor social conditions, religion plays an important role in providing alternative meaning to life which secular institutions are incapable of. However, for this same reason, religious activism tends to focus on local actors (other religious groups or the state) and on the social condition (religious expressions, issues of social justice and access to public goods and services) rather than on external (international) matters.

The nature of Islam to address all human endeavours and to encourage activism makes its adherents more sensitive to matters of public affairs. While religious activism by itself need not be violent or conflictual, the political structure and the social environment in which adherents find themselves could turn activism into violent conflicts between religious groups as well as with the state. Thus religion assumes a dynamic force in response to changing situations and time. The Nigerian situation examined in this chapter reflects this force of Islam.

Yet, since Nigeria and its Muslim population operate in an international system their activism cannot be completely divorced from the currents of the global system. As a result conflicts with other groups and with the state have the potential to take on global dimensions (with the potential for a clash of civilizations). For example, from the simple demand for Shariah law to serve the proper way of worship for Muslims, the demand grew into an oppositional alternative to secular laws in Nigeria considered as representing western and Christian values. This dynamic tendency of religious ideas to metamorphose is evidence of the potential clash of civilizations. However, in the 2007 national elections matters of Shariah or religious issues were conspicuously absent from candidates' campaign agenda.[34] Was this a sign of the limit of religious activism on the potential clash of civilizations? Maybe yes, even though that may not be sufficient to stop the "clash talk" among Muslim leaders, some of whom require it as a legitimating strategy.

8

Somalia—Grievance, Religion, Clan, and Profit[1]

Stig Jarle Hansen

After eleven years of relative obscurity, Somalia resurfaced in the news in
2006. The Supreme Council of Islamic Courts (SCIC), an alliance/union of
Shariah courts in Mogadishu, expanded quickly, first by gaining control over
Mogadishu, then by conquering parts of central and southern Somalia. Ethiopia provided a large segment of the forces facing the SCIC, and in the end
contributed to their defeat in late 2006-early 2007. Because of Ethiopian
involvement in support of the sides opposing the SCIC, several observers
viewed the conflict as a form of "clash of civilizations". Highlighting Ethiopia's
supposedly Christian majority, the support from the Christian United States,
and Somalia's Islamic identity, the German journal *Der Spiegel* went so far as
to brand the conflict "the new East African front in the clash of civilizations".[2]
Superficially the recent history of the region seems to support the existence of
a "clash of civilizations" on the Horn of Africa. During the Ogadeen war
(1977–1978) in which Somalia clashed with Ethiopia, most of the Arab
world supported the Somali side, while most of the African states supported
Ethiopia.[3] Somali resistance towards the Ethiopians, the Italians and the English, all three supposedly Christian states, constituted a significant part of the
Somali nationalist rhetoric during the dictator Siad Barre's reign (1969–
1991), as well as the republic that preceded him (1960–1969). However, the

127

history of these conflicts is far more complex. During the Ogadeen war Somalia's major ally was the Eritrean Peoples Liberation Front (EPLF). EPLF
mobilized a substantial number of fighters and embarked on a large-scale
offensive against Ethiopia.[4] EPLF was, despite having connections with the
Arab world, at the initial stages of its creation dominated by atheist/Marxist
leaders from Tigray, a traditionally Christian ethnic region.[5] The second major
force allied with the Somalis during the Ogadeen war was the Tigrayan People's Liberation Front (TPLF), Maoists from a Christian ethnic group in
Ethiopia. TPLF, together with some closely allied parties, later came to power
in Ethiopia. Indeed many members of the top leadership of Ethiopia today,
including the Prime Minister Meles Zenawi, come from the TPLF, Somalia's
old ally. In this sense the most important allies of Somalia during the Ogadeen
war were Christian/atheist.

The picture of a unified Muslim front against a unified Christian Ethiopian
alliance fades even more when studying the events of the rise and fall of the
SCIC. The supposedly Christian Ethiopians were led by a leadership from
traditionally Christian groups, but the leaders were from highly secularist
organizations formerly allied to Somalia.[6] Ethiopian involvement was partly
prompted by the claims several members of the court union had made on
Ethiopian-controlled territory, as well as the fact that several of the SCIC
leaders had been involved in organizations implicated in bomb attacks and
assassination attempts on Ethiopian soil.[7] Several religious organizations, such
as the Islamist *Harakat Al-Islah* (The Somali offshoot of the Muslim Brotherhood) and the *Ahlu Sunna wal Jama'a* worked against the SCIC, although
there were important defections from these organizations as SCIC's power
rose. Some, if not a majority, of the older Shariah courts of Mogadishu, such
as the old Mogadishu-based Harrariale court, resented the SCIC. Contrary to
popular belief that there was a united movement of all Shariah courts, key
courts defected from the court alliance during battle, never to rejoin again.
Some courts hesitated to join the SCIC, and joined only very late when the
alliance seemed to be unstoppable. Despite the claims of the press, the SCIC
never controlled most of Somalia. The transitional government and other
regional entities, such as Somaliland, and Puntland, as well as Rahanwehin
militias, held sway over roughly two-thirds of the country. Somalia was
divided; the alliance of the courts (which as stated earlier even failed to
include all Shariah courts in Mogadishu), as well as their competitors in the
transitional government, drew heavily on particular clans, while other clans
were under-represented. However, as will be shown later, belief in Islam pro-

vided the SCIC with notable military and economic advantages. Despite drawing mainly upon support from some clans, the SCIC was amongst the most successful Somali movements when it came to recruiting from all Somali clans: they had a *relative* success.

This chapter will argue that one has to examine the rise and fall of the SCIC in Somalia, and the conflict between the SCIC, the transitional government and Ethiopia, using more complex analytical tools than a simple primordialist approach to the role of religion in politics. The chapter argues that there were four major factors that caused the rise of the SCIC: *local grievances, economic interests, clan dynamics* and *economy*, as well as *religious faith*, exploring each of these factors in the above indicated order. Importantly, religion was the focus point that defined the interaction. Religion created and defined specific solutions that became "natural".

Local grievances: creating the building blocks of the courts

When the "enemies or allies" project at the University of Bath surveyed the business community of Mogadishu in 2006, it was—not surprisingly—discovered that the major cause of serious financial crises amongst the Mogadishu commercial enterprises was war and insecurity.[8] The stories from Mogadishu during the years 1991 to 2006 are indeed heartbreaking: crime was rampant, rape was common, and a life was of little value.[9] In the volatile situation of Somalia, trust was an open question. Who should be trusted to handle security? Reputation for religious piety and respect for the *Qur'ān*, perhaps because of the strong condemnation of theft and rape within Islam, was one factor that made Somalis trust fellow countrymen to handle security and justice issues. The activities of religious charities in Somalia contributed to this, creating a positive perception of religious scholars.[10] Indeed, it was this reputation that created the foundation for the rise of the separate Shariah courts of Mogadishu, and thus the building blocks of the future SCIC.

Both Salafists and Sufi religious leaders gained a reputation of trustworthiness, and many of them also acted directly to prevent the injustices they saw around them. As claimed by Ali Mahdi, former—contested—president of Somalia, Islamic scholars were the only option for creating courts, because they enjoyed so much trust and respect.[11] Somalis tended to expect that religious clerics would be well behaved, that they believed in justice, and that the belief system of Islam created an ideational focal point, a solution that felt natural because of the dominating role Islam had in society. When one has little power to defend oneself, the belief that others adhere to norms that could help uphold some form of law and safety becomes vital if one is considering allowing them to handle the task of preventing crime. In this sense, it was no wonder that the Islamic judges were trusted as upholders of the law. To outsiders, their image of strong belief in Islam functioned as the best guarantee available.

It is worth noticing that most of the courts were initially created by a mix of traditional clan leaders, civil society leaders and businessmen, many with little in-depth knowledge of ideological divisions within Islam, and these men appointed judges from most of the religious groups in Somalia, despite the theological cleavages between these groups. This meant that the Islamic *sheiks* (religious leaders) involved in the courts had a varied background, spanning Sufis to Wahhabis.

The history of the first larger courts illustrates how insecurity drove the formation of Shariah courts, but also how the Shariah courts could efficiently make life better for ordinary people in Mogadishu. On 14 April 1994, several traditional and religious leaders met in the northern part of Mogadishu, they all came from the Abgal clan. The leaders were shocked by the rampant crime in northern Mogadishu, and one of their own, Sheik Mudey, had his house attacked by freelance militias almost simultaneously with their first meeting. The 2006–2007 Mayor of Mogadishu, Adde Gabow, had a similar experience.[12] Several of the *sheiks* who participated in the meeting that night later became judges in the courts. These leaders were also famous for their adherence to Islam, a religion that strongly condemns and forbids theft, rape and killings. A system of northern Mogadishu courts was created, of which the largest became known as the Karar court. The Karar court was an extremely efficient remedy against violence and crime, and theft, rape and robbery decreased in the north of Mogadishu.[13] According to Kassahun, the Karar court processed 6,000 criminal cases and 2,000 civil cases between August 30, 1994 and September 1996.[14] However, the punishments for several criminal offences were extreme, and included amputations. In the end the Karar court collapsed. The faction leader controlling the north, Ali Mahdi, felt threatened by it. The business community was scared of what they perceived to be an increasingly political agenda and the court's deviation from the traditional Somali practice of Islam.[15] It should also be noted that the court system at that time was based on a particular clan, the Abgal.

After the fall of the Karar court in 1996, many of the affiliated courts collapsed. The origin of the courts that in the end formed the Supreme Council of Islamic Courts (SCIC), are somewhat similar to the origins of the Karar system (1994–1996); some even originated from courts that were a part of this system. The history of the Sii Sii court is illustrative. Sii Sii initially existed as a part of the northern Mogadishu court system. When the northern Mogadishu court system collapsed, the Sii Sii continued its existence as a shadow court, maintaining a formal leader, but it remained inactive and failed to act against bandits. When the court was recreated, one of its first tasks was to put a stop to an infamous and effective gang that was stealing cars and trucks. This gang fielded a substantial militia, operating out of the Sii Sii area, but was happy to steal cars from the whole of Mogadishu. The Sii Sii Court managed to put an end to the gang despite a growing conflict between the head of the court, later head of the union of the courts, Sheik Sharif Sheik Ahmed, and his militia first commander, Nur Daqle. However, as with all of the other courts, the Sii Sii court was based on one sub-sub-sub clan, and mostly wielded jurisdiction only over this sub-sub-sub clan.[16]

There were several attempts to transcend the clan divisions and to unify the courts, the first as early as 1993. All of the pre-2004 unions of courts were partly created to transcend clan divisions by coordinating and regulating crimes in which the victim(s) and the accused came from different clans.[17] From 2004 and onwards, four courts, the Ifka Halane, the Circola, the Towfiq and the Sii Sii, drove a new process of unification forward, initially relatively unsuccessful, as many courts resisted the dominance of the four. Nevertheless, it was this drive that in the end resulted in the SCIC, and this drive was also said to have started because of the wish to be able to provide justice that transcends clan.[18] However, the fact that the Ifka Halane court members had wanted to play a role in the previous establishment of a regional administration and in deterring the transitional government from marching on Mogadishu in September 2005 indicates that there might have been an additional political motive on behalf of some courts.[19]

The strength and swiftness the four courts had shown in dealing with criminals were admired by Mogadishu's population. During the spring of 2006 the SCIC defeated the warlords. Most of the unpopular warlords of Mogadishu were individuals who had started out as faction leaders, but who, through war profiteering and failure to establish law and order, had alienated their own followers. The SCIC were helped by the wave of sympathy they enjoyed from the ordinary population, from the diaspora, as well as the business community that provided them with support. According to Mogadishu dwellers that witnessed the events, citizens blocked streets with debris to prevent the movement of the warlords, and there was widespread random sniping against the warlord forces. The fact that the courts facilitated security and provided justice created sympathy amongst the Mogadishu dwellers. The peace that followed their victories was astonishing. Even businesswomen, a group that was targeted in the rhetoric of the SCIC, praised the latter's role in re-establishing security in Mogadishu.[20] The provision of security created widespread sympathy with the SCIC, even by the writer of this chapter, who experienced Mogadishu both before and after the SCIC.

The courts started out as security and justice providers; they were created because of the lack of safety in Mogadishu, often by community leaders with little religious interests (but led by religious leaders). Shariah courts provided justice that gave them the popular support, as well as legitimacy and trust needed in order to create larger alliances between separate and originally clan-based Shariah courts.

Economic interests: providing cash for the courts

Sympathy alone does not win wars; economic resources are also needed, and the provision of justice does not necessarily give access to financial resources. However, the SCIC was backed by some of the strongest businessmen of Mogadishu. Abokor Omar Adane, the main shareholder in the El Maan port of northern Mogadishu, provided funds for several of the courts. The reason for his support of the courts, and other justice institutions such as the Karar police station, could have been because of commercial interests. The courts provided relative safety for the transport of goods. In the survey conducted for the University of Bath, the "enemies and allies project", almost 69 per cent of the commercial enterprises reported that they had financially supported the courts: the courts simply made business safer.[21] It is important to underline that the courts also made the businessmen's personal life better. Many of the main financial backers of the SCIC had suffered personally because of insecurity, losing brothers, friends, and family.

An additional factor that made the business community support the SCIC was their need to maintain a good reputation. To keep up appearances as an ardent follower of Islam, going regularly to the Mosque, giving charity to relief foundations, making religious statements, equalled a reputation of trustworthiness, of immense importance in an economy that functions without a state, thus in which reputation is one of the few guidelines consumers can employ in order to avoid cheating on behalf of the businessmen. At the same time, it was advantageous for businessmen to adhere to the Salafist/Wahhabist dogmas of Islam, opening doors for them in Saudi Arabia, but also drawing them closer to the most extreme and militant elements within the SCIC. Salafism/ Wahhabism is in many ways an upper-class phenomenon in Somalia, businessmen gaining important social capital by adhering to its tenets.

The international press failed to comment on the various conflicts over resources that formed a backdrop for the rise of the courts.[22] It was not religion, but a disagreement over cars that sparked the fighting between the court alliance and the warlords. *Shabelle News*, a local media group, reported that Bashir Raghe and the financial backer of many of the courts, Abokor Omar Adane, clashed over the ownership of several cars in the north of Mogadishu in January 2006, a claim supported by interviews with Adane's former militia.[23] The fighting then escalated when the newly formed the Alliance for Restoration of Peace and Counter Terrorism (ARPCT), an alliance of warlords, came to Bashir Raghes' aid, and the major Shariah courts supported Abokor Omar Adane. What was at stake in the initial stages of battle was nothing less than control over one of the biggest sources of revenue in Mogadishu, El Maan port. The control over El Maan port would ensure revenues that could be used for military mobilization, as well as personal enrichment. The SCIC secured control over most of Mogadishu's working airports and seaports as early as in February 2006, and put itself in a position to sabotage inbound flights of the sole airport remaining under warlord control, Dayniile. In this sense they scored an early victory; controlling the major revenues of Mogadishu. Adane provided a substantial number of his own fighters to the union of courts, perhaps making up as much as one-third of the total amount of their forces during the spring of 2006. The members of the Mogadishu business community that supported the courts achieved political influence in return. The power of the business community could clearly be seen in the top leadership of the SCIC. Businessman Abokor Omar Adane's son was the court alliance's head of finance. Prominent Mogadishu businessmen such as Abdullahi Hussein Khaie were members of the executive committee.

In one sense, individual courts gained support, including militia, from the business community, simply because they were good for business.

Clan dynamics

The SCICs successful provision of justice and the economic advantages it provided to the business community were not the only causes of success.

However, clan considerations also drove the development that led to the formation of the SCIC.

Most Somalis traditionally claim to be members of a clan, tracing their ancestry from the father's side. Each Somali clan is divided into sub-clans, which in turn are divided into smaller sub-sub groups, which in turn can be divided into even smaller groups, the smallest group in Somali tradition being a single family. A wife will belong to her husband's lineage, but will still have ties to her father's lineage. The main faction opposing the SCIC was the transitional government, at the time led by President Abdullahi Yusuf and his Prime Minister Mohammed Ali Gedi. The Nairobi conference that produced the transitional government was based on the so-called "4.5 formula", including what the participators defined as the four major clans of Somalia; the Diir, the Darod, The Digil-Mirifle, and the Hawiye. The 0.5 was the quota allocated to the minority clans. There were several problems with this formula. Somaliland, an enclave of Somalia that has declared independence, contains many of the supposedly Diir sub-clans (the concept of Diir is contested), making many see the Diir representation as weakened.[24] The weakness of the Diir was serious for the Hawiye; they felt isolated. The Hawiye were unpopular with the Rahanwehin representatives, since Hawiye factions had looted Rahanwehin properties in the mid-1990s. Ethiopia played a major role in the negotiations. Ethiopia's oldest allies in Somalia were the Rahanwein Resistance Army, and Abdullahi Yusuf, the president, and non-Hawiye organizations. Moreover, most of the parliamentarians supposed to represent the clan had been selected by the unpopular warlords of Mogadishu; indeed some of the warlords themselves became ministers and MPs. The pill was made more bitter to swallow by the fact that the president preceding Abdullahi Yusuf, Abdiqasim Salad Hassan, leader of the Transitional Federal Government appointed after the 2000 Arta conference, was from a sub-sub clan of the Hawiye, the Ayr of the Haber Gedir. Seemingly, the Hawiye had lost power, when the Arta-based cabinet was dissolved. In many ways the Hawiye clan, and especially its Haber Gedir sub-clan, had little ownership over the Nairobi/Mbagathi peace process that produced the government. It is thus not surprising that the Hawiye factions had serious stand-offs with the rest of the transitional government even before the rise of the SCIC.[25]

The Hawiye had alternatives. The Ayr sub-sub-clan of Hawiye was also the clan of one of the most prominent courts in Mogadishu, the Ifka Halane, and all of the courts of Mogadishu were Hawiye-based. In fact, the mobilization of the Hawiyes can be seen as a mobilization against non-Hawiye-dominated

SOMALIA—GRIEVANCE, RELIGION, CLAN, AND PROFIT

political structures. The militias fighting against the court alliance were mainly recruited from three sub-clans, the Majerteen of President Abdullahi Yusuf, the Rahanwheins, and the Marehan. The SCIC forces were dominated by the Hawiye, especially the Haber Gedir sub-clan.

Despite having supporters among all Somali clans, the numbers of non-Hawiye fighters within the SCIC were seemingly small compared with the Hawiye component of the courts.

Religion

In one way, religion interacted with the above mentioned factors. The fact that the courts addressed the security needs and grievances of the common population of Mogadishu contributed to their initial popularity, but this commitment was influenced by the tenets of a relatively stable interpretation of Islam: the addressing of the needs of the poor, and the condemnation of theft have been cornerstones of Islam since the birth of the Prophet Mohammed. *Sheiks* and *qadis* had reputation of trustworthiness and this gained them prominent positions, and also made several SCIC leaders strive to achieve the title. In October 2006, fifteen out of seventeen of the members of the executive committee of the SCIC were sheiks. It was the courts' reputation of trustworthiness, the general legitimacy gained by supporting religious institutions, and the SCIC provision of security to the business community that allowed the SCIC to gain financial support from the Somali business community. Nor can the possibility that the business community supported the SCIC out of their individual religious beliefs be excluded.

The courts were initially divided by clan lines, however, the SCIC managed slowly to transcend the clan-demarcated jurisdiction of the various courts, they established a *shura*, a council that functioned somewhat similarly to a parliament, and also established an executive committee, which had some similar functions to a cabinet, and the nucleus of non-clan-based militia units and police. It is important to make it clear that the court union was more able to transcend clan divisions than any of the political factions before them. During the fierce fighting between warlords and the court alliance in May 2006, militia commander Abdulle Cadar, nicknamed "*Gaal-dile*", meaning "Christian killer", of the Faruqaan court, was killed when he led fighters from all over southern Somalia, even also including some northern Somalis. In the north, many members of the Majerteen sub-clan fought against the Majerteen militias of Abdullahi Yusuf, clans and sub-clans were fighting within themselves.

The extremist wing of the SCIC fully transcended the clan cleavage with leaders from all clans.

Religion provided all of the Shariah courts of Mogadishu, and later the SCIC, with the trust of the general community. Moreover, religious beliefs motivated fighters to fight with a discipline seldom seen in the Somali wars, and for the first time the Somali civil war saw fighters that believed in "paradise": ultimate victory regardless of the outcome of the battle itself. A hardcore of court alliance fighters, frequently recruited in *madrasahs*, often very young, many times referred to as the *Shebabs*, fought with an amazing discipline.[26] Perhaps it was because of the fighting spirit of these forces that the leaders of this group gained their key positions within the court system as commanders of various court militias. The *Shebabs* rose to ascendancy in the Ifka Halane court, the Circola court and many of the new courts formed during the autumn of 2006. The Ifka Halane court had shown signs of having larger political ambitions from the start. The initial leader of the Ifka Halane court, Hassan Dahir Aweys, was a former leader of *Al Itthad Al Islamiya*, a Somali islamist organization that on occasion resorted to militancy. Aweys was also accused by the United States of aiding the al-Qaeda 1998 attack against the American embassy in Nairobi. *Al Itthad al Islamiya* was not popular amongst Somalis, it was seen as extreme. It was within Hassan Dahir Aweys' old court that the most extreme elements in the court union flourished, and the *Shebab* group, a group of young militant Salafists, first gained a major foothold. While the *shura* and executive committees of the Shariah courts were dominated by moderates, even intellectuals, the military apparatus became dominated by a small hard-core of the *Shebab* leaders: Salafist fighters including Hassan Turki, Aden Hashi Ayro (killed during the spring of 2008), Muktar Robow "Abu Mansoor", and Abdullahi Moallim Ali "Abu Qutaiba" (killed early 2007). Hassan Turki was wanted by United States for his involvement in the 1998 attacks on the American embassy in Nairobi, and Aden Hasi Ayro and Muktar Robow "Abu Mansoor", were said to have been trained in Afghanistan before/just after the American invasion in 2001–2002.[27] The group also contained first generation (1980–1989) Afghanistan veterans such as Ibrahim Abid "Al Afghani", and implemented Iraqi-style suicide attacks, with releases of suicide videos, after the fall of the SCIC.

The SCIC had some global connections, both material and more ideological. Foreigners were fighting on behalf of the courts. However, a number of foreigners did not necessary fight for the global jihadist networks causes, but for the independence of several ethnic groups. The Oromo, an ethnic group that mainly lives in regions in Ethiopia and that has traditionally fought for independence from the Ethiopian central state, seemingly made up the largest contingent of non-Somalis.[28] There are concrete facts that confirm the presence of Arab fighters.[29] Nevertheless, the small numbers of Arab captives, and the lack of positive identification of dead Arab fighters, seem to suggest that the presence of Arab fighters was limited, or that the fighters have escaped the Ethiopians and the transitional government. Indeed, little information about the supposed international jihadists captured by the Ethiopians and the transitional Somali government has been released, and little evidence of the presence of foreign jihadists in large numbers has been presented.

Religion did not only provide the SCIC with advantages, it also created problems. There were several indications of an emerging split within the SCIC before the Ethiopian/TFG victory. At one occasion *Shebab* leader Abu Mansoor spoke critically about "the black cat" when former warlord Indohadde was sitting beside him, "black cat" being a metaphor for how Hawiyes followed members of smaller clans in order to force the latter to pay illegal tax, a practice that Indohadde was famous for. Hassan Turki was reprimanded by the SCIC for his pan-Islamic agenda. He claimed that Somali nationalism was less important for him than the resurrection of the Islamic Caliphate, a statement that angered many of the Court leaders. The more extreme jihadist elements interpreted the *Qur'ān* and the *Hadiths* in a way that scared many Somalis, and also Somali religious scholars.[30]

A clash of civilizations?

The SCIC, as well as its wars with Ethiopia, the Transitional Federal Government, and several warlords, were not a product of "a clash of civilizations". The conflict was not a confrontation between Islam and Christianity. The Somali Muslims were disagreeing over the interpretation of what Islam was and many religious groups and even Shariah courts were sceptical towards the SCIC and its version of Islam. Admittedly, the courts' main propaganda argument was that Somalia was invaded by Christian Ethiopia.[31] Yet, several Somali clans provided large numbers of forces that fought against the SCIC.

The tenets of Islam did however contribute to the dynamic of the situation. Mogadishu residents had problems with crime, and Islamic institutions provided one type of solution, and gained support because of their efficiency; the successful provision of security by the courts was essential in bringing them legitimacy as well as economic support. The courts' religious reputation also made businessmen support them to maintain their own reputation; it made the SCIC more able to transcend clan, explaining their relative success, compared with previous Somali rebel groups, in recruiting amongst many clans. Elements of the SCIC army were highly motivated because of their beliefs. However, the more extreme jihadist elements scared many Somalis and also Somali religious scholars.[32]

Religion provided a relatively stable framework of interpretation; in this sense religion was a major factor defining the developments, and it became a catalyst that formed the events, and also the conflicts within the SCIC.

9

Ethiopia—On the Borders
of Christianity

Terje Østebø

Although the presence of Islam in Ethiopia can be dated to before the formal establishment of Islam itself, Ethiopians have often referred to themselves as a "Christian island in a sea of Muslims and Pagans", revealing a self-image of a country situated on the frontier of Christian civilization.[1] The relationship between Christians and Muslims in Ethiopia and, moreover, the status of the country's Muslims were largely determined by the Christians' control of the political and cultural institutions. While the peaceful coexistence between Christians and Muslims in Ethiopia often has been celebrated both by Ethiopians and foreign observers, one should not ignore the fact that history also contains periods of inter-religious hostilities and conflicts. Peaceful coexistence between Muslims and Christians is to a large degree made possible because of an asymmetric relationship between the two, the latter controlling the political institutions, and defining the former as second-class.

Ahmed ibn Ibrahim, nicknamed "Ahmed Granj", is central in the Ethiopian self-perception. Ahmed Granj launched an offensive against the Christian kingdom in 1529. Nearly defeated by the Muslims, the Christians finally managed to drive their enemies back, killing Ahmed Granj in 1542. In addition to the vast devastations caused by the war, this incident can moreover be said to constitute a major watershed in the development of Islam and its relationship to Christian Ethiopia. First of all, it was the final blow to Islam as a political force in Ethiopia, leaving the Christian kingdom the sole dominating political entity in the region. Secondly, as the conquest of Ahmed Granj had led to the formation of a Muslim population within the Christian kingdom, the rulers soon initiated a policy of religious discrimination. Even if Islam ceased to pose any real political challenge to the Christian kingdom, the near-defeat by Ahmed Granj laid the foundation for a perception of Islam as a threat to the kingdom's very existence. Introducing the term the *Ahmed Granj syndrome*, Erlich has argued that the experiences of Ahmed Granj's conquest led to the construction of a religious fault-line, with the perception of Islam as a possible external threat, compelling the Christian rulers to question constantly the loyalty of the country's own Muslims.[2] Combined with a strong nationalistic ideology, where Christianity and the intermarriage between church and state constituted important components, the country's Muslims found themselves subject to subjugation and even persecution. The expansionist policy of emperor Menelik II at the end of the nineteenth century establishing the present borders of Ethiopia led to the incorporation of numerous ethnic and religious groups, and, to the inclusion of a substantial Muslim population under Christian rule. Hence, Ethiopia was increasingly becoming a multi-religious society, forcing the political rulers to follow a policy of more "guarded religious tolerance".[3] Guided by the notion of a unitary Christian state, Menelik and even more so, Haile Selassie, strengthened the policy of cultural dissemination, where the Christian Orthodox faith and the Amharic language continued to be major factors. Though this policy of "guarded religious tolerance" alleviated the situation for the country's Muslims, they were never accepted on an equal footing with the Christians. Muslims remained excluded from employment in public offices and from holding higher ranks in the army.[4] Not easily surrendering to this process of assimilation, Islam was rendered as the antithesis of Ethiopianism; the Christian rulers continuously being cautious about potential alliances between external Islamic forces and the country's own Muslims. Referring to the notion of political stability and national unity, the *Ahmed Granj syndrome* would on occasions be invoked and elevated to a higher level where the political discourse was interwoven with religious prejudices and fear. This has in turn led to encumbering the contact with the outside world and contributed to isolating the Ethiopian Muslims from the rest of the Islamic world.

Parallel to this, the relations between Christians and Muslims in the micro-sphere have been of a more peaceful character. Popular harassment of Muslims has been uncommon, instead friendly coexistence and mutual tolerance is dominant at grassroots level. In some areas, like Wollo, a degree of religious mobility is common. The situation is, however, not one of equality and religious parity. The views and policy of the ruling elite have permeated down to the populace, contributing to sustaining a popular perception of the Muslims as inferior to the Christians. The latter see themselves as the group constituting the very core of Ethiopianness, and the former as neighbours to be tolerated. Thus, this oft-celebrated relationship of tolerance and coexistence in the microsphere is rather complex. The two groups' positions and statuses have been clearly defined, contributing to shaping the identity of each group, demarcating the boundaries between them and upholding a relationship of an asymmetric character. This situation has inevitably affected the self-image of Ethiopia's Muslims, who, deprived of access to the political institutions and lacking real power to challenge the cultural and political subjugation, have had few other options than accepting their position as second-class.

Islam in contemporary Ethiopia

The new policies introduced by the Ethiopian People's Democratic Revolutionary Front (EPDRF) have had far-reaching consequences for the Islamic community in Ethiopia. Starting from 1991, restrictions on *hajj* and the ban on the import of religious literature were lifted, confinement on the construction of mosques was removed and Islamic organizations, newspapers and magazines were legalized. Naturally, this led to much enthusiasm among the Muslims, seen in the mushrooming of mosques, and the establishment of a number of Islamic organizations and magazines in the early 1990s.[5] With basic religious rights increasingly being secured, this contributed to a renewed consciousness among the Muslims, to Islam becoming more visible and to the carving out of public space for Islam. Commentaries in Islamic newspapers and magazines appeared; seeking to refute different allegations and "misinterpretations" of Islam, often answering articles published in local Amharic newspapers and also trying to provide comments on controversies between Christians and Muslims. While many of these writings must be said to be of a defensive nature, more self-assertive sentiments were found in a series of articles in *Bilal* (1992–1993). Dealing with the Axumite *hijrah* and Islam's history in Ethiopia, it was argued that instead of referring to periods of oppressions in the past, the time was now ripe for the modern Ethiopian Muslims to start thinking about their long and glorious history, and to stand forth with pride as Muslims.[6] In addition, several large public demonstrations were to be seen in the streets of Addis Ababa. Whereas many of these demonstrations addressed internal affairs within the Muslim community, there were others more directly concerned with Islam in relation to society and politics.[7] A large demonstration in November 1994 demanded among other things, the inclusion of Shariah law as one of the bases for the new Ethiopian constitution, and challenged the ban on headscarves for girls in high schools.

The emergence of a renewed consciousness among the Muslims, and the questioning of old conceptions and the previous position of Islam in Ethiopia, illustrates how the Muslims actively embarked on a process of identification.[8] Accompanied by revitalization and articulation of religious virtues and a demarcation of religious boundaries, this has inevitably led to increased cultural and religious diversity, to contradictory discourses within the Islamic community, and even to increased inter- and intra-religious tensions, which again have been entangled with the most prominent discourse in contemporary Ethiopia: that of ethnicity.

Islamic reform movements

This increased diversity is clearly seen through the emergence of several Islamic reform movements. Most visible has been the Salafi movement, ideologically affiliated to Saudi Arabia.[9] Emerging in Harar in the early 1940s, the movement made its presence felt among the Oromo in Hararge, Arsi and Bale in the late 1960s.[10] In accordance with Salafi doctrines, the movement attacked popularized Sufi practices, such as pilgrimages to the shrines, celebrations of *mawlid*, the inclusion of indigenous elements in Islam and has in general agitated for a stricter observance of Islam.

The other set of impulses came from the *Jama'at al-Tabligh*, emerging in Addis Ababa in the 1970s.[11] Introduced by South African and Kenyan Indian *Tabligh* missionaries, and facilitated by a certain Hajji Musa, the movement expanded steadily among the Gurage community in Addis Ababa. In accordance with their principles, the *Tabligh* movement has been active in calling people to attend prayers in the mosque, to observe fast, and to uphold the main virtues of Islam. In contrast to the principles of *Tabligh* in general, the movement has in Ethiopia been relatively pragmatic in relation to popularized Sufi practices, thus creating a link of continuity to earlier religious practices, particularly those of the Gurage.[12]

The expansion of these movements was to a large degree checked by the religious policy of the Derg regime (1974–1991). Guided by a Marxist ideology, the Derg sought to curb religious activities in general, which caused religious change to be temporarily postponed in Ethiopia. During this time, Islamic organizations were virtually non-existent, whereas religious activities were strictly controlled and restricted to the mosque. The change in political climate in 1991 paved the way for a revitalization of these reform movements. The Salafi movement, which had already gained a foothold in Oromo-speaking areas, such as Bale and Arsi, soon attracted large number of additional followers in these areas. Similar trends were soon seen in Harar, Jimma, Wollo and Addis Ababa. Obviously, the EPRDF's policy on religion enabled Salafis to strengthen their contact with the outside world. In the case of Bale, this was notable through increased communication with Saudi and through the *qawettis* Oromo returning from exile in Somalia in the early 1990s, advocating reform in line with Salafi doctrines. In the capital, it was the Ethiopian Muslim Youth Association that became the main promoter of the Salafi ideology. Established in the early 1990s and led by Sheikh Sayid Ahmed Mustafa and Muhammed Usman successively, initially the association only had loose connections with Salafi Islam. As funding from Saudi increased, however, and links with the World Association of Muslim Youth (WAMY) in Riyadh were established, the Salafi affiliation became more obvious. As observed by one of my informants; "The Saudis were the only one making funds available at that time". Besides the Muslim Youth Association, the Salafi movement was represented by a group of Oromo *ulama* returning from Saudi Arabia in the early 1990s and settling in Aiyr Tena, one of the suburbs of Addis Ababa. Individuals such as Dr. Jeylan Kadir, Dr. Kamal Galato, Sheikh Umar Walle, Sheikh Abdullatif Hassan and Sheikh Qasim Haji were exerting substantial influence on the young Oromo residing in Addis Ababa. Further, the Islamic Da'wa and Knowledge Association, established in 1992 by Sheikh Tahir Abdulqadir from Bale has been active in the translation and publication of religious literature, construction of mosques and in supporting various forms of *da'wa*. The activities of these Oromo Salafis have, due to linguistic boundaries largely been limited to the Oromo population in Addis Ababa. Moreover, the *Awaliyah* School and Mission Centre has played an important role. Supported by the Saudi controlled World Muslim League since 1966, the ownership of the school was in 1993 transferred to the International Islamic Relief Organization, a branch of the World Muslim League.[13]

Also the *Jama'at al-Tabligh* emerged with increased strength in the post-Derg period. With their *markaz* (centre) in the Kolfe area, *Tabligh* grew to be one of the main movements of Islamic reform in Ethiopia. The *da'wa* was now conducted in more organized and extensive manner, with small groups or bus loads of *Tabligh* missionaries sent out to various parts of the country; on three-day or forty-day journeys. In compliance with the regulations of self-reliance, the missionaries of *Tabligh* support themselves, and the movement itself is not dependent on any outside funding. The movement has improved its contact with the wider *Tabligh* world by receiving *Tabligh* missionaries, particularly from the Indian communities in Kenya and South Africa, and by sending representatives to the annual *Tabligh* conference in Pakistan. Yet, in spite of increased activities, the *Tabligh* movement in Ethiopia has remained within the Gurage community in Addis Ababa. Attempts to establish centres in other areas have met resistance, particularly in Oromo areas, where the Salafis are dominating.

The third movement of reform emerging in the early 1990s is somewhat difficult to categorise. Highly informal and lacking any bureaucratic structure, it evolved around certain individuals advocating a set of ideas rather than initiating a particular movement. It emerged in the campuses of Addis Ababa University and other institutions of higher learning, attracting students in large numbers, thus acting unofficially as the Muslim student movement. Organized in small groups and led by individual figures called *amirs*, the movement was important in fighting for the rights of Muslim students as well as organising lectures and study-circles. Whereas the movement initially had links to the *Tabligh* movement, the ideas of the Muslim Brotherhood, in particular those of Yusuf al-Qaradawi were often disseminated among its followers. The Muslim Brotherhood, however, never established itself in Ethiopia. Outside the campuses, the movement was able to exert influence through the *Bilal* magazine, where many of the contributions were made under the pen-name, Najat Abd al-Qadir.[14] However, the writers were careful never to mention the Muslim Brotherhood or their ideologues by name. Further, prominent members of the movement have also been active in publishing books through Najashi Publishers during the last decade. Although the leaders of the movement are still able to diffuse their ideas through lectures and seminars given to students in Addis Ababa and surroundings, the movement has lost much of its strength in the campuses. Instead, it has remained a rather elitist phenomenon: its leaders and followers mainly being young university graduates and urban intellectuals. Another characteristic is their inclination towards Sufism. Challenging the traditional popularized versions of Ethiopian Sufism, and not affiliated to any *tariqa*, a sort of "modern" Sufism is advocated, emphasizing individual religious practices as enhancing one's inner spiritual life in a materialistic world.

Increased diversity and intra-religious tensions

The emergence of these religious movements has created a situation of noticeable diversity and even of increased tensions within Ethiopia's Muslim community. First of all, the diversity is of an ideological nature, most obvious where former religious practices have been challenged by the emerging movements of reform, and where the movements contest each others' standpoints. Not surprisingly, it is the tensions between the Salafis and the more "traditional" Muslims that has drawn most attention, the former challenging the latter's inclination towards popular Sufism and the incorporation of indigenous religious elements. This has caused a sharp decline in veneration at shrines and celebrations of *mawlid*, particularly in Bale and Arsi, but also in Wollo, Jimma and Harar. In addition, there have been tensions within the Salafi movement; between its seniors and a generation of more zealous Salafis emerging in the 1990s. The issues are in some ways ideological as the youth advocate a stricter observance of Islam, and a different understanding of what should be compulsory and what belongs to the *sunna*. The conflict is also a quest for power, young challenge the positions of the elders. These tensions climaxed with the arrival of the *Takfir wal Hijrah* group in 1994–1995.[15] Introduced by Sheikh Muhammed Amin, returning from exile in Sudan, the movement grew strong in Gondar, northern Ethiopia—before it spread to Addis Ababa, where it gained a foothold in the mosque in Terro, a northern suburb of the city. The *Takfir* was soon able to attract quite a number of followers among the young generation, before the Salafi *ulama* of Aiyr Tena came out with public statements denouncing the movement. In 2002 a young scholar named Hassan Taju published a book fiercely criticizing *Takfir*, weakening the movement further. When its main leader passed away in 2004, *Takfir* had lost its real strength.

Tensions also exist between the Salafi movement and the other reform movements. The Muslim student movement is, because of its attachment to the Muslim Brotherhood, antagonized as detached from the true Islam, and repeatedly labelled as both Sufi and Shia—the favourite insults of the Salafis.

This is a rather puzzling issue. Given the influence the Muslim Brotherhood had on Saudi Salafism from the 1960s and the relationships between Salafis and Islamic revivalist movements in many regions, one would expect a larger degree of mutual acceptance.[16] Yet, in Ethiopia the movement is criticized by the Salafis for its inclusive attitudes towards Sufism. The Muslim student movement on their part, views the Salafis as rigid literalists, as narrow-minded and ignorant of the diversity of Islamic scholarship. The Salafis are using similar derogatory labels for the *Tabligh*, attacking their affiliation with Sufism, and labelling their organized *da'wa* as *bid'a* (innovation). The *Tabligh*, for its part, has in general kept a low profile, focusing on their *da'wa* activities and avoiding any form of confrontation. Whereas their relationship to the Salafis is rather strained, they are at ease with the Muslim student movement. Both have an essentially positive inclination towards Sufism, despite the student movements more critical attitude towards the popularized Sufi practices.

Besides differences of an ideological nature, the religious diversity and tensions have been underpinned by a contemporary discourse on ethnicity. Since 1991, ethnicity has overtly dominated the public discourse, becoming increasingly politicized under the present system of ethnic federalism.[17] While the debate on ethnicity has received much attention, its religious undercurrent has unfortunately been largely ignored. In the construction of ethnic identities, factors such as language, social institutions and common history *together* with religion may serve as reinforcing factors; constructing ethnic identities and drawing up ethnic boundaries.

In the case of contemporary Islam in Ethiopia, the demarcation of ethnic and of religious boundaries have acted as simultaneously reinforcing trends, contributing to the divisions within the Muslim community. In the case of the *Tabligh*, overtly dominated by the Gurage, the derogatory labels applied to them are interchangeably drawn from a religious terminology and characteristics with clear ethnic connotations. In either way, the Gurage are equated to *Tabligh* by the Salafis, where both as an ethnic group and as a religious movement they are labelled as deviators from the true Islam, as Sufis and as *mushrikun*. Similar derogatory representations are used by the Salafis for the Muslims of Wollo; the Wolloyyans as a collective seen as Sufis and neglecters of the true Islam. They are also accused of religious laxness, because of their acquiescence to the Christian Amhara. Among the Salafi (Oromo) themselves, self-representations with a primordial colour can sometimes be detected, emphasizing the quality of the Oromo as a whole for discovering and upholding the true tenets of Islam (i.e. the Salafi doctrines of Islam). The

Salafis are on the other hand despised, particularly by the elitist Muslim student movement, as backward literalists. One of my informants described a prominent Oromo Salafi *alim* as "a Saudi-educated shepherd from Bale", revealing prejudice of an ethnic nature. This ethno-religious diversity was further detectable in the course of Ethiopia's interventions in Somalia in the latter part of 2006. In general, there was a clear, yet silent, opposition to the war from the country's Muslim community, but had the fighting escalated, it could easily have divided the Muslims of Ethiopia. The Muslims of the north, harbouring a stronger nationalistic sentiment, would have been supportive of the regime, while the Muslims in the south (Oromo) would be less so, rather seeing the Somali claim for Greater Somalia as a legitimate, similar to the views held by separatist movements in the south.

Islam and inter-religious tensions

The emergence of Islamic reform movements and increased diversity within the Muslim community have produced an escalation of inter-religious frictions. Such incidents have often evolved around constructions of mosques and churches, and in relation to public celebration of religious holidays.[18] Allocations of plots for churches and mosques have often produced protests from the Muslims and Christians respectively, in some cases leading to clashes between the two communities. Controversies over celebrations of religious holidays were often sparked by spacial proximity, like that of Kamise (Wollo) where the procession of Christians celebrating Epiphany came too close to the Muslims preparing for prayer at the town's mosque, resulting in a skirmish with casualties on both sides. Such incidents have been of a rather local character, and not part of any organized national movement, neither from the Christian or the Muslim side. On the other hand, they need to be seen in relation to a wider pattern of religious revival, increased consciousness and re-demarcation of religious boundaries. During the fall of 2006, tensions between Christians and Muslims exacerbated through violent clashes around Jimma and Beghi (Wollega). Both the scale of the conflict and the level of violence were surprisingly high. There were reports of a grouping calling themselves *Kharijites* who allegedly have connections to other parts of the country and even to Sudan and Yemen, torching numerous churches and even forcefully trying to convert Christians to Islam.[19] Although the conflict was more coordinated than previous ones, and spanned a wider geographical area, it remained of a local character, and not part of a wider organized movement.

147

However, what makes this incident different from others was the clear articulation of the religious dimension; i.e. Christians versus Muslims. In previous conflicts, religion has often been closely entwined with ethnicity, making it difficult to determine the actual nature of the conflict. In many cases, conflicts perceived as religious have in fact been of an ethnic character, or little or no distinction has been made between religion and ethnicity by those involved.[20] Whereas religion was important in the disparity between the Amhara and the Muslims in the south (particularly the Muslim Oromo), and for the discrimination the latter were subject to, this injustice has been, and is still interpreted along ethnic lines. Hence, conflicts very often have distinct ethnic headings. As religious identity is transcending the boundary of locality, and a conceptual distinction between religious and ethnic affiliation is emerging, one sees conflicts with more articulated religious labels—like the ones in Jimma and Beghi. Even if most Muslims in Ethiopia remain largely bound by ethnic boundaries, these incidents demonstrate the possibility of increased inter-religious tensions.

Political Islam?

Along with current regional and global developments, religious changes in the domestic arena have made the country's Christian population increasingly alarmed. Observers outside the Muslim community, both Ethiopian and foreign, have to a large degree interpreted these changes as a process where Islam in Ethiopia is becoming increasingly politicized, and where Islamic fundamentalism is surfacing in the ranks of Ethiopian Muslims. Referring to the growth in the number of mosques all over the country and to the increasing number of Muslims holding governmental and public positions, Ethiopian Muslims are accused of aspiring for political power based on radical religious ideas. Quite stark statements are forwarded in the public debate, where *madrasahs* are charged of being "brain washing sessions and jihad factories nurturing potential bin Ladens..." and where "innocent Ethiopian kids are taken to various countries in the Middle East for military training, and then return home to participate in the meticulously planned and widely coordinated jihad".[21] Not supported by any empirical data, these attitudes could to some extent be seen as the resurfacing of an old pattern of prejudices and fear, triggered by domestic developments and current regional and international events.

As part of the process of increased consciousness and re-demarcation of religious boundaries, grievances related to the perceived mistreatment of Muslims in the past and lack of religious equality in the present are increasingly being articulated within the Muslim community. It would, however, be difficult to equate demands of better representation with a politicization of Islam, or as proof for the emergence of Islamism in Ethiopia. Instead of relying on general assumptions and unfounded charges, we need to look at the contemporary Islamic movements more in detail.

Much attention has been given to the Salafi movement, perceived as the main carrier and promoter of political Islam in Ethiopia. Although ideologically linked to the Salafi doctrines of Saudi Arabia, a state said to be founded solely on the Shariah, the Salafis of Ethiopia do not advocate a similar system. Recognizing the religious plurality of Ethiopia, the prevailing view is that religious freedom for all could only be secured under a secular government. Rather than conveying political viewpoints, their focus has been on the strict adherence to the doctrine of *tawhid*, seeking to purify Islamic practices from Sufi and indigenous elements and to encourage the individual to perform his religious duties with diligence. In general, the Salafi movement in Ethiopia constitutes a rather conservative entity, largely following mainstream Salafi doctrines. Although there have been occasional clashes between young Salafis and Sufis, these have been rare. Both the leaders as well as the followers in general emphasize the dissemination of the Salafi ideology through peaceful means. At the same time, the Salafi movement does not constitute a homogenous entity, and within its rank one might find certain elements following a more conflictual pattern, who would welcome an expansion of the Shariah courts' jurisdiction, and who would seek to distance themselves from the Christians. The Oromo Salafis are, moreover, clearly advocating the idea of an ethnic exclusiveness, rather than that of a religious exclusiveness. Many of them, including the *ulama* at Ayir Tena, do not speak Amharic; to some degree segregating them from the rest of Ethiopian society and limiting their range of influence. Like most of the Muslims, the Oromo Salafis are strong supporters of the Oromo Liberation Front (OLF).

In general, the *Jama'at al-Tabligh*, argues that the individual should seek to Islamize society by making efforts to convert others and by upholding the virtues of Islam, and is at the same time negative to the politicising of Islam and to the views of the contemporary Islamists. Restricted to conducting *da'wa*, the movement has thus claimed to be outside of politics. The networks created by the organization however, have in many areas been exploited by various Islamist groupings, creating a situation where it has often been equated with political Islam.[22] In Ethiopia, *Tabligh* has overtly operated in compliance with the general principles of the movement, and has through its history been devoid of political engagement. Through its low profile and withdrawal to its *markaz* and to selected mosques in Addis Ababa, it has remained rather imperceptible and to a large degree secluded from any involvement in public life.

The Muslim student movement, ideologically affiliated to the Muslim Brotherhood would be assumed to be the movement with the most radical political agenda. Yet, while actively endorsing the many of the ideas of the Brotherhood, the opinions held by its followers in Ethiopia are nevertheless quite different. There is a clear dissociation from the idea of Ethiopia governed solely by Islamic law, as well as a general absence of classical Islamist rhetoric. Nobody is advocating for Islamizing the political and public life of Ethiopia, neither by peaceful or by violent means. This is not to say that the movement is without a political agenda. It remains the movement with the highest political awareness, agitating for improved equality of Muslims with the Christians in Ethiopia, and for Muslims getting involved in political and public affairs— while at the same time emphasizing the need for an environment of mutual respect and coexistence between the two religious groups. And even further, they argue, this could best be achieved through a secular government; protecting the rights of each religious group.

The importance of the local context

Where grand theories are losing ground, the question of locality has gained increased attention in social studies: the local context intersected with other layers of contexts being pivotal for understanding phenomena like religious movements. While there may be factors held in common, the particularities of each movement would only be illuminated by considering the local context. Let us take the Muslim student movement as an example. Comparing the socio-cultural background of the Muslim student movement in Ethiopia with similar movements in other parts of the Muslim world, we see a basis for recruitment among groups of disgruntled and alienated urban Muslim youth, exposed to modern life and education and caught between modernity and tradition.[23] While this in other areas often produces radical Islamist movements, the picture in Ethiopia remains different. Here, this group of educated and alienated youth similarly is caught between dissatisfaction with former religious practices and an abrupt process of modernization initiated during the Marxist Derg regime and increasingly contradictory cultural patterns during the current regime. They may have moved in the direction of modern Islamic reform movements, yet there is an absence of a radical political programme. This obviously calls for a deeper understanding of the Ethiopian context and a thorough consideration of the particularities of this locality.

First of all, the current political environment has had clear implications for the development of Islamic movements. Whereas previous regimes did not leave much space for the civil society to develop, the current EPDRF regime has initiated a more liberal policy, leading to the establishment of a number of civil organizations. However, while these have been allowed to exist, the regime is at the same time cautious of organizations with a more overt political agenda, and sensitive to any form of political statements.[24] With regard to Islam, it could be argued that the regime is even more attentive: actively watching and ready to intervene as they see fit. As a result of these actions, the Ethiopian Islamic Affairs Supreme Council (EIASC) came to be the main Islamic organization. It is said to be the only legitimate representative of the country's Muslims, and at the same time is linked to the ruling party.[25] Any other organized movement is perceived as both challenging the position of EIASC and as opposing the regime. Inevitably, this has affected the development and nature of the Islamic movements, where besides encumbering the establishment of such; the regime's grip over the Muslim community has moreover impeded the articulating of a political agenda.

This is not to say that Islamic movements in Ethiopia have remained detached from politics merely because of fear of repression from the current regime. In fact, there are other underlying currents to be considered. The existing religious plurality and the tradition of relative peaceful coexistence have undoubtedly contributed to a moderation of the Islamic movements. The pattern of shared commonality on the grassroots level, a degree of mutual respect and even, in some areas, transgressions of religious boundaries have served as important resources in preventing inter-religious conflicts. This tradition has also influenced the Islamic movements, making them less likely to embark on a path of a conflictual character. Further, the already mentioned asymmetric nature of Christian-Muslim relations in Ethiopia may be an even more important factor. As mentioned, centuries with Christian dominance, a politico-cultural ideology where Christianity constituted an important part of Ethiopianness, resulted in a repressive policy towards Islam. When Muslims were excluded from participating in political life and denied representation they became secluded from the public sphere and protective of their limited space. This situation has deprived the Muslim community in general, and the emerging Islamic movements in particular of the necessary tools, tradition and experience for involvement in the wider Ethiopian society, affecting both the strength and content of these movements. The Christian politico-cultural domination comprising the perception of the Ethiopian Muslim population as second-class has naturally made an impact on the self-image of the Muslim population; incorporating the image of the other as their own. Absorbing the image of being second-class, it would be possible to argue that this has affected Ethiopian Muslims' resources and confidence to seek representation in political life. Moreover, it has had clear implications for the agenda of the reform movements making them more reluctant to challenge the status-quo and causing them to refrain from articulating political views in a radical direction.

Conclusion

Religion has proved to be force to be reckoned with for popular mobilization, where contemporary developments have shown the emergence of a wide spectrum of religious movements paving the way for inter- and intra-religious tensions. The case of Islam in Ethiopia is a clear illustration of contemporary Islam as a heterogeneous phenomenon, where the local context has determined its emergence and its features. As we have seen, the Salafi movement and the Muslim student movement, both likely to be guided by an activist-political ideology, are not explicitly articulating points of view in this direction. Both have the character of being movements of resurgence: the former seeking to transform the individual's and the community's religiosity in compliance with mainstream Salafi doctrines, the latter seeking to carve out religious space for the young generation caught in-between tradition and modern life. Their ideological preferences are determined by a selective reading of the texts, a selection process very much produced by the context they actually live in. Many so-called Islamist movements in East Africa may have rather diffuse ideological links to global Islamism, and their agenda and objectives are often quite diverse and deviant from what is characterized as Islamism. Univocally labelled as radical Islam, they have in many cases simply been agitating for improved equality and increased representation with the Christian populations. This situation would make it relevant to reassess earlier assumptions about Islamism as a phenomenon. By reducing it to a civilizational phenomenon without duly considering the variety of contextual features produced by the politics of locality, we are restricted in our inclusive understanding of its many facets and components. Admittedly, there may exist shared ideological ground yet, but as this chapter has shown, the locality often determines both the emergence of such movements, as well as their features and agenda.

10

Sudan—Trying to Understand its "Multiple Marginality"[1]

Gérard Prunier

"Border" is a notoriously ambiguous word on the African continent but perhaps no where more so than when concerning the Sudan. The very name of that "country" is not the name of a country but of a zone, of an area. The word derives from the term used by medieval Arab geographers "*beled as-Sudani*" i.e. "the land of the Blacks". For these Arab geographers "*as-Sudan*" was the strip of land extending south of the Sahel, from Senegal to the high plateau of "*al-beled al-Habashiyiin*", the land of the Abyssinians.[2] This perception was so rooted that the Arab classic called *at-Tarikh as-Sudan* (A History of the Sudan) does not deal at all with what we today call "the Sudan" but roughly with Niger, Mali and parts of Senegal. Later during the colonial period, the French called *le Soudan* what is today called Mali, a cause of endless problems for university students looking in library index cards for relevant material on "the Sudan".

In addition, the borders of "our" Sudan, the Sudan of today, are not, contrary to those of most other African countries, the product of twentieth-century European colonial expansion. They are, at least in part, the product of an early nineteenth-century anachronistic revival of Ottoman imperialism. The core of present day Sudan was born in 1821 from the conquest of a chunk of Northern Sudan by the troops of the "Turco-Egyptian" Khedive (king) of

155

Egypt, Muhammad Ali. Muhammad Ali was neither an Egyptian nor even a Turk but an Albanian who had served in the Turkish Army at the time of the Napoleonic conquest of Egypt.[3] Having managed to set himself up as the master of Egypt after Napoleon's departure he then strove for two classical Ottoman political goals, legitimacy and conquest. The Sudan helped towards both: the Khedive hoped to extract gold and slaves from its southern conquest and controlling a new land which had not been under Istanbul's sway previously reinforced his claim to autonomy *vis-à-vis* his Turkish suzerain. Thus from the beginning the Sudan did not exist in itself and for itself but in relation to another entity, entirely organized to satisfy the needs of that other entity. This is why the word "colonization", with its connotation of rational economic exploitation, can hardly be applied to what later became known as the "*Turkiyya*" period in the Sudan.[4] The political and administrative system of that period was purely one of looting and commodity extraction whereby Cairo tried to get as much as it could out of the Sudan without ever investing a penny in the territory. The main item on the Sudan's budget was military expenditure and even that was financed by slaving raids (*ghazzua*) rather than by Cairo paying the army costs. Black slaves were captured by the Turco-Egyptians and press-ganged into the "Egyptian" army, the surplus being sold on the slave markets of the Middle East.[5]

After being defeated by the Egyptian army's superior firepower, Darfur prudently withdrew from Kordofan in order to avoid further clashes. It was not to be conquered and incorporated into the "Egyptian" empire intil 1874. But the Funj Sultanate suffered an even more dire fate and within months of the Turco-Egyptian onslaught it was annexed by Cairo. Thus for a period the occupied territory later to be called "the Sudan" stretched roughly from the western border of Kordofan to the Abyssinian plateau and Khartoum was founded by "the Turks" in 1826. Then the imperial power started to move southward. Its two main goals had been to find gold and slaves. Hardly any gold had been found in the north and since the northern population was Muslim, it could not be conveniently enslaved.[6] The south however, was pagan and therefore belonged to *Dar al-Harb*.[7] From about 1830 "the Khartoumers", as they were called with dread throughout the region, started to launch slaving raids ever further southward. This practice led to an endlessly expanding frontier which, in many ways, was comparable to the North American far west or to what was called in Brazil at that same time "*Bocas do Sertao*".[8] During this process which lasted for roughly half a century "the Sudan" extended in Eastern and Central Africa like a cancerous growth, eventually reaching at its peak a huge territory, much larger than today's Sudan. The southward expansion covered the whole of today's Southern Sudan and large chunks of the present Central African Republic and Northern Uganda. Meanwhile a parallel eastern expansion was pushing Sudan's borders to include Massawa, the eastern part of today's Eritrea, the Harrar region of Ethiopia, the whole Red Sea Coast on to the Bab el-Mandeb and then down the Indian Ocean coast of Somalia all the way to north-eastern Kenya. Westward the Turco-Egyptians occupied the Darfur Sultanate in 1874. Thus the Sudan was not a "country" but rather a kind of ongoing imperial concept. In those pre-Berlin Conference days, Khedive Isma'il (1863–1879) considered that Egypt's "civilizing mission" practically extended to the whole of Africa and at the International Exposition of 1873 the Egyptian pavilion displayed a map of Cairo's [future] African Empire extending westward all the way to the Atlantic and southward down to the Great Lakes. But these grandiose dreams were brought low by two radically different factors: financial overreach and an explosion of Muslim-fundamentalism-cum-proto-nationalism. The financial overreach was not only due to the growing costs of the Sudanese Empire, it was also due to Isma'il's ambitious plans for Egypt's modernization. The Suez Canal, the transformation of Cairo into a Hausmanian European-type capital complete with massive stone buildings and gas lighting, the beginning of industrialization, the construction of railways, all these expenses eventually drove the Egyptian treasury into over-borrowing and bankruptcy. This led to the British occupying Egypt in 1882 to get back the money they had loaned to the Cairo regime. But when they came into Egypt they willy-nilly inherited the Egyptian Empire together with the imperial core. The central parts of that empire, Kordofan and the Nile Valley, were in full rebellion. A previously unknown *fiki* (religious preacher) called Muhammad Ahmad, quickly nicknamed "*al-Mahdi*", had risen against the Turco-Egyptians, accusing them both of being bad impious Muslims and of being oppressors who had imposed high taxes, forced military recruitment and *haram* (religiously forbidden) criminal penalties such as blowing people up after tying them to the mouth of a cannon.[9] Thus good religious practice and the fight against foreign tyranny were all wrapped up into one. This blew the Turco-Egyptian Empire asunder and, in spite of a late British intervention, by 1885 "the Sudan" was independent.[10] Its borders were quite different from those of the former Empire however, since all the non-Arab territories had taken advantage of the Mahdist rebellion severing its ties with Cairo as well as their own subordinate links to Khartoum.

The religious ebb and flow in the Sudan

The Sudan is often considered as a Muslim country with a Christian minority and, as simple statement of fact, this is true. But this simple fact has to be qualified in many ways. Christianity, not Islam, was the first of the Abrahamic cults to come to the Sudan. In the same way as Hellenistic Egypt and neighbouring Axumite Abyssinia, the Sudan was Christianized by Byzantine Greek monks coming from Syria in the first four centuries of the Christian era.[11] The three Christian states that existed in Northern Sudan up to the early sixteenth century were coextensive with the areas now considered as the heartland of Islam in the Sudan i.e. the Nile Valley, Sennar and parts of Kordofan. Contrary to what happened in North Africa, the transformation from Christianity to Islam was not the result of military conquest, it was the result of the expansion of transnational networks. People converted to Islam because after the Islamization of Egypt both international culture and long-distance trade became Muslim preserves. From the top of society—Muslim scholars and traders—Islam seeped down into the more humble strata of formerly Christian Sudan and then on, eastward and westward, into the previously pagan parts of the region. But there are two important caveats to be considered. The first point to remember is that the type of Islam that spread from the Nile Valley outward transformed itself in the process from a highly centralized Caliphate-based Sunni orthodox type of Islam into a popular Sufi type of Islam. In the Sudan one is not simply "a Muslim", one is also (and perhaps first) a member of a *tariqa* (brotherhood) which acts as a kind of sub-unit, almost as a kind of (gentle) sect within the limits of the great Islamic *Ummah* (Community).[12] The *turuq* (plural of *tariqa*) are many things to their members: first a kind of benevolent association (members are supposed to help each other); to some extent a social club; for centuries a matrimonial pool; often a business network and at times an insurance policy. For educated people they are a school of Islamic hermeneutics; and in modern times a political party. But what *turuq* have *not* been are instruments of the state and transmitters of a politico-religious orthodoxy. The Turco-Egyptians, who were indifferent in matters of religion but very keen on political control, tried to have a kind of state-sponsored Islam which would act as a counterweight to the more independent-minded *Turuq*. It was an almost complete failure and the Egyptian-controlled *ulama* (doctors of orthodox Islamic law) were definitely never very popular. The Mahdist proto-nationalist uprising was also hostile to the *turuq* but for different reasons. Mahdism was a fundamentalist movement that considered the popular Islam of the *turuq* to be debased and corrupted. The Mahdi was opposed to the cult of the saints and to the many "pagan" practices that had survived in Sudanese Islam disguised in a pseudo-Islamic garb. An interesting comment on the nature of Sudanese Islam is that, after the death of the Mahdi, his movement, called the *Ansariyya*, became a new *tariqa*, complete with all the trappings of the other *turuq* i.e. an all powerful *sheikh* (religious leader of the same family), strong matrimonial endogamy, political and economic networks and a sub-culture of its own. The *Mahdiyya* had been a theocratic movement and state during its years in power (1885–1898) and later became a potentially theocratic form of counterculture which caused endless headaches for the British colonial system and which remains to this day a politico-religious force *within* the Sudanese polity. The modern Muslim Brotherhood (*Ikhwaan al-Muslimin*) which was born in Egypt in the twentieth century and which has taken power in the Sudan through a military coup in June 1989, is the heir to that theocratic tradition which is a minority one in the Sudan. It has tried to create a new form of state Islam over the last thirty or so years and has largely failed to achieve its aims because it runs counter to the deep Sufi type of Islam that has always been dominant in the country.

The second caveat that has to be kept in mind when looking at the religious evolution of the Sudan is the fact that Islam did not manage to spread beyond the Arabized regions of the Sudan. In the next section we will discuss how Islam has acquired a variegated aspect as it spread together with "differential Arabization" in the non-Arab parts of the country. But the parts which were not Arabized at all, like southern Sudan, did not adopt Islam. This was not due to colonization, since the "African" south resisted both Arabization and Islamization *before* the arrival of the colonialists in 1898. But after 1898, Christianity in its imported missionary form was quickly seized upon by the southern black African populations as a counterforce to the progress of Islam, seen by them as a vector of Arabization rather than as a purely religious movement. There are a few southern Sudanese Muslims. They are mostly the descendants of Turco-Egyptian slave soldier families (*jihadiyya*) or of trading families. But not only have they remained a minority, they have also remained, in their majority, anti-Arab. During both of the north-south civil wars (1955–1972 and 1983–2002) the majority of Southern Muslims squarely sided with the southern rebels.[13] Missionary Christianity in the Sudan was given a prominent role during colonization, partly because the British colonial administration lacked the means of effectively administering the south and largely left that task to the missionaries. Up to the first civil war this new Christianity was largely a cultural marker which even had an added tribal component. To avoid quarrels among the various missionary orders the Condominium authorities carved out missionary territories which were attributed to the various orders. This led to the Bahr-el-Ghazal Dinkas being mainly evangelized by the Italian Comboniani Brothers, while the Nuer became Presbyterians and the Bor Dinkas Anglicans. Most southerners became superficial Christians while keeping a lot of their "pagan" beliefs and practices. The wars, particularly the second one, were to change that. The wars had several completely opposite effects on the religious and cultural scene: Muslim proselytism, seen as a tool of Arabization, was completely stopped. But since population movements had become massive, with internally-displaced persons and refugees numbering in the millions and since English was not widely spoken, the Arabic language on the contrary was increasingly used as a form of *lingua franca*. In addition Christianity radicalized itself, with efforts at purging it from its "pagan" elements and the growth of new forms of radical evangelical Protestantism.

The Sudan's blurred ethnic mosaic

With almost six hundred spoken languages and dialects the Sudan is an incredibly heterogeneous space where the notion of "north versus south", although largely true, *represents only one segment of the truth*. First of all there is the myth of the Arabism of the Sudan. A number of Sudanese do have ethnic Arab blood, but they are a minority and even among them, "Arab" racial traits are deeply mixed with "other" (i.e. Negro Nilotic, Cushitic, Nubian and other Semitic) racial traits. "Arabism" in the Sudan is a cultural fact, not a biological one.[14] The progressive Islamization/Arabization that took place between the seventh and the sixteenth century was first of all cultural, then religious and racial only in a limited way. But since "being an Arab" is essentially a linguistic and cultural matter, the northern Sudanese were accepted, albeit reluctantly, as members of the Arab family. The problem was that they were *never* accepted as fully-fledged members. The Arabs have an ambiguous attitude towards their Sudanese "brothers". On the one hand the Sudanese can always make a claim on the generosity of the white Arabs when they can brandish some kind of a victim status. They have received help from other Arab countries, particularly from Egypt, during both civil wars as they managed to portray these conflicts as attacks on Islam and Arabism engineered by "imperialist" Christian forces. The expulsion of the Christian missionaries from the

Sudan by General Abboud in 1964 was seen in the Arab world as a perfectly legitimate act of cultural self-defence.

When the black Christian rebels of the Sudan Peoples Liberation Army (SPLA) took the northern border town of Kurmuk in 1988, the Khartoum government immediately received a large arms shipment from Saddam Hussein's Iraq to help it reoccupy the town. The fact that the "Christian" SPLA was at the time armed and supported by the officially atheist Communist Ethiopian regime, that Saddam Hussein's Baathist regime was far from being piously Muslim and that the Khartoum government was in the hands of the "moderate" and democratically-elected regime of Sadiq al-Mahdi, did not diminish the underlying ethnic and cultural dimension of the clash between an "Arab" state and a "heathen" rebel group. Here the confusion between ethnicity and religion is massive. That the rest of the Arab world, which hardly considers Sudan to be an "Arab" country, nevertheless immediately feels called upon to defend it if and when this "Arab" status appears to be threatened by non-Arabs, has been one of the trump diplomatic cards of the Khartoum regime in the present Darfur crisis, in which the Islamists have managed to retain the support of the Arab League by presenting the conflict as a "Christian western plot" against the Arab world, even though both killers and victims are Muslims.[15]

The accepted wisdom on the Sudan has long been that it is divided between an "Arab" Muslim north and a "Christian and animist" black African south. This picture obliterates an essential fact: over half of the Muslims are not Arabs. This therefore leads to one inescapable conclusion: the great ethno-cultural groupings of the Sudan are not two but three: (1) Arab Muslims (2) non-Arab Muslims (3) non-Arab non-Muslims. Which makes any kind of "borders", be they racial, cultural or religious, quite blurred. And this even more so if we take into account that each one of the three groups is far from being homogeneous.

(1) The "Arabs" are, as we have seen, racially mixed and are Arabs only at the cultural level.[16] This creates a deep sense of unease towards the international Arab community and a constant need to reaffirm one's Arabism, including through violent means. A large part of northern Sudanese violence towards the southerners can be seen as an urge to "kill the nigger within", i.e. to distantiate oneself from what the Islamist publicist Abd-el-Wahhab al-Effendi once called *"the heathen jungles of Africa"*.[17] And since this brand of Sudanese Arabism is fragile and based on cultural adhesion to a distant outside model, it is internally fragmented. Thus the Nile Valley "Arabs" consider themselves as fully-fledged Arabs (even if their Saudi or

THE BORDERS OF ISLAM

Lebanese brothers do not completely concur). But they do not really bestow that honour on the more marginal "Arabs" of the west, the so-called *awlad al-Gharb* (westerners) belonging to the Baggara tribes and even to less racially-mixed Kordofan tribes. There, the biological criteria which the white Arabs use against their dark Sudanese brothers are used *inside* the Sudanese Arab community to marginalize the "black Arabs" of the western provinces, thus creating what Darfur specialist Alex DeWaal has called a form of "differential Arabism". To paraphrase George Orwell, they are all Arabs but some are more Arab than others.[18] This complex racist situation is at the heart of the present Darfur conflict where the riverine Arab elite is trying to use the fantasized Arabism of the western tribes to set them against the African tribes in an effort at controlling and "arabizing" Darfur before the "heathen" SPLA can build a potentially dangerous political bridge with the black tribes on the base of their "shared Africanism".[19]

(2) The non-Arab Muslims are again another very complex group, so complex that it would be better to call it a "non-group". The one distinctive feature which makes all these Muslim people "non-Arabs" is that they speak as mother tongues what the "Arabs" deprecatingly call a *rottana*. The term *rottana* is purely Sudanese and it is hard to translate. Basically it means some sort of low dialect, a kind of gibberish, a language barely fit for humans and definitely not for civilized people who should speak *lughat Allah*, God's language i.e. Arabic. Among those we find people as different as the Nubians, who are considered largely civilized and definitely marriageable, and some of the smaller Darfur tribes like the Dajju or the Tunjur who are considered neither. The various eastern strands of Beja like the Beni Halba or the Hadendowa are in between i.e. marriageable if they have money. Otherwise they would better stick to their own uncouth brethren.

(3) The non-Arab non-Muslim groups are somewhat easier to define. They are black African tribes of Sudanic and Nilotic ancestry, speaking their own non-Semitic languages and with hardly any trace of Arabization.[20] They are divided into many tribes. But they all share a common past experience in relationship to the centre of power in Khartoum: victims of the slave trade, conversion to counter-cultural Christianity, educational marginalization, social and economic discrimination, and military confrontation with the Arabs resulting in an aspiration towards national independence.

The centre versus periphery paradigm

We have by now a rough idea of what the various "boundaries" are in the Sudan, in terms of land, religion, language and ethnicity between which, the obvious conclusion might be, there is no global coherence. At the same time it is also obvious that the Sudan is a crossroads between the Arab world and sub-saharan Africa, between Islam and Christianity and between the Middle East and Africa. Does this mean that we cannot get any type of general principle on the relationship of these various cultural dimensions? Or should we surmise that in spite of these contradictions some general principle such as "civilizational confrontation" overrides these multiple contradictions? It is our contention in this essay that all of Sudan's complexities cannot be reduced to a simple explanatory paradigm but that all these are nevertheless over-determined by one fundamental contradiction, the one between the centre and the periphery.

This is a contradiction as old as "the Sudan" in its modern form i.e. going back to 1821 and it is closely linked to the fundamental nature of the Sudanese state, which has been the same since the *Turkiyya*:[21]

- Ready recourse to extra-legal military force
- Low performance level on delivering social services and on furthering economic development
- Focus on rough commodity extraction and taxation
- Manipulation of racial and religious identities to reinforce the central government's power

The combination of weakness and violence that has long characterized the Sudanese state and still characterizes it today puts it in a very peculiar position. The state is not perceived by its subjects as an emanation of the population but rather as a kind of superimposition on society, as a kind of internal colonization agent. Therefore, since the state is not geographically, ethnically or culturally neutral, the various subject groups see themselves in fairly different relationships to the central *hokum*.[22] Rather than the abstract letter of the law, it is the religious, ethnic or geographical position of a group of people *vis-à-vis* the state that determines how this group is likely to be treated.

The present Darfur crisis is very much a case in point. Throughout the 1960s, 1970s and 1980s Darfurians served as the military mainstay of a regime dominated by the Nile Valley Arab groups (Shaiqiyya, Danagla and Ja'aliyin). Their being Muslims was used by the central Sudan Arabs as a deceptive bond which united both groups *vis-à-vis* the southern Christians. However, this was enough to keep the Darfurians, both "Arabs" and non-Arabs, on the side of the Khartoum *hokum* in spite of the fact that the radical marginalization their province suffered gave them the same poor socio-economic status that the southerners they were being asked to kill had. Out of habit of political loyalty, out of Islamic devotion and in exchange for a few marginal advantages, they loyally served the state.[23] Two things progressively showed them that although they were Muslims, they were in fact second class Muslims not on par with the ruling group at the centre: (1) starting with the run up to the 1986 elections, they were sold by the central government to the Libyans who started to use the province as a rear base for their subversion of Chad.[24] The result was mayhem, with the Libyan Army and its *Failaka al-Islamiyya* (Islamic Legion) auxiliaries plunging the province into sixteen years of low-intensity racial and social warfare.[25] Khartoum, whether democratically elected Sadiq al-Mahdi or the putschist National Islamic Front never seemed to care. Then (2) the Naivasha negotiations between the Muslim Brothers' government and the southern rebels of the SPLA, which started in 2002, also showed a total lack of interest in Darfur. The Khartoum *hokum*, run by people the Darfurians now considered as unfriendly at best and as enemies at worst, *was allowed to speak for the whole of the "north"*. In other words, when a major peace and power-sharing agreement began to be discussed between "north" and "south", the Darfurians realized that they were "represented" by people with whom they had stopped identifying and whom they now understood to be pitiless manipulators of their religious identity for purposes of political and military gain. This was the last step in understanding that they had been deceived, used and reduced to desperate mute acquiescence. They decided that enough was enough and that they, like those southerners whom they used to kill, had to take up arms and fight the centre which had exploited them as much as it had exploited the *Janubiyin* (southerners). They correctly surmised that if they did not, the government would use their supposed acquiescence in peace as it had used their blood in war. In February 2003 the newly-formed Sudan Liberation Movement (SLM) attacked el-Fasher and began the war. Khartoum's answer was massive and led to a minimum of 300,000 victims, possibly as many as 400,000, during the next four years.

If one had needed a proof of the fact that the various Sudanese conflicts were not religion-driven, one could not have asked for a better (and more horrible) demonstration. Now Muslims were killing Muslims in droves, raping their women, destroying their means of livelihood, burning their villages and forcing them into exile or internally-displaced people's camps.

In the light of this situation it is hardly possible to decide that "Islam" is the cause of the mayhem.[26] The explanation is less grand, less ideologically all-encompassing and less philosophically sweeping. The Darfur conflict, just like the two north-south conflicts that preceded it, is a centre versus periphery conflict in which a crudely extractive regime at the centre first completely neglects a certain part of the country (there is nothing to be extracted there) and then crushes it militarily when it poses a threat to its dominance.

This by the way requires a bit of further explaining: if there is nothing to be extracted from Darfur, then why this extreme violence towards a regional/racial group which is not taking anything away from the state but simply asking for a fair share of its national resources? The answer is both cultural and geopolitical. The Muslim Brothers' regime in Khartoum, like all other riverine Arab regimes before it, has always counted on the loyalty of the Darfurians. The fact that they were Muslims was deemed to be enough. So when they revolted it fundamentally threatened the concept of Muslim political cohesion. Within an Islamist perspective, the Christian southerners had been natural enemies since they were neither Arabs nor Muslims. But the Darfurians were at least one of these things and at times both. Thus the government in Khartoum expected the non-Arab tribes of Darfur to at least remain loyal and if they did not, it expected the "Arab" ones to enter the fray on its side and help it kill the black "African" rebel tribes.

But this did not work as planned even if the government very cleverly managed to deflect the frustrations of the Darfur Arabs from hostility to Khartoum into hostility to their "African" neighbours.[27]

The Darfur revolt was a threat to the myth of "Muslim solidarity" and "Muslim brotherhood"; it was also, much more practically, a potential threat to resource extraction i.e. to the oilfields that have been the mainstay of the regime's affluence since 1999. Nobody has found oil in Darfur so far, although there could be some since exploration has simply not yet been seriously undertaken. But the Naivasha Peace Agreement includes a provision for a referendum of self-determination in 2011, and this could result in the independence of the south, either peacefully or violently.[28] Any eventual return to military operations would leave the oilfields, particularly those around Abyei, dangerously exposed.

Conclusion

These fractured segments of the Sudanese identities remain essential components of any attempt at picturing a global "national" vision of the present situation and its causes. But it definitely does not mean that "Islam" as such is the key defining element in that complicated prism. Islam is *only one* of the elements of the Sudan's "multiple marginality" and, arguably, perhaps not the most important. To the eyes of a careful observer, the centre-periphery relationship and its attendant problems of distance and relation with a predatory form of resource-extracting government, tend to be more fundamental than which God the people pray to. And in addition, in the very recent chronological slot, any attempt at weighing the various components of the identity/ political crisis of the Sudan has to take into account a fundamental new fact: today, with the increased commercialization and monetarization of everything in the Sudan—as well as in the world outside—the key fault line runs between those who have access (to cash, goods, prestige, power, services) and those who don't. The traditional elements of identity, while not obsolete, tend today to pre-select the "haves" and the "have-nots". The "haves" are quite easy to define: Muslim, "Arabs" in the cultural sense and belonging to one of the three tribes of the Nile Valley. But the "have-nots" offer a bewildering variety of types and even include, in addition to those who do not belong to the "have" group, thousands who do but who are economically marginalized. In other words, *real practical membership in the ruling elite is far from being linked with either Islam or ethnicity alone but it also implies certain family connections or, lacking those, certain political ones replacing the missing social graces.* Having all the right characteristics but no connections can go hand in hand with poverty; just as in sixteenth century Spain noble *hidalgos* who had only their name and their *antiguo Cristiano* credentials could well go hungry. Violence, in this context, comes when denizens of the periphery try to occupy by force centre positions they would "normally" be structurally excluded from reaching. Thus "Islam" cannot be viewed as a cultural Behemoth automatically empowering its top ethnic members but rather as a filter pre-selecting some types of access. If it does not combine with others, it is not operative. In today's Sudan the former Muslim radicals who are in power are ironically called *tujjar ad-Din* (merchants of religion) in acknowledgement of this shift in their operating criteria. Correspondingly, young men who, in the early days of the *Thawrat al-Inqaz al-Watani* (Revolution of National Salvation) were ready to die as *shahid* in the jihad, are not any longer. They want employment (including in the security apparatus where organizing the Darfur repression is seen as a job like any other). The actual killings are carried out by lower-ranking members of the semi-periphery who are poor enough to be compensated through the looting of their victims' property. Thus the extraordinary mosaic of the Sudan's multiple marginality is today simply the raw material for a repressive system grounded in a typical resource-rich but technologically-poor increasingly monetarized society. Its exotic complexity, carried over from former pre-monetarized days, should not be allowed to hide the new wiring of an increasingly modern commercial-authoritarian system where Islam is simply a tool of social and political manipulation among many others.

Region III

The "Old" European Border[1]

Stig Jarle Hansen

The migration waves of the twentieth and twenty-first centuries have created *de facto* enclaves within the European Union; many Muslims live amongst atheists and Christians, the most common European beliefs.[2] However, Europe also had "older" borders between Islam and Christianity. In many ways, these borders are the results of the expansion of different empires. In the west of the continent, the forces of the Umayyad Caliphate took control over most of present day Spain, also expanding for a short period of time into present day France. By the eleventh century, internal war made it possible for Portugal, Castile and Aragon, and later Spain to conquer many of the divided Islamic fiefdoms; in 1492 the last Muslim stronghold fell. Further east, the Ottomans came to power in the central lands of present-day Turkey, conquering the smaller Islamic principalities in the area and then attacking the Byzantine Empire, conquering Christian regions. By the nineteenth century the Ottoman Empire was in decline, and ethnic groups such as the Greeks and the Serbs, often supported by their Russian co-religionists, rebelled. Further to the East, the religious borders were defined by the expansion of the Russian empire. During the reign of Peter the Great, Russia's southward expansion drastically accelerated.[3] Ottoman resistance halted Russian expansion, but by the eighteenth and nineteenth centuries, Russian conquests in the Caucasus brought Dagestanis, Chechens, Ingush, and others into the Russian state. Most of Ukraine was conquered in the eighteenth century.

The expansion and retraction of the empires influenced local folk tales, and religion functioned as a unifying factor for many ethnic groups, Serb oral traditions were for example kept by the monasteries and churches that survived the Ottoman occupation.[4] In this way religion became entangled with ethnic self-definition for many of these border groups. Nationalism, imported through the German tradition, was based on the notion of a common language, history, culture and religion.[5] It was during the national awakening after the fall of communism that larger conflicts again surfaced both in the Balkans and in Caucasus.

For Huntington the manifestation of conflict in the Balkans and in the Caucasus became a sign of the fault line that divided Islam from the Christian Orthodox and western civilizations. Indeed the mental frames created by religion were to have influence, but often because religion influenced ethnic self-definition. Religious fault lines proved far from accurate as a foundation for predictions: there were examples of conflict, as in Ingushetia and Ossetia, Armenia/Azerbaijan and several of the cases explored in this book. Islamic provinces such as Dagestan chose to remain within the Russian federation, as did many of the other Islamic areas within Russia[6]. Orthodox Greece is a longstanding member of the European Union. Romania and Bulgaria joined the EU despite their orthodoxy, Bulgaria also bringing a sizable Muslim population into the Union. The Turkish Islamist Justice and Development Party (AKP), desires EU membership. In the chapter covering Chechnya, James Hughes explores how the conflict between Chechnya and Russia initially started as a nationalist conflict, riding on a wave of nationalism amongst the former Soviet republics, but he also explores how the dynamics of the conflict changed over time, with religious rhetoric gaining in prominence. In the following chapter, Tuncay Kardas shows how secularism was used by the elite of Turkey in order to keep power, but also how the Islamists searched for allies in "another civilization", namely in the EU, in order to counter the repressive moves of the secularized Turkish elites. Svein Mønnesland then analyses Bosnia-Herzegovina, highlighting how religion interacted with nationalism in this case, but also how religion was used by belligerents for propaganda purposes. In the last chapter in this part, Elena Arigita argues that the Islamic legacy of Spain constructed a powerful image of Islam as Spain's historical "other" and influenced the ways in which the Spanish identity has been constructed throughout centuries and keeps being revised in the light of present events. However, she also illustrates how the image of Christian Spain struggles with an image of Spain as a country with multi-cultural past, a struggle over the contents of national identity.

11

Chechnya—How War Makes Jihad

James Hughes

In *The Clash of Civilizations* Samuel P. Huntington distinguished "fault line" conflicts from other forms of "communal war" in two key respects: first, they are conflicts defined by religion, and second, they share a propensity for "internationalization" through the involvement of external kin countries, groups and cultural entities. Huntington reasoned that Chechnya exhibited all of the characteristics of one of his so-called "fault line" or "communal" conflicts. It was a conflict for control of territory that involved "ethnic cleansing" and shared the "prolonged duration, high levels of violence, and ideological ambivalence of other communal wars". By categorizing the conflict in Chechnya among those that were defined by religion, between "Orthodox" Russia and "Muslim" Chechnya, Huntington could frame it as one of his "intercivilizational" wars.

The analysis that follows demonstrates that there is little evidence for categorizing the conflict in Chechnya in "civilizational" terms for the period in which Huntington developed his thesis in the first half of the 1990s. The conflict in Chechnya originated not as a historically rooted "fault line" religious war, but as a contingent secular nationalist revolution that was part of the European anti-communist Zeitgeist of the late 1980s and early 1990s that rejected Soviet colonization. As the conflict progressed during the 1990s the degree to which it was framed on both sides as a historically rooted religious and civilizational conflict strengthened, but this framing shift was generated, in the main, by the turn to violent conflict from late 1994 and was a motivational force for only part of the Chechen resistance movement. The key development to be explained in the case of Chechnya is why the secular nationalist movement of the first half of the 1990s was transformed into one which contained a significant jihadist element during the second half of the 1990s. Huntington's indiscriminate imposition of a "civilizational" template on the whole Chechnya conflict obscures rather than explains this transformation.

The infusion of jihadism into the conflict from the middle of the 1990s was, principally, the result of a radicalization of the protagonists following the shift from political to violent conflict. The radicalization of the Chechen resistance in particular is closely correlated with the escalation of Russian military force and its disproportionate use against civilians during the war of 1994–1996. Consequently, the conflict in Chechnya should be understood as a dynamic one, where the key causes, motivations and protagonists change over time. The later development of a jihadist element within the Chechen resistance to Russia should not distract us from testing the plausibility and logical coherence of Huntington's argument within its own time frame of the period 1991–1995. Chechnya is a powerful example of how violence becomes part of the structuring mechanism shaping the radicalization of political conflict and, in particular, the shift from nationalism to jihad.[1]

What is the evidence for an "Islamic" factor driving the Chechen struggle against Russia in the period in which Huntington's thesis was developed? We can explore the salience of Islam in the politics of Chechen secessionism in three main areas. Firstly, we should expect to see the salience of Islam as an *ideological force*, informing the thought, policy and actions of Chechen leaders in the drive for independence. Secondly, we should expect to find Islam playing a *legitimizing function* in how Chechnya was governed by the *de facto* independent regime under Dzhokhar Dudayev, which came to power in October 1991. Thirdly, we should expect to see Islam play a *directional role* in how the Chechen secessionists framed their own case for independence, whether in the bargaining process with Russia or in the attempts to secure international recognition. In sum, if the conflict in Chechnya was a "fault line" war driven by Islam then we would expect to see an Islamist agenda being implemented by the Chechen leadership from the outset of independence, and at the very least during the period in the early 1990s to which Huntington's work referred.

Chechnya's nationalist revolution

Most of the academic and journalistic accounts of the conflict in Chechnya have recurrently framed it in historicist terms, as one that is driven by primordial "ancient hatreds" and historical "ethnic enmity" in the relations between Russians and Chechens that can be traced to the period of Russian colonization of the Caucasus in the early to middle nineteenth century.[2] Russian colonization occurred contemporaneously with the spread of Islam in the North Caucasus. Not for the first time in history, imperialist aggression and expansion and the resistance to it became historically associated with religious differences. The association between Islam and resistance to Russia in this period was strengthened by the fact that periodic anticolonial uprisings by the indigenous peoples against Russia were often led by Islamic religious leaders, *imams*, who were not only local spiritual leaders but also military commanders in the resistance. The Chechens and Ingush are Sunni Muslims of the Hanafi School, a form of Islam that spread from the ʿAbbasid caliphate (present-day Iraq) and that was accommodating of the role of local custom in Islamic law. Sufism, a form of Islam based on orders or traditional paths of mysticism (*tarīqa*) where great importance is attached to the worship of saint-like "holy" figures, and which is organized into brotherhoods became embedded in Chechen society during the turmoil of colonization and resistance in the middle of the nineteenth century. Historically, two orders of Sufism were of importance in Chechnya: the *Naqshbandiia* order, which fused religion and politics to frame the resistance to Russian colonialism in terms of a "holy war" (*ghazavat*) against the Russian infidels, and the more mystical and "otherworldly" *Qadiriia* order. The Chechen Sheikh Mansur who led the revolt against Russia in 1785–1791, and Imam Shamil, who led the "Murid" revolt against Russia in the 1840s were adherents of the *Naqshbandiia* order. Shamil's jihad, moreover, was driven by both the goal of expelling the Russians, and also of purifying and spreading "true" Islam and building an Islamic society based on Shariah.[3] The history of colonial resistance in Chechnya is widely viewed as a critical foundation that shapes the present-day struggle for Chechen independence and the growth of Islamist fundamentalism across the North Caucasus. There was, however, a century of historical development between the resistance to Russian colonialism and the contemporary conflict.

The tendency to view the conflict in historicist terms mistakenly downplays the importance of the context and contingency of the collapse of the USSR in the origins of the conflict. A Chechen nationalist movement only emerged in the late 1980s as part of the regional anti-communist "mobilizational cycle" for democratization and national self-determination in Eastern Europe evoked by Gorbachev's liberalization policies.[4] As in many other parts of the Soviet bloc, in Chechnya the first stirrings of nationalism came from secular academic associations. In Chechnya the academic organization *Kavkaz* (Caucasus) was formed as an "informal" group under Gorbachev's liberalization of 1986–1987, and from it dozens of others were spawned as the USSR imploded in 1988–1991. The informal groups mutated into the more obviously nationalist "Popular Fronts", beginning in the Baltic States, which couched their demands for independence under the slogan of "sovereignty." In this period, Chechen nationalists, as with nationalists elsewhere in the USSR, were inspired by and imitated the Popular Front nationalism of the Baltic States, which was secular and western-oriented. The two leading figures of the Chechen nationalist movement in this period, Zelimkhan Yandarbiev and Dzhokhar Dudayev, epitomized its essentially secular character and were great admirers of the democratic nationalism of the Baltic States. Yandarbiev was a teacher and poet who was a member of the Russian Writers' Union and an activist in *Kavkaz*. Yandarbiev's intellectually-grounded form of secular nationalism of this period would mutate into a radical form of Islamism as a result of the conflict with Russia from late 1994.

The radicalization of Yandarbiev is clearly evident from the content of the two collections of writings that he published in 1994 and 1996: the first mostly drawn from works written or published as part of the "national revolution" in 1989–1992, and the second from works written or published in the run-up to and during the war with Russia in 1994–1995.[5] There are many iconic illustrations of the personal, political and religious journey from secular nationalism to Islam. Photos of the clean-shaven secular nationalist Yandarbiev of the late 1980s stand in contrast with the *papkha-* (traditional sheepskin hat) wearing, bearded Islamist of 1994. More substantively, the early writings emphasise the "national freedom struggle" of the Chechen nation (*natsiia*), and the political struggle for "sovereignty". There are references to an eclectic group of great western and Russian thinkers who had influenced Yandarbiev's nationalism: Hegel, Camus, Nietzsche, Berdyaev, Hayek and the Chechen Soviet dissident Avtorkhanov. Yandarbiev wrote seven articles on nationalist political questions in the period 1989–1992 but perhaps the most emblematic of this phase in Yandarbiev's political evolution is his 1989 essay on Soviet nationalities policy, which was published in 1991. The essay reflected his embeddedness in the Soviet intellectual tradition by its concern with the "dialectics" of social development and its cumbersome title: *Istoki (natsional'nyi vopros: problemy i suzhdeniia)* (Sources [the national question: problems and assessments]). Yandarbiev was part of the multicultural nationalist political ferment in Moscow's academic institutions in the 1980s. Disgruntled with the slow pace of change he and other young radical nationalists broke away from the Popular Front in what was then the Soviet Autonomous Republic of Checheno-Ingushetia to form the nationalist *Bart* (Unity) Party in July 1989. The link between the nationalist movement in Chechnya and those of the Baltic States was such that the first three issues of *Bart's* newspaper were printed in Riga by the Latvian Popular Front's press. Yandarbiev was first and foremost a Chechen nationalist but he also developed an ideology for a regional Pan-Caucasian secular ethnic nationalism (*Kavkazskost'* [Caucasianness]), framed in anti-Soviet and anti-colonialist rhetoric, which he attempted to spread by organizing the first Congress of Mountain Peoples of the Caucasus in late August 1989.[6] Yandarbiev's second book, published in 1996, is bracketed with Islamic rhetoric: an Islamic prayer in the foreword and an Islamic poem at the back. The book is mainly a narrative account of the first years of the Dudayev regime and the struggle for independence from Russia. That Islamism came out of this struggle rather than drove it is never openly stated by Yandarbiev, and indeed his second book contains essays from the period 1989–1991 which illustrate Yandarbiev's secular nationalism of that time. An increasing Islamization of Yandarbiev is evident from certain iconic features and steps mentioned in this book: his visit to Mecca in June 1992 (but apparently he arrived too late to perform the *hajj*); his first mention of *ghazavat* (a synonym for jihad) which came after the Russian invasion of December 1994; during 1994 he refers to Chechen commander Shamil Basaev by the Islamic military title "*amir*"; some photos in the book exhibit Chechen fighters, including Basaev, wearing headbands with the *shahada*. Yandarbiev's rhetoric also shifts to an Islamist vernacular in his writings of 1995.[7]

The indigenous communist elites of the North Caucasus were extremely pragmatic and cautious about calls for independence from Russia for several reasons. They were highly Sovietized and acculturated into a Soviet elite network, and consequently saw their own self-interest and security in a renewed Russian Federation in which they would have greater autonomy. All of Russia's ethnic republics, except for Chechnya and Tatarstan, signed up to a new federal treaty in March 1992.[8] Moreover, the so-called "titular" ethnic republics of the North Caucasus were among the poorest in the whole of the former

Soviet Union and faced bleak developmental prospects without Russian economic support. The success of a nationalist revolution in Chechnya was highly exceptional within the region, and there were a combination of circumstances that account for this. Across the Soviet Union and some parts of Central and Eastern Europe, the struggle against Soviet occupation and for national self-determination was often characterized by generational conflict between radical young nationalist groups led by intellectuals and the indigenous elites of careerist collaborators with the Soviet regime. The secular "Baltic-style" nationalism that drove Yandarbiev and his group in this period is evident from the nature of their opposition to the indigenous Soviet leadership of Checheno-Ingushetia, installed by Moscow in 1989 under the leadership of the regional communist party secretary Doku Zavgaev. Zavgaev and his nomenclatura allies favoured preserving union with a reconstituted USSR, or failing that with Russia. From early 1990, in the wake of the Eastern European revolutions and as the USSR began to implode, Yandarbiev opportunistically attempted to intensify the nationalist mobilization for an independent Chechnya. In March he established the Vainakh Democratic Party (VDP), one of the first secular nationalist parties to be formed in the USSR with the express goal of achieving independence.

The emphasis on nationalism as opposed to Islam in the political mobilization in Chechnya is clear from the proceedings of the first Chechen National Congress (CNC) that was convened on 23–26 November 1990, which was nominally under the auspices of the Zavgaev leadership. About 1,000 Chechens and several members of the Chechen diaspora in Turkey and Jordan attended the gathering in Grozny. The event marked the beginning of what became known as the "Chechen national revolution". Zavgaev hoped to steer the CNC in a moderate and unionist direction, but Yandarbiev and a number of close associates (including Movladi Udugov and Sait-Khassan Abumuslimov) led a VDP takeover of the organization.[9] The final resolution adopted by the CNC was thoroughly secular nationalist in content and tone. It provided for the adoption by the Supreme Soviet of the Chechen-Ingush Republic of a declaration on "State Sovereignty", which was subsequently passed on 27 November 1990. This declaration was, in fact, one of the last in the so-called "parade of sovereignties," where most of Russia's autonomous republic's declared their sovereignty, though nearly all did so with the proviso that they remained "within the RSFSR." Article 1 of the declaration stated: "The Chechen-Ingush Republic is a sovereign state, created as a result of the self-determination of the Chechen and Ingush peoples." No mention was made of the RSFSR, though a commitment was expressed to sign a new federal treaty with the USSR, on equal terms with the Union Republics. Provisions were made for protecting and promoting the Chechen language and culture and Islam but these were listed below other grievances such as territorial disputes with the neighbouring republics of North Ossetia and Dagestan, and the demand for compensation from Russia for its historical injustices against Chechnya (notably the genocidal deportation of 1944).[10] Chechnya's first significant statement of a nationalist agenda was, therefore, very much in line with the declarations made by the most Western-oriented nationalisms of the USSR, those of the Baltic States, and focused on the moral legitimacy of the claim to independence through the principle of national self-determination, underpinning this claim by reference to the historical injustices perpetrated by the Soviet Union and Russia.[11]

The emergence of Dudayev as leader of the nationalist movement was also inspired by Yandarbiev. A serving Soviet air force major-general, Dudayev had name recognition throughout the Soviet Union because of his open and active support for Baltic nationalism. As commander of the Soviet nuclear bomber air base at Tartu in Estonia, Dudayev found himself at one of the epicentres of nationalist resurgence in the USSR in the late 1980s. The Baltic nationalist Popular Fronts involved the mass mobilization of support around secular nationalism and a commitment to moral pressure on the Soviet authorities based on the legitimacy of the claim to national independence as an expression of democracy. To understand Dudayev's nationalist consciousness we must recognize that it was a late conversion. Any sense of Chechenness was subsumed within a Soviet identity. Although he was born in Chechnya in 1944, just prior to the violent Soviet deportation, Dudayev was raised in Kazakhstan and did not live in Chechnya until late 1990 at the age of forty-six. While he retained a working knowledge of the Chechen language, his first language was Russian. He was thoroughly Sovietized by a military career which had seen him join the CPSU in 1966, marry a Russian military officer's daughter, and serve with distinction against the Mujahedin in Afghanistan in the 1980s. His conversion to nationalism and the idea of an independent Chechnya came about as a result of his observations of the rise of the Estonian nationalist Popular Front while he was based in Tartu in the late 1980s.[12] As the senior Soviet military commander in the district, he was *ex officio* a member of the city party executive committee (*gorkombiuro*), which would have brought him into close contact with local and national politics.

Dudayev was elected leader of the executive committee of the CNC in December 1990 for several reasons but, as the recollections of his wife and others make clear, Islamism played no role whatsoever.[13] His seniority was one factor, but he was also an outsider to the client networks that operated within Chechnya and thus perceived to be a good compromise candidate. Yandarbiev had visited Dudayev in Tartu to encourage him to accept the leadership of the nationalist movement for good logical reasons. Dudayev's military authority and experience would bring strong leadership, charisma, respectability, discipline and organizational skills to the nationalist movement. Most important, Dudayev had proven himself to be a committed nationalist and charismatic speaker at the congress. His nationalist credentials were affirmed when just weeks later Dudayev foiled Gorbachev's violent clampdown on the nationalists in the Baltic States by closing off Estonian airspace, and assisted Yeltsin's security during the Russian president's visit to Tallinn.[14]

When Dudayev retired from his air force commission and returned permanently to Grozny to lead the executive committee of the CNC in March 1991, the struggle within Chechnya was by then polarized into a conflict between the unionist Chechen party nomenclature elite under Zavgaev and the nationalist secessionists. This was a struggle about competing visions of secular Chechen nation-building. The unionist forces under Zavgaev favoured the reintegration of Chechnya into either a reconstituted USSR or, failing that, a reformed Russian Federation. The nationalists aspired to self-determination and independence.

Dudayev accelerated the radicalization of the nationalist movement. In May 1991, on the basis of the declaration of sovereignty, he dissolved the Zavgaev-dominated Chechen-Ingush Supreme Soviet and declared the executive committee of the CNC to be the only legitimate provisional government in Chechnya until elections could be held. A new "Common National Congress of the Chechen People" (OKChN) was established in July 1991, with Dudayev as chairman. Some have argued that the moderate nationalists and unionists were routed by a "coterie of extremists" led by Dudayev, who advocated "the creation of an Islamic state."[15] There is no evidence for such an intention. As will be demonstrated later, in our discussion of Chechen state-building, Dudayev, Yandarbiev, and other nationalist leaders at this time were driven by a secular vision of nation-state building; beyond occasional Islamic symbolism, such as the traditional cries of "Allah Akhbar!" by the more vocal anti-Russianists, there was no significant Islamic content to the nationalist drive for independence. Dudayev's nationalism was rooted in the Baltic model, and he was keen to position it within a global experience of anti-colonialism. He rejected "colonial freedom" or any other "hybrid" version of sovereignty, and demanded a treaty with Russia that would legally recognize Chechnya's national independence. The executive committee of the OKChN, headed by Dudayev, declared itself the only legal government of Chechnya (and named the new republic Nokhchi-cho). At this time Dudayev had a tactical alliance with Beslan Gantemirov, a former Moscow-based criminal boss turned leader of the "Islamic Path" party, whose militia formed a hard core of the new National Guard. This appears to have been an Islamic party in name only.[16] In fact, of forty-six political parties and movements identified by Timur Muzaev at this time in Chechnya, only three were self-declared "Islamic" in orientation, and all of these had been dissolved by 1993, including Islamic Path. Consequently, the evidence suggests that the "Islamic" factor in Chechen politics was residual, if not marginal. We should also note, however, that the opening up of Chechnya in late 1991 to the outside world meant in the first instance openings to Chechen diaspora communities, in Turkey and Jordan in particular, countries where strong traditions of secular nationalism were being challenged by the rise of political Islam. The opening up of Chechnya also brought opportunities for proselytizing influences from the wider Islamic world through new funding, mainly Saudi in origin, for religious-cultural activities.[17]

The nationalist revolution in Chechnya occurred with the direct support of the Yeltsin-led democrats in Moscow including the parliamentary speaker Ruslan Khasbulatov (also an ethnic Chechen). When Zavgaev wavered during the August 1991 coup in Moscow, Dudayev seized the opportunity to launch a nationalist uprising. Yeltsin declared a state of emergency in Chechnya and ordered local Russian military garrisons to arm and support the nationalist forces. Leading members of Yeltsin's administration, including Gennadii Burbulis and Khasbulatov, visited Chechnya to support Dudayev and ensure that Zavgaev resigned so that there was a peaceful transfer of power from the Supreme Soviet to an OKChN-dominated Provisional Supreme Council. The international post-communist Zeitgeist of the period 1989–1991 saw nationalist movements in Eastern Europe, the USSR and Yugoslavia legitimize the assertion of independence through the democratic expression of national self-determination. Positioning Chechen nationalism within this broader movement, Dudayev and the OKChN called presidential and parliamentary elections in Chechnya in October 1991. The fairness of the elections was disputed, but according to official Chechen sources Dudayev was elected president of Chechnya with 85 per cent of the vote on a 77 per cent turnout, and even allowing for vote-rigging, most observers accepted that Dudayev was the clear winner.[18]

If Islamism was a significant ideological, legitimizing, or directional force for Dudayev then we should expect his regime, once in power, to act accordingly. In fact, even as Yeltsin's new Russian administration turned against Dudayev in the weeks following the national revolution, the conflict with Chechnya was not framed as a problem with "Islamists". Rather, the Yeltsin regime took the very typical policy response of colonial regimes by criminalizing the nationalist resistance. The discursive process determining the security threat on both sides at the outset made no reference to "Islam" as a factor. For the Russians, Dudayev represented a problem of "separatism" and the seizure of power by "bandits" and "criminals".[19] Dudayev and his ministers in turn increasingly embedded their anti-Russia rhetoric in a historical narrative of Chechen resistance to Russian "colonizers," and often succumbed to racist outbursts against Russians, often likening them to "Nazis."[20] Both idioms resonated vibrantly with the respective national constituencies: with Russian stereotypes of Chechens, and vice-versa, both of which had their origins in the Russian form of Orientalism derived from its nineteenth-century colonial experience in the Caucasus and embedded by its "Golden Age" literature such as Pushkin's *Kavkazskii plennik* ("Prisoner in the Caucasus") and Tolstoy's "moral" novel of the "Murid" war, *Hadji Murat*.

Chechen nationalism and state-building

What did Dudayev and the nationalists do with political power? Was there in any sense an Islamist state-building project? Dudayev's decrees and policies after the formal declaration of independence and his assumption of the presidency on 1 November 1991 through to the Russian invasion of December 1994 offer plenty of grounds for analysing his regime as a classic post-colonial secular nationalist state-building project. Dudayev's overwhelming concern was to achieve recognition of Chechnya as a sovereign state, primarily from Russia but also internationally. Over the next three years of negotiations with Russia on the status of Chechnya he consistently grounded Chechnya's right to independence within a secular legal framework of Soviet constitutional law and international law. In numerous interviews to Russian and other foreign journalists at this time, Dudayev held that the Chechen people had expressed their "will for self-determination and freedom" at the ballot box. He stressed that the USSR laws passed in April 1990 established the constitutional right of an Autonomous Republic to decide its own fate, whether it was to refuse to sign up to Gorbachev's draft new Union treaty of May 1991, or to secede from the USSR in circumstances when this state was already in the process of disintegration, as was the case after the August 1991 coup. In the absence of a constitutional ratification of the new Union treaty (which Zavgaev had signed, but the ratification of which was pre-empted by the August coup), Chechnya remained *de jure* outside the USSR within the terms of constitutional law. After his election as president, Dudayev pushed through a number of radical decrees to complete the repatriation of Chechnya's sovereignty. By the end of November 1991, all federal property in Chechnya had been nationalized and payments of taxes and revenues to the Russian federal budget were stopped, though Russian state transfers of pensions and social payments were still processed. Russia, for its part, was reluctant to terminate the transfers, since this would compromise its claim to sovereignty over Chechnya.[21]

Following the speedy rout of a Russian military intervention in early November 1991, Yeltsin turned to a twin-track strategy alternating between sporadic military attacks and the isolation of Chechnya by blockade, and the use of Chechen loyalist proxies to destabilize Dudayev's regime. Russian policy on Chechnya became absorbed by propagandistic attempts to demonize Dudayev's government as "criminal" and "terrorist". Comparisons especially favoured by Yeltsin and other Russian politicians were with Panama's former ruler General Noriega and Russian propaganda branded Chechnya a "bandit state." As a former general, and assisted by a former Soviet artillery colonel, Aslan Maskhadov, as his chief military commander, Dudayev devoted much time to the organization and training of Chechen armed forces to resist a Russian attack. The militarization of Chechnya was secured by an agreement between Dudayev and corrupt elements in the Russian General Staff for an equal division of the quite considerable Soviet-era military stocks based in Chechnya, which included huge quantities of infantry weapons.[22]

Dudayev viewed religion pragmatically and instrumentally as one of the potential unifying forces that would assist state-building and the construction of a national identity. He was sensitive to the need for the development of sound social values, and aimed to use Islam among other religions for this purpose. Moreover, there was an understandable desire to rejuvenate religious life in Chechnya, which after all had been suppressed for decades under Soviet occupation. Most importantly, he attempted to harness the authority of societal leaders and religious elders in support of his regime. His establishment of a Supreme Islamic Council in September 1991, almost immediately following the revolutionary overthrow of Soviet power, was an attempt to unify the religious establishment, which like Chechnya's political establishment, was deeply divided over the question of secession. The Supreme Islamic Council was regarded by the former religious establishment as being too dominated by the Sufi *Qadiriia* order, and the rival *Naqshbandiia* order set up its own "Spiritual Administration of Muslims". Dudayev attempted to create a unified "Muftiate" in August 1992, but when Chechnya became embroiled in a civil war between Dudayev's secessionist presidential administration and a more moderate parliament that was willing to compromise with Russia in the spring of 1993, the religious establishment, including the Muftiate, sided with the parliament against Dudayev.[23]

We should not confuse Dudayev's instrumental use of religion, and the growth of religiosity in Chechnya in the early 1990s with political Islam, in the sense of an ideology to embed Islam within the political fabric of the state. Many Russian and western observers exaggerated the role of Islam under Dudayev, based on a small number of seemingly iconic facts, such as that he swore his presidential oath on the *Qur'ān*. It is logical for a nationalist leader to mobilize forces around ideas that have popular legitimacy and such topics were a natural response to independence from Russia, which brought freedom to express national identity, and an increased consciousness of identity. Moreover, contacts with the Chechen diaspora and the Islamic world intensified the Chechen's search for a post-Soviet identity. Besides, there was a sudden outburst of religiosity across the whole of the former Soviet Union, in reaction to the Soviet oppression of religion. What occurred in Chechnya was part of a wider post-Soviet trend. Some have argued that Dudayev was a Sufi adept characterized by "adherence to Islam and piousness", but without providing any evidence for such assertions.[24] Dudayev's use of Islamic rhetoric, such as the term "*ghazavat*" (holy war) was almost always correlated with moments of extreme urgency such as during the Russian invasion of December 1994. There is no evidence that Islam played a major role in Dudayev's personal life, and even as other nationalists, such as Yandarbiev, adopted traditional dress forms such as the Chechen *papkha* (sheepskin hat) and Islamist rhetoric during the conflict of 1994–1996, Dudayev preferred the Soviet military officer's field hat (*pilotka*) or a homburg or trilby hat. It is important also that we do not confuse religiosity with fundamentalism.

There was no attempt to construct a Shariah state under Dudayev. For Dudayev the chief policy priorities, apart from the constant threat from Russia, lay in building an efficient secular state administration, organizing the armed forces, and preventing socio-economic collapse and internal disorder. He presided over the drafting of a new constitution for Chechnya, which was approved by the Chechen parliament in March 1992. The Chechen constitution was a standard model of a secular nationalist parliamentary constitution. The preamble states that the constitution is guided by the "idea of humanism" not Islam. Article one states: "The Chechen Republic is a sovereign and independent democratic law-based state, founded as a result of the self-determination of the Chechen people." Article two affirms: "The people of the Chechen Republic are the only source of all power in the state." Many aspects of the constitution would not look out of place in any other constitution informed by the ideals of secular republican nationalism. That the constitutional commitments to democracy and openness were not just a sham is suggested by the report of a fact-finding mission conducted by the well-respected London-based NGO International Alert, published in October 1992, which stated: "Chechen society is characterized by a remarkable degree of political openness and freedom of expression."[25] Even the new official symbol of the Republic, the wolf *couchant* under a full moon, was un-Islamic, supposedly created by Dudayev's Russian wife Alla from traditional Chechen animist iconography.

It was difficult to tar Dudayev with the brush of Islamic radicalism in the face of such a secular nationalist constitution. The separation of the state and religion was affirmed in Article 4, and the constitution provided for complete freedom of worship and opinions. The shift from secular constitutionalism to Shariah in Chechnya occurred much later under president Maskhadov's rule in 1998–1999 and Article 4 was amended to make Islam the official state religion only in February 1999. Dudayev wrote elsewhere that the "ideal" Chechen state would be one based on Islamic Shariah law, where a traditional council of Chechen elders would make decisions, but this was not the principle on which the constitution was formed.[26] He explicitly claims that Chechnya should become a constitutional secular state.[27]

If the use of Islam was anything other than pragmatic and instrumental, one would have expected Dudayev to issue decrees and orders to promote the infiltration of Islam into the state and society. Again, there is no evidence for this. For example, when we examine the sixty presidential decrees, four acts, and forty-seven orders in the critical period of state-building following the revolution and the promulgation of the new constitution in 1992, we find no attempt to Islamize Chechnya's state structures, or public life.

While journalists, in particular, have often stressed the role of traditional kin ties and "clan" (*teip*) in Chechnya, the sociological evidence and political reality demonstrates that this is a misunderstanding of "patron-clientelism".[28] Dudayev employed clientism in his personnel policy to build a following of loyalists in the state administration. His secular vision of state-building was set out in a long treatise published in April 1993. The text began with a formal reference to the "will of Allah," but that is the only religious reference. His goal was to develop Chechnya into a successful capitalist country, which would be free from Russia's "imperial diktat" and be "enlightened and civilized."[29]

There were several subtexts to the outbreak of war between Russia and Chechnya in December 1994, none of which concerned the "Islamic" factor. Firstly, there was undoubtedly an "oil" subtext. This had less to do with Chechnya's role as an oil producer, as in 1993 its production was some 1.25 million tons (less than 1 per cent of Russia's total output), or even the then current volumes (120,000 tons) pumped through the Russian pipeline from Azerbaijan. Rather, Russia perceived an independent Chechnya to be a strategic threat to its dominance of Caspian energy and its capacity to fend off the escalating western penetration into the region, which was demonstrated by a western consortium's "deal of the century" with Azerbaijan over Caspian oil in September 1994. Secondly, Russia saw in the crushing of Chechnya an opportunity to affirm its own state integrity after the federal destabilization inherited from the Soviet collapse. Negotiations between the Yeltsin and Dudayev regimes were conducted for two years in an attempt to resolve differences, but it proved impossible to reconcile Russia's offer of autonomy with Dudayev's claim to independence. Thirdly, there was also the motive of revenge. Crushing Dudayev by military means would go some way to undoing the humiliations inflicted on small scale Russian military incursions in late 1991, 1992 and November 1994. Furthermore, Dudayev's general arming of the male Chechen population in late 1991 and early 1992 led to an escalation of social disorder and abuses. Many of those armed were unemployed highlanders who faced poverty as a result of the difficulties of finding work in Chechnya or in Russia and the loss of their traditional seasonal work in other parts of the USSR due to the economic crash. Anti-Russian sentiment led to a spontaneous ethnic-cleansing of Russians who did not have kin or clientelist protections. A decade-long process of Slav emigration was suddenly accelerated as about 90,000, about one-third of the total number living in Chechnya, were expelled or left in 1991–1992, and most of these were critical for the proper functioning of the state social sector and oil and petrochemical industry.[30] It seems odd to confuse this ethnic expulsion with "religious war" when there were so many more valid explanations derived from the political and social context of ethnic power relations and how these were dramatically transformed by the collapse of the USSR and the Chechen national revolution.

Conclusion: the making of jihad

After the invasion of December 1994 Russian leaders began to extend the frame of the conflict with Chechnya to include the "Islamic factor" and even borrowed elements of Huntington's "civilizational" framing device. In his memoirs, Yeltsin blamed the conflict on both Dudayev's attempt to secede from the Russian Federation *and* his goal of creating an "Islamic republic."[31] More recent Russian academic studies of Russian policy in the Caucasus acknowledge, however, that "there was no 'Islamic national project' in Chechnya" and that at the beginning of the 1990s "the Islamic republic in Chechnya seemed to be a myth."[32] Much of the attention on the "Islamic factor," consequently, came from a concern with the growth of Islamic radicalism in Chechnya as a result of the first Russian-Chechen war in 1994–1996.

One of the themes of this book is the impact of violence on faith. There was a well-documented drift to Wahhabist and Salafist jihadism among some sections of the Chechen resistance during the first war, which grew and strengthened in the late 1990s and came to dominate the resistance movement during the second war beginning in late 1999. Under Dudayev, the struggle for Chechen independence was, in essence, a classic example of a secular nationalist and anti-colonialist movement. Once the conflict escalated into a brutal war, both sides gave little quarter and the Russians employed disproportionate military force against civilians, while the Chechens responded with sporadic acts of terrorism. War produced a a shift to Islamism occurred. Dudayev was intent on building a secular state in Chechnya, and it was only after his death and the expulsion of Russian military forces from Chechnya that his successor as president, Yandarbiev, introduced a Shariah court and began the reconfiguration of Chechnya's political structures in a more Islamist direction.[33] We can identify three main factors for this growth. For some of the more radical Chechen field commanders, like Shamil Basayev, the ideological pull of jihadism actually predated the all-out Russian military attack of December 1994. Basayev and a small group of followers traveled to al-Qaeda's Khost camp in the summer of 1994 to undergo ideological and military training. As we noted earlier, Yandarbiev began to refer to Basayev with the jihadi title "*amir*" (commander) in late 1994.[34] Basayev, however, was a contradictory figure. The depth of his commitment to political Islam remains questionable. Whereas the secularist Dudayev placed a portrait of Mansur (the great Chechen resistance leader of the late eighteenth century) in his presidential office, Basayev reportedly preferred to cast himself in the mould of a Chechen "Che" and placed a portrait of the Argentinian internationalist in his home in the early 1990s.[35] The importance of Basayev lies in the fact that he exercised enormous authority within the resistance movement because of his aggressiveness and success in attacking Russia (notably in destroying the Russian armoured column that attacked Grozny in December 1994), and his drift to jihad lured many others. Secondly, the attraction of jihad as a countermovement to Chechen secular nationalism can also be attributed to disillusionment within the Chechen resistance with the "West", in particular the USA and the EU, which rather than support Chechnya's bid for democratic national self-determination, tolerated or sympathized with the Russian policy of crushing Chechen secessionism. The collapse of the USSR was treated according to the legal norms devised for decolonization, notably the principle of *uti posseditis juris*. Potential for international influences on the early negotiation of a peaceful resolution to the question of Chechnya were sacrificed to the national interests of Western governments in supporting the reformists under Yeltsin and demarcating Chechnya as an "internal" matter for Russia. Even though there were periodic criticisms of Russia's "excessive" use of force in Chechnya, an indelible mark on the reputation of the West among Chechens was left by President Clinton's absurd comparison of Boris Yeltsin and Abraham Lincoln. Thirdly, bin Laden's interest in Chechnya (as with Bosnia) as a front in the strategy to globalize jihad was not sparked until 1995. That is to say, not by the presence of a nominally Muslim community *per se* but by war and what he interpreted as the "destruction and slaughter" being meted out to Muslims in these places by "Crusaders".[36] In early 1995 bin Laden sent financial support to the Chechen resistance, and a small group of well-trained Arab jihadis commanded by the Saudi *amir* Khattab, called the "Islamic International Brigade", came from Afghanistan to Chechnya, mostly via Dagestan. Khattab was certainly welcomed by the Chechen resistance at this critical time in the war, and he was appointed to important military command and training posts by Dudayev. Khattab's principal connection, however, was with Basayev. He became Basayev's deputy commander and chief advisor and remained in Chechnya until his assassination by the FSB in March 2002.[37] Khattab also brought al-Qaeda's skills in the information war to bear on the conflict in Chechnya. The exaggerated attention paid in Chechnya, Russia and internationally to the role of the jihadis in the conflict was in no small part due to Khattab's deft use of video recordings of successful attacks on the Russian military, which were then copied and distributed and also propagated globally by the burgeoning number of al-Qaeda controlled or influenced websites, including sites specifically devoted to the conflict in Chechnya.[38]

During the second war, and after 9/11 facilitated the Russian propaganda machine's demonization of the Chechen resistance as part of the "global war on terror", Dudayev's former aide and successor as nationalist leader, Aslan Maskhadov, often spoke of how the presence of "international terrorism" in Chechnya was an "invention". By then, however, Islamists linked to al-Qaeda, such as Khattab, played an important role in the resistance to Russia, but the term "invention" is appropriate to the extent that the superior capacity of al-Qaeda to fight an informational war exaggerated the role of its adherents in the conflict in Chechnya and downplayed the part of the nationalist resistance. By then the conflict in Chechnya could more readily be located within Huntington's paradigm of "clash of civilizations". But this was a self-fulfilling prophecy. What had begun as a secular nationalist conflict that was misinterpreted by Huntington, Gurr and others as a "religious" or "fault line" war, became so because of the way that Russian policy opted for a security solution to a political problem of secession, and moreover did so in a most brutal manner that guaranteed a drift into extremism on the part of the resistance.

12

Turkey—Secularism, Islam, and the EU

Tuncay Kardas

Turkey is traditionally seen as a pro-western parliamentary democracy, and a "success story of secular nationalism"; one which has served as "the paragon of secularism across the Muslim world".[1] The dramatic rise and ascent to power of the so-called "moderate Islamist" Justice and Development Party (JDP) challenges this perception. Questions surrounding the coming to power of an "Islamist government" gained a new resonance and further political importance beyond Turkish polity in the wake of the 9/11 terrorist attacks and the ensuing "war on terror".

Samuel Huntington admits Turkey's complexities by categorically defining it as a "torn country", divided between the ruling modernizing secularist state establishment and the larger Islamic populace. Secularism in Turkey is the dominant identity of the secularist establishment (composed mostly of extra-political actors from the military, the judiciary, public prosecutors, the constitutional court, and the upper echelons of civilian bureaucracy, including university presidents), and it lays the groundwork for extra-political methods of action against Islamic identity. Islamic identity is upheld by the general public and by certain political parties that react to such state-imposed secularism. The resultant political and social confrontations between these both orientations of identity often hit the headlines and have clear implications for both the present day and the future of the country. Contrary to Huntington's positioning, this chapter claims that the process of transforming political

Islam in Turkey shows that Islam is not a monolithic, dogmatic, essentialist, transhistorical, and ontologically different religion on a collision course with the western world. Secondly, it argues that Turkey's major predicaments spring not from its relations with a "Christian civilization" but from the confrontational positioning of secularism and Islam within the country itself. It shows that Turkey's salient social and political confrontations are mostly a by-product of state policies rather than unchanging cultural or natural givens. Put differently, domestic political conflicts largely emerge from the extra-political methods of securitization of secular and Islamic identities by the state, which generates a fertile ground for confrontational politics between the secular state elites and the Islam-sensitive socio-political actors.

Turkish state secularism

Turkish state secularism does not correspond to the Anglo-American experience of secularity, but rather stems from the anti-religious French model that seeks to eliminate or control religion.[2] The western tradition that separates the private sphere (interior thoughts, beliefs, emotions) and the public sphere (government, market) serves as a protective legal umbrella for the Church-State separation and the tensions that might arise between the two.[3] This has hardly been the case for Turkey. That is, the oft-cited liberal characterisation of secularity as the separation of Church and State does not apply to Turkish state secularism. The state's secularization programme, from its embryonic stages onwards, displayed a mode of authoritarian state control over the religiosity of the people.[4] Various representations of Islamic identity have been used as a recurring excuse for state intervention into society and polity. The well-known scholar Ali Fuat Basgil has pointed out that this misplaced-secularism in Turkey led to a clampdown on various religious freedoms, generating a system of "state dependent religion".[5] In this sense, the Turkish state is not separate from religion: it attempts to control and define it.

Since the setting up of the modern republic, secularism became, in large measure, the embodiment of the belief that Islam was inimical to the logic and development of modernization, and is an "obstacle" in the process of westernization. The religious-cultural elements were seen as the remnants of the Ottoman state and society and, as such, were represented as having vigorous resistance to westernized innovation. Starting with the new republic, secularization attempts, in the Turkish context, appeared as an overtly elitist project to foster individual secular subjectivities in society.[6] After the establishment of modern Turkey in 1923, the state secularization project embarked upon the formation of a new identity for the people through corresponding legal and institutional practices. These changes "aimed at destroying the symbols of Ottoman-Islamic civilization and substituting them with their western counterparts".[7] Instead of Ottoman-Islamic civilization and traditional-religious identity, the western identity soon became the only "agent" of the Turkish modernization project. The modernizing bureaucratic elites were of the conviction that, in order to generate new modern subjectivities, the personal identity of a Muslim Ottoman should be replaced by a secular, ethnically defined and homogenized (Turkish) nationality.[8] In this process, the ruling elites sought to embed secularism in the minds and hearts of population and strove to foster a secular subjectivity through legal and political reforms in order to combat a resistant and powerful Islamic identity.

Political Islam in Turkey

Observers of Turkish politics have generally been fascinated about the talk of the "resurgence" of political Islam at various times and from all quarters.[9] Characterizations of political Islam are often couched in such terms that see religious awakenings as a "natural" reflection of "reactionary" religious groups, which were always against the country's progressive march towards modern civility, especially after the establishment of the republic in 1923.[10] As mentioned, the project of state secularization attempted to establish an all-encompassing secular-national identity through a legal/political reform process. However, the overall result of this ambitious project was that the state was able to diffuse such stringently upheld secularism mostly into "important but minority sectors of Istanbul and Ankara bourgeoisie, political, professional and media elites".[11] That is, despite its attempts at exclusion and marginalisation, Islam remained a strong personal and social source of identity for the non-elite and the general public.[12] Placed in this context, the rise of Islamic-politics can be better seen as a response to the predicaments of social and political change in Turkey induced by modernization-from-above, a state-led political project which enforced secular nationalism as a social identity.[13] Particularly in the 1990s, the various reversals and difficulties in these projects helped Islamists to form, and represent themselves as, an alternative to secularist westernization. Sharing some elements of the post-modern critique of the nation-state and modernism on a global level, Islamists launched their criticism by pointing to the authoritarian, bureaucratic tendencies of westernization. Furthermore, contrary to the lack of social and political alternatives in the "cynical and nihilist" post-modern critique, the Islamists proposed an alternative political philosophy as well. As in some other countries, the latter proved especially appealing in the context of harsh economic liberalization and rapid industrialization programmes, which often failed to heal social wounds and bring in a "quick-fix" between democracy and economic development.[14] In order to cure the problems associated with the ever-enlarging concentration of social groups in urban centres particularly after the advent of industrialism and nationalism, the Islamists resorted to solutions founded in social welfare policies in their local environments.[15] Concerning personal and religious dimensions, Islam provided meaning to human existence and filled the emotional, personal, and ideological void often generated by such rapid modernization, atomized individuality, and subsequent alienation.[16]

The successful cultural and political expression of these Islamic sensitivities in the 1990s was made increasingly vocal through "the popularization of knowledge through mass communication...by a new class of intellectuals based in the print and the electronic media, and of the [Islamic] party's internal organizational flexibility and ideological presentation of the [Islamic] 'just order'."[17] Indeed, the "new Islamist intellectuals" employed an effective counter discourse against that of the established secularist state.[18] Overall, with the help of Islamic business groups and networks in society what can be called a moderate social Islam was brought into being.

Consequently, these developments helped form a new "consciousness" by and through mass and higher education, and an ever expanding vista for mass communication through print and electronic media that resulted in an increasing influence of the Islamic identity upon otherwise politically detached people.[19] This new socio-religious environment gradually turned into a politically rewarding supply line for the politicians of the centre and religious right parties (i.e. the majority of the political spectrum). Not surprisingly then, the parties in question politicized Islam by competing over the Islamic electorate. They employed religiously informed rhetorical strategies and located Islamic discourse within the political debate. Thus, particularly in the 1990s, although Islam had not been "the language of modern Turkish politics, Turkey's political language has been Islamicized".[20] In fact, political uses of Islam had already started with the institution of competitive party politics in 1950; centre-right parties closed in to the religious groups for political purposes and (partially) voiced their demands. It was the brief Refah Party government (1996–1997), however, which was able to flesh out the demands of the religious expression of the electorate.[21] And it was their Islam-centred political discourse and policies that touched the raw nerve of the secularist establishment of the state. Moreover, this discourse provoked the ensuing security measures and confrontations, which in only one year led to the ousting of the party from government in 1997, and the outlawing of the party a year later.

Secularism, Islam and security: Logic of confrontation

As indicated, Turkey's "civilizing project", along with the importation of western values, carved out a socially and politically bipolarized space for confrontation between the secularists and Islamic identity holders to such a degree that it is often seen as a natural fact of life.[22] But what are the sources of this bipolarization? Starting with the formation of the modern republic, the state secular discourse constructed the role of the bureaucratic elites as civilizing agents, leaving the ruled as the blank slate. As Nilufer Gole argued, the secularist elites undertook a governing and civilizing mission over their "primitive" counterparts in the society, who lacked their "western" attributes.[23] This confrontational space has in turn been used for the state's intervention into the deeds and lives of the masses in the name of "rectifying" those who decline to adopt "western" attributes. For example, headscarf-wearing female students are still banned from the universities as their Islamic subjectivities are seen as a threat to the state and society.[24] Instead of understanding this pre-eminent litigious issue as being about extending the benefits of citizenship to women with headscarves, or freedom of religious expression, or democratic and constitutional rights to education, Islamic (female) public visibility is explained as "creat[ing] such a malaise because it has corporeal, ocular, and spiritual dimensions".[25] The headscarf, then, becomes first and foremost a visible threat to the idealised imagery of the state project in creating a westernised and modern womanhood. It is, crucially through this type of threat construction that the attribution of "normal" to secular and "abnormal" to (political) Islam breeds a security dimension, which helps to frame the debate on secular versus religious in Turkey in terms of the safety of the state. This particular security logic foresees that "abnormal" attributes of a society could be detrimental to the existence and strength of the state. Thereafter, a binary logic prevails. That is, the secular/western identity of the state elites (notably the military and civilian bureaucracy) is constructed as "normal" against the religious/non-modern attributes of society or lay-people, who are thought of as "pathological" and/or "abnormal". This juxtaposition also becomes a recurrent theme in the discourse of the Turkish state. The utilization of this theme, in turn, continues to constitute one main component in contemplating the (legitimacy of) subject positions of actors in politics. In short, it becomes commonplace to polarise identities as subordinate/hierarchical and (under) privileged in the wider political space.

Furthermore, these connotations about secularism in Turkey are conceived first and foremost as a political requisite for the state to survive. In other words, as mentioned, secularism's essential value-laden connotation for the Turkish state elites does not seem to derive from being a necessary facilitator of personal, national, economic, and democratic development, but rather from its relation with the security of the political identity of Turkish state. Secularism of the state elites, in this context, is further informed by historical memories of insecurity, which stemmed particularly from the experiences of dismemberment of the theocratic Ottoman political structure.[26] So construed, secularism is hence securitized: the basis of the state's survival: fortitude and endurance is expected to come only with sticking—at all costs—to the secular nature of the state.

Despite the lack of any militant tendencies, Islamic political identity is consequently seen as an "obscurantist" political orientation, bent on destroying the secular foundation of the modern Turkish Republic. Nothing best summarizes the general view of the secularists about the Islamists than the words of Turkey's former Chief State Prosecutor, Vural Savas. In his application to the Constitutional Court for disbanding the Refah Party, Vural Savas accused it of posing the greatest danger to the constitutional foundations of the Turkish state, calling its members, "vampires feeding only on blood".[27] He put particular emphasis on the party's views regarding the need to relax the strictly-observed controversial ruling on women's dress (i.e. the ban that forbids women wearing the headscarf in vaguely described "public spaces" including, for instance, universities). Hence, anyone carrying an explicit Islamic political identity is rarely been taken a legitimate actor. They are instead assumed to be representatives of religious sects and/or orientations, whose "repulsive", "retrogressive", "obscurantist" and "dangerous" political intentions are to eventually destroy the state's existence. Attributing such images as "obscurantism" to otherwise vigorous political movements, the state elites render Islamic sensitivities as relics of a pre-modern past or as the bearers of an "irrational" past. In the secular state discourse, the simple individual appearance of religious identities in public space is seen neither as an occur-

rence of freedom of expression of individual citizens, or as religious obligations, nor as personal choice. Instead, these socio-religious sensitivities appear
as subversive political practices and as "security threats" to the foundations of
the state. Secularism has been construed not simply as a timeless radical political principle, but as a matter of "life and death" particularly in the face of
emergent popular political parties determined to extend the benefits of citizenship to vast segments of the religious Muslim public.

Changes in Islamist political identity

Particularly since the collapse of the Islamist Refah government in June 1997
(as a result of the military's post-modern intervention), the manifestations of
a major change in Turkey's Islamic political identity have become all the more
evident.[28] Indeed, the ascent to power of the "Islamist-rooted" JDP has confirmed the prospect of a change of political identity at a nation-wide level.
How can we account for this dramatic change in Islamic political identity and
what are its implications for the identity dimension of confrontations in
Turkey?

The issue of change in Islamic political identity is a rather perplexing one.
Deliberations by analysts and political scientists over the underlying economic
and political factors that can account for such a change have been
flourishing.[29] The issue of change should, perhaps primarily, be couched in the
confrontational security space between the secularist forces (i.e. the military)
and Islamist (party political) forces. First though, it is necessary to go beyond
the discourse of "religious awakening" by briefly surveying various social, economic, and political factors that played significant roles in changing the
Islamic political identity in Turkey.

Behind the recent upsurge of changes in the Turkish polity were social and
economic troubles that included the catastrophic effects on large segments of
society of rapid inflation in 2001, global competition, and the economic
recession that "narrowed opportunities for spoils" and generated "large and
persistent pockets of poverty" and further unemployment.[30] In the early
2000s, a palpable and widespread dissatisfaction with the ineffective parliamentary system, together with rampant cronyism, highly personalized political battles between party leaders, blatant populism, political patronage, and
corruption all led to an alienated electorate and an ailing political system.[31]
The change in Islamic political identity in recent years is also closely related to
the decreasing power of the Kemalist state ideology in dominating state-

society relations.[32] In essence, the historically dominant position of the Kemalist state ideology and bureaucracy was weakened as a result of the neo-liberal economic transformation process introduced during the early 1980s by the then PM Turgut Ozal.[33] Ozal managed to circumvent the powerful state bureaucracy by his own style of politics (e.g., bold leadership and ruling by decrees for bypassing normal parliamentary constraints) that led to "the weakening of the bureaucratic or state apparatus". The shrinking of state control over the economy and politics was furthered by the advent of democratization and economic liberalism supported by the EU membership process. Over time, these weakening factors led to the loosening of the tight grip of the state over society, which in turn allowed Islam to occupy an increasingly central place in public space. In short, liberalism opened the door for moderate Muslims to step in.

Transformation of political Islam: JDP

That the general election of 3 November 2002 has transformed the Turkish political landscape has become the commonplace argument amongst political analysts.[34] Between 1986 and 2002, no one party was able to win a majority of seats in parliament. In the November 2002 elections, the electorate ousted the incumbent governing parties of the centre-left and right-wing tripartite coalition, whose members could not win even a single seat this time in the new parliament.[35] A new and untested party, namely the JDP, achieved electoral victory despite the fact that it had never competed in Turkish national elections before.[36] The JDP was one of "the parties that Turkey's politically powerful military least wanted to see win".[37] The results of the local elections in March 2004 confirmed that majority of the electorate embraced the JDP's political message. This triggered a whole new debate as to what exactly the hopes of the party and the masses were. Contrary to the "politics of fear" that have been prevalent for a while, the economic policies and the general political performance of the JDP government has surprised even the most unrepentant cynics and staunch critics of the party.[38]

How can we account for the success of the JDP? An answer can be found in an overview of the emergence of the party. After the military's post-modern coup against the Refah government in 1997, the future of the Islamists was further clouded by the judiciary. In addition to the military campaign, on 22 May 1997 the Public Prosecutor, Vural Savas, applied to the Constitutional Court, asking for the closure of the party, on the grounds that it ran foul of secularist principles.[39] Furthermore, the pressures of the military-led campaign were accompanied by the erosion of the coalition government's majority by resignations from the partner True Path Party. As a result, the first Islamist PM, Erbakan, resigned on 18 June 1997. Later, in January 1998, the Constitutional Court closed down the Refah Party and banned Erbakan from politics for five years. Alerted by the impending closing net on their party, most of members of the Refah Party joined the Fazilet (Virtue) Party, which was founded by the confidantes of Erbakan on 17 December 1997. Having taken up a relatively more moderate language of politics than the Refah Party's earlier inflammatory religious rhetoric, the successor Fazilet Party ran for general election on 18 April 1999, but in the end secured only 15.4 per cent of the national vote. Despite the fact that the Fazilet Party adopted from the onset a more moderate political discourse declaring its commitment to secularism, the Constitutional Court once again stepped in and announced the closure of the party in June 2001 on the same secularist grounds that closed its predecessor. The Public Prosecutor applied to the Constitutional Court on 7 May 1999 for the closure, claiming that the party was undermining the secularist principles of the state, a reference to the headscarf issue.[40]

Particularly after its unsuccessful election results in April 1999 and the Constitutional bans, signs for a new initiative within the Islamic political cadres became all the more visible. It had become clear that the Islamist political movement could not survive these fatal blows from the military and the judicial establishment. The movement split into two separate parties. The older generation loyal to the founder of the movement Necmettin Erbakan formed another successor party under a different name: the Saadet (Felicity) Party. The younger generation of the movement headed by Tayyip Erdogan and Abdullah Gul, on the other hand, staked their bid higher by establishing a wholly different party: the Justice and Development Party on 14 August 2001. Significantly, the JDP, unlike previous Islamist parties, has since then repeatedly underlined its commitment to secularism and has waved the flag of democratic institutions and, last but not least, has striven more than any other government to further Turkey's bid for EU membership.[41] By aligning its message to the mainstream centre, the JDP has transformed itself "into a politically sophisticated, progressive and moderate participant in normal politics".[42] The party immediately disowned its predecessors' more contentious Islamic demands and adapted an avowedly democratic and centrist political stance.[43] The new JDP then came to power by winning a landslide victory in the November 2002 national elections.[44]

What lies behind this change? Graham Fuller, an observer of Turkish politics, has argued that one key principle behind the revival of political Islamic movements has been the conviction on the part of the actors, who "attribute the past achievements and past durability of Islamic civilization to the very message and implementation of Islam itself".[45] In this logic then, any straying from that faith might be perceived "as a direct source of decline and failure".[46] If this is a yardstick against which we can question the political principles and style of the JDP it is clear that the latter does not constitute yet another version of political Islam. The JDP ideologues now clearly represent the party as a typical "conservative democratic party" that signifies not "a status quo but is open to change and future oriented modern conservatism, which defines change in an evolutionary transformation of society...a space for conciliation".[47] Hence, the result is a transformation from political-religious discourse to a western style (conservative) democratic discourse that corresponds more to an "eclectic and liberal" ideology than to religious tenets.[48]

The JDP and the EU membership process

This dramatic rise and ascent to power of the JDP, with a massive majority in what is an avidly secular and strategically key NATO member, as well as an official EU candidate state has been seen by many observers as somewhat "perplexing".[49] The fact that the JDP became a driving force in the process of obtaining Turkey's membership in the EU was even more astonishing.[50] The transformation from the Refah's Islamist party ideology to the JDP's EU-endowed discourse of democracy and human rights signals a momentous change in the contemporary identity of the Islamic political movement. It is in part this change that has consequently set the wheels in motion to transform the politics of security. It seems that Tayyip Erdogan, Abdullah Gul, and the JDP as a party mostly employ a political discourse attuned to a full EU democratic conditionality, by means of which they target (without overt political confrontation) the security or "reason of state" rationality and interventionist techniques of the state.[51] They articulate their EU-centred discourse by embedding it within a placid socio-cultural "Islamic" identity rather than sticking either to a previously defended but vaguely defined "Ottoman golden age" argument, or to criticisms of the capitalist credentials of the EU.[52]

In fact, the changing contours of EU membership criteria in the early 1990s significantly helped to shore up the democratic political discourse of the JDP and other democratic socio-political forces against that of state security. The basic formula to do so lay in the efforts of the party to cross-fertilize both the needs of the party and of society into real politics, with the help of the sense of direction offered by the EU.[53] The EU membership conditions set out in the Copenhagen criteria presented (from a policy-transfer perspective) an institutional-discursive niche that helped the JDP to thwart domestic "uncertainty when imitation provides a means to avoid lengthy and controversial policy debates over ambiguous situations at home".[54] For instance, the human rights and democratization drives faced less opposition on the grounds that the EU membership was conditional on the acceptance of these related reforms. Such discourses as the EU democratic membership conditionality enabled and empowered the JDP to put forward an EU-oriented democratic (counter-) discourse against the security-driven discourse of the secularist establishment. Turkey's relations with the EU made it evident that the global conditions of international politics have increasingly blurred the boundaries between the national and the global. As a result, Turkey's secularist establishment has increasingly been left in an anachronistic position that fails to withstand the test of the long-cherished state target of reaching the level of "contemporary western civilization" that is the EU.[55] Such a pro-EU move by the JDP exposed the state elites to the charge that the establishment is still embedded in the "modernization project" of the nineteenth century that seems irreversibly eclipsed by the contemporary EU's post-modern project.[56]

Indeed, the JDP capitalizes on EU membership by not only presenting the EU as "the twenty-first century phase of modernization" but also by repositioning itself as a modernizing Islam-sensitive force, moving its socio-cultural identity from the fringes of policy into the centre.[57] While the secularist state elites have increasingly found themselves less in touch with the EU project as a whole, the dominant Islamist political movement under the JDP has come to the fore as a pro-EU political force in the system. Hence the JDP strives to realize its political stature first by giving up on confronting the secular sensitivities of the state at the domestic level, and, secondly by enforcing its sensitive political position by synchronizing its preferences with the EU conditionality. By so doing, the JDP has successfully integrated itself into the internal and international channels of legitimacy.[58]

Emerging successfully out of the fringes of the anti-systemic Islamist Refah Party, the JDP government has crucially found a politically rewarding refuge in discourse of the EU membership process, which is utilized against the politically influential discourses of state security. In the process of engaging and eventually transforming the state security practices, EU membership conditionality has proved particularly useful in helping to shape the JDP's democratizing policy preferences without it having to denounce its Islamic sensitivities, letting the latter comfortably stay within frames of the electorate's socio-religious identity. It is crucial to note that Turkey's recent struggle for the EU membership was fervently upheld by the country's once notorious and maverick "Islamist", the incumbent PM, Recep Tayyip Erdogan, and his party's previously Islamist members.[59] Indeed, the EU membership struggle the party's reputation in international circles and the media to such an extent that some argued that PM Erdogan "has staked his political future on the EU".[60]

Overall (and in line with the EU membership requirements), the JDP government under the leadership of Erdogan passed a series of radical reforms with a view to harmonizing the country's civil-military relations, judicial system, and human rights practices. These measures included: increasing the ratio of civilians to military officers on the National Security Council, electing a civilian to head the NSC's secretariat, removing military representatives on the boards of the Council of Higher Education (YOK) and the Radio and Television High Council (RTUK), granting Kurds broadcasting and cultural rights, and breaking traditional inflexibility over the Cyprus question.[61] Thanks to the synergy generated by EU membership, reforms in almost all walks of life, and an impressive grass-roots network, the JDP government was able to switch from confrontational identity politics to service politics providing crucial social and economic services to a larger populace such as more accessible health care and housing credits and better infrastructure for poorer regions.[62] Lastly, it should be noted that prior to the July 2007 national elections the JDP government was anxious to take further hold of the political centre and also prove once more its transformation from an "Islamist" party into a "western-oriented" one. Due to these aims, it reshuffled its internal party structure by boldly replacing 160 parliamentary members with newcomers "who appealed to different segments of society such as women, social democrats, liberals, Alevis, Kurds, and non-Muslims".[63] Consequently, it seems reasonable to claim that Islamic political identity has been changing under the JDP government. Can a similar change be detected in secularist state identity and policies?

Changes in secularist state identity

As mentioned, secularism is one of the constitutive dimensions of the political rationality of the Turkish state establishment. Indeed, the state ideology concedes a tenacious weight to secularism, which produced a considerable normative justification for the military interventions in the past and continues to do so.[64] In general, such excess gives rise to a politics of "militant secularism".[65] As Feroz Ahmad—a prominent historian of Turkey—wrote: "the possibility of another coup [after the 12 September 1980 coup] is always present so long as the Turkish army perceives itself as the guardian of the republic and its Kemalist legacy".[66] One can argue that more than ten years on, Ahmad's prediction continues to hold ground with an important caveat: the military does not have to bother staging direct coups to uphold its political muscle because of the availability and efficiency of extra-political techniques of political intervention. Out of a repertoire of such intervention techniques, the military has used the power of mainstream print and visual media to hype-up concerns over the "secular nature of the state" by way of securitizing Islamic identities in order to topple or change governmental policies governments as it did in 1997.[67] The basic credentials of parliamentary democracy, have, meanwhile clearly been sidestepped. This is particularly visible when we compare the reactions by the military towards the electoral successes of two Islamist parties, namely the Refah Party in 1997 and the JDP in 2002. The military stage-managed the 1997 coup, with the help of the mainstream media that acted as "functional securitization actor" in representing the Refah government as an "*Islamist* domestic threat" to "the *secular* nature of the state".[68] Yet this kind of dismissive and outright reaction has not appeared against the so-called "moderate Islamist" JDP government. Instead, the military openly "accepted" the landslide victory of the JDP in the November 2002 general elections by plainly declaring the electoral result as the "will of the people".[69] The possibility of another open military coup against Islamists is believed to be unpopular amongst the military top brass.[70] However, opting "not to block" the JDP cadres from coming to power never means an unconditional toleration of its policies by the military.[71] The point often missed is that the military does not need to block the JDP in the first place anyway, because with the help of mainstream media and its alarmist security-savvy discourses and techniques, it is able to continue to exert its traditional influence to let or block certain policy initiatives by any government it deems "anti-secular". The military also manages such securitizations not simply by acting at times against the legal constraints, but precisely by using such legal precepts that provided the space to take up such securitizing moves.

What drives the military and other secularist state elites including certain segments of judiciary to cast a constant watch on the parliamentary democracy and the religious representatives of the people? The custodial non-democratic role of the state elites and military and their institutional political interventions are sustained by a security-informed task of "maintaining national unity".[72] The crucial ingredient in the military's role has been its constitutional-legal capacity to find political latitude by acting in the capacity of being the "guardian and guarantor of national security for maintaining national unity".[73] The latter is officially defined in relation to the "internal threats to the state unity" or "threats to Turkey's unitary state quality and secularism".[74] Behind its mistrust of politics and politicians also is the military's low esteem for the institution of party politics in general and the professional political class in particular. It is important to note that this mistrust has persisted in the EU candidacy period including the period of JDP government since 2002.[75] This attitude was particularly evident in the initial secularist reaction to the JDP by the military: the so-called "young officers" crisis that broke in the early 2003. Columnist Mustafa Balbay from the daily *Cumhuriyet* reported in a series of articles that some influential officers within the military were "uncomfortable" with the idea that a "moderate Islamist" government could take hold of the state with its "anti-secular inclinations".[76] Given the fact that the JDP government was newly formed, it was not clear as to what "anti-secular inclinations" the military had in mind other than the earlier political experiences of its leadership. Another example of secularist reaction that showed the continuing prevalence of the secularist identity of the military-led state elites can be given in relation to the EU-induced "University and Education Reform". According to the newly-established JDP government, the latter reform was designed in line with the EU reforms to "democratize" the higher education system by transferring more power to the lower-level representatives of universities from their state-appointed rectors, which necessitated changing Article 2547 of the Higher Education Council (YOK) Law.[77] Unsatisfied with this EU-induced reform initiative, some secularist university rectors and other representatives of YOK strove to bypass the JDP's political authority by acting as "functional securitizing actors". The activities of the latter included provoking the secularist sensitivities of the military by presenting the university reform not as one of a democratic necessity but of an "Islamist threat to secularism".[78] Playing with the raw nerves of the high ranking, secularist army officers by visiting their military headquarters, the representatives of the YOK sought refuge in the military's "political autonomy and authority in the system".[79] The military took the visit at the highest levels possible, namely by the offices of then Commander of the Army Aytac Yalman and Chief of Staff Hilmi Ozkok himself.[80]

Later, in April 2007, another secularist intervention into politics came amid the presidential election process in the summer of 2007. This intervention came in the form of a so-called "e-coup" or "online memorandum" that was staged from the Turkish Chief of Staff's official website, which declared that the army would not tolerate the governmental support given to (then Minister of Foreign Affairs and second man in the party) Abdullah Gul to become Turkey's next president[81]. This "online ultimatum" was issued amid the efforts of the secularist opposition party the Republican People's Party (RPP), which had earlier fuelled the allegations surrounding Gul's candidacy, claiming that his presidency would amount to an end of the secular Turkish republic and the start of an Islamist state. The RPP then applied to the Constitutional Court to annul the presidential election process on shaky legal grounds in an attempt to block Gul's presidency. Later the court decided to halt the presidential election process through "hitherto unapplied interpretation of the related constitutional provisions", which necessitated a call for early elections required in such deadlocks on a presidential selection.[82] While the military's ultimatum declared Gul's presidency unacceptable, he was nonetheless elected as the new President of the Turkish state. So even though the latest involvement by the secularists backfired, the spectacle of such an "e-coup" or "online ultimatum" and a whole series of legal sideshows and manoeuvrings, together with other media-savvy interventions, ensued for weeks. The episode showed that the secularist establishment has not cast away its right to make interventions or shed control over the government of people.[83]

Despite all the efforts of the JDP government to prove that it is not a threat to secularism, the unaccommodating attitude of the secularist establishment still lingers on. One recent example is the secularist "judicial coup" that appeared in the form of a crucial decision taken by the Turkish Constitutional Court (a central institution of the secularist state) to accept the case for closing down the AKP on the grounds that the incumbent government runs foul of the Republic's—narrowly defined and dogmatically protected—principle of secularism.[84] The Court eventually decided not to close down the party. But the crisis of government it yielded was of a catastrophic nature. The case for closing down the AKP was earlier strengthened by the Constitution's verdict on 5 June 2008 annulling the Parliament's amendments to Articles 10 and 42 of the Constitution that was supported by a clear majority of 411 MPs from several parties. The amendments aimed at strengthening equality before the law and eliminating the unconstitutional denial of the right to education of women wearing the headscarf. It is clear that the Court's attitude towards democratic politics not only bypasses popular will but also "legalizes arbitrary restrictions on the right to equal access to education, and erodes the separation of powers by permitting itself to act outside of the legal order".[85] In addition, the news that broke about a recent unofficial meeting between one of the top ranking generals of Turkey's secularist army and the vice president of the Constitutional Court has also given fuel to the allegations that the Court's decisions are affected by the military's well-known negative attitude towards democratic politics.[86] In all, the activism of the secularist establishment risks creating a system of an "undemocratic juristocracy" that is accountable to no one.

Consequently, it is clear that the secularist identity of the military-led state elites continues to punctuate the negative perception of democratic politics. The same is also true for the EU membership struggle. The secularist state elites in general, and the military in particular, have viewed democratic politics and EU membership largely from a security-based outlook and declined to appreciate the help of democratic politics in recasting domestic problems in non-security logic and language.[87] The elites have not fully embarked upon EU membership as a primarily political project, which is bent on changing the internal-political structures of aspirant states through "EU policy transfer". According to the state elites, the issue of a fundamental change in Turkish politics—that would change the political power structure at their expense—could be avoided by construing the EU membership process as a security-based bilateral negotiation process. This, in their view, would only invest the country's "material power sources" or invoke potential "security contributions" to EU security, rather than embracing a different political logic and agenda. The main reason for holding this kind of perception stems chiefly from the military-led state elites' reduction of national and international politics to a sacrosanct security mentality and statist discourse.[88] This standpoint on the EU widens the rift with the JDP government.

This is not to say that the military is openly against the EU membership. The military asserts that it is not against the EU. It has repeatedly sought to assure the national and the international public that it supports Turkey's bid for EU membership.[89] If so, should one not expect fewer interventions from the military in politics? We know that the EU's "civilian power" is bent on changing the non-democratic political behaviours of the aspirant candidate states.[90] In Turkey's case this includes an especially ambitious plan for transforming the exigencies of the non-democratic security outlook of the military and civilian bureaucracy.[91] Despite that and behind its ostensible official support the military views the EU political membership conditionality as potentially undermining of the national unity and integrity of the state.[92] In other words, the kind of EU membership the military espouses is not quite one which includes fully embracing the EU as "civilian power". Consequently, at a deeper level, it is rather uncertain whether the military will ever fully embrace the more pluralist democratic public space that the EU promotes. Bearing in mind past examples of damaging democratic politics, one can even argue that the military is likely to retain its "militant secularists" trepidations and interventions into domestic politics.[93]

To summarise, if we accept the definition of consolidation of democracy by a Turkish student of democracy as "a situation in which democracy becomes the only game in town, when no one can imagine acting outside democratic institutions", the securitization of Islamic identity reveals a salient truth: secularism often trumps basic features/institutions of democracy in Turkey.[94] Thus, in practice the civilian and military bureaucracy's secularist proclivity becomes the Achilles heel for any government in power. Also, when considered in this fashion, the military's identification with secularism attains a persistent political purchase that well exceeds the capacity to make or break the governments within the confines of electoral democracy. Indeed, it is this constantly active secularist gaze that endows the military with the necessary power to outperform the functions of a direct military coup. This type of action, well outside democratic institutions, is still evident even at the apex of the EU membership process, throughout which the military has craved to preserve its own power.[95]

The changing engagement of JDP with the secularist establishment

Critics of the JDP are right to point out that the above mentioned process of change lost its initial momentum after 2005, leading to a period of "reform fatigue" which strengthened the hands of the secularist establishment. During this period we have seen the slowing pace of democratization, a marked failure to pursue a democratic civilian solution to the Kurdish problem, and a retreat into growing nationalist demands after the increasing reluctance of some powerful EU states (France and Germany) to go ahead with accession talks. Some even take these developments as showing that the JDP "lacks a practical democratization agenda independent from the EU membership requirements".[96] It is also true that PM Erdogan's short-lived attempt to criminalize adultery in 2004 and his appointment of religious conservatives to certain bureaucratic positions handed ammunition to the politics of Islamophobia employed by the secularists. In all, however, such weak spots in the JDP are insufficient to explain the extra-political interventions. Such weaknesses are better seen as signs of a centre-right political party "based on an eclectic coalition of interests" acting by survival instinct and constantly influenced by domestic and global dynamics.[97] Besides (and despite) all these "bumpy" roads, the JDP government acts in line with the necessity of undoing the contexts and pretexts for the military's securitization attempts as a means to enhance its political capacity. Having being alerted by previous experiences of the military's politically devastating intervention techniques, the JDP has been largely vigilant in its steps and political moves, and in insisting by its assertions that it does not challenge "the security of the state", despite occasional protests to the contrary. The fact that JDP leader Erdogan strove to make peace with the military, judiciary and secular circles before coming to power attests to this cautionary stance.[98]

Consequently, a profound result of the newfound "liberal-democratic" orientation (and discourse in Islamist political identity in Turkey) is that it helps release the Islamists from the habit of providing ammunition for the secularist military to justify their interventions into the workings of democratic politics. Thus, after an ill-founded confrontation with the secularist establishment under Refah party rule in the mid-1990s, the new political movement of the JDP hedged its political bets by cleansing itself of any religious identity-driven security rows with the military-led state elites.[99] In large measure, the JDP has refrained from the discursive and institutional confrontations with the secularists, most visibly the military and the mainstream media. Therefore, it seems that the JDP is employing a "strategy of confrontation avoidance" because it is particularly aware of the unsettling confrontational identity dimensions in Turkey.[100] The JDP also seems "skilful" in not evoking any identity confrontations between "Islamists" and "secularists", since inflammatory securitizing discourse (with the secularists) can well lay the groundwork for extra-political and non-democratic state practices. As to the secularist state elites, devoid of any of the avenues/elements that were available to them (like previously-employed fiery rhetoric or religiously-informed policies) they seem to have found it increasingly difficult—albeit not impossible—to penetrate the governmental political domain.

In all, the politically unsettling identity dimension in Turkey (which helps to make Turkey seem a "torn country") is rendered increasingly superficial by the JDP's prudent and non-confrontational democracy orientated discourse induced by the EU membership process. Hence, the changes in Islamic political identity have been based on the changing contours of the "Islamist" discourse and policies that are successfully articulated by the JDP party elites and executed by the intermediary party officials.

Conclusion

This chapter has argued that Turkey's political conflicts emerge mostly from the securitizations of secular and Islamic identities by the state. Securitization generates a ground for the ongoing politics of identity between the secular state elites and the Islamic socio-political actors. Particularly since the Islam-rooted JDP government formed the government in 2002, the ongoing palpable anxiety and the misgivings inside and outside the country about Turkey's modern and Islamic identities are misplaced.[101] Since Turkey gained official candidacy status, Islamist political identity has been significantly transformed, whereas such transformation has not taken place in the secularist identity of the military-led state elites. As shown, the changing Islamist political identity bears significant ramifications for the future direction of the country.

We have seen that the formation and workings of the new JDP government challenge the monolithic view of Islam; they also challenge Huntington's thesis. The JDP carries out its political aims in part through the EU membership process, which requires Turkey to democratize its extra-political establishment and politics. It is in this sense that the JDP's interest in carrying out reforms in order to achieve EU membership seems particularly meaningful. EU membership offers not only an invaluable opportunity for stripping the military of its political weight and power but also for a fuller democratization of the political system. In the process of the EU membership struggle, the JDP also hopes to open up a legitimate political space for its religious electorate's demands for recognition.[102] In sum, the JDP aims to curb the political role of the security actors including the military by replacing the chronic and politically divisive security discourse and logic of state security, which wreck the social and cultural cohesion and diminish efforts of democratic consolidation.[103] The JDP's struggle for EU membership is hence closely related to its own survival instincts. On the other hand, the EU membership process systematically helps the "Islamists" to carry out a transformation both in "Islamist" party politics and in state policies because the process requires adopting democratic membership conditionality in all walks of life and abandoning religiously-articulated policy choices and fiery political rhetoric.[104]

In all, the chapter argues that all this transformation amounts to a significant "makeover" of Islamic discourse, changing it toward an openly "liberal-democratic" discourse. While the previous Islamists voiced their opposition by claiming that Turkey was not religious enough, the moderates now basically claim that Turkey is not democratic enough, and that the way to democratize is mainly through EU membership.[105] By so arguing, they seek to free themselves from often unfounded secularist charges and/or characterizations.

13

Bosnia—Religion and Identity

Svein Mønnesland

Samuel Huntington uses Bosnia as an example of a state situated on the borders between the Islamic, the western, and the Orthodox civilization that shows how the border interaction between these civilizations create conflict.[1] The main thesis of this chapter is that the deep underlying differences in religion and concepts of history found in the Balkans have been engraved into conflicts, but are not in themselves the cause of the conflicts in our time.

Bosnia was a feudal state in the Middle Ages, ruled by a *ban*, later king. Due to its geographical isolation, the ties with the Catholic Church and the Pope became looser, and a special Bosnian church organization, called the "Bosnian Church" (later wrongly termed "Bogomils") developed, organized as a monastic order. The Pope called it "heretic" and "dualist".[2] In addition there were Catholics in the north and west, and Orthodox in the east and south. Bosnia was a borderland between Catholicism and Orthodoxy, and although outside forces, especially Hungary, made invasions in order to include Bosnia in the Catholic world again, Medieval Bosnia was characterized by religious tolerance. The Bosnians seem to have found a way of coexistence of the three faiths. The people called themselves Bosnians, not Serbs or Croats. The religious picture in the Balkans gradually changed through the Ottoman expansion from the fourteenth century onwards. In the fringe areas, just outside the Ottoman Empire, Turkish expansion was a constant threat. The epic poems of ethnic groups living in these areas glorified the fight against the Turks.[3]

Among the Christian population living under Ottoman rule, no such epic works could be written, but here epic folk songs flourished. This heroic epic tradition was to dominate Serbian culture and mentality until the present time. During these centuries, the division between the Eastern Ottoman Empire and the western states was indeed conceived as a clash of civilizations: a struggle not only between states, but also between Christendom and Islam.[4]

The urban centres in the Balkans became completely orientalized. This oriental urban culture, with its bazaars and artisans, had an enormous impact on Balkan culture and mentality. The peoples of the Balkans, Slavs, Albanians, Greeks and Rumanians alike, were deeply influenced by the centuries under Ottoman rule. Their food, folk music and language were shaped under Turkish influence. It is reported that in Bosnia under Ottoman rule, there was a fusion of Christian and Islamic customs and practices among ordinary people. There was a peaceful coexistence of religions, but intermarriage was not practiced until the twentieth century. In the Ottoman period there was no internal warfare based on religious grounds. The internal hostilities were the result of the economic and social inequalities, between the (mainly) Christian peasantry and their Muslim landowners.

By the end of the seventeenth century the Ottoman Empire began a slow but steady contraction. The Balkans became an area of rivalry between the great powers: Austria, Russia, and the Ottoman Empire. Within the Ottoman possessions in the Balkans, revolutionary national movements increased in strength, aided by the general popularity of nationalist ideology. New states, such as Serbia and Greece, gained independence. In the second half of the nineteenth century, the concept of ethnicity or nationality spread to the Balkans from Western Europe and to Bosnia from the neighbouring nations, Croats and Serbs. The religious differences were increasingly interpreted as a sign of national identity. Being Orthodox meant also being a Serb, and Catholics were classified as Croats. Within this context the Bosnian Muslims too were increasingly aware of their specific identity.

The new Balkan states that emerged during the nineteenth century were conceived as nation states. Nationalism, imported through the German tradition, was based on the notion of a common language, history, culture and religion.[5] The cornerstone of nation building was the liberation of the Christian peasants from their Turkish overlords, and the struggle of the Orthodox churches against Islam. Turkish rule was depicted in black colours. The demonizing of the Turks and celebration of the pre-Ottoman states was the very foundation of the new states.

In the new national states the mixed nature of the population presented a problem. Minorities, especially Muslim ones, had no place here. From the very beginning of the emergence of new states, there was a steady flow of Muslim refugees, especially Turks, to areas still held by the Ottomans. This was partly a forced migration, often resembling ethnic cleansing. The slogans were, at least implicitly, Greece for Greeks, Serbia for Serbs etc. Ironically, although demonizing the Turks, the different Balkan nations, Slavs, Greeks, Rumanians, and Albanians, continued to live and be deeply influenced by the Ottoman legacy in their way of life, mentality, food, music, and language (oriental loanwords). Even today this Ottoman legacy is what distinguishes the Balkan cultures from Central or Western European culture.

During the Second World War, 1941–1945, Bosnia was a battleground in what was both an occupation and a civil war. But the origin of the conflict was not in Bosnia. When Hitler and Mussolini occupied the Kingdom of Yugoslavia in 1941, Bosnia was included in a great Croatian state called "the Independent State of Croatia", and ruled by the notorious Ustasha regime. The Germans used the "divide and conquer" method, letting the Ustashas massacre Serbs. The Ustashas, who wanted to present themselves as real Croats, "the flower of the Croatian nation", did not persecute the Bosnian Muslims, except for some anti-fascists. Serb extremists, Chetniks, mainly from Serbia, committed massacres against the civilian Muslim population in Bosnia. In addition there was a civil war along political lines with two resistance movements: the Communist-led Partisans and the royalist Chetniks, who gradually collaborated with the occupants. The conflict in Bosnia during these years was not primarily a clash between Christians and Muslims. It was a struggle for power in the future, post-war Yugoslavia: should it become a Communist state or not? There was indeed a clash between Catholic Croats and Orthodox Serbs, where religion played an important role. The Ustashas demanded forced conversion of the Orthodox to Catholicism. Extremist Serbs committed atrocities against Muslims. But the main struggle was between a multi-national, non-religious communist liberation movement, the invaders, and their supporters. Notably, the atheistic Communist ideology did not prevent huge swathes of the population, of all religions, joining the Partisan forces.

In the first decades after the Second World War, the Muslims in Bosnia had to declare themselves in censuses as Serbs, Croats, or "Yugoslavs in the sense of nationality". In the 1971 census, after a long discussion in the Communist Party, it was decided that the term *Musliman* (with a capital letter) should be introduced as a national designation (as distinct from *musliman* denoting religious affiliation). The Bosnian Muslims would have preferred the traditional name Bošnjak (English "Bosniak"), which became the official term after the fall of Communist Yugoslavia.

The break-up of Yugoslavia and war in Bosnia

After the collapse of the Yugoslav Communist Party in early 1990, the break-up of the Yugoslav Federation was difficult to avert. Serbia's communist leader, Slobodan Milošević, had turned to nationalism and wanted a centralized state, while Slovenia and Croatia wanted a looser federation. Different political forces came into power in the six republics and two autonomous provinces during the first multi-party elections in 1991: former Communists and anti-Communists, but all of them more or less nationalistic. Slovenia, Croatia and Macedonia declared independence, while Serbia (still called Yugoslavia), under Slobodan Milošević, wanted to keep as much as possible in a rump Yugoslav state (thus ensuring that all Serbs would be living in one state) but also including territories without a Serb majority. The brief war in Slovenia in the summer of 1991 led the Yugoslav People's Army (JNA) to be dominated by the Serbs. In Croatia, Serb-inhabited areas declared autonomy and clashed violently with Croatian forces, especially since the JNA intervened on the side of the Serbs.

After the fall of Communism, the tradition of multicultural rule continued in Bosnia. The government of 1991 had nine Bosniak, six Serb and five Croat members. President Alija Izetbegović was the leader of the Muslim (or Bosniak) party SDA (The Party of Democratic Action), a man without any political experience, like most of the new politicians after the fall of Communism. He tried as long as possible to keep Bosnia-Herzegovina together, advocating multicultual coexistence. In 1991 Bosnian Serbs started to declare autonomous areas and the civil Serbian population was being armed. Propaganda sharpened the tensions between the national groups. However, even after the war broke out in 1992, a third of the defenders of Sarajevo against Karadžić's Serb forces were Serbs, and the commander of the defence of Sarajevo was a Serb, Jovan Divjak.[6]

In 1991, before the war broke out in Croatia, the Serb leader Radovan Karadžić met with president Tudjman of Croatia for "secret" talks about Bosnia and Herzegovina. Both wanted to include parts of the territory in their respective republics, a reflection of the century-old aspirations from the Serbian and Croatian sides towards Bosnia. The problem, however, would be to decide how to divide the territory. The fate of Bosnia was to be situated between two rival nations, each of which had a part of their nation inside Bosnia and Herzegovina. The war in Croatia in 1991 troubled relations between Serbia and Croatia, but the aspirations to include parts of Bosnian territory did not weaken. After the peace settlement in Croatia in early 1992, the situation in Bosnia-Herzegovina was tense, with the republic having two choices. Bosnia-Herzegovina could either become independent or join Serbia and Montenegro in a Yugoslav state. This was a contested topic, on which the European Community imposed a referendum on 1 March 1992. Although 70 per cent of Bosniaks and Croats voted for independence, the Serb leaders could not accept this, and began military actions in order to keep the republic under Serb control. This was met by spontaneous demonstrations in Sarajevo, and war was inevitable. Serb forces encircled the city to make the government give up, but the siege lasted for three and a half years. Serb paramilitary units started the ethnic cleansing of Bosniaks and Croats. Supported by the Yugoslav People's Army they established a Bosnian Serb army. A Bosnian Army (mainly Bosniak, but including Serbs and Croats), loyal to the Bosnian government, was put together to resist it. The Bosnian Croats led by the nationalist party The Croatian Democratic Union (HDZ), formed their own army, the HVO (Croatian Defence Force). After an initial alliance against the Serbs, in 1993 the HVO fought the Bosnian Army in Central Bosnia, but in 1994 the USA pushed through the "Washington Agreement" to impose a new Croat-Bosniak alliance. In 1994 Muslims also fought Muslims in the Bihać enclave, where a popular politician, Fikret Abdić, carved out his own mini state, rejecting Sarajevo's authority, with support from the Serbs.

The rhetoric of war and the war of rhetorics

Although religion and national affiliation was not the root cause of the war in Bosnia, these aspects certainly played a key role in the war rhetoric. This was the case especially when nationalist policies were accompanied by extensive propaganda efforts to demonise the enemy. In Serbian nationalistic rhetoric in the 1990s, the Ottoman past was revived and the present conflicts between Serbs and Muslims interpreted as Serbia defending European values. This was even more the case for Kosovo than Bosnia. The well-known Serb historian Dušan Bataković used the term "clash of civilizations" about the Serb-Albanian conflict even before the publication of Huntington's first article.[7] Bosnian Serb leaders like Radovan Karadžić invoked the Kosovo battle, consequently calling the Bosnian Muslims "Turks". This rhetorical strategy was aimed at making a convenient historical enemy out of the Bosnians. The Bosniaks were portrayed as Islamic fundamentalists, who allegedly planned to create a "green transversal"—a strip of connected Muslim-held territories from Macedonia through Kosovo and Sandžak to Bosnia—in order to strike jihad into the heart of Europe. A useful resource to the propagandists was the earlier labelling by the Yugoslav Communist Party of Bosniak dissidents as "pan-Islamist," "fundamentalist" and "nationalist" Muslims. Such claims were repeated by journalists, politicians and academics.[8] Radovan Karadžić knew that "such images would strike a nerve with a western audience"[9] and that it found resonance in a European tradition of "Orientalism". The war in Bosnia was therefore often portrayed in western media as a conflict between Muslims and Christians, between eastern and western civilizations. However, both in the beginning of the war, in 1992, and towards the end, in 1995, Catholic Croats and Muslim Bosniaks joined forces against Serbian (Christian Orthodox) forces. One of the groups in Bosnia, the Muslims, was referred to in religious terms so western observers easily got the impression that religion was the main controversy. It was not known that this was in fact the official term imposed by the Tito's Communist regime.

The Serb propaganda machinery referred to Alija Izetbegović as a fundamentalist and terrorist. It is true that he had been jailed by the Communists as a fundamentalist, after a political trial in 1983, for his text *The Islamic Declaration* (a rather fundamentalist call for an "Islamic order" in states with a Muslim majority, written in the 1960s). In fact, this publication, as acknowledged by renowned expert on Islam, Gilles Kepel, showed that Alija Izetbegović at the time was a part of the intellectual Islamist revival amongst the whole Islamic umma.[10] However, his writings became more moderate in the 1980s, and his political appeal was mainly to the secularized urban classes and intellectuals in Sarajevo. As a politician in the 1990s he started as a moderate, but was forced by the circumstances into a more and more defensive line, in the end even defending a rump-Bosnian state with a Muslim majority.

As a result of the conflict, Bosniak extremists developed an Islamic propaganda similar to the Serbian one, creating myths and demonizing their enemy. Historians tried to present Bosnia as a land belonging mainly to the Muslim Bosniaks, while Catholics and especially Orthodox were described as newcomers. The Muslims of Bosnia were presented as victims to Great Serbian hegemonism. The Islamic tradition of Bosnia was emphasized, a cultural tradition that had been prohibited until now. Oriental words were introduced in order to underline this eastern tradition. Islamic leaders became more visible in the public sphere than before, and new mosques were built, mostly with support from Islamic states. Many people became interested in religion and their roots, as a natural response to the horrors of war.

Since religion, and not language, was what divided the groups in Bosnia, religious monuments and symbols were made into available targets for nationalistic forces. Mosques, churches, and monasteries were burnt or torn apart. Because of the anti-Muslim rhetoric, it is difficult to identify the extent to which the religious dimension contributed to the conflict. Nationalist Serb propaganda was certainly made easier due to the fact that the enemy was Muslim. It was possible to make present-day propaganda a continuation of Serb nationalistic rhetoric, known to every Serb, even the most uneducated. The Kosovo epic was revitalized, and the Serbian Orthodox Church participated in the propaganda. Historical myths became a part of the political discourse.

On the Croatian side, the old notion of Croatia being the *antemurale christianitatis* was used in the rhetoric. Bosnia, and especially the Bosnian Muslim population, was again "crucified" between two rival nationalisms. But was this really a clash of civilizations? Many Bosnians, regardless of their religious or national affiliation, would say that this was an artificial situation, created by the warlords, for whom it was important to impose a negative picture of the enemy. The best proof against such a clash argument is the fact that the interethnic relations in Bosnia improved very soon after the war. Not that the political problems were solved by the Dayton agreement, as extreme politicians continued to try to split the population. But ordinary people soon began to communicate and have normal contact. There were almost no incidents of ethnic hatred, terrorist acts etc., as one would have expected after a bloody war. And this was not due to the presence of international forces and police. Ordinary people very soon started to behave in a pragmatic way. The interethnic relations could not be compared to the tense situation among Catholic and Protestant neighbours in Northern Ireland. The war was not conceived, by ordinary people, as a clash of hostile civilizations, but as the result of cynical politicians and competing elites in the former Yugoslav republics.

For years the international community was not able or willing to put an end to the war in Bosnia. The Srebrenica massacre of some 8,000 Bosniaks by the Bosnian Serb army under General Ratko Mladić in July 1995 led to NATO air attacks on Serb positions later that summer. When Croatia conquered the Serb-held areas in Croatia (entailing massive "cleansing" of Serbs),

Croat and Bosnian government forces in Bosnia came on the offensive. American diplomacy stopped the Croat-Bosniak military advance, bringing the Bosnian, Serbian, and Croatian presidents together to negotiate a peace in Dayton, Ohio, in December 1995. The Dayton peace accords provided for Bosnia to be divided into two "entities", the Bosniak-Croat Federation and the Serb Republic, leaving few prerogatives to the Bosnian state level. The Federation was further divided into ten cantons dominated by Bosniaks or Croats. In this way the international community followed the logic of the nationalists, that a state should be organized according to ethnic or national affiliation.

The rest of the Islamic *Ummah* attempted at times to intervene in the conflict: the Muslim Brotherhood of Egypt declared a jihad against Serbia, Iran sent *pasdaran* forces in support of the Bosniaks, and there were Bosnian mujahedin, the most famous being Abu Abdel Azis "Barbaros", fighting as a detachment of the 7th Brigade in the Bosnian army.[11] But the differences between the Bosniaks and the "holy warriors" mainly from the Arab world were large, and the mudjahedin force had to be separated into a special unit (the *El-Mudzahidun* Brigade) to avoid problems. Attempts to impose the veil, and beards on men, were highly unpopular locally. Moreover, the Afghan experience had scared potential Arab government sponsors, who wanted to maintain strict control in order to avoid the formation of extremist groups that could be used against them. When Bosnia attempted to get support from the West, and specifically from the United States, the pan-Islamic military units were disbanded.

Huntington's fault line: an assessment on the sources of the conflict

Was the war in Bosnia a war between Christians and Muslims? If the previous analysis is correct, the cause of the war in Bosnia can hardly have been ethnic hatred or centuries-old conflicts, but a disagreement about the political affiliation of the republic, and rivalry between two neighbour states over Bosnian territory (and even rivalry between Muslim fractions). In other words, the war in Bosnia was for classical motives of war: territories, natural resources etc. The outcomes of war and ethnic cleansing would probably have been the same even if the part of the population that resisted Serb aspirations had belonged to any other religion or ethnic group. The aim was not to extinguish a certain religious group, but to have control over territories and expel the population belonging to the other nations there.

In the Balkans, religion and nationality are closely interwoven. However, the conflicts in the Balkans in our time have not been exclusively between Christians and Muslims. The war in Croatia was between Catholics and Orthodox, and we have even seen deep conflicts between Orthodox brethren in Montenegro, i.e. even within the same state. Also between other Orthodox groups there have been conflicts, for example between Macedonians, Serbs and Bulgarians. An indication that the religious split between Muslims and Christians does not in itself lead to conflicts can be found in the tolerant situation among Albanians. Of all the Albanians in the Balkans, about 70 per cent are Muslims, about 20 per cent Orthodox, and about 10 per cent Catholics, but religion has never been a source of tension or conflict. Nor has it been possible for neighbour states to use this split in order to achieve political goals.

More specifically, the Bosniaks were traditionally "European" Muslims, liberal Sunnis. They stayed away from radical Islamist ideas. Also, as in the rest of Yugoslavia, half a century of Communist rule with strong secularising pressure had made a strong impact on the Bosnian Muslim population. By the time war started, a whole generation was strongly secularized. Their lifestyle was not different from that of their Yugoslav compatriots. For many Bosnian Muslims only their first name was a signal of their cultural identity. But when that turned out to be a sufficient cause for being ethnically cleansed, a new wave of nationalism and interest in their identity arose. After the war broke out, radical, anti-modernist tendencies became visible. Those groups associated with the "Islamic awakening" of the Middle East, often called Wahhabis by their opponents, constituted, however, a fringe phenomenon. The resurgence of religion was a phenomenon observable all over Yugoslavia as a result of the fall of communism and the experiences of war.

Although oversimplified, it cannot be denied that there is a historical division between the peoples of South Eastern Europe who for centuries lived under the Ottoman Empire, and those who lived outside, in Western Europe. In a macro-historical perspective, Huntington's description illuminates important cleavages. The peoples living inside the Ottoman Empire were excluded from the main cultural, political and economic currents in the West. However, when applied to the present-day situation, the situation Huntington himself claims to explain, and when his argument is transformed to the security level (that is the "clash" level) by seeing cultural divisions as triggering conflicts, this description does not contribute to the understanding of the situation. When explaining political events in Western Europe, few would resort to historical events that took place many centuries ago. Furthermore, what Huntington says about economic development has already turned out to be false. The "Orthodox" countries Bulgaria and Rumania are EU members, while the "western" country Croatia is not. And most importantly, the conflict lines in the 1990s did not follow the "fault line" between western nations on one side and Orthodox-Muslim nations on the other.

Conclusion

Two conclusions would obviously be false: to present the coexistence of the religious groups in Bosnia during the centuries as purely harmonic, or as an example of centuries-old hatred. The picture is much too complicated for such simplified statements. It is not true, as is sometimes stated, that people in Bosnia did not fight each other until the most recent war: during the last 150 years alone there were armed conflicts in 1875–1876, 1878, 1914–1919 and 1941–1945. However, the crucial point for our discussion here is that most of these conflicts were caused by outside forces: the Austrian occupation in 1878 and foreign occupation during the two world wars. Earlier, in the seventeenth and eighteenth centuries, wars in Bosnia were fought between Austria and the Ottomans. Armed conflicts were imposed from the outside. Not the civilizational fault lines but the politics of the Great Powers made Bosnia a battleground. The nearest Bosnia came to a civil war was during World War Two. But again, the roots of the conflict did not stem from Bosnia itself, but from the outside.

In spite of a common language, it was never possible to merge the Bosnian population into a common national identity. In some periods, this seemed to be sustainable, and some individuals succeeded in attaining a real Bosnian identity, but as a whole the population remained deeply divided. Due to the religious cleavages in Bosnia, as a borderland between East and West, the forces behind the wars could use these differences for instrumental purposes and for mobilizing their potential forces. Political entrepreneurs exploited religion, old myths, prejudices and national pride, aiming to split the population and divide the country. The rhetoric of the warmongers presented the war in Bosnia as a clash between Christian, pro-European forces and Oriental fundamentalists. It did not make it easier for the Bosniaks that they were called "Muslims" in western media. Serb nationalists used the traditional Balkan term "Turk", meaning Muslim. Historical myths were a part of the political discourse. Many misconceptions of the nature of the conflict were thus spread by the propaganda and less informed journalists. In one sense religion became a part of national identity.

In the recent history of the Balkans, there have been no religious wars in the sense that religion has been the cause of the conflict. Nor was there a conflict between pro-European and pro-Oriental forces. The conflicts in the Balkans should therefore be interpreted as more "normal" than is usually the case; as conflicts between competing interests, similar to conflicts found in other parts of Europe at various times. However, since nationalism was of paramount importance in the conflict, and religion was a part of nationalism, religion had causal power. Religion was to a certain extent used as an instrument by fanatical leaders. Civilizational clashes had some influence, since they could be used to mobilize support. In Bosnia, there is a complicated relationship between the existing animosity amongst the different groups and the cultural and religious background of Europe's melting pot.

14

Spain—The al-Andalus Legacy[1]

Elena Arigita

The historical legacy of al-Andalus and its different interpretations throughout history gives Spain distinctive characteristics within the European context. Following the scheme of what was termed by Huntington as a "clash of civilizations" Spain could be defined as not just the geographical periphery of a "Christian world" but also, and above all, as a border area of conflict between two civilizations, Christianity and Islam. The 2004 terrorist attacks in Madrid and so-called "jihadist" literature distributed through web pages, which claims al-Andalus as a territory of Islam, help strengthen this perception of Spain as a battlefield of two civilizations defined essentially by religion. In fact, in public debates in Spain, the existence of cultural values and identities forged by belonging to a given civilization/religion are increasingly assumed as an axiomatic and irrefutable truth. Both the "alliance of civilizations" proposed by President Jose Luís Rodriguez Zapatero in the aftermath of 11 March 2004 and the opposing idea of a "clash of civilizations" rely on and strengthen this discourse.

This chapter will examine the complex dynamics that emerge from an accumulation of negative images through the centuries and which fuel public perceptions of Islam today. The institutional regulation of Islam as a religion by the state in contemporary Spain, and the place it occupies within the current public-political debate, will be analysed.

Religion, state and the interference of the Islamic legacy of al-Andalus

al-Andalus represents a unique legacy within the context of Europe. From a historical standpoint, eight centuries of continuity, and the remarkable cultural and scientific achievements make al-Andalus unique. The ideological connotations of the interpretation of this period with respect to the formation of the modern state and Spanish national identity are also very important. Eight centuries of Islamic domination in the Iberian Peninsula, the historiographic interpretations of that legacy built from the Middle Ages to the present day, the powerful orientalist imagery it offered to European Romanticism, and its image in Arab literature make al-Andalus an inescapable and at the same time complex reference for reflecting on a world defined schematically by opposing civilizational blocs.

The Islamic legacy of al-Andalus has been (and still is) the object of substantial historiographic controversy that is repeated in different periods in Spanish history and which transcends the limits of a single academic discipline to become a core part of the definition of Spanish identity against "the other" Muslim identity. The Arabist María Jesús Viguera describes al-Andalus as an interference in the medieval historiography of the Iberian Peninsula that materialises into two apparently different images which serve the same purpose: to alienate al-Andalus, to turn it into something foreign, dangerous and necessarily incompatible.[2] Viguera distinguishes two periods: from the eighth to the eleventh centuries, al-Andalus and Islam enjoyed their greatest preponderance in the peninsula and were perceived as a danger by Christian historiography; from the eleventh to the fifteenth centuries, when the Christian monarchs gradually strengthened their position, al-Andalus started to be projected as a problem that had to be resolved, and it became necessary to "know" the enemy. This second stage was also characterized by what Viguera describes as an "erroneous idealization" that aimed to extol the enemy in order to magnify the eventual victory over the latter.

In modern times, al-Andalus disappeared from the "history of Spain" and was defined as an exceptional period in the broader narrative of a Spanish identity whose essence was Catholicism.[3] The official historiography of Spain was in turn strengthened by the religious identity of the state, which was traced back to the sixteenth century's embryonic "modern" state shaped as confessional and even exclusive, and where the Catholic Church already played a pre-eminent role that continued for centuries. As evidence of the link between Spanish identity and the Catholic Church, José Álvarez-Junco mentions the 1812 Constitution of Cadiz, inspired by the liberal revolutionaries, which, in his opinion, stated "with shocking bluntness" that: "The Roman Apostolic Catholic religion, the only genuine one, is and shall perpetually be, the religion of all Spaniards".[4]

The short-lived Republic introduced by the 1931 Constitution marks the first and only time that a separation between Church and state was considered. The abrupt end to the Republic and the new legislation introduced by the Francoist dictatorship in 1945 reaffirmed the confessional state even more strongly, and at the same time reconfirmed a Spanish identity essentially linked to Catholicism. Thus, under Franco's regime, Catholicism once more became the religion of the state, as Principle II of the Law of Principles of the National Movement of 1958 recognized that it was the "only one true religion, inseparable from national conscience, which will inspire its legislation".[5] Despite the severe restrictions imposed by the dictatorship on religious freedom, it was paradoxically the regime's recognition of the Catholic Church which opened the door, following the Second Vatican Council in 1965, for the rights of confessional minorities to start to be recognized, albeit with restrictions, although the religious identity of the state continued to be guaranteed.

The institutional regulation of religions in contemporary Spain introduces the separation between Church and state, and could be considered to denote a break with the historical legacy of the confessional state. However, the current 1978 Constitution contains a specific reference to the Catholic Church in an article that lends itself to a certain degree of ambiguity. The Constitution explicitly mentions the separation between religion and state, but it also introduces a formula that allows for privileged collaboration with certain confessions.[6]

The Organic Law on Religious Freedom develops the modalities of that privileged relationship between the state and certain confessions that must fulfil the condition of *notorio arraigo* (being well established), a concept that represents the legal recognition of a specific confession taking into account its "scope" and "number of believers". The definition of the concept of *notorio arraigo* is complex and uncertain, giving rise to open interpretations that have allowed history or "historical scope" to be included as arguments. Thus, and despite the numerical and organizational limitations of the incipient Muslim community in Spain at that time, in 1989 *notorio arraigo* was granted to Islam precisely for historical reasons and in the following terms: "Islamic religion is one of the spiritual beliefs that has configured the historical personality of Spain. Our culture and tradition cannot be separated from the religious foundations that have forged the most profound essences of the Spanish people and character".[7]

Thereafter and until 1992, the basis of a dialogue was established between the State and the Muslim community. At the same time, parallel agreements were concluded with Protestants and Jews that culminated in the 1992 Cooperation Agreements. Once again, the signing of the agreements with the religious minorities entailed a review of the historical legacy, this time to repair what was perceived as a historical injustice, since 1992 marked the 500th anniversary of the taking of Granada, the last Muslim kingdom, by the Catholic monarchs. The Cooperation Agreements signed with the confessional minorities must therefore be understood as part of the logic that has gradually forged the historical pre-eminence of the Catholic Church, and its example inspires the relations between different religious faiths and the state.

The signing of the Cooperation Agreement with the Muslim community was but one of several events in 1992: the commemoration of the "discovery" of America, celebrated as "The Meeting of Two Worlds"; the inauguration of the King Abd-el Aziz Al Saud Mosque in Madrid by the King and Queen of Spain and Prince Salman Ben Abdul Aziz of Saudi Arabia; the "Sefarad 1992" ceremony in Toledo; the World Expo in Seville; an exhibition at the Alhambra on the Andalusi legacy and the peace conference in Madrid. All these events aimed to show the world that Spain had become a "normal" democratic country through a re-reading of its history, promoting al-Andalus as a mythical period of the coexistence of three cultures—Judaism, Christianity and Islam.

Making Islam visible in contemporary Spain

It is said that the Muslims were absent from the Iberian peninsula for four long centuries. This absence is usually traced back to the order to expel the Moriscos in 1609 and lasted until contemporary times, when so-called "immigrant Islam" appeared. In an important sense, the modern state is therefore built on rejection, and Spanish identity has, at the same time, been shaped in the absence of and in opposition to Islam.

However, before looking at when and how Muslims became visible in contemporary Spain, it is important to underline that Muslims have never been entirely absent from the "Spanish imaginary" during those three centuries following the expulsion of the "Moriscos" in 1609. Quite the opposite, they were

consolidated as the image of the "other history" although their religious identification came to form only one part of a ensemble of attributes and "Muslims" started to be identified primarily as "Moors" in artistic, cultural, festive
and literary manifestations.[8] Furthermore, the persistence of a stereotyped
image should not be considered as indicating the existence of homogeneity or
linearity; in contrast, the interference of the Islamic legacy has been updated
and adapted to circumstances to function always as a mobilising element and
a legitimating instrument at the service of political power.

Thus, the nineteenth century opened the door to the colonial experience in
Morocco and once again the interference of al-Andalus resurfaced to exert a
special influence on Hispano-Moroccan relations, since the orientalization
of Spain in the Romantic imaginary in Europe through its Islamic legacy
was interiorized so that the colonial adventure would be justified as a type
of reunion.[9]

The polarization of Spain into two sides—Nationalists and Republicans—
during the Civil War (1936–1939) also rendered the stereotypical image of
"Moors" ambivalent and made it work within the logic of the fractures caused
by the Civil War. On the one hand, the rejection of "Moors" was consolidated
with the participation of Moroccan troops alongside the pro-Franco troops,
coupled with the accumulation of the negative image of "Moors" that already
existed as the "traditional enemy" who now also became "traitors" collaborat-
ing with the National Front to overthrow the legitimate government of the
Second Republic.[10] On the other hand, Franco justified the mobilization of
Moroccan troops against the Republic as a new "crusade" of believers against
an "infidel" government.[11] Thus, the perception of Islam from every corner of
a Spain divided into two sides is extremely paradoxical but basically inherited
and reaffirms the cumulative image of the "historic other".

The consolidation of democracy during the 1980s, the economic development, the new immigration laws and the achievement of religious freedoms
enabled the installation, consolidation and also the emergence of visibility of
an incipient associative Muslim network, although this network was perceived
until the 1990s at that of "immigrants". In fact, the categorization of different
forms of Islam, which was to be developed in the 1990s, once again introduces
a dichotomy between an imported and alien religious tradition and another
that legitimately can claim its rootedness in Spain and Europe. However, this
time the dichotomy concerns different strands inside the Islamic tradition
(and not Islam in opposition to Christianity). This categorization is present
in literature on Islam in contemporary Spain, where a distinction is made

between Islam practised by immigrants and that of converts, but it also has been articulated by Spanish convert groups. Since the 1970s, small Spanish and European Muslim communities have been formed in Spain. Over time, they have achieved stability, a very visible presence in Spanish society, and are prominent interlocutors with the Spanish state. These groups vindicated a Spanish identity that rejected the still very recent legacy of Franco's National-Catholicism in the late 1970s and sought their legitimating reference as Spaniards *and* Muslims in the Islamic legacy of al-Andalus. Here, the memory of al-Andalus serves, once again, as a source of legitimacy to define a dissident identity, which also vindicates Islam as another part of the cultural heritage of Spanish and European identity.[12]

The conclusion of the 1992 agreement can also be understood as an attempt by the state to transform "immigrant Islam" into an "Islam of Spain". In fact, ethnic, doctrinal, and ideological differences characterise and differentiate between the Muslim communities that have formed in contemporary Spain, as well as their establishment in different locations and also their visibility. The institutional development that has taken place since the late 1980s led to the creation of national federations and an Islamic Commission of Spain in 1992 which constitutes the official representative body before the state, aimed at overcoming these differences.[13]

The current form of representation through an Islamic Commission of Spain led by the Cooperation Agreements of 1992 is certainly deemed to be very deficient in general, although the whole frame of the agreements it is not considered either by Muslim leaders or political actors and observers as having entirely failed.[14] While the failure of this system of official representation is systematically attributed by observers to the internal fragmentation of the communities and to the absence of clear leadership,[15] it is at least equally important to consider the deficiencies of the institutional model adopted for regulating Islam in Spain. In fact, this model, usually considered as very progressive, is probably a key factor that explains the inadequacy of the Islamic Commission of Spain as the only interlocutor to represent Muslims to the state.

As pointed out above, the agreements signed with the three minority confessions were formulated (and imposed) following the model of the historical relationship established with the Catholic Church. Among the latter, however, the absence in Islam of structures comparable to that of the "Church" and of ecclesiastical hierarchies is often advanced as an argument to criticize the state-sponsored form of institutionalization. Looking at all the tensions that emerged throughout the process of constitution of the Islamic Commission and its inoperativeness throughout its fifteen years, one can conclude that the model of representation through a single representative organ has proved to be weak to the point that even though this representative body continues to be the official interlocutor with the state, state agencies have opened up new informal means of dialogue with Muslim leaders. A second phase in the process of interaction between the administration and the Muslim communities after 2004 thus led to the gradual and continuing development of new forms of organization at the national level, as well as new forms of representation at the local and regional levels.

The interference of "security" in the aftermath of 11 March 2004

The impact of 9/11 caused a growing concern about Islam as a potential threat to Spain, as happened in other western countries, and this concern was infinitely heightened by the attacks of 11 March 2004 in Madrid. Subsequent to this, Spanish Islam has been directly articulated with a variety of security issues. Although various debates on Islam and Spain had existed for a long time, the effect of the events of 11 September 2001 and 11 March 2004 and their influence in the global public sphere reinforced in Spain the claim of a supposed clash between the West and Islam, assuming that a certain Islamic specificity makes integration impossible. Media and political intellectual debates on Islam and Muslims in Spain and Europe increased dramatically during the years that followed. Discussions, polemics, new interpretations with a very essentialist approach of Islam and the Muslim legacy in Spain in the light of present events took place; there was also a renewed interest in how Muslim communities are organized in other European countries and especially in the features and goals of the Muslim population of Spain.[16]

Right after 11 March, Spanish Muslim representatives were placed at the centre of attention in the course of a polarized political debate on the causes of and responsibilities for the attacks in Madrid. During the weeks that followed, Muslim leaders contributed to this discussion with statements to the press condemning the attacks and expressing their concern about the possibility that the Muslim population at large could suffer the negative impact of these acts in their daily life, but also acknowledging the general positive response of Spanish society. The associations encouraged their people to actively participate in blood donations and the demonstration against terrorism that took place two days after the attacks. While these specific initiatives need to be acknowledged, a lack of participation of Muslim voices can in general be noted in the Spanish public sphere; an absence which helps to reinforce the clichéd uniformed image of the Muslim as immigrant, poor and, in any case, alien to the Spanish society.

The attacks in Madrid had another effect on Muslims living in Spain through the implementation of various counterterrorism strategies that were to determine the ways in which the government interacted with the Muslim representatives. On the one hand, right after March 11 increasing attention was paid to the imams, to the point that they were considered partly responsible for the radicalization, or integration, of the Muslim population in Spain. On the other, the influence of certain Muslim countries was pointed out as a problem for furthering the integration of Muslims in Spain.[17]

The responsibility and influence of the imams upon the Muslim population was in general overemphasized during the months that followed the attacks. On the one hand, they were portrayed as the principal figures of religious authority within Muslim communities simply because of the fact that they lead prayers in the mosque. On the other, they were assigned an important role in the cultural or social mediation between Muslims and the host society.[18] This sort of stereotyped image of imams as leaders of Islam in Spain is contradicted by the remarkably diverse group of persons acting as imams as well as their variously defined responsibilities within the communities. Nevertheless, during the months that followed the attacks in Madrid, different proposals coming from the Interior Ministry saw the light concerning strategies to control radical preaching in prayer rooms across the country, but each of them provoked much controversy for different reasons. The early announcement of controlling *khutbas* and imams in May 2004 led to protests by certain Muslim representatives. They drew attention to the negative consequences of such initiatives, which implied a biased perception of Islam, and questioned their effectiveness with regard to the aim of combating terrorism.[19]

In relation to the influence of foreign countries on Muslim immigrants Wahhabism in particular has been pointed out as a possible source of radicalization.[20] Saudi Arabia has a stable diplomatic relation with Spain, and also promotes cultural and religious activities in Spain, which basically consist of the distribution of translated works of outstanding Saudi *ulama* and, above all, the creation of endowments to establish big mosques. Saudi Arabia also gives small donations for the establishment of prayer rooms. Although Saudi influence is evident in some of the big mosques, it is less evident when it comes to an effective influence in local associations and prayer rooms that have benefited from private donations from Saudis obtained through informal personal contacts. While financial contacts with Saudi Arabia or Saudi citizens are openly admitted by Muslim leaders, the claim to Wahhabi influence on Muslims is often rejected by them and it indeed appears to be less evident at the grassroots level of mosques and associations. Thus, the link between the funding on the one hand and an effective influence of Wahhabi teachings on Spanish Muslims and their radicalization can currently not be affirmed and requires more evidence and systematic research.

Morocco, is in important and complex ways, related to Spain, because of the historical and geostrategic relations linking both countries and also due to the fact that Moroccans constitute the largest segment of immigrants in Spain.[21] Both countries have established a range of cooperation in economic, cultural, immigration and anti-terrorist issues. However, while the post-11 March government announced its cooperation with the Moroccan authorities in order to tackle extremism and "increase our understanding of the Islamic community of Spain", studies conducted with Muslim leaders show that an official influence from Morocco is broadly rejected both by Moroccan and other Muslim leaders.[22]

Paradoxically, given the profound concerns that, according to opinion polls, the Spanish public harbours with regard to the integration of Muslims into the so-called Spanish lifestyle,[23] studies conducted inside Spain's Muslim communities highlight the extremely positive valuation of democratic values and civic rights by Muslims.[24] All in all, this asymmetry between the negative and stereotypical image of Muslims on the one hand and the findings of scientific studies about their integration points not only to the need for more systematic research about Muslims in Spain, but also underlines how highly ideologized the perception of Islam and Muslims as a "threat" is.

An alliance to counteract the "clash"

As has been shown above, 2004 marked a new turn for Muslims living in Spain, mainly in terms of visibility but also, and partly as a consequence of it, in terms of the internal organization of the community, all of which was influenced in different ways by the attacks in Madrid. The events in 2004 also modified Spain's objectives in international relations and its position in the so-called "war on terror". While Spain had taken a very active pro-American position right after September 2001, in April 2004 the new socialist government that won the elections of 14 March ordered the withdrawal of Spanish troops from Iraq, and just several months later Prime Minister Zapatero reoriented Spanish foreign policy by launching the concept of an "alliance of civilizations" in his first speech in the UN (in the 59th assembly of the UN, on 21 September 2004).

Since then, his proposal, which has also drawn sharp criticism, has gathered important support at the international level. The "alliance of civilizations" theme was later endorsed and used by UN Secretary General Kofi Annan and co-sponsored by the governments of Spain and Turkey. A basic document of November 2005 produced by the Spanish Ministry of Foreign Affairs specifically tackles the thesis of a clash of civilizations by proclaiming as one of its aims to "increase world awareness of the risks that a wall of misunderstanding may arise between the West and the Arab/Islamic world, and thus the threat of the 'clash of civilizations' may become a reality and put at risk the many positive aspects of mutual relations, and even imperil the whole framework of international relations".[25]

The specific reference to the clash thesis, as well as the concept of "alliance" as a means to counteract it, is not mere rhetoric, but it is an attempt to intervene in the ongoing debate on Spain's historical identity (in relation to Europe and Islam) and to reconfigure the spectrum of political strategies that are made possible by the latter. More precisely, the concept of alliance of civilizations needs to be situated in relation to the deeply rooted polarized understanding of Spain, which is defined either as a conflicted border zone that keeps back the Islamic threat from Christendom (or the West), or a fruitful crossroads of civilizations in which coexistence among religions/cultures is possible.[26]

These antagonist visions of Spain as either a crossroad of cultures or a "frontier state" of Christian-western civilization that has had to fight Islam over centuries becomes very clear when reading Zapatero's speech compared with one by former Prime Minister José María Aznar given the same day. While Prime Minister Zapatero was presenting his proposal "as representative of a country forged and enriched by different cultures" (21 September 2004) in his speech to the UN, José María Aznar emphasized in his inaugural lecture as visiting scholar in Georgetown a vision of an eternal Spain essentially Christian and eternally threatened by Islam:

"The problem Spain has with al-Qaeda and Islamic terrorism did not begin with the Iraq crisis. In fact, it has nothing to do with government decisions. You must go back no less than 1,300 years, to the early eighth century, when a Spain recently invaded by the Moors refused to become just another piece in the Islamic world and began a long battle to recover its identity. This *Reconquista* process was very long, lasting some 800 years. However, it ended successfully. There are many radical Muslims who continue to recall that defeat, many more than any rational western mind might suspect. Osama bin Laden is one of them."[27]

The term "alliance" was not only used by Zapatero, but also by Aznar, however, in a totally different approach. While the former was proposing an alliance of civilizations between the "western world and the Arab and Islamic world" to avoid "a new wall of hate and misunderstanding", Aznar suggested an "alliance for peace, security and prosperity, putting together all liberal democracies willing and able to act and fight terrorism"; an alliance for Americans and Europeans as a "community of values and common interests" that should be transformed into a "community of common actions".

The important point to make here is that both speeches, in spite of their essential divergences, share in a civilizational logic that perfectly coheres with old stereotypes of the historical other for the Spanish imagination. In the words of Gema Martín Muñoz, the stereotype "shares the *consensual culturalist paradigm* that the European and western world has forged about the Muslim world and the feel of western cultural supremacy" which traces its origins back to a long process beginning in the Renaissance and reinforced during the colonial period in the nineteenth and twentieth centuries. Thus, both terms either calling for an alliance of civilizations or an alliance of Americans and Europeans draw on a vision of two distinct and ahistorical cultural/civilizational regions "Islam" and "Europe" (or "The West"). In the case of Spain, this vision is reinforced by the conflicting visions of the Islamic legacy of al-Andalus.

This brief overview of the conflicting relation of Spain with the Islamic legacy of al-Andalus shows how a powerful image of Islam as the historical other for Spain and the Spanish identity has been constructed throughout centuries and keeps being revised in the light of present events. Thus, what Zapata-Barrero has addressed as a "historical anomaly" when referring to the interpretations of al-Andalus with regard to the history of Spain, is constantly revisited and updated in service of the political mobilization.[28] The stereotype functions on different levels, whether at the state level, in intellectual and academic production or in public debates, and it helps to reduce Muslim identities to one single stereotype which is basically perceived as unable to adapt to the Spanish lifestyle. While the academic research on Muslim communities living in Spain demonstrates a very diverse and plural reality as well as the explicit will of a wide majority of the immigrants from Muslim countries to fully develop their rights and duties as citizens of the country to which they have migrated, the stereotype persists and contributes not only to distorting this reality, but also to the frustration of their expectations.

Region IV

The New Borders

Atle Mesøy

The expression "the new borders" will here refer to several "entities". Firstly the new borders are within the western countries to which Muslims emigrated during the twentieth and early twenty-first centuries. If Huntington's claims are correct there will be conflicts and wars where the West and Islam meet, and today the West and Islam meet even within Western Europe and the US. Indeed, Huntington claims that the frontlines have been drawn at this new border.[1]

The burning of Salman Rushdie's novel *The Satanic Verses* and the strong reaction to the cartoons of Muhammad printed in a Danish newspaper have demonstrated differences between large parts of the Muslim population and ethnic westerners. However, the Muslim population in the West is far from homogenous. The duration of time that a group has settled in a country will influence how integrated the group in question is; some groups, such as the Pakistanis in Norway, came early and some, such as the Somalis in the UK, came at a later time; this influences their socioeconomic situation.[2] A variety of different traditions and relationships influencing Muslim emigrants' relationships with their new host countries, as well as variations in traditions and the history of the countries, ensures that it becomes harder to generalize between the various Islamic ethnic groups within the new borders. Moreover, ethnic groups often choose favourite countries to emigrate to, in many cases travelling from former colonies to the former colonial power, ensuring that the composition of Muslim communities in the West varies from country to country.

The second reference for the concept "new borders" will in this book be the virtual world of the Internet. The Internet is a system for communication and access to information. In its name, the World Wide Web (www), lies the concept of global availability, and with its growth rate of 80 per cent per year it is becoming the world's most extensive communication network.[3] The possibilities of the Internet are wide, and it has the potential to tie groups together on a global scale, enabling individuals of the same belief system to come together, and by Internet interaction strengthen or weaken their own perceptions of the world, including perceptions of a clash between civilizations.

Importantly, Islam is undergoing a process of redefinition within the new borders. The struggle over Islam is dynamic, and the frontlines are shifting. Islamic traditions are weak, the Islamic religious institutions are new and do not hold an age-old authority as similar institutions do within traditionally Islamic countries, thus opening up the faith for new interpretations of the Qur'ān and the Hadiths.

The authors of the following chapters will examine the above described issues and patterns of conflict within the new borders. Dominique Thomas will describe the most important reasons for the radicalization that a relatively high number of Muslim youth have gone through in the United Kingdom. These are youths that have gone through what Thomas describes as different types of ruptures including the disruption of ties to society. In the case of France it will be demonstrated that the jihad movement is closely connected to social class and the feeling of being excluded. The contributor on France, Farhad Khosrokhavar concludes there is a clash, but not the same clash Huntington describes. Atle Mesøy and Stig J. Hansen explore Scandinavia, a region that often has been perceived as lacking the interests and the connections western great powers have with the Islamic civilization. However, they show how globalisation has put Scandinavia on the borders of Islam. Scandinavia has problems with integration and Islamophobia, but has also benefited from the Muslim communities, a point that will be explored in chapter sixteen.

Even if the US suffered 9/11, the worst terrorist attack ever, and another earlier failed terrorist attack on the World Trade Center, radical Islamism has not developed in the same way within the US borders. The explanation according to Allen Hertzke lies partly in the culture of religion in the country and the way in which the US's traditions and laws support a freedom of religion and religious expression. The last chapter in the book introduces the virtual border on the Internet. Stephen Ulph demonstrates how the virtual community in one sense contributes to a global imagined community, a pick-and-choose "virtual civilization" that is unbothered by local conflict dynamics, creating a world where the fault lines between civilizations are re-invented and re-constructed in a clear form, far from the alliances of power within local contexts described in the previous sections, creating a deadly world-wide belief system.

15

Britain—Rejecting Western Modernity?

Dominique Thomas

The impact of recent events and the influence of radical preachers and clerics are two major factors that account for the considerable changes in the Islamist milieu in Britain over the last decade. Measures taken by the British authorities to contain the development of radical movements in the United Kingdom took the shape of laws against violent groups, be they Islamist or others identified as terrorist. These amendments brought about a series of arrests and repressive measures aimed at the jihadists (the closing of radical mosques, the freezing of private accounts, and the banning of certain organizations) under the umbrella of the Terrorism and Public Order Acts, which are considered unjust by many among the British Muslim community (both radical as well as moderate). Actually this policy played an important role in reinforcing a climate of tension and suspicion between Muslims and the British authorities. The Policy Exchange Report underlines that the increasing tension between a faction of the Muslim community and the British authorities accounts for the growth of radicalization and the development of the phenomenon of "rupture" between a number of British Muslims and the British mode of life.[1] Some emblematic figures of "Londonistan"[2] have been arrested, and some radical preachers have left the United Kingdom. Places of worship, such as the Finsbury Park mosque, the Fatima Centre, or Brixton mosque, have been

transformed and transferred to Muslim authorities known to be more concili-
atory in their dealings with the British authorities. In spite of these changes
within the Islamist field, the radical discourse has remained highly influential
among the believers who are dispersed throughout the United Kingdom or
who have joined jihadist fronts elsewhere.[3]

Radical Islamic preachers were widely influential in the process of radicalization, particularly among the younger generations. The Islamic associations
founded by preachers such as Abu Hamza al-Misri (Supporters of Shariah) or
Omar Bakri Muhammad (al-Muhajiroun) recruited mainly among young
people between the ages of 16 and 26 at mosques, prayer rooms, schools, and
universities. This generation represents a favourite target since it proved to be
the most receptive to the radical discourse already rooted in Britain.

The radical Islamist discourse revolves around two major lines. The first
aims to dissuade British Muslim youth from adopting the model of British
society by denouncing the very essence of western society and its moral and
cultural values. In this light, radical Islamist discourse seems to be in keeping
with the thesis of the "clash of civilizations" dearly defended by Huntington,
though with a major diverging point; indeed like Huntington the radical
Islamists believe that the clash of civilizations does exist, yet it takes place
between a modern corrupt western society and a virtuous Muslim world
whose ideals should be encouraged because they are noble.

The second line of this discourse defends the idea of an open war between
the Muslim world and the West by referring to the recent crisis between Islam
and the western world. This idea is currently nourished by the conflicts in Iraq,
Pakistan, and Afghanistan, and mobilizes many British Muslims since they
perceive these conflicts to be manifestations of a jihad against Islam.[4] Indeed,
for some radicalized youths, 9/11 is seen as a kind of revolutionary struggle
under the aegis of al-Qaeda; in this sense radical discourses exploited this
event as a catalyst to the process of radicalization.

The arrest of leading radical preachers has not curtailed their wider influence. It should be underlined that the spheres of radicalization among British
Muslims vary widely and do not depend only on a jihadist discourse. This
chapter seeks to demonstrate that more established Muslim groups living in
Britain have been trying to redefine their relation to British society and its
main values, namely secularism, democracy, and modernity. Their attempts
take the shape of protests or "rupture". Also explored are the ways in which
British Muslims' radicalization is far more complex than a mere clash of civilizations, since it also encompasses a clash between different generations of

British Muslims competing to put forth a redefined Muslim identity. It is worth noting too that radical Muslims reject the foundations of a traditional Islam adopted by the earliest generations of Muslim immigrants, hence the double rupture with the official representatives of British Islam on the one hand and the British authorities on the other hand. In the light of all these factors it will be argued that the phenomenon of radicalization in Britain is the result of a process peculiar to Islamic minorities living in the West and differs markedly from radicalization in Muslim countries.

Spheres of influence in radicalization

The spheres of influence in radicalization are widely varied and range from the ideological to the social, professional, and existential. For instance the profiles of the men responsible for the London attacks of 7 July and 21 July 2005 reveal that most of them attended some of the venues where radical sermons were preached. Thus Mohammad Sidiq Khan and Shezad Tanwir, who took part in the first attacks, had attended the meetings of the *al-Ghuraba* group formerly known as *al-Muhajiroun*.[5] The group that organized the attacks of 7 July espoused a strategy similar to that of the attacks of 9/11: that is they acted like normal citizens and developed clandestine contacts. That said, the protagonists of these attacks were ideologically and militarily prepared, either through the Internet or through spending time among the Islamist milieu in Pakistan. Indeed some British radicals of Indo-Pakistani origins had been arrested previously, which bears witness to the fact that radicalization was already well established among some British Muslim communities.[6]

The discourse of radical preachers such as Abu Hamza al-Misri, Abu Faysal or Omar Bakri Muhammad had Muslim immigrants recently settled in Britain as its main target.[7] Yet gradually some Muslims born in Britain who attended the Finsbury Park and Brixton mosques were convinced by this discourse, which aimed to explain why their integration into western society failed and much more importantly how any attempt at integration is synonymous with the weakening of their Muslim identity. This weakness is presented as the main cause of their reluctance to defend the Muslim community in general and the Islamist movements of their homelands in particular.

Radical discourses are particularly influential among Muslim immigrants who had recently settled in Britain. Thus the organisers of the failed attacks of 21 July attended sites of radical preaching such as the Finsbury Park and Brixton mosques yet neither demonstrated a high degree of engagement nor played an important role in these places. Some radical militants organized on the basis of national and religious factors. For instance, a broad Afro-Muslim identity played an important role in mobilizing the participants in the failed attacks of 21 July. The six members of the cell are all Africans (Ethiopian, Somali, Ghanaian) and none was born in the United Kingdom: Manfo Asiedu, Hussein Othman, Yassin Omar, Moktar Ibrahim, Adel Yehya, and Ramzi Mohammad came to Britain in the 1990s as political refugees.

Ties of solidarity effected through professional circles differ from the usual frameworks of social contacts and organizations among Muslim activists, such as mosques, college societies, or charities. Thus it was that members of the medical profession played a key role in mobilizing the cells that were dismantled after the failed attacks on London and Glasgow in July 2007.[8]

Other radical groups disrupted in Britain recently proved the importance of geographical proximity in the process of radicalization. Some groups lived in the same district, attended the same Islamic venues of worship or socialisation and became acquainted there. This is the case of most of the young men arrested in July 2006 for a failed plot to place bombs on aircraft and who hail from the London suburb of Walthamstow or from High Wycombe (Buckinghamshire).[9]

Radical British Muslims are characterized by their extreme heterogeneity. The perpetrators of the attacks of 7 July are from groups of British Muslims who have been living in Britain for decades now; some of them were even born in Britain.[10] This statement is confirmed on examining the backgrounds of the arrested members of the *Badat, Khayam*, and *Barut* groups or again that of the members of the cells dismantled in July 2006 and January 2007. Here again British Muslims of Indo-Pakistani or Afro-Caribbean origins were involved. This said, even though being British Muslim is a determining factor, the radical militants—except for those of 21 July 2007—have different sociological backgrounds. The average age of these militants ranges from 20 to 35. For some of them, and more particularly the Afro-Caribbeans, radicalization is a result of some trauma related to a social deprivation. For others radicalization is a consequence of social exclusion. Radicalization may also be caused by problems of integration, by unemployment, disillusion concerning the educational system's (failing) role in ensuring integration, and some feeling of injustice and discrimination.

Besides this, radical Islamist materials on the Internet are undoubtedly the second major sphere of influence. Two key facts help explain this trend: first, the arrest of the principal radical preachers in 2001 led to the transfer of radical discourses from mosques to web sites; second, is the coming to age of a new generation of the Islamist intelligentsia who have adopted the new technologies to disseminate their message. Having adopted the cyber-preaching model or the broadcast of Islamist news in the Muslim world, these groups focused their activities on the Internet—and as a consequence they no longer enjoy the same level of grassroots support in the United Kingdom.[11] Their supporters are web readers. This phenomenon has developed progressively since the 1990s, with the appearance of the earliest Islamist sites and forums in London.[12] Islamist groups, be they radical or moderate, have mostly developed their political communication strategy through the Internet. They have chosen this medium for many reasons: first, easy access to a virtual space on the web; second, a widespread readership; third, an opportunity for networking information and communication in such a way as to create a globalized Islamism; fourth, finding a route into mass communication after having been excluded from the traditional media.

The influence of the jihadist discourse from real and virtual places of radical preaching plays an important role in the process of radicalization. Yet the crisis of identity among British Muslims is another determining factor in the latter. This crisis is the origin of what I refer to as the "double rupture".

The phenomenon of "double rupture"

Radicalization is often synonymous with a disruption of ties with national and cultural identity and this is expressed through withdrawal into oneself. When the radical Islamists, whether born in Britain or recently settled there, criticize western society, contest its values and political authorities, they engage in a conflictual relationship that confirms Huntington's thesis. They call for an Islamic communitarian society to confront the western social model that presents itself as modern and universal. However, when some British Muslims question their own identity and culture, they also engage in a conflictual relationship with Muslim culture itself. Their agenda is to reform Islamic society by calling for a revival of the foundations of Islam. The particularity of the religious minorities in the West is that they intend to found a Muslim community in the West and to contest western ideals from within. This is an agenda that undermines the binary schemes of Huntington's theory.

Every single western country, indeed all western societies, are different, and none of them share exactly the same values and models. This is also the case for Muslim communities in the West since they emanate from many different countries. Even though Islam is a monotheist religion, the Islam practised in Pakistan differs markedly from that in Morocco. Moreover, the Muslim world is itself prey to the conflictual relations between different countries, doctrines, and cultures. Diversity within Muslim societies and cultures plays an important role in the mechanisms of radicalization and it has to be taken in to account if we are to obtain a fuller and more nuanced understanding of this phenomenon.

Thus, in Britain the Islamist milieu is considerably different from the one found in Spain or France in the way it encourages rupture. The Barelwi, Deobandi, Jamaati, or Tablighi schools in Britain may serve as a basis for radicalization and rupture if some of their pupils decide to break away from their families, friends and places of social interaction and accept a doctrine in opposition to the traditional Islam of their parents.[13] Most of these groups took part in the protest movements during the Salman Rushdie case in 1989, which was also an opportunity for British Muslims to draw the attention of the authorities to their aspirations to exercise political power at local council level and above.[14] Their involvement was a means of responding to their political and social demands: redefining places of worship and halal eating practices, establishing free private Islamic schools, developing electoral representation, reforming the representatives of Islamic institutions, and establishing a specific community response to deal with anti-Muslim aggression. At the time the Rushdie case was regarded as a form of humiliation and an attempt to secularize Islamic values. It also revealed the existence of westernized Muslim elites whose principal aim was to establish a regime of peaceful cohabitation with non-Muslim Britain. Even if this case was at the origin of a conflict it led to the reorganization of Britain's Islamic communities under the umbrella authority of the Muslim Council. From that episode also local associations were founded that participate in the wider Muslim Council of Britain, the official representative body. These associations do not question the political orientations of the British authorities. Nevertheless, they have their own agenda of social and religious objectives. Unlike the radical jihadists they do not preach for armed jihad in Iraq or in Palestine. These official associations are not opposed to taking part in political life in Britain and hence are willing to participate in parliamentary and local elections. They adopt a strategy of integration and concentrate their demands on improving the daily lives of Muslims[15] in a way that they deem respectful of their faith.

A new wave of British Muslim activism was inaugurated to campaign against certain governmental measures perceived as being harmful to Islamic values.[16] Such measures, along with the difficulty of integrating into British society, prompt some Muslim youths to reject it altogether. Their rupture is expressed through means different from those of the integrationist associations. For instance, internal signs of radicalization such as very regular mosque attendance, and outward personal manifestations such as public displays of piety are some of these, but they are not the most important signs of radicalization. We can refer to the tendency to revert to origins, as is the case with some British Pakistanis. Yet this can also be understood as a desire to mark one's difference from other members of one's native community as well as from the codes of British society, in the logic of a double rupture.

The rejection of national identity

The most important reason for radicalization among these British Muslims is that they do not identify with the traditional pillars of authority of British Islam.[17] Most of them, and particularly those militants in groups such as SOS or Ahl al-Sunna, reject all forms of national identity and withdraw from the places and activities that usually allow close contact with their fellow citizens. Importantly, these groups represent a small minority that probably does not exceed more than 5 per cent of the entire British Muslim population. Other radical militants, such as those close to the Pakistani jihadist movements in Kashmir, identify themselves as Pakistanis, even though they contest the political regime of their native country. A third wave of radicals are to be found among recently settled immigrants, mainly those who came from Iraq, Afghanistan, the Balkans and East Africa, and they do indeed identify with their original national identity. These communities are often aware that the problems of integration they encounter are caused by cultural barriers, yet they still stick to the religious teachings of their Islamic scholars.

This sense of exclusion is widely reinforced by the geopolitical context in the Middle East/Asia (Iraq, Palestine, Afghanistan) and by Muslims' belief that, since 2001, the British authorities have passed oppressive laws against them (the Terrorist Act, the Public Order Act). This feeling is reinforced by the provocative reaction of some elements of the British media with regard to Islam: the Danish cartoon controversy is a case in point. The fact that the Internet is being mobilised to fight Islamophobia means that this phenomenon is becoming widespread; indeed the rise of Islamophobia has become a major contributory factor for radicalization.[18] This perception of British society, a perception exploited by groups such as Hizb ut-Tahrir and Supporters of Shariah and the former al-Muhajiroun, accounts for the radicalization and recruitment of some British Muslim youth.

Social and ideological rupture

In some cases, personal experiences may lead the radical militant to turn to a discourse that answers his expectations and fulfils his repressed social frustration. In this sense radical discourse restores order and gives sense and identity to British Muslim youth. For some of them, discovering the earliest teachings of Islam corresponds to retrieving a kind of serenity, acquiring moral values and even answering some existential questions.

Radicalization often engenders a rupture with society, a rupture that marks the beginning of a process of discovery of another form of Islam. This Islam is different from the traditional Islam practised by most Muslim communities in Britain. It is an Islam that is founded on the teachings of the Sunna. A wide discrepancy exists between this radical teaching and the disciple's previous and feeble knowledge of Islam, often the legacy of traditional teachings. The new teaching is therefore the antipode of the traditional referents of a young Muslim, namely those of his family and community, and is closer to the earliest teachings of Islam. As a consequence, the new militant no longer identifies with the Islamic values of his parents or with the traditional representatives of his country.[19] Other youths break off from their parents because they do not practise Islamic religious rituals. In spite of their attachment to their origins, it is neither the language nor the national identity of their original country that matters but its link to Islam. Hence some Indo-Pakistani youths search for a new Islamic identity without necessarily trying to strengthen their ties with the Indo-Pakistani community. This complex behaviour is even more obvious when it comes to Afro-Caribbean radical youths who often abandon their original identity after their conversion to Islam.

The ideological rupture with traditional Islam is not the result of a modern discourse produced by a new generation of Muslims born and brought up in the West. Indeed, Islamists all over the Muslim world, be they the jihadist groups in Pakistan, Salafist reformists in Saudi Arabia, or the Muslim Brotherhood in Egypt, preach a revolutionary and reformist discourse that calls for a breaking off from the traditional cultural and ideological model of the countries where they live. They are calling for a modern Islamic society more respectful of the teachings of traditional Islam and critical of traditional religious practices.

The discourse of double rupture (with the traditional Islam and the corrupt West) is often used to form a new Muslim identity. Radical militants exploit this point to introduce the link of the Muslim to the *Ummah* differently. Rather they present themselves as defenders of the *Ummah* and of its Islamic values, regardless of national and regional differences. This explains why a Pakistani or black Muslim may accomplish a suicide attack in the name of the Iraqis, the Palestinians or any other Muslim people considered as being oppressed.

These radical militants' relation with the West is paradoxical. On the one hand they do not reject its technological modernity or for example western clothing, on the other hand they contest many of the principles of western society that they consider contradictory to their fundamentalist reading. This is the case with political principles such as democracy and secularism, with social principles related to education, women's role in society, or cultural practices related to moral values. It is in this sense that they emphasize the opposition between Islamic values and those of western society.

Radical militants manifest their rupture not only with western society but also with some traditional Islamic authorities. They are critical of certain Islamic texts and are keen on reforming them. The Salafists, the Muslim Brotherhood, and the jihadists alike are convinced that they are part of a vanguard community whose objective is to re-establish an authentic Islamic faith. Their movement takes the shape of an Islamic Renaissance, based on the earliest interpretations of Islam, namely that of the prophet and his four caliphs.

Conclusion

Since 2001, radical groups and Islamist networks mobilized young British Muslims as well as Muslim migrants recently settled in the United Kingdom. By studying the profile of their new recruits two levels of radicalization are revealed: first, a simple radicalization expressed through a cultural break from the local social order; and second, a violent radicalization that is expressed in a twofold rupture from national politics and the regimes of certain Muslim countries that are deemed illegitimate.

In addition to these two types of radicalization, we have noted that the new radical militants have converted to a radical form of Islam. There are many different types of conversion, for instance many British Muslims have espoused a radical and at times extremist ideology and have thus undergone a kind of second conversion to a new Islam different from any they have known so far. Some white British converts to Islam have become radicalized after having attended Salafist circles in "Londonistan", such as the group at Brixton mosque, followers of Abdullah el-Faysal, the Afro-Caribbean radical preacher. Other Muslims, who used to practise a traditional Islam (such as that preached by the *Barelwi*), became radical for political or existential reasons. The last type of conversion concerns a lesser number: it has to do with those Muslims who became radical after many intermediary phases, from affiliation to a traditional Islam (for example, the *Deobandi* school) to a break with the national and traditional referents under the influence of a local or online preacher or after a journey to Saudi-Arabia, Pakistan, or Chechnya, to a violent jihadist activism related to al-Qaeda. This is the case for the activists of 7 July.

The radicalization of the Muslims in Britain is complex because it springs from a phenomenon of rupture from western society on the one hand and from the original community, its referents, authorities and traditions on the other. At times, this radicalization is the result of a conflictual relation between Islamic and western values. But more often it is the result of a protest against a traditional Islam adopted by traditional Muslim societies and regimes. Both causes are sometimes inextricably related. This twofold rupture is accompanied by a search for a new Islamic referent and authority which may be embodied by radical Salafist doctrine or by other moderate Islamist movements having the same goal, namely a modern Islamic society that rejects the traditional Islamic model as well as the western one. In this sense, radicalization among the West's Muslim communities cannot be explained merely as the result of a clash between two civilizations.

16

France—The Clash of Civilizations?

Farhad Khosrokhavar

The notion of the "clash of civilizations" has found in journalistic and socio-logical literature a much wider meaning than the one originally intended by Samuel Huntington, which was as a cultural conflict between distinct civiliza-tions embodied in different religions within different territories.[1] The clash of civilizations can mean many different things, sometimes complementary, sometimes antagonistic to each other. The first is the inevitability of conflict between the world of Islam and the western world. Another version of the clash of civilizations is that the old class conflict promised by Marxists gives way to a new, culturally precipitated conflict between different "civilizations", the Chinese versus the American, the Islamic versus the western. This meaning is a subcategory of the first, applied this time to different "civilizations" in dif-ferent time-frames. The third version, distinct from the other two, is that the clash of civilizations is not the conflict between two distinct entities but between fundamentalist parts of the very same civilization or different civili-zations. In this respect, moderate Muslims and moderate Christians or secular people are closer to each other than fundamentalist or extremist strata of the Muslim and western world.

The notion of civilization in itself can be understood in different manners as well. In most cases, the clash is not between civilizations but those strands that claim to be the bearers of their civilization in an imaginary sense. The al-Qaeda members who claimed to be the representatives of the "genuine" Mus-

THE BORDERS OF ISLAM

lim world were not from a traditional Islamic civilization but were influenced by the West not only in their technology and organization, but also in the very style of their antagonism, marked by a long war against the former Soviet Union in Afghanistan and the relations of Egypt and Saudi Arabia to the West, mainly America. Ayman al Zawahiri and Osama bin Laden are familiar with western civilization, and their Islamic civilization as distinct and opposed to the West is an imaginary entity coined through their "perverse modernization" rather than being a reproduction of the traditional Islam. In a different way, most of those who fight the "West" within Europe, be it in France or Britain, are either citizens raised or educated in the West, or migrants in close touch with it. In most cases in Europe, radicalized Muslim youths are part and parcel of western civilization, but with a "distortion" in their thinking due to racism, Islamophobia and economic exclusion. Those who belong to the lower middle classes identify with a "Muslim" community that is denied dignity and full social participation by the host society. Here, contrary to the Muslim world, jihadism means distorted participation in citizenship and identification with the radical version of Islam, ending up in the praise of violence as the sole way of achieving their goals.

Perverse modernization and the subculture of death[2]

If we take Islam as being one of the major polarities in the clash of civilizations the problem arises as to what kind of Islam is being brandished by its protagonists as being at war with the West. The notion of "perverse modernization" is crucial in this respect. By this concept I mean a notion with a four-fold characteristic. It is primarily a type of social change that induces total violence as the exclusive way of dealing with the group of actors that are seen by the ego as opposed to its aims and aspirations. The second characteristic of perverse modernization is the sacralization of one's ideas and feelings in such a way that no "compromise" is possible with the adversary. The only way to tackle the latter is to fight endlessly against him in order to impose one's views. The third feature of perverse modernization is the centrality of death as the major and non-negotiable factor in the radicalization process. To die or to put to death, to subdue the enemy by accepting death and to kill him unless he submits to the ego and accepts its terms in a dichotomous way is the result of this type of modernization. In this sense, within the Islamic realm, al-Qaeda-type ideologies are fascinated by death (they are literally "mortiferous" in the centrality they accord to death and the meaning they give it that overshadows life). They build up a subculture of death within the Islamic world that horrifies not only the West but also many devout Muslims as well. The fourth characteristic of perverse modernization is the "de-humanization" of the adversary in such a way that killing and maiming innocent people is not seen only as the "collateral" aspect of the fight but also as its "desirable" aim, at least for the most radical proponents of it (many of their proponents, though, see the death of the innocent people as a by-product but not desirable outcome of the fight).

Perverse modernization implies a strong desire not only to fight against the West as the enemy, but also to annihilate it and to savour the victory even at the price of one's life. In the West, the decline of leftist ideologies has left a vacuum that can be filled with Islam as the only ideology that can still claim to be the bearer of conflict with the West. In Europe, Islam has become the "ideology of the oppressed" for many people who believe themselves, rightly or wrongly, not to have any future in that society. Most of them are of Muslim descent but some are converts who choose Islam to legitimize their fight against an "impious" and "depraved" West. The "perversity" of their attitude lies not so much in its rejection of the West but in the way violence is granted an absolute value and no compromise is accepted in dealing with the "Satanic" western order. In contrast to Muslim countries where Islam is rooted in a historical situation with a culture immersed in the Islamic soil, in France (and more generally in Europe) the Islamic reference of many people is the result of their uprootedness. Second generation French citizens of North African Islamic descent (the so-called "Beurs") did not refer, at least till the early 1980s, to any Islamic identity. They referred to "citizenship" and "laïcité" to lay claim to equality and freedom. It is at the end of the 1980s that the reference to Islam began to gain currency in France. This was not the consequence of the permanence of Islamic culture but the discovery of Islam as a new identity, with the name of Allah's religion as the motto of new social movements. The 1990s saw the appearance of Islam as an ideology justifying war against France and more generally, against the West. Here, internal and external problems intermingled through globalization, but the major cause of Islamic radicalization was the social and economic failure of many second and third generation people of Muslim descent within French society and their lack of integration as fully-fledged citizens.

France, Muslim communities, and jihadi terrorism

France, with around 4.5 million Muslims, has the largest Muslim community in Europe, most of whom come from France's former North African colonies (around 1.5 million Algerians, 700,000 Moroccans, some 350,000 Tunisians). There are many voluntary associations among them, some of them regarded as fundamentalist (in French, "*intégriste*", although the former word is used as well). These are groups that do not promote violent action against society or the West and would like to be recognized as part and parcel of French society with their particularism: that is, the recognition of the "French-Islamic" identity in the public sphere. Among them one can distinguish between moderate fundamentalists and the hyper-fundamentalists. The first subgroup (the religious associations like UOIF—*Union des Organisations Islamiques de France*—and the *Tabligh* among others) does not seek total separation from society, whereas the second campains to set Muslims apart from non-Muslims in two segregated entities (the so-called Salafi groups in France). Another group, much smaller in number, but having some followers in the poor suburbs (the "*Banlieues*") and among some converts, promotes violent action against "heretical" French society as such. This group is related to jihadi terrorism.

Two factors played a major role in the radicalization of a minority of Muslims in the name of Allah in France. The first is related to Algeria and the politics of that country. The second is based on the problems of the Muslim "diasporas". At the beginning of the 1990s, the FIS (*Front Islamique du Salut*) became the most popular political party in Algeria and won the elections but its government was overthrown by the military with the approval of the French government in 1991. The failure of the post-independence national government in Algeria to promote social participation and a balanced distribution of the oil wealth pushed many people towards Islamic political parties which promised social justice in the name of Islam. After its overthrow, the marginalized FIS gave birth to a set of terrorist groups under the name of GIA (*Groupe Islamique Armé*) which, during the next ten years, murdered some 100,000 people in their attacks inside Algeria. In France, where Muslims of Algerian origin are the largest Muslim population the GIA conducted some major attacks, the most significant being the blowing up of the Saint-Michel Metro in Paris in 1995 (in which eight people died and 150 were wounded). Activists of Algerian origin such as Boualem Bensaïd, Khaled Kelkal, Karim Koussa and Smaïn Aït Ali Belkacem played important roles.[3] Another bomb attack, in which twenty-six people were wounded, occurred on 17 October 1995 at the Maison Blanche metro station in Paris, also the work of the GIA. The third attack was perpetrated at the Musée d'Orsay station in Paris on 17 October in which thirty people were wounded. Other projected attacks were neutralized by the police. Prior to them, three members of the French consulate were abducted in Algiers in November 1993. That was the beginning of the hunt to shut down the networks in France that were supporting GIA: eighty-eight of their supporters were arrested, others were deported. During Christmas 1994 an Air France Airbus was hijacked in Algiers by a GIA group and three passengers were executed. The French specialist anti-terrorist police (GIGN) intervened and four kidnappers were killed. Six months later, Bensaïd and Belkacem were sent to Paris in order to organize the jihad in France. They were supported by Ali Touchent who recruited young men in the poor French suburbs to conduct terrorist attacks.

The plight of Muslim communities is partially the cause of resentment and frustration for second and third generation Muslims. As in many other parts of Western Europe, most Muslims came to France as unskilled blue collar workers from the 1960s onwards. Many of their sons and grandsons are stuck in poor suburbs where they suffer from economic exclusion and cultural stigma. Such "disenfranchised" youths are often influenced by jihadism. A minority of Muslims achieve a middle class or lower-middle class status but precisely because of this, part of this new middle class is deeply moved by the fate of their excluded brethren and is prone to radicalization, to save a "suffering *Ummah*" inside France and overseas (Palestine, Iraq, Afghanistan, Chechnya...).[4] These Muslims act as the vanguard of a "persecuted *Ummah*" which from their point of view has submitted to domination and alienation by the French and, more generally, westerners.

The study of jihadi activists reveals their multiple social origins: some are from the lower-middle classes, many are from the so-called excluded and disenfranchised youth; most of them are of Muslim origin, some are converts with a Christian or secular background. They are young but many are in their thirties. The overwhelming majority of them are male but a few are women and in the future one might expect the number of the latter to rise. In addition to their social characteristics (social class, generation, gender or ethnic and national origin), their cultural and ideological frame of mind brings us closer to an understanding of their enrollment into Islamic terrorism.

At the end of the 1980s a major cultural change occurred in France. Up to then, most French of North African origin defined themselves as "secular" citizens in the public sphere and their claims were put in terms of "equality" and "fraternity", according to the "*laïcité*" political culture. Since then, many second or third generation Muslims have defined themselves in religious terms through a change of denomination. Up to the 1970s, they longed for integration in France, holding some features of their countries of origin. The "Arabs" perceived themselves as North Africans (Algerian, Moroccan, Tunisian) in France, in transition to French cultural identity. From the end of the 1980s on, the reference to their origin has been overshadowed by their new self-definition as Muslims. This does not necessarily mean being a devout Muslim. In many cases, knowledge of Islam is at best sketchy among them and the lack of knowledge about Islam often plays a role in their radicalization. They easily shift their hatred of society into a religious duty (jihad) without a real understanding of its religious meaning. In this respect, hyper-secularization of society has been a facilitating factor in the promotion of jihadism among Muslim youth. In most cases, radicalization occurs before Islamization and once under the spell of jihad, they try to acquire religious information and knowledge.

The notion of the "suffering *Ummah*" as the major justification for jihad is built up in a new way, borrowing some notions from tradition but, in the main, espousing many features of the extreme left and extreme right mottoes. Probably for the first time in history, it is possible for a Muslim to feel oppressed "at home" and "far from home" within the framework of a world-wide *Ummah*. The media showing in real time what is going on in other parts of the world (Palestine, Chechnya, Iraq, Afghanistan), the new networks through the Internet allowing the creation of groups with almost no previous physical contact, the capacity of Islam as the only major monotheistic religion among the others (Christian, Jewish) to mobilize new generations for the ultimate sacrifice in the name of their lost honour and dignity and their glorious past, all of it gives an input to an imaginary *Ummah* that would oppose the rest of the world in order to restore the honour and the hegemony of Muslims.

Two sets of facts determine jihadism in France. First the situation of the so-called "*banlieues*" where there is a high concentration of second or third generation youth from North Africa or Black Africa and where the rate of unemployment is very high (up to 50 per cent, that is five times more than the average). A subculture of rupture with the rest of the society prevails there. Within the *banlieues*, new generations of French believe that they have no future in terms of employment and integration within French society. Those who succeed in finding a job and become "normal citizens" leave the suburbs and those who remain harbour the idea that the society is against them and that they are victims of a racist France that stigmatizes them. This feeling of absolute victimization is contradicted by the facts, since a proportion of the second or third generation migrants from North Africa join the middle classes, within or outside the *banlieues*.[5] Some turn to Islamic terrorism in the same fashion as in the 1970s: in Europe, some middle class people joined leftist groups like *Action Directe* (France), Red Brigades (Italy) or *Fraktion Roter Armee* (Germany). They set themselves the goal of protecting the "persecuted *Ummah*" in the same fashion as the middle class leftists proclaimed themselves as the vanguard of an imaginary proletariat. The major difference with the radical movements of the 1970s is that in the current case many people from the lower classes join them (the "youth" from the poor French suburbs) whereas, in the leftist movements of three decades ago, there weren't many lower class people. Islam, then, has become in France and more generally in Europe the religion of the "persecuted people".

The "suffering *Ummah*" is coupled with a high level of victimization in a peculiar way. Many "Arabs" (that is French of North African origin) from the *banlieues* believe that they are being oppressed by French society in the same fashion as Palestinians are being persecuted by the Israeli army. The crisis of the Muslim world combined with the economic exclusion of the "Arabs" in France (that is, the French of North African origin) paves the way for total violence against French society and beyond that, the West. The imaginary neo-*Ummah* which is supposed to suffer worldwide in the same way as the youth of the French suburbs, is at the root of a dichotomized world where the good people (the Muslims) are being oppressed by the bad and godless people (the West).

The fact that in Europe people of Muslim origin have the highest rate of imprisonment (between five and ten times their proportion in many European countries, where statistics are available), the lowest education and the lowest expectancy in terms of social promotion makes the projection easier.[6] New apartheids in the school system and racism in terms of employment and job opportunities give some justification for this sombre self-victimization. The imaginary "suffering *Ummah*" goes hand in hand with the persecuted self of young male Muslims and paves the way for jihadi ideology.[7]

Between 1992 and 2006 a few hundred of people were arrested in France under the heading of the so-called "Association of criminals preparing a terrorist action", among whom 150 were sentenced to jail terms[8]. Many of them are of North African origin. Some are converts. Many have had ties to jihadi organizations outside France, in particular the different branches of the GIA in Algeria. Some have been at the heart of other terrorist groups, with ties in Germany, England, Morocco and the Middle East. Many also belong to what is being called "home-grown terrorism": that is, people born or raised in

France who build up terrorist cells in an almost autonomous manner, without necessarily being related to the outside world or at best, being only marginally related to it.

The intermingling of "home-grown terrorism" and transnational jihadism is the prominent feature of the new wave of terrorism in many European countries. In some cases, the terrorists have a multinational background, in others they have travelled and stayed in different European and American countries. The case of Zaccarias Moussaoui is one example. Born in France of Moroccan parents, he was raised in a secular fashion, with his parents divorcing after a few years and his mother managing to work and create a home of her own. His brother and two sisters were raised in the same fashion. After completing his schooling, he went to England in order to improve his English and study business in London. There, jihadi groups influenced him, in particular preachers such as Abu Qatada and Abu Hamza al-Misri. He became an intransigent Muslim and cut off ties with his former friends, unsuccessfully pushing his mother and sisters towards a rigorous Islamic practice. His trip to the US and his involvement with al-Qaeda show the itinerary of a Frenchman of North African origin getting enmeshed in terrorism mainly through his stay in London (the so-called "Londonistan" of the fundamentalist Islamic groups). Zaccarias Moussaoui's situation is that of a young boy from a deeply fragmented family where the father torments his wife and children and extorts what his wife earns to spend it on a disorderly life. Moussaoui's two sisters and his father suffer from schizophrenia. Other terrorist cases do not show the same deep psychopathology within the family.

In other cases, the ties are built with Algerian cells. The case of Khaled Kelkal is particularly significant. Born in Algeria, raised and schooled in France from the age of five, he discovered Islam in secondary school where he was exposed to racism and was stigmatised. He went off the rails and in prison embraced a jihadi version of Islam. Later he fell in with a GIA-related terrorist group that blew up the Metro at Saint-Michel in Paris in July 1995, killing eight people.[9]

Nowadays, a new type of jihadi terrorist is becoming a threat in France, related to the French policy on the veil issue on the one hand, and the war in Iraq on the other. In January 2005 a young and charismatic Muslim preacher, Farid Benyettou, aged 23, was arrested in Paris for having sent a dozen French Muslim citizens to Iraq to fight against the American army.[10] Seven seem to have died there and two were imprisoned.[11] Another group, *Ansar al Fath*, mentored by Safé Bourada, an Algerian jihadist already condemned for his relations to the GIA in 1995, was broken up in September 2005 in the Paris suburbs (Merisiers in the city of Trappes in the Yvelines). Another group appears to be related to Belgian networks. A 27-year old Tunisian was arrested in November 2005 in the Paris suburbs for his alleged membership of a Belgian jihadi group whose members had committed suicide attacks in Iraq. Preventive arrests are frequent against people suspected of money laundering for jihadi groups or trying to extort "Islamic taxes" on their behalf. In December 2005 some twenty people were arrested in the Oise (greater Paris region) within an inquiry into the illegal financing of jihadi groups.

The terrorist groups belong either to Algerian, or to national or transnational groups. National boundaries do not limit them at all, and increasingly their ties to North Africa, England, Belgium, Germany and other European or Middle Eastern countries or even Australia make them really transnational. In this respect not only Muslims by birth but also converts play a significant role. For instance Pierre Richard Robert (Yacoub under his Islamic name), born in 1972 in a town close to Saint-Etienne, who converted to Islam in 1990. He went to Afghanistan in 1994 and then to Tangier where he married a Moroccan girl and became the father of two children. He was involved in terrorist acts in Casablanca on 16 May 2003 which caused thirty-three deaths and twelve supplementary deaths of the terrorists themselves with around a hundred wounded. This "blue-eyed Emir", as the Moroccans called him, denied the charges brought against him by the Moroccan authorities but was found guilty and sentenced to life imprisonment. Another convert, Willie Virgile Brigitte, a Guadeloupean of French citizenship, became a Muslim and was in touch with radical Islamists in the Paris suburbs. He appears to have travelled to Yemen, Pakistan, and Afghanistan after 9/11. It was there that he fought the American army before travelling to Australia. He was extradited from Australia to France in 2003. Another convert, Jérôme Courtailer, was arrested in September 2001 in Holland as he prepared terrorist acts in Britain.

In all cases, the modernization is obvious. None of them is "traditional" or a conservative Muslim in the sense of deep sense of religion rooted in a tradition. The people in question are mostly from Muslim backgrounds but they have suffered uprootedness and their knowledge of Islam has been, in their childhood, at best sketchy. Their self-consciousness as "Muslims" has been the result of antagonism towards an imaginary France (and by extension, the West). The combination of racism, Islamophobia and the colonial past push towards radicalization and Islam, as the sole available ideology (leftist ideologies are discredited), that proposes a legitimate means to justify the fight against France. This is not the result of the clash between two civilizations, it is much more to do with the distorted image of the West among those who feel "oppressed" because they are not at home where they are born or raised. Even those who are from the middle classes feel alienated because of their disturbed identity.

The clash of French and European subcultures

In France, jihadism is neither purely external (the case of 9/11 in the US) nor purely internal, although "home-grown terrorism" increasingly plays a major role. It is at the crossroad of the internal (national) and external (transnational) world. The external transnational world, the bonds linking the activities in France with events and groups outside France, can be of two kinds: either real links with other parts of the world in terms of networks or finances; or an imagined tie to the external world with an underlying imaginary neo-*Ummah* as a "persecuted *Ummah*". The imagined tie transcends the boundaries of France and encompasses the entire West and the East as the "domains of war" (*Dar al-harb*) in order to restore Islam to its glory and divine right as a universal religion for all. Anthropological studies of these Muslims underlines the fact that the internal situation (poor suburbs, stigma, Islamophobia) plays a significant role in a situation where a sizeable number of Muslim citizens believe themselves to have no future prospects and feel condemned to a situation of inexorable exclusion. Even those who succeed are exposed to this predicament: they might end up as a vanguard for the "oppressed *Ummah*". Contrary to the United States where white Muslims are middle class with a high prospect of social and economic promotion, the overwhelming majority of the French (and more generally European) Muslims are from the lower classes and many, in the second and third generations, feel downtrodden, disenfranchised, and stigmatized. They transfer their feeling of humiliation into radical Islam to raise their self-esteem by fighting the French—and more generally western—infidels.

Their fights in France today cannot be explained by the clash between Muslim and western civilizations. Most French youth that take part in jihadi activities are born and raised in France, have gone to French schools, been socialized through French TV and the subcultures of the *banlieues* and, therefore, are ignorant of Islamic civilization in its depth or even its language (the Arabic of their parents is most often a simplified version of literary Arabic, so-called "dialectal" Arabic). They become prey to Islamic radicalism not so much in order to fight against the "arrogant West" as to denounce racism and Islamophobia in their country. They feel rejected by the French and have no "Algerian", "Moroccan" or "Tunisian" identity either. Islam becomes a kind of imaginary identity to fill a major gap between a denied identity (Frenchness) and a non-endorsed one (the identity of their parents or their grandparents). It is not so much the knowledge of Islam, its history, or its civilization but the utter ignorance of it that pushes them towards a jihadism that gives them a sense of belonging to an imaginary community, without real roots in the past. Their "imaginary Muslimhood" is not based on the same mechanisms as the "imaginary communities" analysed by Benedict Anderson.[12] It is imaginary in the "diasporic" sense: no real community (there is no closely knit "Islamic community" in France, neither in terms of voting system nor in the sense of any neo-*Ummah* based on a neo-caliphate). The Islamic *Ummah*, in the minds of most of the radical Islamic youth, is there to fill a vacuum created by their own torn identity: rejected by the majority of the French citizens as not French and having no substance to be treated as "Algerian", "Moroccan", or "Tunisian" due to their lack of identification with the latter countries. Islam has the function of a "vacuum filler" without any reference to a real community: most French Muslims are either secular (the rate of attendance at mosques is around 20 per cent, one in five), or attached to local communities or belong to major groups (the UOIF, the FMNF, the *Mosquée de Paris*, or *Tabligh*) that define themselves as French Muslims. The jihadi groups are at best a very tiny minority of a few hundred or a few thousand (if we include the sympathizers who do not participate actively in jihadi terrorism). The jihadi fight within France (and more largely, Britain and Holland) is espoused by a subculture of those who feel rejected, stigmatized, marginalized and denied dignity rather than those bearing a distinct identity within a distinct civilization. In Europe, there is no distinct "Islamic civilization" among the second and third generations of Muslims. There is a social, cultural, and economic problem related to marginalized communities whose identity is jihadi not in terms of a distinct civilization but in terms of an identity problem within the framework of Europe. They develop a "perverse identity" where heroism in the name of a sacred death (martyrdom) and antagonism towards the West is the result of their rejection by the host society. In this respect, their "perverse modernization" is distinct from that of many Muslims within the Muslim world who are denied participation in the political system and denied the opportunities within the social system that would allow them economic and social advancement. Their experience in France occurs in a non-Islamic setting, in an area governed by a non-Islamic government. Western misunderstanding of their problems and aims only compounds their opposition such that it becomes "civilizational" due to the failure of secular regimes in the Muslim world and political short-sightedness in the West.

17

Scandinavia—Alienation or Integration?[1]

Atle Mesøy and Stig Jarle Hansen

A clash of civilizations in Scandinavia? The proposition might seem strange. It was not until the 1960s that a substantial Muslim immigration to the Scandinavian countries took place. Scandinavian industry needed workers; some were actively recruited by Scandinavian industrialists, in some cases they were recruited by travelling agents in their own countries, and some came on their own initiative.[2] More recently, refugees from violent conflicts in Iraq, Somalia, Bosnia-Herzegovina, Kosovo, and Iran settled in Scandinavia. Many migrant workers as well as refugees successfully applied for permission to bring their families to Scandinavia. In all Scandinavian countries family reunification is the largest single cause leading to the granting of permanent residence permits.[3]

The number of Muslims in Scandinavia is currently estimated to be 590,000 to 740,000 persons.[4] Most of the Danish Muslims come from Turkey, Iraq, Bosnia-Herzegovina, Lebanon, Pakistan, and Somalia.[5] The majority of Sweden's Muslims originate from Turkey, Iran, and the Balkans.[6] In addition, other large groups of Muslims have Arab, African, and Pakistani origin. The largest Muslim groups in Norway come from Pakistan, Iraq (mainly Kurds), Somalia, Bosnia-Herzegovina, Iran, and Turkey.[7] With the growing number of Muslim immigrants in the last fifty years the lack of understanding and knowledge (of both the Scandinavians and the new groups) resulted in distrust and examples of fear of the unknown; in this sense there is a relatively high degree of Islamophobia (fear of/discrimination against Islam) in the Scandinavian countries, as well as a tendency for crude stereotyping. A Swedish survey for example shows a correlation between the income of immigrants and their decision to change their names into Swedish names.[8] However, there are indications that education removes some of the fear of other social groups. Statistics from Norway show that a lower educational level, both amongst Muslims and non-Muslims, is correlated with a larger amount of fear directed towards other religious groups.[9]

To be surrounded by a more or less secular population does have an impact over time. Westernization, "modernization", secularization, and liberalization are confronted by Muslim scholars and imams, many brought directly from the home countries of the various ethnic groups adhering to Islam, with strong demands to stay committed to the "correct faith". Nevertheless, the impact of such calls is limited. In several surveys conducted amongst the Muslim population in Norway in 2006, a majority of Norwegian Muslims perceived Norway as a moral society, despite being governed by relatively liberal laws.[10]

Socio-economically, Scandinavian Muslims are hard to stereotype as a group. Firstly there are few statistics on religious communities, partly because of reluctance to undertake such studies, thus one is often forced to generalize using statistics focusing on ethnic groups that are traditionally Muslim, with all the problems to which such generalizations can lead. Using such data, one discovers that there are large socio-economic variations between groups that come from traditionally Muslim areas. In Scandinavia, Bosnians are often highly educated and high earners; Iranians also in general have a high education level. Somalis, a relatively recent ethnic group in Scandinavia, often tend to have low income and receive more benefits than other groups.[11] Indeed, there is a strong correlation between the time the various groups have remained in a country, their education, and their employment rate. An ethnic group that has been settled in Scandinavia for a longer period often has a lower unemployment level, as well as a larger percentage enrolled in higher education, than groups that are new to the countries.[12]

As for most Muslims worldwide the situation for Muslims in Scandinavian countries changed after the attacks on the World Trade Center and the Pentagon on 11 September 2001. A combination of suspicious reactions from ordinary people, new amendments in the criminal laws, and an increased level of surveillance of many Muslim individuals and networks increased the stigmatization of Muslims. The topic of integration is often merged with a "clash of civilizations" discourse, and the subject of Islam has become dramatized and "hot"; perhaps this is the reason that more ethnic Scandinavian youths have converted to Islam post-9/11 than before, as well as being the reason for the growth of new "experts" on the issue, ready to publish dramatic comments to gain the attention of the press.[13]

One of the few times Denmark has been in the headlines globally was in early 2006 when strong reactions from Muslim communities around the world emerged as a reaction to twelve cartoons published in the Danish news-paper *Jyllands-Posten* in September 2005, which many Muslims perceived to be insulting. In October a delegation of ambassadors from Arab countries demanded to discuss the cartoons and the situation for Muslims in general with the Danish Prime Minister, Anders Fogh Rasmussen. He refused to meet with them and argued that freedom of speech is guaranteed in the Danish constitution and that it was neither appropriate nor possible for him to dis-cuss such topics. The delegation returned to their home countries with the message that they were poorly received and consequently argued for actions against Denmark. The spiritual leader of the most influential mosque in Den-mark, the late Imam Ahmed Abu Laban, a member of the governing council of the Islamic faith society in Denmark, emerged in the media as one of the major critics of the cartoons. Laban participated in a group led by Ahmed Akkari, an imam in the central Danish city of Aarhus, which travelled to the Middle East in November-December 2005 and gained more support for their case. According to the group itself, this was a protest against the lack of dia-logue with the government.[14] However, several of the pictures they presented were taken out of context in order to document anti-Muslim discrimination in Denmark. The result was worldwide Muslim protests against Denmark, and later Norway, the latter due to publication of the cartoons in a small right-wing Christian magazine.[15] Shops, factories, consulates, churches, and embas-sies were set on fire, and more than 150 were killed during the riots worldwide. Norwegian soldiers in Meymaneh in Afghanistan became involved in a fire fight when an angry crowd attacked the military base there.[16] Most of the violent actions took place in Lebanon, Syria, Iran, Pakistan and Nigeria. Many Mus-lims boycotted Scandinavian products.[17] Danish losses alone were estimated by Aarhus School of Business to be 1.9 billion Danish kroner, approximately $368.7 million USD.[18] On 2 June 2008 Denmark experienced a suicide attack against its embassy in Islamabad, Pakistan; al-Qaeda argued that it was a pun-ishment for the humiliation of Muhammad in the Danish cartoons.[19]

The cartoon episode illustrates how Scandinavian minority groups that feel marginalized can use religious ties to drum up foreign support. It is interesting to note that Sweden had a similar case one year later. On 19 August 2007, the *Nerikes Allehanda* newspaper published Muhammad caricatures drawn by an eccentric Swedish artist, Lars Vilk. However, while there were demonstrations, they were of a small scale compared to the highly dramatic reaction sparked by the Danish cartoons.[20] The Swedish Prime Minister reacted fast, visiting prominent mosques in Sweden, and called in Muslim ambassadors to explain that the Swedish government was unable to censor Vilk due to the right to freedom of speech enshrined in the Swedish constitution.[21] Muslim communities in Sweden actively tried to minimize the potential damage that could be caused by the cartoons. A Muslim group even took the initiative of exhibiting the cartoons to spark a discussion, and to challenge the stereotypes of Muslims.[22] Denmark can be regarded as the country with the strictest immigration laws in Scandinavia, with a strong emphasis on forced integration; the Danish approach might have contributed to the dramatic situation by refusing dialogue with the delegation that first approached them. Denmark also deployed forces to Afghanistan and Iraq, which could have been another continuing factor.

The example illustrates how globalization has led to new international ties that can be manipulated in order to get support in what essentially seems to have been a local Danish conflict. In this sense it illustrates new cross-border ties: not directly a clash of civilizations, but rather the existence of ideational links that can be used by efficient and inspired individuals. The ideational links need not lead to conflict, as the Swedish example shows, but might, if not handled with care, contribute to the escalation of local conflicts. Importantly, the Danish and Swedish cases demonstrate that many local variables as a more generally hostile situation and lack of dialogue, as well as the existence of instrumentalists with an interest in the expansion of conflict can escalate a tense situation, these variables were present in Denmark and not in Sweden.

Militancy?

Several Scandinavian Muslim organizations are frequently accused of being militant, but concrete proof has never been presented.[23] However, groups which preach and, on rare occasions, plan violent actions exist. In Denmark, there are two lines in the "jihad tradition", the first being the Egyptians with links to *Gamaat Islamiyyah*, and the second North African-linked al-Qaeda-like networks.[24] The country has been used as a safe haven for Islamists banned in their own countries.[25] At the time of writing one terrorist-related trial is taking place in Denmark, the Copenhagen case.[26] Two other terrorist cases have ended. The first, nicknamed the "*Glostrup*" case by the Danish press, involved the Bosnian-Swede Mirsad Bektašević ("Maximus") and Cesur Abdulkadir, born in Denmark, who were suspected of planning a terrorist operation in Europe, and who were found guilty of planning a suicide attack in Bosnia and sentenced (in a Bosnian court) to fifteen and thirteen years respectively. Four young Danish men were indicted of assisting Mirsad Bektašević and Cesur Abdulkadir to obtain the explosives for the operation. Only one of them, 17-year old Abdul Basit Abu-Lifa, was found guilty in the Danish court system and received a seven-year jail sentence for his supporting role in the terrorist plot.[27]

In the second case, the "*Vollsmose*" Case four persons have been convicted of planning a terrorist operation that was to be carried out in Denmark.[28] According to the Danish Security Services, explosives were found in a flat where one of the convicted persons lived. The explosives were TATP, and fertilizer. The court case was taken all the way to the Supreme Court. Two of the men were sentenced to twelve years and the third man, five years. They were found guilty of planning and preparing an act of terrorism. The fourth man was acquitted.

A third case was brought against Moroccan-born Said Mansour, who later became a Danish citizen. He allegedly had contacts with European leaders in al-Qaeda such as Abu Qatada, and al-Barakat Yarkas.[29] Mansour was found guilty of instigating militant jihad through the material he was distributing. The material included CDs on which infamous terrorists such as Osama bin Laden and Ayman Al-Zawahari were proclaiming their war messages and encouraging people to join in violent international jihad, including suicide missions. Notably, Mansour was sentenced to three years and six months in prison, despite the lack of evidence that his influence had led to actual terrorist operations.[30] Only a minimum of information has been made available to the public, especially in the "*Vollsmose*" and Copenhagen cases.

In Sweden, a branch of *Ansar Al-Sunnah* has published incendiary statements on its website, and during[31] the nineties Stockholm also became a base for GIA (*Groupe Islamique Armé*), where they published their *Al-Ansar* bulletin.[32] However, the clearest examples of possible terrorism/terrorists with international connections in Sweden are the previously mentioned Maximus (Mirsad Bektašević). A home-grown group, the so-called "boys' room terrorists" also planned attacks on a Christian sect, as well as threw Molotov cocktails at Iraqis voting for the Iraqi election in Sweden. The "boys' room terrorists", all very young, put an al-Qaeda-inspired film on the internet (that was how they were caught), and were in one sense an example of childish self-radicalisation.[33]

A major issue has been the transfer of money from Sweden to organisations operating outside Sweden. In 2005 two Iraqi Kurds were convicted in Swedish courts for channelling money to *Ansar Al Islam* in Iraq.[34] In 2001, there was a case involving the then blacklisted Somali Al Barakat money transferring company; it was, however, blacklisted by the United States without any trial or possibility of appeal, but in the end the blacklisting was also lifted. In 2008, three Somalis were suspected of money transfers to the *Al Shebab* group in Somalia, but later released. Ethnic non-Swedes with Swedish citizenship have also been arrested outside Sweden for alleged terrorist-related activities, such as planning, training or recruitment. Oussama Abdullah Kassir, was for example arrested in Prague for helping to set up a jihadist camp in the United States, and was extradited from the Czech Republic to the United States.[35] Several individuals have also been expelled from Sweden, but often information about these expulsions is lacking.

The closest Norway has been to politically and religiously-motivated violence was the failed assassination of William Nygaard, the Norwegian publisher of Salman Rushdie's novel *The Satanic Verses*, on 11 October 1993. He was shot outside his home in Oslo. According to Odd Isungset the investigation centred on employees of a foreign embassy, but the case remains unsolved.[36] In Norway, the case of Najmuddin Faraj Ahmad, often known by the name Mullah Krekar, the former military leader of an Iraqi/Kurd organisation, *Ansar al-Islam*, has gained international attention. According to the United States authorities, a group of captured *Ansar Al-Islam* fighters caught with suicide bomb vests after a failed attack during the spring of 2003 told interrogators they were working for Krekar.[37] Americans asked for his extradition, and according to *Newsweek*, even discussed the possibility of a military intervention (special operation) in Norway in order to capture Krekar.[38] However, the court case against Ahmad (Krekar) collapsed when the witness of the prosecutor, an Iraqi captured after the initial attack, claimed that his initial statements had been given under torture. Despite the fact that he was never sentenced for terror links, another court made a decision to extradite him to Iraq, claiming that he posed "a threat against national security". This verdict was appealed as far as to the Supreme Court, where the sentence was confirmed. The verdict has so far not been implemented, because of fear for Najmuddin

Faraj Ahmad's life if he is returned to Iraq. Najmuddin Faraj Ahmad is increasingly unpopular in Norway, partly because of his statements in the Iraqi press in support of Osama bin Laden, and the late leader of al-Qaeda in Iraq, Abu Musab al-Zarqawi, as well as his public display of anger when he was manhandled by a female Norwegian comedian during a TV appearance.[39]

On 5 October 2001, the police raided the Somali money-transferring agencies "Hiirad" and "Al Barakat," suspected of channelling money to the Somali *Al Itthad Al Islamiya* organisation, which again has been claimed to be connected with Osama bin Laden. In the end all suspects were released because of lack of evidence.[40] In Norway there was also a case against what the police define as a previous member of the criminal street gang, Young Guns, and two accomplices, accused of planning an attack on the US and/or Israeli embassy, and firing with an automatic rifle at the main synagogue in Norway.[41] On 19 September 2006, Arfan Qadeer Bhatti, a former member of the Young Guns, was arrested and charged according to Norway's terrorism legislation. A police-monitored conversation in which Bhatti and another person seemed to be discussing how to attack the American and/or the Israeli embassy was published in one of the tabloids in Norway.[42] Bhatti was convicted of criminal offences, but not under the terrorism legislation. His lawyers focused on the way that the security police interpreted taped conversations between Bhatti and other individuals, as well as the fact that some of his expressed anger at specific world events, especially the Palestinian/Israeli conflict, were also common amongst the general Norwegian population.[43] The last "terror" case in Norway, still in the legal system at the time of writing, concerns three Somali Norwegians; accused of supporting the radical *Al Shebab* group, as well as the Shariah courts of Mogadishu (see the chapter on Somalia). Interviews with many Somalis indicated support for the general insurgency in that country, as they see it as a fight against Ethiopian occupying forces, and were generally unaware of *Al Shebab's* links with al-Qaeda.[44] However, interviews indicate there were some radical elements amongst the Norwegian-Somali supporters of *Al Shebab*.

The trends in Scandinavia underline how migration has brought Scandinavians closer to the world; events in Scandinavia can lead to reactions in such countries as Syria and Lebanon, while political events in Somalia may have legal consequences in Scandinavia. Denmark so far is the country that has had the most serious terrorism cases, perhaps a paradox given its strict policies. It is interesting that at least half of the terror-related cases that have led to police action in Scandinavia have concerned alleged terror attacks or support for alleged terror related organisations taking place/being active outside Scandinavia. Nevertheless, it is not suggested that the above examples illustrate a clash of civilizations, as the majority of Muslims in Scandinavia are seemingly more moderate than the more extreme groups that have caught the attention of the police. It also illustrates that extreme groups in general are less interested in planning action in their new homelands than their old or a third country. The new globalised world creates challenges for the police in Scandinavia, since many cases involve events and organisations outside the region, demanding competence and complex knowledge of far-away conflicts, where at times potential partners, the local police forces, are malfunctioning or even use torture.

Conclusion

Several facts are of importance when exploring the interaction between Muslims and Scandinavian societies in the light of Samuel Huntington's clash of civilization thesis. The first factor is that, so far there have been no successful terror attacks in Scandinavia. The most serious attack against Scandinavia, the one against the Danish embassy in Islamabad, took place outside the Scandinavian countries. A second factor is that both ethnic Scandinavians and the Muslim population within the Scandinavian countries in general hold moderate views. Notably, the ethnic groups holding Muslim faith are integrating deeper and deeper into Scandinavian society over time, with the exception of intermarriage.

Rather than a global clash of civilizations, what we see in Scandinavia is the existence of smaller belief systems that tie some individuals with peers outside Scandinavia, at times leading to extreme and violent actions, or the planning/funding of such actions. Not all of the individuals within such extreme belief systems are motivated by a jihadist world view: they can also be motivated by patriotism, or even a blurred mix between the two. The interaction between faraway wars and conflicts and actions in such conflicts planned in, or funded from, Scandinavia, creates challenges for the police, who have to develop new expertise, and in some cases even have to be able to distinguish between propaganda from belligerents in war (as well as confessions extradited under torture), and well-founded terror accusations.

As shown by the Mohammed cartoon incident a multi-cultural/multi-religious society creates challenges, and these challenges have to be met with interaction and dialogue. Cultures are not divided by eternal separations, nor are religions. Through interaction and respect, individuals will understand any similarities between the groups, and indeed change. The alternative, non-interaction and non-dialogue, will enable extreme groups to gain respect; they can claim to defend something legitimate, Islam itself. Scandinavia has grown into a region on Islam's borders; global belief systems situated within the Islamic world, of which a minority is extreme, have reached Scandinavia. However, the Scandinavian "border" is not yet "bloody". Admittedly, some of the diaspora communities are vulnerable. Dialogue and transparency, as shown in the Swedish cartoon incident, might defuse further serious situations.

18

The United States of America— American Muslim Exceptionalism

Allen D. Hertzke

This chapter argues that the interaction between Muslims and other groups in the United States has been generally peaceful. The USA has never had Muslim riots, and, compared to European countries, the extremist groups are smaller and less significant. The strong pull of economic and political opportunity, plus the increasing scrutiny of outside influences, generally mute the militant voices in the United States.

Estimates of the current size of the US Muslim population vary widely, from under three million to over six million. The lower figure, which may come closest to the actual number, represents about 1 per cent of the US population.[1] Thus the US Muslim presence is still modest compared to some European countries. Nonetheless, high fertility rates alone ensure that it will grow rapidly, making the Muslim community an increasing part of the American mosaic. American Muslims remain a heavily immigrant community. According to a major survey conducted in 2002, only 36 per cent of the adult Muslim population were born in the United States. That percentage, however, will grow as second and third generation youth come of age. The remaining 64 per cent hail from no less than eighty countries, making the American Muslim population the most diverse in the world. By origin 32 per cent are South Asians, 26 per cent Arabs, 20 per cent African Americans, and 7 per cent Africans.[2]

American Muslims represent the full range of traditions—Sunni, Shia, Sufi, Ismaili, Ahmadi, and the different Islamic schools of thought. To a degree this means that highly diverse Muslims intermingle in unprecedented ways. On the other hand, different communities maintain institutions that cater to their ethnic or religious particularities. Thus not only are relations sometimes strained between Shias and Sunnis, but between "indigenous" (African American) Muslims and immigrants, and between first generation émigrés and their American-born children.

One of the most striking features of the American Muslim community is its relatively high socio-economic status. This flows from the fact that most immigrant Muslims came to America not as labourers (as in France or Germany), but as college students and professionals in such lucrative fields as medicine, engineering, and business. Thus the Muslim population in the United States is a solidly middle-class community, with educational and income levels at least equilivant to typical Americans, and perhaps higher.[3] We do not see in the United States, as in parts of Europe, the spectre of large numbers of alienated, unemployed Muslims living in ghettos. Indeed, American Muslims represent the most highly educated Islamic community in the world. High socio-economic status helps explain the relatively limited appeal of separatist or hard line Islamic expressions.

American Muslims also represent a very young and family-oriented group. Muslim adults are more likely than average Americans to be married with children and they have larger families. Few are over the age of 65.[4] Thus the community is heavily nested in the web of activities associated with child rearing—school projects, athletic leagues, youth groups, and the like. American Muslims have created a vibrant civic community in America, replete with institutions and habits that generally channel energies, aspirations, and discontent in voluntary endeavours and democratic outlets. In addition to an estimated 1,200 mosques there are a host of charities, civic organizations, publishers, private schools, boy scout troops sponsored by mosques, college clubs, and political groups.

Leaders of American Muslim groups have sometimes flirted with Islamist radicalism.[5] But exposure by watchdog activists has combined with the shock of 9/11 to temper the different advocacy organizations. The Council for American Islamic Relations (CAIR), for example, which was formed by a Palestinian group and at times evinced solidarity with Hamas,[6] now focuses on fights against domestic defamation and discrimination. Its residual reputation for militant sympathies, however, has resulted in a precipitous drop in membership since 9/11.[7] Other organizations have carved specialized niches. The Muslim American Society (MAS) focuses on grassroots mobilization; the Muslim Political Affairs Committee (MPAC) on interfaith relations, lobbying, and working with government agencies; the American Muslim Alliance on promoting office seekers; the American Society of Muslims on initiatives in the black community; and assorted political action committees (PACs) on financing electoral campaigns. In addition, a host of professional associations represent Muslim lawyers, doctors, scientists, professors, etc.

A key umbrella organization is the Islamic Society of North America (ISNA) which seems to have evolved from its wahhibi roots. Its annual convention attracts an estimated 30,000 participants. Part scholarly conference, part religious gathering, and part cultural fair, the convention features diverse topical panels and noted authors, along with hundreds of booths featuring such diverse fare as international relief exhibits, *hijab* fashion, Islamic investment plans, glossy magazines, and colourful displays of Islamic-theme comic books and tapes for children. Despite widespread complaints about certain US government policies, the tone of the 2006 convention was notably upbeat, confident, and even self-critical. Speakers championed a greater role for women, more father involvement in child rearing, better race relations, voter mobilization, Islamic movie making, care for the poor, and environmental activism. Muslim leaders heard admonitions to critically appraise them of the troubled state of Islamic societies abroad.[8] Notably, the members elected Ingrid Mattson, a woman who had criticized the community for lack of female inclusion, to head the association. A professor at Hartford Seminary in Connecticut, Mattson aims to "give worshippers more control over who preaches in their mosques" and intends to "help keep out extremists."[9]

In addition to general civic engagement, American Muslims have become increasingly active participants in democratic politics. Despite the fact that two-thirds of the Muslim population is foreign born, a remarkable 82 per cent reported in 2004 that they were registered to vote and of those nearly all said they *intended* to vote. A majority of survey respondents also said that they had called or written to a politician or the media, or signed a petition, and healthy numbers reported attending political rallies or volunteering time or money to candidates.[10] College students, active on their campuses, show every sign of continuing this pattern.

As a political community American Muslims are ideologically complex. They oppose gay marriage, unrestricted abortion, and pornography, while supporting public vouchers for families to send their kids to private religious schools.[11] This cultural conservatism—combined with elevated socio-economic status, high marriage rates, and entrepreneurial proclivities—make Muslims look like typical Republican voters. And indeed, before 9/11 many Muslims were drawn to the Republican Party, whose operatives actively courted them. In fact, in 2000 a coalition of American Muslim leaders made a strategic decision to flex their political muscle by collectively endorsing George W. Bush, who won a plurality of the Muslim vote against Al Gore.[12] This gained Muslim leaders invitations to White House functions and some access to executive branch agencies. White House sensitivity to the Muslim population continued in the immediate aftermath of the attacks of 11 September 2001. President Bush proclaimed Islam a religion of peace, called upon Americans not to discriminate against Muslim citizens, and spoke felicitously about protecting "women of cover." He also hosted end-of-Ramadan *Eid* celebrations at the White House. By the end of 2001 the majority of Muslims gave what turned out to be short-lived approval of Bush's handling of the war on terror.

But Muslim attitudes never fully conformed to the economically libertarian agenda of the modern Republican Party. Perhaps reflecting both their immigrant status and the social justice tradition of Islam, American Muslims overwhelmingly favour universal health-care, government assistance to the poor, stricter environmental laws, funding for after school programmes, and increased foreign aid to poorer nations.[13] These liberal views incline Muslims toward the agenda of the Democratic Party, and as sentiment toward the Bush administration soured with the war in Iraq they moved with alacrity into the Democratic camp. Indeed, American politics has seldom seen such a rapid turnaround as the shift in the Muslim electorate from one presidential election to the next. Perceived excesses of the Patriot Act, the round-up and detention of several thousand Muslim émigrés, and the war in Iraq combined to make the Bush administration highly unpopular with American Muslims by 2004. Not only did they overwhelmingly give their votes to John Kerry, but increasing numbers identified themselves as Democrats.[14] This pattern should repeat itself in 2008, as Democratic nominee Barack Obama is popular in the Islamic community, even though some Muslims expressed dismay by the vehement way he denied rumours he was a Muslim.

As this narrative suggests, the Muslim constituency, while in certain ways still in its political infancy, is beginning to come of age. Organizational leaders admit that they still lack extensive access to members of Congress, nothing like the legendary Jewish lobbies.[15] But that may change with the growth and increased sophistication of the Muslim population. This is illustrated by the way deep discontent with American policies has been largely channelled into democratic participation—news conferences, letters to the editor, litigation, lobbying, and voting.

Discontent has been fuelled by both domestic and foreign policies. By 2004 more American Muslims said that the US was fighting a war on Islam (38 per cent) than a war on terror (33 per cent). The vast majority opposes the war in Iraq and sees it as contributing to terrorism and instability in the Middle East. In addition, reports of the mistreatment and humiliation of Muslim detainees, including American citizens, reverberate widely through the community. While such grievances have provoked violence by Muslims elsewhere, this has not been the general pattern of response in the United States.

By far the most successful response to the perceived assaults on the Muslim community at home and abroad has been electoral mobilization. During the 2006 congressional elections Muslim organizations mounted unprecedented voter registration drives, endorsed prominent Democratic challengers, and employed classic get-out-the-vote techniques to ensure a robust turnout. Their efforts were rewarded by the Democratic takeover of both houses of Congress, widely seen as a repudiation of Bush policies. Given the hairbreadth Democratic victory in the Senate, Muslims were able to take credit for the margin of victory. In particular, they touted their decisive impact on the senate race in Virginia, which gave the Democrats control of the upper chamber. In Virginia, Muslim PACs endorsed Democrat James Webb against the incumbent George Allen, and the Muslim American Society turned out its constituency by conducting automated phone calls and recruiting over 200 volunteers to get their people to the polls. Of the estimated 60,000 Muslim voters who turned out in Virginia, over 47,000 voted for Webb, who won by a margin of only 7,000 votes.[16] Muslim press also celebrated the historic election of the first Muslim—Keith Ellison of Minnesota—to Congress. In a potent symbolic gesture, Ellison took the oath of office with his hand on a copy of the *Qur'ān* owned by Thomas Jefferson.

In sum, despite widespread frustration about domestic discrimination and profiling, and despite the growing view that the US war on terrorism is a war on Islam, Muslims generally have not abandoned—indeed have intensified— democratic participation as the outlet for their grievances. Nearly all mosque leaders agree that "Muslims should be involved in American institutions," with 77 per cent strongly agreeing.[17] And among lay Muslims a strong majority believes it is important to "seek a place at the political table." More remarkably, some 51 per cent in one survey said that it is a "good time" to be a Muslim in America.[18]

Part of what produces this outcome is the nature of American civic and religious culture. For one thing, the American version of nationality is not tied to ethnicity or religion, owing to the long tradition and routine legal process of immigrant naturalization and democratic assimilation. Thus Muslim immigrants are following the same paths as waves of Catholics, Jews, and now Hindus and Buddhists. The Constitution's protection of religious freedom and prohibition against state churches powerfully shape civic life in the United States. Freed from the paternalistic hand of government and unencumbered by harassment, religious communities in America have flourished in dizzying pluralism.[19]

Many Muslims have discovered that this American civic culture is congenial to their religious life. The entrepreneurial openness to opportunity rewards people—like American Muslims—who emphasize education, strong families, and tight-knit communities that generate social capital. This explains why over 70 per cent of American Muslims believe in the "American Dream" that "most people who want to get ahead can make it if they work hard."[20] Moreover, if Muslims suffer discrimination on the basis of their faith they have access to the courts. Or as one Muslim woman put it, "My daughter can wear her headscarf to school and if they won't let her we'll sue."[21] In contrast to more secular nations of Europe, religious practice in America is routine and accepted. In the words of one young Muslim, average Americans "don't think I'm hallucinating when I say, 'It's prayer time.'"[22] Immigrants are often pleasantly surprised by the piety of American people.[23] Moreover, some Muslims, like Shias from Sunni lands, Sufis, or moderates, find they can practice their religion more freely in the United States than in their home country, where minority expressions are suppressed by the state or dominant culture.

The draw of American civic culture has inspired Muslim thinkers to lay the intellectual groundwork for an authentic Islamic understanding of citizen participation in a pluralist democracy. In particular they are challenging the traditional Islamic division of the world into the realms of *Dar al-Islam* (the abode of peace governed by Islamic rule) and *Dar al-Harb* (the "realm of war" that exists outside of Islamic governance).

Instead, a number of scholars explicitly articulate Islamic principles that they believe vindicate natural rights and democracy.[24] New York imam Feisal Abdul Rauf, for example, argues that there is a concordance between "what's right with America"—provision of rights and constitutional checks on abuse of power—and "what's right with Islam"—the consultative and social justice spirit of the *Ummah*'s self governance.[25] Similarly, Taha Jabir Al-Alwani, president of the *Fiqh* Council of North America, argues that a new interpretation of Shariah is required to guide the engagement of Muslims as minorities in western democracies. This new *Fiqh* (Islamic legal system) would draw upon the higher values of the *Qur'ān* and the power of human reason to script cordial relations between Muslims and non-Muslims. In particular, Al-Alwani suggests that whenever Muslims are free to practice their faith, as in the United States, a kind of *Dar al-Islam* obtains, in part because Muslims have the opportunity to enlighten non-Muslims about the "straight path."[26] Other thinkers have attempted to capture their experience in America by coining such terms as *dar ul-sulh* (place of alliance or treaty), *dar ul-aman* (place of order) or *dar ul-da'wa* (place of calling).[27] Perhaps the most felicitous phrase comes from a Sufi movement that promotes democratic citizenship as *dar ul-hizmet*, or an "abode of service."[28]

One of the most important intellectual enterprises seeks to advance the full participation of Muslim women in civic life. While men continue to hold the majority of leadership positions—and a number of them promote traditional gender roles—a cadre of assertive women academics, writers, and professionals serve as key voices of reform within the *Ummah*. Keenly aware that in the western imagination Muslim women often represent a synecdoche for "backward" Islam, these thinkers plumb Islamic history to distill what they see as the enlightened essence of Qur'anic teachings about women's capacity.[29] And average Muslim women overwhelmingly share their view, with 71 per cent saying that "Islam treats members of sexes equally well."[30]

The 9/11 watershed

American Muslims experienced the attacks of 11 September 2001 as a shock and a watershed in their life in the United States. For one thing, the events of that day and their aftermath dramatically heightened the visibility of the Muslim community. Muslim leaders found themselves frequently invited to explain their faith at churches and community forums, and they participated in diverse efforts—such as producing documentaries and movies—to portray Islam in a positive light. To an unprecedented degree they opened their mosques to non-Muslims and increased interfaith dialogues. They also engaged in media outreach to the Muslim community abroad, appearing on *Al-Jazeera* and other international news outlets to condemn terrorism and explain their participation in American democratic life.

The events also heightened the self-consciousness of American Muslims. Casual believers embraced the faith more deeply, some women started wearing the *hijab*, and many studied Islamic precepts to explain them to curious co-workers and neighbours. But American Muslims, especially the young, don't blindly follow the teachings of the local imam; like fellow citizens they often tailor their religious practice to their lives in the United States[31]

The experience of being thrust suddenly into intense civic engagement spurred the rapid maturation of Muslim political organizations, which raised more money, expanded their operations, and got additional followers involved. As one scholar put it, "despite prejudice and hate crimes we hear the increasingly confident voices of American Muslims in the public sphere," and "calls for adherence to the Constitution and civil rights."[32]

But if the shock of 9/11 mobilized the community, the war on terror brought unprecedented scrutiny of Islam, which led some of the American faithful to be apologists for any Islamic regime abroad, no matter how despotic or illiberal.[33] Much to the consternation of Muslim leaders, the US government shut down half a dozen charities, such as the Holy Land Foundation, that allegedly funnelled money to terrorist organizations—and individuals were prosecuted for doing the same. While in a few cases links were found to al-Qaeda networks, most focused on ties to such Islamist movements as Hamas in Palestine and Hezbollah in Lebanon.[34] Listed as terrorist organizations by the government, Hamas and Hezbollah enjoy some sympathy among American Muslims as social service providers and advocates for besieged Palestinians and Shias. In the wake of Israel's 2006 war with Hezbollah, for example, Arab-Americans in Dearborn, Michigan, demonstrated in support of Hezbollah's cause, some holding up pro-Hezbollah placards. But any tangible backing for these groups resulted in prosecution, as was the case of a prominent Dearborn restaurant owner, who fled to Lebanon after being indicted for funnelling some 20 million dollars to Hezbollah.[35]

Both domestic converts and immigrants were swept up in massive law enforcement efforts against terrorist networks, which have brought long jail sentences. Some of those charged did not see themselves fighting against the United States. For example, former civil rights coordinator for CAIR, Randal "Ismail" Royer, fought on behalf of Bosnian Muslims and later joined a Pakistani group that trained to fight in Kashmir. He said that he did not think his actions were illegal because the group "wasn't on the US terrorist list at the time." But under the doctrine of "preventive prosecution" authorities have pursued any who train with Islamic militant groups, "fearing that they could return and form sleeper cells."[36]

In certain cases aggressive prosecutions have exposed and rooted out extremist impulses among a few Muslim leaders. The head of the now-defunct American Muslim Council, Abdurahman Muhammad Alamoudi, a highly visible leader of the community, was sentenced to twenty-three years in jail for his association with terrorists. Ali Al Timimi, a lecturer at the *Al Arqam* mosque in a suburb of Washington D.C., was sentenced to life for "urging a group of congregants after September 11 to travel to Afghanistan to fight US forces alongside the Taliban."[37] And Sami Al-Arian, an engineering professor at the University of South Florida, plead guilty to a charge of helping finance the Palestinian group Islamic Jihad.

In addition to law enforcement agencies, robust networks of think-tank fellows, scholars, and polemicists scrutinize the American Islamic community and expose any extremist impulses.[38] Epitomizing this is Daniel Pipes, the *bête noire* of Muslim leadership, whose blog highlights Islamist declarations or supposed terrorist sympathies in the Muslim community.[39] A consistent target of his is CAIR, which by his count had five former employees or board members "arrested, convicted, deported, or otherwise linked to terrorism-related charges."[40] Another watchdog is Steven Emerson, who produced the documentary "Jihad in America" about home-grown terrorists. This act made him a target of threats from international radical groups and necessitated living at a clandestine address.[41] While Muslim leaders view much of this scrutiny as unfair and distorted, it does act as a check on the germination of Islamist networks. After 9/11 Muslims live in a fishbowl.

Nowhere is this more evident than in the exposure of militant Wahhabi teachings promoted by Saudi money. For years the Saudi Arabian Embassy's Islamic Affairs Department ran a multi-million dollar campaign in the United States, building mosques, distributing Salafi-commentary *Qur'ans* and bringing in "foreign imams to lead congregations." As one scholar charged, this "oil-nourished plutocracy" was warping American Islam.[42] In the wake of the discovery that fifteen of the nineteen hijackers on September 11 were Saudis trained by Wahhabi teaching, there were exposés of this influence and the US government ultimately revoked diplomatic visas of Saudis involved in "religious outreach."[43]

This action helped close out the programme, but continuing Saudi influence remains under the microscope. In 2005 Freedom House issued a report detailing the scathing depictions of non-Muslims and the West in Saudi-financed literature found in American mosques. According to the report, America was depicted as the "abode of the Infidel" and good Muslims were urged to dissociate from Jews and Christians, "hate them for their religion," and prepare for bellicose jihad against unbelievers. Enmity for Jews was especially prevalent, with the forgery *Protocols of the Elders of Zion* treated as historical fact. Democracy, freedom of thought, and religious tolerance were also condemned in the literature, and Muslims who rejected such Wahhabi teachings became "apostates" whose blood can lawfully be spilt.[44] The report got wide play in the press and sparked initiatives by other watchdog entities, such as the US Commission on International Religious Freedom, which took Saudi Arabia to task for its role in fertilizing militant Islam around the world. The embarrassing glare of this exposure led some mosque leaders to scrutinize literature in their houses of worship, which is one of the several ways the community has begun policing itself.

The promise of living on the borderlines

American Muslims live on the borderlines between civilizations, "their feet in the West, their hearts with Islam."[45] Many are conscious of how this thrusts them into a unique global role as a potential bridge between Islam and the West. They are both the "best ambassadors" from the United States to the Islamic world and the best "ambassadors to the US from the Islamic world." Or as one young Muslim put it, because Islam is in the spotlight "you are an ambassador whether you want to be or not."[46]

This unique role creates a special responsibility. Sulayman Nyang, professor of African Studies at Howard University, suggested that American Muslims could "play an important role in the cultural development of their brethren elsewhere" and thereby become "one of the major pillars" of the Islamic world.[47] Salem al-Marayati, director of MPAC, similarly asserted that his organization could "be more powerful than so many other Islamic groups" abroad because it enjoys the freedom to organize politically and to "help others elsewhere."[48] Ahmed Younis, former Washington director of MPAC, contends that American Muslims are positioned to lead the "reform conversation" in the Islamic world and by doing so help to change negative images of Islam. A young attorney, Younis epitomizes the growing consciousness among American Muslims that their strategic position creates special obligations.[49]

Public intellectuals mirror this sense of destiny for the American Muslim community. Muqtedar Khan wrote that demonstrating "to the rest of the world the relevance of Islamic values to a modern/postmodern society" is the "manifest destiny of American Muslims." He goes on to say that the task of "manifesting a moderate, peaceful, tolerant, inclusive, compassionate and moral model of Islam falls on the American Muslim community." American Muslims, in other words, can serve as the *Mujaddid*, or "reviver," of Muslim culture.[50] Ideed, there are many Islamic organizations working with the promotion of human rights and democracy within an Islamic framework. The most notable effort on this front has been mounted by MPAC. Challenged at its first convention in December 2001 to create a Muslim human rights organization, MPAC resolved to grade Muslim nations on their human rights practices. But leaders realized that to be meaningful such a critique must come from within the Islamic tradition, not be derivative of western or secular human rights organizations. This led to a major effort, spearheaded by Maher Hathout, one of the elder statesmen of the community, to link human rights with Islamic jurisprudence. The product is a weighty book that systematically grounds rights—such as freedom of speech, religion, association, and civic participation—in teachings of the *Qur'ān* and *Hadith*.[51]

The shock of seeing Muslim militants declaring jihad against their own country has greatly emboldened moderate and liberal voices in the American Islamic community. As Scholar Karen Leonard observes, these Muslims "are increasingly confronting their conservative co-believers."[52] UCLA law professor Khaled Abou El Fadl, for example, has been a prolific critic of hard liners and literalists—whom he calls "puritans"—while pressing an Islamic justification for civil liberties, women's rights, and democracy.[53] Reza Aslan, a young émigré from Iran, explores the rich historical tradition of Islam to make his case for sweeping reform.[54] Emory law professor An Naim calls for nothing less than a "reformation" of Islamic law to make it compatible with the imperatives of modern life.[55] Imam Hamza Yusuf, a popular international lecturer and media personality, seeks to reclaim the tolerant "spirit of Andalusia" among Muslims.[56] Another prominent imam, Zaid Shakir, counsels against Muslim chauvinism—what he terms a "false sense of moral superiority"—and implores his brethren to embrace the positive aspects of the American constitutional guarantee of rights.[57] Zuhdi Jasser, a former US naval officer, founded the American Islamic Forum for Democracy as an alternative to groups like CAIR that he sees as too sympathetic to Islamists, a posture he shares with another reformist group, the American Islamic Congress, headed by Zainab Al-Suwaij.

Most consequentially, in response to the London bombings of 2005, the authoritative *Fiqh* Council of North America issued an important *fatwa* categorically condemning "religious extremism," suicide bombings, and "all acts of terrorism and targeting of civilians." Also "*haram*" (or forbidden) is cooperating "with any group or individual involved in terrorism or violence." The *fatwa* concluded by proclaiming that it is a "civic and religious duty to cooperate with law enforcement authorities to protect lives of all civilians."[58]

Nurtured in the laboratory of American civic life, the Muslim community is clearly poised to play a crucial role in the relations between the Islamic world and the West. But to fulfil their "destiny" American Muslims must overcome several challenges.

Challenges

One challenge involves negative views of Islam among non-Muslims, which increased as the conflict in Iraq descended into grisly sectarian violence. Interestingly, most Americans distinguish between their fellow Muslim citizens, or whom they have generally favourable opinions, and the Islamic religion, which elicits more disparaging sentiment. For example, favourable views of Muslim-Americans actually rose in the immediate aftermath of the 9/11 attacks. Perhaps taking cues from statements by President Bush and Muslim leaders, fully 55 per cent of the public hold favourable opinions of Muslim-Americans. Some analysts, however, believe that the nation's tradition of religious tolerance may lead some respondents to give "socially desirable" responses in surveys, inflating the actual sympathy for the Muslim population.[59]

A better gauge of sentiment might be attitudes towards Islam. Here the trend has been downward. Between 2005 and 2006 unfavourable opinion of Islam surpassed favourable, and now approaches a majority (46 per cent) of the American public. Prominent right wing polemicists fuel this sentiment. In a statement practically designed to confirm Islamic paranoia about American intentions, commentator Ann Coulter said of the Muslim world that "We should invade their countries, kill their leaders, and convert them to Christianity."[60] Within the American religious community negative sentiment is highest among evangelicals, many of whom see the war against terror as in effect a conflict between "Islam and the Christian West."[61] Incendiary remarks by some visible leaders of the evangelical community have contributed to this view. Franklin Graham, son of the famous evangelist Billy Graham, referred to Islam as "a very evil and wicked religion." Former Southern Baptist Convention president Jerry Vines said that the Prophet Muhammad was "a demon-possessed paedophile." Pat Robertson referred to the prophet as a "wild-eyed fanatic," while Jerry Falwell termed him "a terrorist." Richard Cizik, Washington director for the moderate National Association of Evangelicals, worried that Islam has replaced the Soviet Union as the "modern-day equivalent of the Evil Empire."[62] Indeed, one finds in the literature of some "Christian solidarity" groups the spectre of aggressive Islam—not only its militant outgrowth—posing a mortal threat to persecuted Christian minorities. Muslim leaders fear that this Islamophobia swells the perception of Islam as an alien culture in the United States and undermines their ability to build bridges with fellow citizens. Similarly, moderate Muslim scholar Akbar Ahmed is concerned that inflammatory rhetoric by non-Muslims fuels the "sense of siege" already felt in the Muslim community.[63]

Battling negative portrayals is made more challenging by remaining pockets of militancy in the community. In a widely-reported 2007 survey, the Pew Research Center identified a small but persistent group of American Muslims with militant sympathies. Some 5 per cent have at least a "somewhat favourable" view of al-Qaeda, for example, while 8 per cent say that suicide bombings are sometimes justified to defend Islam and 7 per cent say that the 9/11 attack was the result of a conspiracy involving the United States government or the Bush administration.[64] Though these figures are much lower than those in Western Europe and the Middle East, they give concern. Pockets of extreme Islamist ideology have sprouted up in the United States. After 9/11 the government crackdown swept up disparate militants: the "Lackawanna Six"—Yemeni-Americans who visited a terrorist training camp in Afghanistan; the "Portland Seven" who attempted to join the Taliban during the war in 2001; Randal Royer and other conspirators in a jihadist group in Northern Virginia who trained in the use of weapons and explosives; members of a New York City sleeper cell of *al-Muhajiroun* (a British radical Islamist group); two members of the US armed forces who attempted to aid al-Qaeda; and three immigrant Muslims in Ohio charged with plotting to fight American troops in Iraq.[65] Another splinter group, The Islamic Thinkers Society, located in Queens, New York, praised the 9/11 hijackers[66] and posted a video on YouTube showing members desecrating the American Flag while shouting that Allah is great.[67]

Scholars and pundits disagree about how extensive and dangerous actual domestic jihadist networks are. Daniel Pipes contends that home grown terrorism is a significant problem. He identified some thirty American converts "suspected, arrested, or indicted of terrorism," and by a somewhat questionable extrapolation concluded that an additional 175 immigrant Muslims have "turned to terrorism."[68] Two other accounts echo Pipes' assessment. In *Holy War on the Home Front*, Harvey Kushner and Bart Davis chastise government officials for slighting the threat of Islamist networks operating through bogus charities, prisons, and internet sites. More expansively, in a 2002 book titled *American Jihad*, journalist Steve Emerson assembled hundreds of hours of video documenting American networks that support Hamas, university-based Islamists, jihad recruiting cells, and publications that preach hate toward non-Muslims. Less polemical than Kushner and Davis, Emerson acknowledges that the vast majority of American Muslims have not embraced radicalism, but he believes that "extremists have disproportionate influence."[69]

Taking issue with these pessimistic assessments, Spencer Ackerman contends that America's pluralist culture diffuses militant appeal, which is why American Muslims generally "haven't turned to terrorism." In contrast to the British-born jihadists who carried out the London bombing, the few instances of American Muslims becoming terrorists "are better explained by individual pathology" than "group disaffection." Epitomizing this are John Walker Lindh, the "American Taliban," Jose Padilla, former gang member and attempted "dirty bomber," Mohammad Reza Taheri-Azar, who ploughed his vehicle into a pedestrian crowd, and Adam Gadahn (formerly Adam Pearlman, son of a psychedelic musician), who became an al-Qaeda spokesman.[70] Ackerman points to a *Washington Post* finding that since 9/11 just thirty-nine individuals have actually been convicted of terror-related charges, and only fourteen of those had links to al-Qaeda.[71] Tellingly, there were no American riots in the wake of the Danish cartoon controversy; instead Muslims appeared on television talk show programmes and wrote op-ed pieces denouncing the derogatory depictions of the prophet Mohammad.

Though concerned about domestic Islamic radicalization, the US Office of Homeland Security seems to share this less alarmist view. In Senate testimony the agency's chief intelligence officer concluded that "it is more difficult for radicalized individuals in the United States to turn their ideologically-driven violent inclinations into successful terrorist attacks," in part because linkages between international criminal cabals and disaffected Muslims are much weaker in American than Europe.[72] And the sheer scale of the threat is profoundly less in the United States. As Senator Joseph Lieberman observed, officials in Great Britain "identified more than 200 cells, with a total of 1,600 individuals who are plotting or facilitating acts of terrorism in the UK"—a figure that dwarfs even the most pessimistic assessment of the situation in the US[73]

While the scope of jihadi appeal is apparently small, some Muslim leaders do see an important task of countering extremist or reductionist interpretations of Islam. Maher Hathout complains about how *Qur'ānic* literalists ignore the great Islamic tradition of independent reasoning, or *ijtihad*, which he promotes in his writing and lecturing.[74] Ahmed Younis admits worrying about some mosques fermenting extremism, but he pointed to his organization's ongoing efforts to provide the tools to prevent militant interpretations of the *Qur'ān* and *Hadith*. In particular, MPAC sought to amplify the Islamic message against terrorism by producing guidelines to prevent mosques from being used by "saboteurs." And the organization cooperates with law enforcement officials in "legitimate" anti-terrorism efforts.[75] Younis believes that authorities are coming to understand that the American Muslim community must be at the "apex of counter-terrorism" because it can identify pathological individuals better than anyone. But he fears that "profiling" by law enforcement officials may alienate law-abiding Muslims and make them loath to cooperate in counter-terrorism initiatives.[76]

While plentiful economic opportunities and democratic outlets blunt the appeal of militant Islam in America, growing opposition to American foreign policy could lead more youth to embrace Islamist ideology. The protracted wars in Iraq and Afghanistan, the use of torture and extraordinary rendition against Muslim detainees, the festering Palestinian quandary, and US "unconditional" backing of Israel combine to increase negative assessments of America's place in the world. Ominously, the percentage of American Muslims who feared that the war on terror had "morphed into a war on Islam" increased from 38 per cent in 2004 to over half by 2006.[77] This perception makes it more difficult for Muslim leaders to meet another challenge: fostering a positive American Muslim identity, especially among the next generation. In the wake of the 2005 London bombings, shockingly perpetrated by "homegrown" terrorists, the question resounded: "could it happen here?" To find out, MPAC conducted a survey of Muslim youth between the ages of 15 and 25. While the vast majority believed that Muslims should be invested in the political process, nearly half (46 per cent) said they felt at least some "conflict between their Muslim identity and their American society."[78] More ominously, the Pew Research Center found that 15 per cent of Muslim youth (more than double the figure for elder Muslims) believe that suicide bombings can sometimes be justified. So in spite of exceptional educational and economic status American Muslim identity remains fluid, a subject of great concern to leaders in the community. The degree of Islamist appeal thus remains an issue of dispute. Critics of American Muslims, especially some neo-con-servatives, point to the "supremacist" expressions of some Muslim leaders about replacing "the US Constitution with Islamic Law."[79] Others dismiss alarmist warnings. Muqtedar Khan argues that before 9/11 there were pockets of the triumphal view that over time American Muslims could turn the United States into an Islamic state. After 9/11, he contends, there is little such talk: "Any reminder of the pre-9/11 vision generates sheepish giggles and snorts from Muslim audiences." Instead, Muslims have been compelled to reconstitute their identity as citizens connected "more intimately with Ameri-can mainstream society."[80]

Conclusion

By their affluence, education, thriving intellectual life, and citizenship, Ameri-can Muslims occupy a unique place on the borders of Islam. Most disagree with Huntington's belief in an inevitable clash between Islamic civilization and the nation in which they reside. And many no longer see themselves on the periphery of the Islamic world but as key players in its evolution. As the above discussion suggests, whether or not American Muslims can "fulfil their destiny" and serve as a bridge between civilizations depends both on develop-ments abroad—such as the outcome of the Iraq war or the Middle East peace process—and on the actions of Muslims and non-Muslims in the United States. In a sense we see two possible contending forces. On the one hand, the abuse of civil liberties in the war on terror, ostracism by other Americans, and the unpopularity of the United States in the Islamic world could converge to produce defensiveness, alienation, or militant sympathies, especially for Mus-lim youth. On the other hand, clear pathways to high status careers, demo-cratic outlets for discontent, and the election of Barack Obama can counteract those impulses.

Law enforcement restraint can fortify the work of moderate Muslims. Aggressive prosecutions, in some cases, have resulted in long incarcerations before defendants were found innocent of crimes.[81] Partnerships with the Department of Homeland Security, the Justice Department, and local officials can achieve two purposes—identifying violence-prone individuals and build-ing trust between the Muslim community and the government. Muslim lead-ers should work assiduously to get more of their young people involved in government. The US government could also do more to support moderate Muslims and promote the flow of their ideas to the Middle East and Europe.

While the situation is fluid one thing is clear: the Islamic community has become heavily invested in the nation's democratic institutions. We see this in how thinking and practice have evolved. As late as 1986 a number of Muslim leaders still thought of themselves as residing only temporarily in the United States, a "place of unbelievers" (or *dar ul-kufr*). But by the end of that year ISNA issued a declaration "favouring citizenship and participation in mainstream politics".[82] This participation accelerated rapidly after 9/11, with the further jolt of the London bombings spurring efforts at democratic socialization of the young. Thus American Muslims find themselves modelling by their lives—as well as their by intellectual effort—the ideal of Islamic citizenship "rather than rulership."

The community is also increasingly financing its own institutions, cutting the tether to Saudi Arabia and "desert Islam."[83] Though not complete, this transformation is significant. The Muslim Students Association, the 1960s forerunner of other Islamic organizations, was almost entirely financed by Saudi money, and CAIR also received substantial funding from abroad. Today such organizations as MPAC boast of not taking "a dime" from foreign sources and reformist groups are entirely self funded. This increasing self-financing should work to blunt the reassertion of Salafi doctrine and better reflect the aspirations of the majority of Muslim citizens. Treasury department enforcement of guidelines for non-profits—including the freezing of assets of some charities—has also spurred Islamic organizations to operate with better board oversight and guidance. A sterling example is Islamic Relief USA, which is ranked among the top 4 per cent of all charities in the United States in terms of fiscal responsibility and effectiveness.[84]

In sum, by increasingly taking positive steps, forging relationships of trust and reciprocity with fellow citizens, and maximizing their talents to model a vibrant democratic community, American Muslims may indeed serve as a unique bridge between Islam and the West.

19

A Virtual Border Conflict

Stephen Ulph

When examining how the issue of conflict has come to occupy centre stage in radical identity, one notable element is how this issue repeats itself in a particular way in an environment where Muslims form a minority group: that is, where Muslims are found in societies outside the heartlands of Islam.

That there should be any border conflict of this nature is, of course, not a *fait accompli* and depends on how soon progress is registered in the resolution of tensions within Islam, tensions that have taken on the magnitude of an intellectual civil war. And in focusing on these potential areas of conflict, we are naturally deliberately selecting those tendencies and groups in the Muslim communities that see their relationship with non-Muslim states as one of hostility. For these, the idea that a conflict exists is a self-evident truth that needs little explanation.[1] This is the radical wing of Islamic belief, and there are certain features unique to this environment. A sense of siege has first to be established for the act of defence to have any meaning. Radical elements on the Internet can wage a border conflict only on certain terms, that is: *notionally*. And it is here that the "border conflict," however abstract, is actually at its most thoroughgoing for being personalized. The reason for this is that for the radical believers, nothing less than Islam's very identity and survival is at stake. How Islamic radicalism works out its struggle on the Internet—where the Islamic model is confronted with statistically powerful social and political, as well as intellectual, adversaries (Muslim and non-Muslim) that do not challenge it so comprehensively in the Muslim heartlands—will form the pattern for future, yet more intensified, struggles in the broader contest over Islam's place in the modern world. It is therefore worth examining this abstract or "virtual" border conflict in some detail.

The first border: Muslims versus the *jāhiliyya*

Since the challenge to Muslim consciousness by the cultural onslaught of the West, the defining feature for a truly "authentic" Muslim society has been not just the self-definition of Muslims in the daily fulfilment of religious obligations, but the reinstatement of the conceptual and normative supremacy of Islam, untainted by starting points hailing from outside its own tradition. This is represented at its clearest in the call for the re-establishment of Islamic Law, the Shariah. Failure to implement the Shariah, or implement it comprehensively, underscores the failure of that society to maintain Islam's supremacy, and underlines the society's "contamination" according to its own definitions. Rallying to the standard of the Shariah forms the centre point about which more than one radical tendency meets, as a sort of national cause for the new *Ummah*. Scholars both of the Salafist and Salafi-jihadist tendencies share the starting point of rejecting the present reality of Muslims living under post-Islamic, and hence apostate, legal systems or Muslims participating in political processes that imply governance *bi-ghayr mā anzal Allāh* "other than what God has decreed". Scholars of either pietistic, or militant tendencies, differ only in the tactics of their rejection.

The failure to date to establish a Sunni Islamic state has not dimmed the energies of radical Islam. These energies are being channelled into the "preparatory" phase for the future state. Works are already circulating on the future characteristics and policies of this state, such as *The Constitution Project for the Caliphal State, International Relations in Islam* and *Finance in the Caliphal State*, but the main focus is on religious preparation.[2] This focus is also prominent in works ostensibly given over to tactical issues in the waging of jihad. Scholars and ideologues from the jihad strategist Abu Mus'ab al-Suri to the Salafist thinker Abu Baseer al-Tartousi have identified the weak doctrinal training, and the far too elementary understanding of Islam among activist militants as causes of their failure.[3]

Reformist-minded Salafists in particular identify the necessity of religious training on the Salafi *manhaj* preceding militancy, on the grounds that God will only grant victory to true believers, and that common sense dictates that jihad can only be carried out incrementally, matching the means to the attainable ends. The *Da'wa-Hijra-Ummah* paradigm is adduced to defend this sequence. Under this formula present day society is associated with the earliest *da'wa* phase of the Prophet's *sīra*, where the true believers are a small island in a sea of *jahiliyya*. Jihadi Salafist thinkers, on the other hand, are at pains to push the interpretation of current affairs at least to the *hijra* stage, where the argument for simultaneous jihad is less difficult to square with historical precedent. Indeed, in a masterfully rendered projection back to Prophetic times of the circumstances of the contemporary jihad—the chaos and disarray of Afghanistan and Somalia—the strategist Abu Bakr Naji identified a "stage of barbarism" that predates the successful establishment of the *Ummah*:

"One can consider the first phase of the Medinan era—before its consolidation and the establishment of a state to which *zakat* (alms tax) and *jizya* (tribute tax) were rendered and neighbouring dependent provinces set up and agents and rulers appointed—as one where Medina was administered according to the 'management of barbarism' system."[4]

But even if the timing is disputed, the argument on jihad postponed is an entirely pragmatic one since, according to jihadi Salafists, holy war as a tactic of religious transformation cannot as such be rescinded in Islamic law. While radicals criticize the behaviour of the mujahedin for their tactical errors, reformist opponents therefore have recourse to the legal precepts of *al-masālih*, the broader "interests" of the nation. Any violent activities that might provoke vigorous responses from state authorities that would hamper the propagation of the Islamic faith have to be censored, since this would constitute "an evil that is replaced by a greater evil" and is thus religiously forbidden.[5]

Whether the jihad is against Arab regimes or western states, for pietistic Salafis the priorities must for now remain education in *'aqīda* (articles of faith) and purification, that is, the correction of contamination from un-Islamic systems and practices. This may take the form of the piecemeal conversion of legal methodology to Shariah-compatible positions, but as the centre of gravity in Salafist thought shifts away from territorially focused activism in favour of personal development in this much longer-term endeavour (a more abstract and transnational concept of a virtual *Ummah*)—self-isolation and re-Islamization of the individual, rather than political or social activism, become all the more pressing.[6] The re-Islamization programme is ambitious and, given the established position of traditional Islam, might appear to be an improbable task. But if consciousness of this new *Ummah* identity is a recent phenomenon, the lines of communication in this endeavour are equally modern. The traditional role of the mosque in educating and regulating the identity and practice of the Muslim is being sidestepped and replaced by the Internet. As a borderless, *passepartout* tool of a younger generation, the new technology is the ideal vehicle for fuelling the virtual community of believers detached from a specific nationality or culture. It is fast becoming the method of choice for disseminating ideas and is instrumental in establishing alternative networks of scholars to defend the surfer's new culture and articulate his allegiance to the "virtual civilization".[7]

The range of materials available to the Salafist-minded browser is very broad—from web sites promoting an Islamic lifestyle to doctrinally-focused sites that provide "ask the scholar" *fatwa* services on points of law, to more hard-edged endeavours to refute heresy or heterodoxy, or a combination of all these. The combination of maximum access with minimum control enables scholars of all stamps and competencies to communicate freely with like-minded individuals and establish cultural groups.

The use of the Internet comes into its own in the coordination of activism. This was well demonstrated during the controversy over the cartoon images of the Prophet Muhammad. Here entire campaigns of demonstrations, boycotts and death threats were organized online, appearing almost overnight. At such moments of crisis the influence of the scholar websites peaks. This is particularly the case with regard to the activities of jihadist-Salafis, where veritable electronic pamphlet wars can take place on the web, waging ideological conflicts that can have a direct bearing on the behaviour and activities of militant mujahidin in the field.[8] A good example of this is the extended controversy over the July 2005 London bombings, where the Syrian Salafist scholar Abu Baseer al-Tartousi cast doubt on the Islamic propriety of the attacks, provoking serious disarray on the chat forums and some fierce responses.[9] Another prominent example of this operational dependency was the heated controversy over the criticism of the Jordanian al-Zarqawi's tactics against the Shia communities in Iraq by his erstwhile doctrinal mentor Abu Muhammad al-Maqdisi.[10] Al-Maqdisi's comments set in motion a potentially damaging debate as jihadist scholars and clerics responded to the anxieties expressed by confused jihad-minded youngsters in online forums. Indeed the continuing debate over the propriety of suicide bombings has exercised the minds of many scholars, either concerned about the morally deleterious effects of the tactic or anxious to maintain their Islamic validity.[11]

Media commentators on radical Islam too often overlook the crucial position legality holds in the rise and practice of jihadist organizations. The centrality of legality permeates the procedures of militant Salafists and imposes limitations on the spectrum of activism. The issue of Islamic legality is such a pressing one that considerable space on the net is given over by the jihadist thinkers to defending their case, point for point if necessary. A random perusal of apologetic works circulating online gives an idea of this endeavour:

"We Are 'Ignorant Deviants', so then Please Teach Us, Guide Us and Correct Us!"

"Guide for the Perplexed on the Permissibility of Killing Prisoners"

"Voices of the Scholars on the Killing of Ambassadors—Refutation of all Opponents of the Mujahidin"

"A Clarifying Voice on the Concept of [Using Humans as] Shields and its Religious Verdicts"

"An Investigation into the Judgement on Mutilating the Dead Bodies of Infidels and Apostates"

"Despite the state scholars, we *will* burn Americans and Jews and abuse the bodies"

"Reviving the Doctrine on Slaughtering the Infidel"

"Treatise on the Verdict of Using Weapons of Mass Destruction Against the Infidel."[12]

The problem of legitimacy became particularly pressing in 2004 when the mujahedin came under attack for their bombing activities in Saudi Arabia, which resulted in the deaths of many Muslims. The sense of danger posed by scholarly censure led to the compilation of *Questions and Uncertainties Concerning the Mujahedin and their Operations*, an exhaustive e-book which aims to give an answer to every conceivable question on the jihad and the behaviour of the mujahedin, drawing its support in each case from Islamic law.[13] It insists defiantly at the outset that "the mujahedin are following the path of the *Ahl al-Sunna wal-Jama'a* in matters of belief, that is, the path of the *Sahaba* (the earliest 'Companions' of the Prophet) and those who followed them" and is at pains to warn the public against the propaganda from the state scholars:

"Do not to be led astray by the scholars of evil and the preachers of error, read the books of the mujahedin, and weigh the mujahedin's actions in the scales of the Qur'an and the Sunna before you turn away, and cause others to turn away, from the path of *tawhid* and jihad."[14]

The work is, in fact, an entire library on this topic, and testifies to the importance given by the mujahidin to maintaining the legal and moral high ground.

In many ways the jihadists' enthusiastic embrace of the Internet reflects the impetus towards forming a "virtual" community among the broader Salafist communities. In the case of the jihadists, the transferral of focus to the web dates back to the loss of Afghanistan, following which the impet us to create a new, virtual Afghanistan, to maintain a sense of cohesion and morale was realized by groups such as *Sawt al-Jihād* in Saudi Arabia. Their publication *Mu'askar al-Battār* ("Al-Battar Training Camp") in particular set out to replicate the syllabus and culture of the Afghan training camps, and "serve the mujahid in his place of isolation" with:

"the publication of the military arts among the youths, so as to fill a gap at a time when the enemies of the faith are hastening to expand ... so that you may meet your obligations and embark on the legal duty enjoined upon you by God."[15]

Participation in this virtual community can take a number of forms. The most conspicuous manifestation is the jihadi chat forum. In a typical example, the sections divide themselves equally between proactive reader communication and contribution, and elements of information and guidance. A good proportion of the traffic is propaganda focused, featuring sophisticated Internet media productions, much of it illustrating the activities and progress of jihadist groups in the field through up-to-the-minute press releases and statements, slick productions of online weekly and monthly magazines, video clips, full-length films and televised news broadcasts.[16] Exploiting the Internet's reach, media coordinating groups enlisted the efforts of armchair mujahedin across the globe for news monitoring, translating and distribution, in one case giving these functions suitable "military" titles to present the image of frontline activism.[17] Surfers sympathetic to the jihad are also encouraged to use their technical skills in the cyber-war, and jihadi chat forums have hosted their own "electronic jihad" sections specialising in the relevant technology. Much attention has also been focused on the jihadi use of the Internet as a nimble distribution tool for military technology and technical training in the form of manuals and online encyclopaedias.[18]

At least half of all Internet endeavour, whether on chat forums or literature download sites, is taken up with this function, in the form of publications, treatises and essays, which are accessed through the various sections devoted to *da'wa*. The sheer wealth of such materials now made available on the web may perhaps not be generally appreciated. This is partly due to the fact that to date the culture of Internet jihad remains a predominantly Arabic-language phenomenon. Indeed, from surveys taken on Internet jihad usage, the epicentre remains the Middle East, which provides most of the doctrinal materials and accounts for the lion's share of traffic to jihadist materials on the web.[19]

The ideological materials circulating on the net form the intellectual underpinning for what a recent study[20] has termed the "self-identification" and "indoctrination" stages of radicalization. The first of these corresponds to the "first border" mentioned earlier, the awakening of consciousness of the encircling *jāhiliyya* and the new impetus towards re-authentification. As a subsection of the Salafiist movement, jihadi-Salafist radicalization on the net exhibits the full complement of Salafist themes—the western "marginalization of the natural order" ethically, religiously and intellectually, the curse of free-thinking and secularism, how "man-made legal systems" and the separation of religious and political spheres stand in contradiction to Islam.

The Internet activism of jihadi-Salafism, however, naturally focuses more closely on the political implications, and it is in this second "indoctrination" stage where the imperative towards action intensifies. Here, ideological primers re-orient the candidate reader away from the prevailing modern order by casting doubt on the "false promise" of democracy—establishing how inequality is built into the system, how it is responsible for the persistence of dictatorships in the Islamic world and how acquiescence in this order compromises the target reader's own self-view as a Muslim.[21] In this phase of what one might term the "antechamber to jihad", individuals or groups:

"... are likely to begin proliferating jihadi-Salafist ideology online along with consuming it. The Internet becomes a virtual 'echo chamber'—acting as a radicalization accelerant while creating the path for the ultimate stage of jihadization."[22]

By far the largest category of works in this indoctrination stage naturally centres on the core interest of jihad. From the sheer size of the online endeavour, and the number, wealth and quality of the works circulated and re-circulated, with recommendations provided by the question-and-answer correspondence on the Internet forums, the materials are enough to seamlessly guide the reader on a journey of progressive radicalization, from passive supporter to potential foot-soldier. They amount to nothing less than a jihad "curriculum".

The works of this curriculum begin with promoting the "fundamental obligation" of jihad through the use of religious texts and classical legal literature to argue the doctrinal case.[23] A whole body of literature then prioritizes the physical struggle over the spiritual interpretation that moderates give to the term "jihad,"[24] and defends the obligation to this over other religious priorities, such as obligations to family and the community.[25] The duty of jihad is then introduced, progressing the candidate through from the uncontroversial defensive jihad (against invaders and heretics), to jihad against unjust rule with its more controversial *takfir* (anathematization) of fellow Muslims, through to the more problematic case for *jihād al-talab*, offensive jihad for the expansion of Islam's political domination.[26] In practical terms the focus of this last duty primarily concerns Muslim sympathisers in non-Muslim states. The interest of these radicalizing works is in the methods by which the ideologues succeed in arguing for absolving the mujahid student of the moral obligation to heed the law of the host nation, and eventually for the practice of active "enmity to the infidel".[27]

Once the student has been fully reoriented politically and culturally, and provided with the confidence of religious backing, a major focus in the radicalization process is psychological training for his status and self-image as a mujahid.[28] These materials include "manuals" that embrace both doctrinal preparation to maximize morale, motivation and practical courses in psychological and personality training, all part of building up the new species of "Mujahid Man".[29] Once "enlisted into the ranks" the armchair mujahid surfer is also provided with a range of literature that aims to contextualize the struggle in broader strategic terms—with the governments of the Muslim world and with the western powers—all with the same overriding message: that the jihad is Islam at its most authentic since it is modelled on the original community, and the mujahedin are simply reapplying a long lost policy, the loss of which has caused the Muslims to decline in the modern age.

How successful this online radicalization endeavour is may be judged from the frustrations of security organizations at the role the Internet is playing in replenishing the ranks of jihadi activists and sympathisers.[30] For security officials this is statistically far more significant than the use of the net for circulating information on DIY munitions production—since radicalization education is an activity that is far broader in reach and uncriminalized. Analyses of the part the Internet is playing in jihadist activities support the conclusion that its primary function is in the provision of intellectual resources—the support and maintenance of the entire process of radicalization.

Reports of arrests of suspects now frequently illustrate the transformational effect of the Internet. French authorities in Montpellier uncovered a cell that had formed after "self-radicalization from Web sources but where they previously were in no way interested in religion at all"[31] and a recent report from the Dutch Ministry of the Interior highlighted how an 18-year old youth who had issued threats against Member of Parliament Ms Ayaan Hirsi Ali, was found, on arrest, to have "gone through the entire process of radicalization and recruitment seated in front of the virtual world of his PC screen."[32] And the pull of the Internet is strong enough equally to radicalize the unsuspecting, according to security authorities in Singapore. Having to deal with one of the most wired countries in the world, the Singaporeans are particularly preoccupied with this phenomenon whereby Muslim surfers of entirely mainstream interests seeking information on Islamic issues become "easily sidetracked onto one or more of the estimated 6,000 websites espousing radical ideologies."[33]

The level of Salafist and jihadi-Salafist traffic online has now reached the point where it competes vigorously for exposure with mainstream Islam.[34] It would be no exaggeration to say that the Internet serves as the mediator of an entire parallel culture, hosting and transmitting entire libraries of doctrinal, ideological and educational materials underpinning the jihad.[35] This function in the jihadists' struggle is of such an importance that it may be confidently said that the battle for Muslims' minds is being fought by radicals not in the mosques or on the university campus, but on the net.

Creating the border

In broad terms the creation of new virtual borders takes the following sequence:

1) Establish an enmity

For the act of defence of a border to have any meaning there first has to be established the sense of a siege. At a basic level this is already provided by the perception, held in common with the Islamists, that the West is degenerate. If for no other reason, this is from the fact that the West's starting point—Man—perversely sets up a competition to God as the primary reference point. This starting point is tantamount to apotheosising mankind and consequently constitutes *shirk* (polytheism[36]). As such, this represents an extension of the pagan environment that confronted the early Muslim community. The analogy with seventh century Arabia is useful, since it acts to delegitimize any potential respect for an environment of pluralism, tolerance and diversity that western societies appear to offer, and which make the concept of enmity difficult to establish. For instance, the Salafist thinker Abu Anas demonstrates how the society of Arabia observed religious tolerance between the differing beliefs prominent at the time (idol worshippers, Zoroastrians, Jews and Christians), but then ascribes this to a form of *secularism*. Their own ritual acts, he maintains, they viewed as being separate to other actions which:

"only regulated certain aspects of their life and hence various ills were committed outside of them. The Arab *mushrikeen* [polytheists] were secularists in that they would implement a few rituals as part of their belief but would not extend this to other aspects of life, namely their political system."[37]

Such an arrangement, for all its apparent success in tolerance, must therefore be shunned. This is a fixed, impassable border. If western societies promote tolerance and diversity, it is for the same reason, to recreate this ancient, anti-Islamic secularism. Thus, legislation for pluralism, far from protecting the Muslim, is effectively recast as an infringement of this new border.

Similarly, it has to be established that western cultural norms are not elaborated purely from internal historical, social and political experiences, but aggressively constructed as a specific targeting of Islam. The most common technique for buttressing this argument is to establish a link as soon as possible with the behaviour of western states in their dealings with the Muslim heartlands. This is done easily enough by having recourse to the language of the "global Muslim *Ummah*", whereby oppression of any Muslim in the world constitutes a direct oppression of every Muslim here at home.

These are added to the ideology of essential enmity to western culture, as expressed in secularism, democracy and religious pluralism. All of these, and not just the last, tend to be subsumed into a single language, conceptually easy for the Salafist to maintain, of a "religious threat". This accounts for the use of terms such as "Crusaders" to denote westerners, a word which has the advantage of couching the opposition in terms of an eternal struggle and allows cultural or inter-faith dialogue to be dismissed as "Crusade by other means".[38] By viewing through the lens of a religious threat the Salafist can also refer directly back to scriptural definitions of the dualistic confrontation between Islam and *Kufr*. Works of this kind take for their basis the theme, mentioned above, that the western starting point comes from something other than God, a fact which implies the prioritization of man-made authorities—such as a state's constitution over that of the *Qur'ān*, or submission to the rule of humans—and the consequent "worship" by these humans of the handiwork of other humans. The result of these approaches for the radical is intellectually satisfying, since it provides validation and justification for a reaction, and one that is construed as *self-defence*. It also provides a new self-image. If the radical Muslim could find validation for his position in the Muslim heartlands in his battle against *jāhiliyya*, in the *Dār al-Kufr* or "Land of Disbelief" the émigré can achieve no less heroic status as a "traveller in enemy territory".

2) *The Obligation to Hijra*

The problem for the Muslim radical in the West is that, strictly speaking, the Salafist doctrine places an open declaration of enmity to the *jāhiliyya* as a requirement of paramount importance. It comes under the category of "openly displaying one's religion" amongst the disbelievers, and is much more than a matter of praying, fasting and reading the *Qur'ān*. According to Shaykh Abd al-Azīz al-Jarbū' many Muslims in the West fail to realise that this obligation, supported by scripture, requires them:

"to openly display [hostility] in any way that would get the message across in the clearest and most well-understood manner ... that our enmity is for them, and that if we were to gain the upper hand, we would not leave them on the face (of the Earth)."[39]

This "hostility and hatred for ever", in conformity with the Qur'ānic text, is therefore the only thing that legally should provide the Salafist his residence permit in the Land of Disbelief. With such polarities as these the Salafist in the West finds himself in an uneasy position. Is he to create constant tension and confrontation with the non-Muslim environment? Or must he risk the taint of collaboration with the *jāhiliyya* and of abdication of his religious responsibility to perform *hijra*? The dilemma goes some way to explain the concern to create conditions where an *internal hijra* is possible, where the Salafist can claim that he is indeed under siege and not compliantly resident in an infidel environment. In this sense the highlighting of examples of "Islamophobia" is a vital part of this programme, since it helps to validate his residence status in the Land of Disbelief.

3) *Institutionalise the isolation*

Once it is established that the community must be, *a priori*, isolated and under siege, the campaign can begin for the institutionalization of this isolation. On this the Salafists and Islamists converge. Issues familiar from the struggles in Middle East states persist, issues of "Islamising" codes of behaviour and dress, or particular requirements with regard to education and the work environment. But the unfamiliarity of the concepts in the host communities has demanded a necessarily more gradualist approach, a piecemeal, progressive establishment of autonomous Islamic structures within western states, sidestepping open confrontation.

Once again the issue of Shariah forms the central point of reference for the institutionalization of this isolation. If finding a reason for victimhood is not so straightforward in a society that guarantees pluralism, it can be done by

THE BORDERS OF ISLAM

identifying a figure for the role of *tāghūt*, one who by nature is impeding the natural progress of divine dispensation, the natural just law. In practical terms this can be any leader of a western state.[40] The cogency of the cause, and its ability to garner support outside Salafist circles, is illustrated by the successful insertion of Shariah-friendly adjudications in western legal systems. Two cases in point are the recent adjudication, in January 2007, by a German judge that a Muslim woman could not divorce her Muslim husband who had been beating her on the grounds that the *Qur'ān* permits this behaviour, and the temporarily successful embedding of Shariah courts within some western legal systems.[41] Since programmes for legal autonomy of this nature have not been unequivocally outlawed, and opacity on the vulnerability of democratic structures persists in the host communities, we are likely to see more of the same; that is, less overt political platforming and more piecemeal special pleading in favour of constructing parallel infrastructures in the legal, educational, and social spheres.

The cultural border

The value of Salafism in an environment such as Europe is as a rallying point for Muslim youth, whether immigrants or progeny of immigrants, who feel that their ethnic origins are limiting them but who, in rejecting these origins consequently suffer problems of identity. Salafism as a whole offers an identity that is both locally practised and universally valid. Stripped of its obligations to ethnic and religious heritage, it is doctrinally leaner and easier to shape into a uniform "transnational" culture. The slogans of the movement—social justice, moral discipline, and an anti-corruption stance—are broad enough to make this an easy ideological platform to ingest, while the effect-driven political radicalism, with its conspicuous symbols of beards and dress, or female headscarves, offers an immediately attainable gratification of pride, purpose, identity and belonging. It thus allows them to occupy a self-confident position in western society, even if this position is radical and rejectionist. Yet the rejection of cultural roots is not total, and the result is far from unalloyed universalism. Salafism itself still maintains a geographical centre of gravity, a new "old country" where original starting points are shared in common. This centre is the Middle East, and the identity is heavily dominated by Arabic cultural norms. As the arena for Qur'ānic Revelation, such identification might appear to be expected. But there is more to this identification than historical tradition. The clash with the host cultures of the West is brought all the more into relief by their counterposing of a Middle Eastern cultural model, even where the universalist Islamic ingredient does not demand this. As a system that is highly suspicious of intellectualism, particularly Muslim intellectualism, Salafism takes the *imitatio Prophetæ* at its most superficial levels. In addition to matters of doctrine, perceived social practices of seventh century Arabia and the early period of Islamic conquests are established as models to attain to; complete with dispensations on the keeping of slaves, the ransoming of prisoners, and the treatment of concubines, and the contemporary expression of Salafism proudly parades its anachronism:

"If the infidels live among the Muslims, in accordance with the conditions set out by the Prophet—there is nothing wrong with it provided they pay *jizya* to the Islamic treasury ... that they do not renovate a church or a monastery [and] do not rebuild ones that were destroyed, that they feed for three days any Muslim who passes by their homes ... that they rise when a Muslim wishes to sit, that they do not imitate Muslims in dress and speech, nor ride horses, nor own swords, nor arm themselves with any kind of weapon; that they do not sell wine, do not show the cross, do not ring church bells, do not raise their voices during prayer, that they shave their hair in front so as to make them easily identifiable ... If they violate these conditions, they have no protection."[42]

The new "old country" answers to the need to repudiate the local setting, to draw authenticity from outside the West. The new nation thus still has roots "elsewhere", and the foreign idiom of this culture is its most validating factor. In an environment such as the United Kingdom, where the Muslim immigration is mainly Asian, this "elsewhere" validation is very pronounced.

The intellectual border

Essentially, this domination of Arabic as the determining idiom of the ideology derives from an imperative governed by what Mohammed Arkoun terms Islam's *logosphere*, the linguistic mental space in which Islamic thought was early elaborated and which came to be jealously guarded by religious scholars faced with the widening philosophical horizons of the expanding Islamic *oikoumene*.[43] This logocentrism has been a defining characteristic of much intellectual discourse throughout the history of Islam—to the irritation of progressive Muslim thinkers—and has provided the conceptual eyeglasses through which profane reality has been systematically subordinated to the archetypes of Revealed Truth. Islamist thinkers of the modern period have given a more sloganic treatment to this centralising sacralization of knowledge process with the broad application of the term *tawhīd*, God's unity or oneness, the exclusivity of the source.

Yet it is the Salafists who have taken this tendency to its limits and made a particular feature of setting the borderlines of Muslim identity tight up against the literalism of the text. Under this identity all human endeavour and intellectual discourse is placed within the enclosure of the *Qur'ān*, the foundation and origin that is to be endlessly consulted for authentication and legitimization. The disdain for those who exercise reasoning outside this enclosure is visceral:

"They worship 'Reason' over and above God Almighty, and prioritise corrupt Reason over sound Tradition ... They are led astray by the scholasticism, philosophy and logic they were brought up with, and they set these above the science of the Qur'ān and the Sunna, and delve into things that it is not permitted to delve into. Their distortions and perversions resulting from this they call 'interpretation' and 'rationalism', so as to spread it among the masses and the naïve ones!"[44]

The obligation to authenticate, to go back to the original reference, stems from the epistemological naivety of the harmonization concept. This holds that scientific truth and Revelation must be identical, and is based on the medieval premise that science, like scripture, is a finite body of knowledge awaiting revelation rather than a dynamic process of discovery subject to continual revision. In contrast to this dynamism, Salafism makes of religion a perfect stasis with the result that, with each new development in science and technology, the tension inevitably raised can only be assuaged by a process of mental compartmentalization.[45] The threat of contamination of this *logosphere* by foreign cultural and linguistic idioms, of having the mental grammar stolen away from them, must inevitably provoke antagonism and throw up barriers to "no-go areas". The liberal use of Arabic, for example in the Salafists' English or French discourse, serves this purpose as gate-keeper, by disqualifying the employment of western conceptual language, and insulating Muslims from the threat of applying thinking to what must remain unthought. Textual literalism, for the Salafist mindset, is a protection against the *fitna*, the "divisive turmoil" that this contamination will cause.

The educational border

The task of radical Islam is a considerable one—to re-educate from the very basics an entire generation of Muslims. As mentioned earlier, the task is primarily one of re-authentication in the face of over a millennium of Islamic scholarly tradition. But the challenge of minority status in western states makes equally urgent the filtering out of "western" concepts from the mental universe of the Muslims, particularly since these concepts are reinforced by the daily patterns of a western lifestyle. It is but a small step from manning the educational frontiers against pollution, to the demonization of the entire package of the western cultural and political system, and the particular dangers it poses to Muslim residents in these systems. Muslims are to be given to understand that the only purpose of these educational systems is to target Islam:

"Muslims are forced to abide by the national curriculum which has the effect of indoctrinating the new generation of Muslims with the western culture by teaching them ideas such as the theory of evolution, the big bang theory, interfaith, free mixing, liberalism, biased western history, citizenship etc. Even Islamic schools are obliged to adhere to the national curriculum to ensure that even those who receive Islamic education are infected with the diseased culture of this society."[46]

The re-education process has to go in deep. A particular target are the "westernized Muslims" who, Salafists feel, have uncritically taken on board the debate on "moralising" and "democratising" Islam in order to appear modern to their neighbours. It also licenses, by extension, the cherry-picking of those elements of the Shariah which happen to be to the taste of western liberals. Any Muslims who call for the re-examination of the Shariah are thus colluding with the enemy, since the enemy is aware that Shariah is the real obstacle to their destructive intentions. Indeed, Muslims should shun the whole practice of self-examination and speculation on the morality of Islam's religious and political practices: "A wise Muslim should never be lured into such traps, because this would make the Muslim nation more likely to be lured into more moral challenges."[47]

The reach of westernization is long, and extends to the very conception of history. True Muslims, according to the Salafists, are to dispense with the false, subversive distinctions of modern and ancient, since this distinction implies, disastrously, the concept of improvement upon an already perfect prototype. Nor are they to accept new "symbolic interpretations" of the core religious texts on the grounds that there is a conflict between the life and legislation requirements of seventh century Muslims and that of their contemporary fellows in faith.[48]

The true border conflict

For jihadists, Islamic political and legal doctrines, elaborated over history from the standpoint of supremacy, have opposed any form of political mechanism that does not take the religion of Islam as the starting point for the delineation of rights. For jihadist Islamist thinkers, systems extraneous to Islam—the rotation of power, elections, the equal rights of the individual irrespective of religious denomination—lack authenticity and should form no part of Muslim aspirations:

"Muslims should reject [democracy] entirely, for it is filthy; it is the rule of a tyrant, it is *kufr* ['disbelief'], with *kufr* ideas, *kufr* systems and *kufr* laws, and has nothing to do with Islam."[49]

That these concepts have, whether through attraction or imposition, become entirely familiar territory to Muslims only renders them all the more dangerous. Indeed, it turns them into active instruments for the purposeful destruction of Islam. Nationalism, democracy, pluralism, human rights, freedom or even free-market policies are nothing more than dangers and fallacies that the infidels are using to finish off Islam.[50] Such things, however, are more problematic for the Islamists than for the democracies they may inhabit. The "vertical" relations between government and citizen—the right to vote and acquire political power by the ballot box, the separation and decentralization of powers, the principle of majority rule in political decision-making, the fundamental rights of the person and of minorities, the public nature of the administration under the rule of law and the aloofness of the government from the privacy of citizens—these things are easy enough to identify and ring-fence. And radical Muslims in western states are aware that no Muslim communities, even if they were remotely so inclined, are in a position numerically to re-shape the political systems of the host countries towards an Islamist model. Besides, even the most confrontational among Salafist Islamists concede that Islamic law mandates the Muslim's obligation to abide by the law of the non-Muslim state if he finds himself there by consent.[51]

By stripping off the accumulations of a more inclusive, traditional Islamic culture, Salafism leaves its exponents less willing or able to integrate socially with the wider Muslim communities, let alone with non-Muslim communities. Overtures of tolerance and co-existence generated by the democratic culture of the citizens can only be greeted as suspect. For the community of the pure and the saved, tolerance derives from moral insincerity and weakness, and the Muslim thinker is explicitly warned against the beguilements of offers of understanding:

"They call for 'co-existence' ... for the 'coming together of faiths', for 'inter-faith dialogue.' Not in order that Truth should be distinguished from Evil and thereby followed ... but for the co-existence of Truth *alongside* Evil within one garment, so that principles, concepts and values become mingled with each other ... so that the conflict between Truth and Evil be removed, [a conflict] that is ancient, and dates from when God Almighty created Adam and Iblis, and which shall continue to the Day of Resurrection!"[52]

One more border in the making: "intellectual apostasy"

The broad thrust of Islamist thought, fixing the life of the Muslim in closer harmony with the Shariah, is naturally predominantly focused on the societies of the Muslim heartlands. However, as mentioned earlier, increased rubbing of shoulders with western patterns of society and thought is presenting the Islamist programme with new and unexpected points of tension, principally the fear of re-importation of these western patterns into the Muslim heartlands. If this was not a preoccupying issue in the mid-twentieth century, second and third generation Muslims brought up within these patterns, and who have refused the call to isolation, present a new source of threat: a community that does not take as its starting point that western culture and mores, or the model of the separation of secular and religious affairs, are *a priori* antithetical to Islam. For the Salafists this presents no problem, since individuals who take this view are simply part of the encircling *jāhiliyya*, or worse, partake of the worldview of the atheist *zindīq* (freethinking sceptic),[53] the mindset that is:

"... infidel, licentious and foul, which does not give any consideration or value to faith, and which is outside the fold of Islam even if it claims to be Muslim."[54]

But for the intellectual constituency of the Islamists the situation is complicating. The West, with its intellectual curiosity and relatively unfettered cultural mingling, is providing the oxygen for such thinking to develop and thus risks emerging as a key arena for the war of ideas.

The threat of a growing rift within the Islamic fold is significant enough to promote the construction of yet another border, one between modernists and those of a more traditionalist stamp. The formation of western-based Shariah councils, such as the *Fiqh* Council of North America (FCNA), and the European Council for Fatwa and Research (ECFR), are symptoms of this developing dilemma, so is the mushrooming of Internet sites.[55]

It means that radicals can no longer view the West simply as virgin territory awaiting Islamization from the Muslim heartlands, nor western Muslims universally as compliant frontiersmen in this enterprise. Instead, western Islam has just as much capacity to emerge as an ideological competitor. The new frontier to be manned, therefore, is Europe and the United States, against the baleful influence of liberalism. At stake, then, is a new *Ridda*, a movement of apostasy, only this time, according to Shaykh Yusuf al-Qaradawi, it is one committed by those who "wrap their apostasy in various coverings, sneaking in a very cunning manner into the mind, the same way that malignant tumours sneak into the body".[56]

Radical Islam has proved itself highly successful in "operating behind enemy lines" and gaining ascendancy among the Muslim communities in western states. To date Islamists have been able, largely unimpeded, to establish a position of influence among Muslim communities in the West that is fast approaching normative. Both Islamist and Salafist influence can be discerned in most of the organizations claiming to represent the interests of western Muslims, and their influence continues to grow. It has been able to achieve this influence through the lack of ideological and intellectual self-confidence of western Muslim constituencies and the financial weight of its Gulf state backers. But in the final analysis, their model for Islamic authentification—the early Muslim community—cannot accept accommodation with non-Muslim structures and societies on any terms other than those of a provisional "truce".[57] The process of forcing through an adjustment to this starting point will therefore be fraught with difficulty.

At the same time, for the other side of the border dispute, there remain limits to the accommodation it is able to make. As time progresses and the establishment of radical Islam makes further, more overt, challenges, the legal position of a liberal state *vis-à-vis* the demands made by an Islamic jurisprudential environment that is still attempting to adapt from an intellectual space of political and social supremacy, will need to be clarified with more urgency.[58]

Meanwhile, challenges such as those by Amina Wadud and Tariq Ramadan, if so far statistically limited, nonetheless place a question mark on how long western Muslims will be content to see themselves as an ideological "annex" to the Muslim heartlands. Nor are the conditions in the West automatically conducive to the elaboration of a single, unifying resolution on the pattern of radical Islam. As the impetus to form official *fatwā* councils in Europe and the United States illustrates, the opportunity that western society presents to radical Islam is proving an open challenge to the latter.[59] Al-Suri's comments in this respect are revealing:

"There has spread among the circles of so-called 'Islamic thinkers' and those held in the West to be *'ulamā*, some antinomian, distorted ideas, ideas of religious tolerance and Islamic-Christian dialogue ... *fatwas* which are entirely freethinking [*zindīq*] and deviant ... that the Americans and the westerners will ... come to our lands as the victorious bearers of an Islam risen in the West! For theirs will be the military power and they will be the ones to hold high the banner of Islam!"[60]

The question is how the race develops. At the moment, the radicals have demonstrated that they have the organization, motivation and the funds to outpace the moderates. If and when this western Islam does begin to develop enough self-confidence and momentum to challenge the consolidating position of radical Islam, overtly promoting a form of Islam that is publicly and explicitly at home in the western political, cultural and social environment, it is here that solutions will be drawn for the resolution of the border conflict—a border not between civilizations, but between civilization of whatever philosophical and religious stamp, and currents destructive to civilization.

Conclusion

Stig Jarle Hansen and Atle Mesøy

Samuel Huntington claimed that religion and religious identity are becoming increasingly essential as political factors.[1] He pointed to the border of what he defined as Islamic civilization, as especially important: He claimed that the borders of Islam would be increasingly filled with conflict.[2]

Although he did suggest that Islam was warlike, he was far from being the primordialist of which he has been accused, arguing that conflicts would be driven by specific social mechanisms that would become more relevant in the future. The most crucial social mechanisms were the weakening of national and local identity, the decline of alternative ideologies, and the uncertainty surrounding safety and security in the modern world, these factors combining to leave a void for religion to fill, "out-competing" other identities. In addition, he suggests that explosive population growth amongst Muslims could lead to problems in the future.[3] In this sense Huntington does not say that religious identity is something static; quite the opposite, its significance will change. Moreover, he explored mechanisms, such as the weakening of other secular alternatives to religion, a theory that has been supported by other researchers more recently.[4] Indeed, Huntington has a much more complex message than many of his critics would have liked us to believe.

As illustrated in the introduction, Huntington's critics can roughly be divided into three: first, those focusing on *cleavages within a civilization* (including multiple identities), claiming that multiple identities and cleavages will prevent unity; second, those pointing to a supposed underestimation of the prevailing *power of states*, claiming that states will remain the key actors in

309

international relations; last, those highlighting his ignorance regarding the influence *grievances* have on the creation of pan-civilizational loyalties. The two first approaches claim that Huntington's idea of a clash of civilizations, including his claim that Islam's borders are especially violent, is wrong, the latter will suggest that there are alternative mechanisms at work, but that Huntington's understandings of a bloody border, and of a clash between Islam and especially the West was correct.

The intention behind this book was to go in-depth at state level to study what Huntington claims are the borders of Islamic civilization, exploring and finding new forms of interaction neglected by Huntington, as well as his critics. This process benefits our understanding of the connection between religion and politics, the "resurgence" of religion and the influence of globalization on this resurgence. It does this by highlighting historical factors, as well as the interaction between many variables over time, with new ones emerging and old variables becoming less important.

Some of the findings of the contributors confirm common knowledge, or have been controversial at earlier stages, but have by now ceased to be contentious, such as the following: that religion and politics do interact, that local mechanisms are vital factors in explaining differences between cases, that there are large variations in the interpretation of Islam, but that the religion also has certain core values that are less open to local interpretation and change. However, other findings, such as those pertaining to the interaction between faith, conflict, poverty and weak institutions over time, are quite new to the debates surrounding Huntington. This conclusion suggests that new mechanisms and new concepts are fundamental in order to understand the dynamics at the borders of Islam, and that some of the mechanisms suggested by Huntington are too weak to have the impact he suggests.

The cleavages of Islam

The findings of this book support the critics of Huntington in saying that the term "civilization" is too wide a concept to generalize inter-faith relations. There is not a single case studied in this book where Islam presents a unified face towards other religions; in all cases there are notable political fissures within Islam, often creating divisions even within supposedly homogenous sub-groups of Islam. There have been many efforts to impose homogeneity upon Islam, even from within the religion, but so far all of them have failed. In this sense, the term "civilization" imposes a homogeneity that does not exist, and Huntington's critics score a point. The influence of local cultures will further ensure that future attempts will face difficulties. This does not mean that mobilization along religious lines is impossible, nor that religiously-based group identities, as suggested by Huntington, give comfort in a changing world; rather it means that civilizational political mobilization is unlikely and that various groups within a religion will develop highly different internal discourses and social rules that hinder wide alliances to promote more complex political targets.

Identity, state and state power.

How important would state interests be in the face of religious factors along the borders of Islam? The power of the state structures studied in this book varies: some are strong and some use religion as a tool, often to create unity, or to attempt to get strategic allies. Others are weak, the state being an arena where several elites can fight their battles: in some cases a so-called state government controls little of its supposed territory, de facto being one out of many factions in a civil war. However, in most cases, state interests, including the interest of states outside the explored state, will be of relevance. While states do still matter, religion becomes a tool in the toolkit of the ruling elites. This seems to suggest an instrumentalist interpretation of religion. However, when religion is used politically, it becomes more than an instrument, as suggested by the constructivist approach presented in the introduction.[5] For the leader has to follow at least a minimum of requirements stipulated in the religion to be believed. On the borders of Islam, state interests do matter. States within Islamic civilization are heavily at odds with other states of the same situation, and intensively employ religion as an instrument in their foreign policy, but they are formed by their tool in return.

Religious identity might be a vital part of a national or local identity, making it more valuable as a potential political instrument. Indeed, religion is, as demonstrated by the chapters of Mønnesland, Hughes, Arigita and Bou Nassif, often a defining factor in ethnic/group identity. Religion may become an identity marker, demarcating a group, employable as a tool to strengthen the loyalty within this ethnic group versus other groups of different religions. As illustrated by the chapters exploring Afghanistan, Indonesia, the Philippines, Somalia, Ethiopia, Nigeria, and Bosnia, resurgence in religiously-inspired rhetoric is often connected with clan/ethnic mobilization. The kind of implication this has for Huntington's thesis is that religious rhetoric is motivated as much out of a need to stress a national identity, as by religious beliefs. In some cases the two are hard to distinguish.

Grievances

What about grievances such as poverty, and repression? Critics of Huntington argued that such factors caused some of the civilization conflicts explored by Huntington. Interestingly, the grievances emphasized by Huntington's critics were pan-Islamic: occupation of Islamic land (including Palestine), and western support for suppressive regimes. As illustrated by the chapters concerning the new borders, such grievances do create anger and attract sympathy from many Muslims. However, the number of individuals motivated actually to act on such grievances seems relatively small compared to the number of individuals with a local background involved in a conflict on the old border. The difference in numbers does not mean that individuals motivated by pan-Islamic grievances, real or perceived, are unimportant: their actions can have serious consequences; such grievances will also aid the recruitment to smaller more extreme groups.

Often the belief in the clash is a result of a simplification of relations on the border of Islam. In the safe computer room, one might conveniently apply a pick-and-choose approach to local conflicts all across the world. While one needs to take clan conflicts into consideration when dealing with local politics in Somalia, what Ulph calls the armchair 'mujahid surfer' might disregard it from the safety of his room. The same dynamics hold true for small groups, they can reconfirm their own beliefs by confronting similarly-minded individuals in their own setting; as described in the chapters of Khosrokhavar and Thomas many terrorist groups are recruited through friends and families. Consequently, small group activism might be combined with Internet jihadism to create a perfect social construction of a *perceived* "clash of civilizations". It should be noted that this will not constitute the global clash Huntington envisaged, but will be "the clash" believed to exist for the people in question, and might spark radical action. One might here talk about radical and global belief systems, in a way created by the mechanisms described by Huntington, such as the new information technology, uncertainty in a new environment, mobility weakening old identities, as well as the weakening of ideological alternatives. These systems will not necessarily be formed into organizations (although they can be), but will rather consist of individuals sharing a set of perceptions: perceptions that can motivate action. Such belief systems might span the globe and create loyalties crossing borders and ethnicity. However, the belief systems do not include an entire civilization, they are often small, and exist in rivalry with other belief systems, and they might also have non-religious foundations. Within Islam, the more extreme belief systems are often heavily at odds with other older traditional approaches to Islam, often, dogmatism makes them inflexible, and promotes fragmentation. Moreover, they are vulnerable to fragmentation when group dynamics are weakened, when some of the grievances that influence their perception are addressed, and when members receive information at odds with their perception.

Interestingly, both Huntington and his critics downplayed the role of poverty as a cause of problems at the borders of Islam. However, the findings in this book suggest that poverty, as well as institutional collapse, are vital factors in explaining why religion has become more important at the borders. Poverty and lack of institutions can potentially explain an interesting phenomenon explored in this book, namely that the prominence of religion might vary from stage to stage in a conflict. A conflict might become redefined as a religious conflict; religiously inspired factions might emerge after the conflict has gone on for years; whereas in some cases the importance of religion might decline. The chapters by Johansen and Rigby, Kardas, Bou Nassif, Schultze, Jarle-Hansen, Hughes and Prunier as well as Arigita illustrate how religious factors, including religiously-based propaganda, vary in importance over time.

Huntington explained the increased centrality of religion by referring to disappointment in previous ideologies, as a way of handling personal emotional insecurity, as well as a result of globalization and the weakening of other identities. This anthology suggests the existence of other mechanisms. In conflicts such as Chechnya, Somalia, and Israel-Palestine the relevance of religion has increased. The argument that low per capita income is related to conflict is common amongst conflict researchers; low per capita income might also be related to the "resurgence of religion" in politics amongst several entities on "Islam's bloody borders".[6] Prolonged war leads to poverty, as well as institutional collapse, and this might subsequently lead to the increased political importance of religion. Both Christianity and Islam stipulate certain commandments that deal with social justice, and promote solidarity with the weak and poor in society. These values have not dominated all Muslims and Christians at all times, but are values to which even instrumentalists (people who use religion for their own interests) have to adhere to in order to keep up their appearances as pious persons. Johansen and Rigby, Kardas, Bou Nassif,

Schultze, Jarle-Hansen, and Mahmud's chapters all illustrate the potential of religion to fulfil not only needs for spiritual comfort, but also needs for social and justice institutions. That is, Islam could be employed to create courts, and it could be used to prevent corruption in political institutions, as Islamic tenets do contain harsh condemnation of crime and corruption, and religious leaders might be perceived to be less likely to engage in illegal and corrupt activities. The World Bank for example discovered that religious leaders were amongst the most trusted in developing countries.[7] Role expectations converge around religious leaders, since they are often seen as just and able to fulfil justice functions in societies with weak state structures, also characteristics of an ideal political leader. Therefore, in a society with weakly developed or corrupt institutions, and little public help for the needy, Islam will be a potential political force, at times providing much needed help to local citizens. Conflict has the potential to create poverty and weaken institutions. Armed conflict might become prolonged, as poverty becomes more widespread and institutions break down, therefore setting in motion a process making religious institutions more important. Likewise, religion might offer hope in a terrifying day-to-day context, leading to more emphasis on religion. Indeed, the supposed prevalence of conflict on the borders of Islam might have more to do with poverty than with Islam itself. Religious factions can draw advantages from the trust they have in society to become important actors on the political stage, this development will not lead to a clash of civilizations. The emerging religious groups will have a variety of interests: some will look to the West for support, and some will be at odds with other religious groups within Islam.

There are older, but equally important grievances that both Huntington and many of his critics fail to underline. Significantly, of the nineteen cases explored in this book, twelve are taken from states that used to be parts of larger empires in a relatively recent past. A common strategy in colonial as well as imperial governance was to employ members of ethnic minority groups in order to govern larger ethnic groups. Initially, Christian groups had a large advantage when dealing with western power: they had the same cultural references. Indonesia's Ambons were for example granted advantages by the metropolitan power. Later, social and demographical changes, as well as decolonization, threatened privileged groups and, as highlighted in the chapters written by Schultze and Reid sparked conflict. Significantly, the lack of western support for Christians in Indonesia and Lebanon, shows how common religious leanings failed to attract support after decolonisation, for religious leaning is far from a blank cheque that can be used to obtain international/civilizational support. It is true that Huntington, in addition to scholars such as Haynes, highlighted alienation as a part of the cause for the resurgence of religion. However, they fail to see that the roots of such alienation in many cases lay in the past, in a colonial master's manipulation of one subject group against another subject group, and the changes of the balance of power in this game.[8] In this sense it is a particular form of grievance, but not the central grievances described in the more general criticism of Huntington.

Huntington, his critics, and the borders of Islam

So where does the discussion of Huntington and his critics lead us? Huntington's concept of civilizations might be crude, but he reintroduced us to the connection between religion and politics, the resurgence of religion, and the influence of globalization on this resurgence. The value of Huntington's work rather lies in the mechanisms he explored, of which many remain essential than in his all encompassing "civilizational thesis".

While the findings in this book disagree with the concept of a "clash of civilizations", it nevertheless seems that some of the mechanisms explored by Huntington point to politically significant processes. It is true that religion seems to have become more important in politics at the borders of Islam and that there are specific bonds that span the Muslim community. However, the cases suggest that different mechanisms are at play, and that the bonds between Muslims are weaker and more complicated than suggested by Huntington. Overall, mechanisms as consequences of poverty and conflict, lack of/weakening institutions and a colonial past might hold explanatory power in analysing the relevance and the resurgence of religion at the borders of Islam.

The findings in this book suggest that alternative social mechanisms should be taken into account in order to understand how religion and politics interact at the borders of Islam.

Glossary

Amir	Ruler
Ahl al-Sunna wal-Jamāʾa	The followers of the sunna; also a Somali organisation
Bidʿah	Sinful Innovation
Dar al-Harb	House of War
Dar al-Islam	House of Peace
Daʿwa	Missionary work
Dhimmi	Non-Muslim
Fard	Religious duty
Fatwa	Legal opinion
Fedayeen	Those who sacrifice themselves (Freedom Fighters)
Fiqh	Islamic jurisprudence
Fitnah	Schism
Hadith	Oral traditions regarding the sayings of the Prophet
Hajj	Major Pilgrimage
Hijrah	The emigration of the Prophet and his followers from Mecca to Medina
Ijtihad	the process of making a legal decision by independent interpretation of the legal sources, the Qur'an and the Sunnah
Ikhwan	Muslim Brothers
Imam	Islamic leader
Inftifada	Uprising
Islamism	Political Islam is another word for Islamism, an ideology that combines Islam and politics, "the understanding that since Islam is part of everything, Islam must also be part of politics or guidance for arranging the society".

Jahiliyyaa	Ignorance, barbarism
Jihad	The concept of Jihad is heavily discussed, often translated "Holy war", also translated as "struggle/personal effort"
Jihad-e-Akbar	The greater jihad against one's soul (nafs) at personal level
Jihad-e-Ashgar	The lesser jihad; struggle in self-defense in the way of God
Jirga	Council
Jizya	Tax
Kafir	Infidel
Khalifah	Head of Muslim state
Kuffar	Unbelievers
Kufr	Rejection of Islamic rules
Khutba	Primary formal occasion for public preaching in the Islamic tradition
Madrasahs	Religious Schools
Mahdi	Guided One
Manhaj	"Method", "methodology". For the Salafists, it is defined as "the methodology of implementing the beliefs and laws of Islam".
Masjid	Mosque
Mawlid	A term used to refer to the observance of the birthday of Prophet Muhammad
Mufti	Religious scholar
Muhajiroun	Early Muslim emigrants from Mecca to Medina
Mushrikin	Those who formally worship idols and do not follow any holy book
Murtad	The Muslim who rejects Islam in word or deed
Muslimun	Muslims
Naskh	Abrogation
Pasdaran	Revolutionary Guards
Qadi	A religious judge ruling in accordance with Shariah
Qawettis	Refugee (Somali; but also much used amongst Ethiopian Oromos (Oromfied spelling))
Qital	Fighting
Ridda	Apostasy
Salafi	Muslims of the first three generations of Islam taken as exemplary models
Salam	Peace
Salah	Righteousness

Salat	Prayer
Shahid	Witness/Martyrdom in Islam
Shariah	Islamic law
Sheik	Honorific term in the Arabic language that literally means "elder". It is commonly used to designate an elder of a tribe, a lord, a revered wise man, or most commonly an Islamic scholar.
Shia	Minority faith group within Islam
Shirk	Worshipping other than Allah
Shura	Council, used for Islamic institutions with parliamentary functions
Sufi	Followers of a mystic Islamic tradition
Sunnah	Deeds of the Prophet
Sunni	Majority faith group within Islam
Surah	Chapter in the *Qur'ān*
Tafsir	Interpretation of the *Qur'ān*
Takfir	The practice of declaring unbeliever
Tariqa/Turuq	Schools of Sufism based on teachings of a spiritual leader (founder)
Taqlid	Following the verdicts of scholars without knowing the evidence. Also refers to repetitiveness and lack of ijtihad of some ulama.
Tawhid	Monotheism in Islam
Ulama	Islamic Scholars
Waqf	Endowment
Zakat	Charity/the giving of alms
Zindiq (Zindī)	Freethinking Atheist

Notes

INTRODUCTION

1. BBC Monitoring, "Bin Laden statement-excerpts", *BBC News*, 7 May, 2004. http://news.bbc.co.uk/2/hi/middle_east/3693969.stm (accessed 11 November 2006).
2. Ronald Rovers, "The silencing of Theo van Gogh", *salon.com*, 24 November 2004, http://dir.salon.com/story/news/feature/2004/11/24/vangogh/index_np.html (accessed 11 November 2006).
3. *Ibid.*
4. Bernard Lewis, "The Roots of Muslim Rage", *Atlantic Monthly*, September 1990.
5. Samuel P. Huntington, "The Clash of Civilizations?", *Foreign Affairs*, 72, no. 3 (1993), 22.
6. Samuel P. Huntington, *The Clash of Civilizations And the Remaking of World Order* (Simon and Schuster, 1996), 98.
7. *Ibid*, 254.
8. Richard Bonney, *Jihad—From Qur'ān to bin Laden* (Hampshire: Palgrave MacMillan, 2004), 357.
9. Huntington 2002, 13.
10. Ibid., 4.
11. *Ibid.*, 64.
12. Samuel P. Huntington, "Try Again: A Reply to Russett, O'Neal and Cox", *Journal of Peace Research*, 37, no. 5 (2000): 609.
13. Huntington, 2002, 128.
14. *Ibid.*, 96.
15. Huntington, 1996, 96–7, 109–14; Gilles Kepel, *Revenge of God: The Resurgence of Islam, Christianity and Judaism in the Modern World*, (University Park: Pennsylvania State University Press, 1994), 2.
16. *Ibid.*, 44.
17. Faisal Devji, *Landscapes of the Jihad* (London: Hurst, 2005), 64.
18. Gilles Kepel, *The War for Muslim Minds* (Cambridge: Harvard University Press, 2004b), 62–5.
19. Huntington 1996, 256; In one of the articles Huntington refers to, Gurr explicitly refutes the "clash" hypothesis. However, it seems as if Gurr neglected to define wars

321

that had religious cleavages involved as "clash" wars. Ted R. Gurr, "People Against States: Ethnopolitical Conflict and the World System", *International Studies Quarterly*, 38, no. 3, 1994. See also Ted R. Gurr, *Ethnic Conflict in World Politics* (Boulder: Lynne Rienner, 1994).

20. Huntington 1996, 263.
21. According to Savage, Muslims will comprise 20 per cent of the population of Europe by 2050. Timothy M. Savage, "Europe and Islam, Crescent Waxing, Cultures Clashing", *The Washington Quarterly*, 73, no. 3 (2005).
22. *Ibid.*, 254.
23. Monica D. Toft, "Getting Religion?", *International Security*, 31, no. 4 (2007), 97.
24. Andrej Tusicisny "Civilizational Conflicts: More Frequent, Longer, and Bloodier?", *Journal of Peace Research*, 41, no. 4 (2004).
25. Tanja Ellingsen, "Towards a Revival of Religion and Religious Clashes", *Terrorism and Political Violence*, 17, no. 3 (2005), 318.
26. Jonathan Fox, "The Increasing Role of Religion in State Failure", *Terrorism and Political Violence*, 19, no. 3 (2007); Jonathan Fox, "The Rise of Religion and the fall of the Civilization Paradigm as Explanations for Intra-State Conflict", *Cambridge Review of International Affairs*, 20, no. 3 (2007).
27. Fred Halliday, "A New World Myth", *New Statesman* 10, no. 447 (1997); Brian Beedham, "The New Geopolitics: A Fading Hell", *The Economist*, 31 July 1999; Masakazu Yamazaki, "Asia, a Civilization in the Making", *Foreign Affairs*, 75, no. 4 (1996); Yamazaki (1996); Stephen N. Walt, "Building Up New Bogeymen", *Foreign Policy*, 106 (1997); Ted Robert Gurr, "People Against the State: Ethno Politic Conflict and the Changing World System", *International Studies Quarterly*, 38, no. 3 (1994); Jackob Heilbrun, "The Clash of Samuel Huntingtons", *The Amercing Prospect* 39 (1998); Zerougui Kader, "The Clash of Civilizations and the Remaking of World Order", *Arab Studies Quarterly*, 20, no. 1 (1998); Richard Rosecrance, "The Clash of Civilizations and the Remaking of World Order", *American Political Science Review*, 92, no. 4 (1998); Frederick S. Tipson, "Culture Clash-ification: A Verse to Huntington's Curse", *Foreign Affairs*, 76, no. 2 (1997). Amartya Sen, *Identity and Violence: The Illusion of Destiny* (New York: WW Norton, 2006).
28. Jonathan Fox and Shmuel Sandler, *Bringing Religion into International Relations* (New York: Palgrave, 2004), 132.
29. Daniel Brumberg, "The End of A Brief Affair?: The United States and Iran", *Carnegie Endowment for Peace Policy Brief*, 14 (2002). The main allies of the Northern Alliance were Russia, Iran and the United States. For an overview of Russian and Iranian support see Human Rights Watch, "Crisis of Impunity: The Role of Pakistan, Russia, and Iran in Fuelling the Civil War", *Afghanistan Report*, 13, no. 3 (2001).
30. Sufism developed around 1200–1300 AD and focused on asceticism, self-purification and had boarding houses resembling monasteries. Several Sufi masters withdrew from secular life and became leaders of Sufi orders, in which members took upon themselves to transfer the knowledge from their masters to new students. Sufis pray through the founders of their order, as Catholics pray through saints; they also emphasize meditation and good works.
31. Stig Jarle Hansen, "Shariah Courts Holds Sway in Mogadishu", *Foreign Report*, 10 (2006).

32. Oliver Roy, *The Failure of Political Islam* (London: I.B. Tauris, 1994), 93–4.

33. For example World War I, World War II and the Napoleonic wars.

34. Faoud Ajami, "The Summoning", *Foreign Affairs*, 72, no. 4 (1993), 6; John Gray, "Global Utopias and Clashing Civilizations: Misunderstanding the Prosperity", *International Affairs*, 74, no. 1 (1998); William Pfaff, "The reality of Human Affairs", *World Policy Journal*, 14, no. 2 (1997). It is not surprising that this criticism is levelled against Huntington: his *Clash of Civilizations* explicitly attacks the realist stand within international relations theory for its focus on states as the major actor in international politics. Samuel P. Huntington, *The Clash of Civilizations And the Remaking of World Order* (New York: Simon and Schuster, 1996), 33–4.

35. David M. Witty, "A Regular Army in Counterinsurgency Operations: Egypt in North Yemen, 1962–1967", *The Journal of Military History*, 65, no. 2. (2001).

36. Huntington 1996, 34–5.

37. Staff writer, "Islam poses a threat to the West, say 53 per cent in poll", *The Daily Telegraph*, 25 August 2006.

38. Huntington 1996, 130.

39. *Ibid.*, 131.

40. Israel also bombed Qana in 1996.

41. It formally ended on 8 September 2006 when Israel lifted their naval blockade of Lebanon.

42. Staff writer, "Anti Israel rally takes place in Mogadishu", *Shabelle News*, 11 August 2006.

43. Shireen T. Hunter, *The Future of Islam and the West: Clash of Civilizations or Peaceful Coexistence?* (Westport, Connecticut: Praeger, 1998).

44. Scott Thomas, *The Global Resurgence of Religion* (London: Palgrave, 2005), 42. Thomas bases his work on the so-called "English School of International Relations".

45. Bobby Sayyid, *A Fundamental Fear: Eurocentrism and the Emergence of Islamism* (London, New York: Zed Books, 1997), 117.

46. Mohammed Ayoob, "Challenging Hegemony: Political Islam and the North-South Divide", *International Studies Review*, 9 (2007).

47. Human Rights Watch, *Egypt Human Rights Developments* (Annual Egypt Report), 1992; Human Rights Watch, *Egypt Human Rights Developments* (Annual Egypt Report), 1995.

48. Staff writer, "How the US Helped Create Saddam Hussein", *Newsweek*, 23 September 2002; Helen Metz, *Iraq, A Country Study* (Washington: Federal Research Division Library of Congress, 1988).

49. Azzam Tamimi and John Esposito, *Islam and Secularism in the Middle East* (London: Hurst, 2000), 9–12.

50. Osama bin Laden, "Bin Laden's Letter to America," *The Observer*, 24 November 2002.

51. The movement in focus was only amongst a minority of Islamist organizations. Some organizations, such as the Egyptian *al-Jamaa al-Islamiyya* in 1997 and the Libyan Islamic Battle group (LIFG) in 2001, have accepted ceasefires. According to Gerges it was even controversial within al-Qaeda, but the shift nevertheless meant a large-scale change of focus that contributed to the 9/11 attacks. Fawaz A. Gerges, *The Far*

Enemy: Why Jihad Went Global (Cambridge: Cambridge University Press, 2005), 1; *Ibid.*, 19.

52. Oliver Roy, *Globalized Islam: The Search for a New Ummah* (London: Hurst, 2004).

53. Thomas Hegghammer, "Global Jihadism After the Iraq War", *Middle East Journal*, 65, no. 1, (2006).

54. For the impact of the global news media, see for example, Robert M. Entman, *Projections of Power: Framing News, Public Opinion, and US Foreign Policy* (London: The University of Chicago Press, 2004); Piers Robinson, *The CNN Effect* (London: Routledge, 2002).

55. Hegghammer, 2006, 18.

56. Sean O'Neill, and Daniel McGrory, *The Suicide Factory, Abu Hamza and the Finsbury Park Mosque* (London: Harper Perennial, 2006), 271.

57. "Anti-Semitic 'Elders of Zion' Gets New Life on Egypt TV", *New York Times*, 26 October 2002; "Israel Protests Airing of Anti-Semitic Egyptian Television Series", *CNS News.com*, 17 October 2002; "Saudis Airing Anti-Semitic TV Series for Ramadan Based on Protocols of the Elders of Zion", *The National Post*, Canada, 7 December 2001.

58. Edward Said "Islam and the West are Inadequate Banners", *The Observer*, 16 September 2001.

59. A survey of articles in four leading international relations journals over the period 1980–1999 finds that only six or so out of a total of about sixteen hundred featured religions as an important influence. Daniel Philpott, "The Challenge of September 11 to Secularism in International Relations", *World Politics*, 55, no. 1 (2002).

60. Karl Marx, *Critique of Hegel's Philosophy of Right* (Cambridge: Cambridge University Press, 1970).

61. Michael Doyle, *Ways of War and Peace* (New York: W.W. Norton, 1997); Even twentieth-century "Christian realists", like Reinhold Niebuhr, a personal believer and a theolog, were sceptical that state action could be properly understood as motivated by deep religious concerns: in a world of power any attempt by states to pursue seriously a religious or transcendent ideal would ironically come to naught. He counselled leaders to act according to a calculation of the lesser of two evils. Reinhold Niebuhr, *The Irony of American History* (New York: Charles Scribner's Sons, 1952); Reinhold Niebuhr, *Christian Realism and Political Problems* (New York: Charles Scribner's Sons, 1953).

62. Philpott 2002, 80.

63. Peter L. Berger, *The Sacred Canopy* (New York: Garden City, 1967).

64. Scott Thomas, *The Global Resurgence of Religion and the Transformation of International Relations* (New York: Palgrave Macmillan, 2005).

65. Andreas Hasenclever and Volker Rittberger, "Does Religion Make a Difference? Theoretical Approaches to the Impact of Faith on Political Conflict", *Millennium: Journal of International Studies*, 29, no. 3 (2000), 641–74.

66. Serious examples of this tradition are hard to find, which are often repudiated by the very scholars that are accused of holding such views. The proponents of primordialism are often to be found amongst extreme Christian sects, or extreme secularists. For an example of the secularist argument see Sam Harris, *The End of Faith: Religion, Terror,*

and the Future of Reason (London: The Free Press, 2005). For an example of the Christian version of the argument see Don Richardson, *Secrets of the Koran: Revealing Insights into Islam's Holy Book* (New York: Regal, 2003).

67. Hasenclever and Rittberger 2000, 644–7.
68. *Ibid.*, 644–7.
69. *Ibid.*, 647–9.
70. Elisabeth Kier, *Imagining War* (Princeton: Princeton University Press, 1999).
71. A Christian today would have significant problems with the strictures and views of a Christian from the fourth century, for example.
72. Jason Burke, *al-Qaeda: Casting a Shadow of Terror* (New York: I.B. Tauris, 2003).

REGION I

1. I would like to thank James R. Vaughan for his valuable comments on this introduction.
2. In 2007 Bangladesh's Muslim population was 129,987,365, India's was 151,402,065, Indonesia's was of 207,000,105; and Pakistan's was 159,305,441. The Muslim populations of even the larger Muslim countries of the Middle East (e.g. Egypt's 69,755,180 or) are comparatively small compared to the Muslim population in South and South East Asia. See Bureau of Democracy, Human Rights and Labor, *International Religious Freedom Report* (Washington, DC: State Department, 2006).
3. See for example Osama bin Laden, *Messages to the World. The Statements of Osama Bin Laden* (New York: Verso, 2005).
4. See for example Osama bin Laden, "Resist the New Rome" in Osama Bin Laden, *Messages to the World: The Statements of Osama Bin Laden* (New York: Verso, 2005).
5. Nikki R. Keddie, *An Islamic Response to Imperialism: Political and Religious Writings of Sayyid Jamal al-Din "al-Afghani"* (Berkeley: University of California Press, 1968).
6. Anne S. Roald, *Islam* (Oslo: Pax, 2004), 163.
7. Dilip Hiro, *Islamic Fundamentalism* (London: Paladin, 1988), 51; indeed Mohammed Abdu put Islamic concepts such as *shura* (consultation), *ijma* (consensus), and *mashala* (choosing the interpretation of Shariah that will bring the greatest good to the population) in a utilitarian framework.
8. Roald 2004, 165.
9. Gilles Kepel, *Jihad, the Trail of Political Islam* (London: I.B. Tauris, 2004), 28; Brynjar Lia, *The Society of the Muslim Brothers in Egypt: The Rise of an Islamic Mass Movement 1928–1942* (Reading: Garnet, 1998), 79–81, 167.
10. Sayed Kathab, "Al-Hudaybi's Influence on the Development of Islamist Movements", *The Muslim World*, 91 (2001), 451.
11. William Sherpard, "The Development of the Thought of Sayyid Qutb as Reflected in Earlier and Later Editions of 'Social Justice in Islam'", *Die Welt des Islams* 32, no. 2 (1992).
12. Bin Laden 2005.
13. Quintan Wiktorowicz distinguishes between the rationalist *Salafiya*, which is said to be the philosophy of the late nineteenth- and early twentieth-century reformers such as Rida, Al Banna, Al Afgani, and Salafism. Wiktorowicz illustrates the difference by

giving an example provided by one of his Salafi respondents, according to whom the *Salafiya* scholar Muhammed Abduh's understanding of the *jinn* as microbes or germs demonstrates his rationalist credentials: not only does it indicate a metaphorical approach to the *Qur'ān*; but it also implies the influence of the West on his thinking. Quintan Wiktorowicz, "Anatomy of the Salafi Movement", *Studies in Conflict and Terrorism*, 29 (2006), 212.

14. This dated from Eisenhower's efforts to promote Saud as an alternative regional leader to Nasser after the Suez Crisis and the enunciation of the Eisenhower Doctrine.
15. Kepel 2004, 142.
16. Faisal Devji, *Landscapes of the Jihad: Militancy, Morality, Modernity* (London: Hurst, 2007), 24.
17. Mark Urban, *War in Afghanistan* (London: MacMillian, 1988), 244.
18. Laila Bokhari, "Radikal Islamisme i Pakistan og Kashmir—fra lokal til global jihad", *FFI Rapport* 2004/01583.
19. International Institute for Strategic Studies, *Strategic Survey 2003–2004* (Hudson: Noram International Partners, 2005).
20. Thomas Hegghammer, "Global Jihad after the Iraq War", *Middle East Journal*, 60, no. 1 (2006), 14.
21. Bin Laden 2005.
22. Hegghammer 2006, 15.
23. Ahmed S. Hashim, *Insurgency and Counter Insurgency in Iraq* (London: Hurst, 2004), 269.

CHAPTER 1

1. See Jonathan Fox, "Are Middle Eastern Conflicts More Religious?", *Middle East Quarterly*, 8, no. 4 (2001).
2. *Settlement Report* 6, no. 4, July 1996. Accessed at http://www.fmep.org/reports/vol06/no4/02-netanyahu_promises_a_new_look_for_israeli_policies.html (5 April 2007).
3. Ehud Sprinzak, "Gush Emunim: The Tip of the Iceberg", *The Jerusalem Quarterly*, no. 21 (Fall 1981). Accessible at http://www.geocities.com/alabasters_archive/gush_iceberg.html.
4. *Ibid.*
5. Rabbi Hecht, 19 June 1995, quoted in A. Brownfeld, "Mirror-image Jewish and Islamic religious extremists threaten Israel's movement toward peace", *Washington Report on Middle East Affairs*, January/February, 1999.
6. http://soitgoes.typepad.com/so_it_goes/the_middle_east/index.html (accessed 20 June 2007).
7. Quoted by Donald Wagner, "Bible and Sword: US Christian Zionists Discover Israel", www.informationclearinghouse.info/article4950.htm (accessed 13 March 2007).
8. Quoted in Richard Greene, "Evangelical Christians", *BBC News*, 19 July 2006.
9. http://www.aipac.org/about_AIPAC/Learn_About_AIPAC/default.asp (accessed 5 April 2007).

10. The Speaker of the House of Representatives, Nancy Pelosi, commented, "With all due respect to former President Carter, he does not speak for the Democratic party on Israel." Quoted on *CBC News*, 9 December 2006, www.cbc.ca/canada/story/2006/12/08/carter-israel.html (accessed 5 April 2007).
11. Quoted from Robertson: "God punished Sharon" on ynetnews.com http://www.ynetnews.com/articles/0,7340,L-3195952,00.html.
12. The name "Hamas" was first used in January 1988. There are credible accounts that Hamas received tacit support from the Israeli security services during its early life— Islamic Jihad was seen as a greater threat and the emergence of an Islamic movement that might divide and weaken the mainstream Palestinian nationalist movement was a desirable outcome from the Israeli perspective, See Andrew Rigby, *Living the Intifada* (London: Zed Books, 1991), 36–7.
13. Covenant of Islamic Resistance Movement, Article 11.
14. Covenant of Islamic Resistance Movement, Article 6. Quoted in Hisham Ahmad, *Hamas* (Jerusalem: Passia, 1994), 53.
15. *Ibid.*, 54.
16. *Ibid.*, 56.
17. *Ibid.*, 107.
18. *Ibid.*, 107.
19. According to some reports Hamas has claimed responsibility for the killing of more than 400 Israelis in about sixty suicide bombings since its formation. Chris McGreal, *The Guardian*, 27 January 2006.
20. Windham and Gardiner *Journal of Comparative Legislation and International Law*, 3rd Ser., Vol. 20, no. 3, 188–92 (1938).
21. Personal communication with Andrew Rigby, January 2007.
22. One consequence of the rise of Hamas, alongside the worsening living conditions, has been the shrinking of the Christian community within Palestinian society. Historically Christians constituted around 10 per cent of the Palestinian population. But in recent years their numbers have shrunk as they have emigrated to join their relatives overseas, the prime push factors being the worsening living conditions and concerns that a Hamas government might codify and incorporate into legislation aspects of Shariah law and Islamic practice.
23. Quoted by Chris McGreal, *The Guardian*, 24 June 2003.
24. The complete text in English can be found at: http://www.informationclearinghouse.info/article6537.htm.
25. Quoted in Michael Slackman, "Bin Laden says West is waging war against Islam", *New York Times*, 24 April 2006.
26. Events in the second half of 2007 both in Gaza and the West Bank confirms the need to have dialogues with all main actors. With regards to Palestine, the failure to engage with Hamas has resulted in lethal damage to the Palestinian project.

CHAPTER 2

1. Samir Khalaf, *Persistence and Change in 19th-century Lebanon: A Sociological Essay* (Beirut: Imprimerie Catholique, 1979).

2. *Ibid.*, 54.
3. For an account of the 1860 events see Tarazi Fawaz Leila, *An Occasion for War, Civil Conflict in Lebanon and Damascus in 1860*, (London: I.B. Tauris, 1994).
4. Pierre Rondot presents the following estimates of the demographical weights of the different Lebanese communities at the time of the creation of the Lebanese Republic:

Communities	Number	%
Maronites	199,182	32.7
Greek Orthodox	81,409	13.3
Greek Catholics	42,426	7
Other Christians	12,651	2.1
Sunnis	124,786	20.5
Shias	104,947	17.2
Druzes	43,633	7.2
Total	609,034	100

See Pierre Rondot, *Les Institutions Politiques au Liban*, in Elizabeth Picard, *Lebanon: A Shattered Country* (New York: Holmes and Meier Publishers, 2002), 33.

5. Meir Zamir, *The Formation of Modern Lebanon* (Ithaca, NY: Cornell University Press, 1988), 124.
6. It is important to note that the Sunni Muslims were the natural interlocutors of the Maronites due to the political irrelevance of the Shias who at that time were only slowly emerging from centuries of political, social and economical marginalization under the Ottomans. It was not until the sixties that the Shias became players on their own right in the Lebanese arena. At the time of independence, however, they were still considered to be almost an appendix of the Sunnis. See Fouad Ajami, *The Vanished Imam: Mussa al Sadr and the Shia of Lebanon* (London: I.B. Tauris, 1986), and Tamara Chalabi, *The Shi'is of Jabal Amil and then New Lebanon, Community and Nation-State, 1918–1943* (New York: Palgrave, 2006).
7. Caroline Attie, *Struggle in the Levant: Lebanon in the 1950s* (London: I.B. Tauris, 2004), 177.
8. It could be mentioned against this conclusion that the head of the Maronite church, Patriarch Paul Mauchi, was actually against President Chamoun, while the Sunni Prime Minister Sami al Sulh was on his side. It is worthy to remember however that the position of the Patriarch isolated him among the ecclesiastical hierarchy of the church while Sami al Sulh was ex-communicated from the Sunni community. In fact, his pro-Chamoun stand ended his political career.
9. Michael Johnson presents an interesting analysis of the attitude of the Sunni elite *vis-à-vis* Nasserism in his *Class and Client in Beirut: The Sunni Muslim Community and the Lebanese State 1840–1985* (London: Ithaca Press, 1986). See notably pp. 77–8.
10. *Ibid.*
11. Document of the Lebanese Front "The Lebanon we want to build" promulgated on 23 December 1980.
12. Farid el Khazen, *The Breakdown of the State in Lebanon 1967–1976* (London: I.B. Tauris, 2000); Samir Kassir, *La Guerre du Liban, de la dissension nationale au conflit*

    régional (Paris: Khartala, 1994) and Alain Menargues, *Les Secrets de la Guerre du Liban* (Paris: Albin Michel, 2004).

13. The Lebanese Economist, George Corm, not known as a warm supporter of political Maronitism, states nonetheless that at the eve of the civil war the great fortunes in Lebanon remained actually in the hands of the large Shia landlords and the urban Sunni notables. Georges Corm, *Géopolitique du Conflit Libanais* (Paris: La Découverte, 1986), 166–83.

14. Huntington, 1996, 254.

15. *Ibid.*

16. Jean Pierre Valognes, *Vie et Mort des Chrétiens d'Orient de l'Origine à Nos Jours* (France: Fayard 1994). Valognes writes "L'opinion publique occidentale, aujourd'hui largement déchristianisée, ignorante de la parente culturelle qui la rapproche des chrétiens d'Orient, ne ressent a l'égard des minorités chrétiennes aucune affinité particulière, bien au contraire (...) Le remords d'avoir persécuté les juifs et colonisé les musulmans les incline (les occidentaux) paradoxalement à ajouter aux erreurs du passé de nouvelles injustices, cette fois au détriment de leurs frères orientaux", 190–1.

17. The first republic lasted from the adoption of the constitution (1926) to the end of the civil war (1989–1990). Though it ended in bloodshed, its peaceful decades (1926–1975) are still largely remembered as Lebanon's "Golden Age" in which the country was a model of democracy and prosperity in a turbulent region, despite the three months of fighting in 1958. The second republic began after the constitutional amendments of the Taef Agreement (1989) and was characterized by the heavy rule of "Pax Syriana".

CHAPTER 3

1. Samuel P. Huntington, *The Clash of Civilizations and the Remaking of World Order* (New York: Simon and Schuster, 1997), 247.

2. See Antonio Giustozzi, *Afghanistan: Transition Without End* (London: Crisis States Research Centre, 2008).

3. See Kaneshka Nawabi et al., *Religious Civil Society: The Role and Functions of Religious Civil Society in Afghanistan* (Kabul: CPAU, 2007), 15.

4. Senzil K. Nawid, *Religious Response to Social Change in Afghanistan, 1919–29: King Aman-Allah and the Afghan Ulama* (Costa Mesa: Mazda Pub., 2000).

5. Steve Coll, *Ghost Wars: The Secret History of the CIA, Afghanistan, and bin Laden, from the Soviet Invasion to September 10, 2001* (New York: Penguin, 2004), 65, 67; George Crile, *My Enemy's Enemy* (London: Atlantic Books, 2003), 236, 340–1.

6. Gilles Dorronsoro, "Pakistan and the Taliban: State Policy, Religious Networks and Political Connections", (Paris: CERI, October 2000) http://www.ceri-sciencespo.com/archive/octo00/artgd.pdf, 11–12.

7. Olivier Roy, *Islam and Resistance in Afghanistan* (Cambridge: Cambridge University Press, 1990) and Gilles Doronsoro, *Afghanistan: Revolution Unending* (London: Hurst, 2005).

8. Milton Bearden and James Risen, *The Main Enemy* (New York: Ballantine Books, 2003), 232, 272; L. Peter Bergen, *Holy War, Inc.* (London: Weidenfeld and Nicolson, 2001), 71–2.

9. Anthony Hyman, "Arab involvement in the Afghan war", *The Beirut Review*, no. 7 (Spring 1994), 85–6.

10. Brynjar Lia, *Architect of Global Jihad: The Life of Al-Qaeda Strategist Abu Mus'ab Al-Suri* (London: Hurst, 2007), 236.

11. That was at least the view of a leading Islamist, Al-Suri. See Lia, *Architect of Global Jihad*, 236.

12. See Ahmed Rashid, *Taliban* (London: I.B. Tauris, 2000).

13. Lia 2007, 238, 291–2.

14. Lia 2007, 239, 242, 269, 287, 293.

15. There were at least fourteen separate jihadist groups in Afghanistan at that time, not counting the Pakistani ones (Lia, 247).

16. Bergen 2001, 112, 177; Roland Jacquard, *Les archives secretes d'Al-Qaida* (Paris: Jean Picollec, 2002), 48–9; *Cracks In The Foundation: Leadership Schisms in Al-Qa'ida from 1989–2006* (West Point: Combating Terrorism Center, 2007), 13.

17. Berger, 179; Lia, 278, 282, 292, 295; Jaquard, 67.

18. Massoud Sayyid, *Pasht-e barde kasi hast*! (Kabul: Ahmad Printing Press, 2003); Lia, 2007, 281, 284–6.

19. See for example Michael Scheuer, *Through Our Enemies' Eyes* (Washington, DC: Brassey's, 2002), 154.

20. The 8–9 months delay in organising the insurgency in 2002 and its slow start seems a clear indication that the Taliban had indeed suffered a blow (see Antonio Giustozzi, *Qur'an, Kalashnikov and Laptop: The Neo-Taliban Insurgency in Afghanistan 2002–2007* (London: Hurst, 2007), chapter 1.

21. Fawaz A. Gerges, *Journey of the Jihadist* (Orlando: Harcourt 2006), 174.

22. See Giustozzi, *Qur'an, Kalashnikov and Laptop*.

23. For more details see Giustozzi, *Qur'an, Kalashnikov and Laptop*, 35 and 131.

24. See note 25 above and several declarations of the leader of the Taliban, Mullah Omar; for example: staff writer "Taliban Only Fighting to Expel Foreigners—Omar", *Reuters*, *11 February 2008.

25. See Giustozzi, *Qur'an, Kalashnikov and Laptop*, 12, 14, 43–4, 49.

26. See Giustozzi, *Qur'an, Kalashnikov and Laptop* 43; Nawabi, *op. cit.*, 52–5.

27. On Pakistan see C. Christine Fair, "Who Are Pakistan's Militants and Their Families?", *Terrorism and Political Violence* 20, no. 1 (2008), 49–65.

28. See Giustozzi, *Qur'an, Kalashnikov and Laptop*, 40–5

29. *Ibid.*, 52–5.

30. *Ibid.*, 111 and 52.

31. *Ibid.*, 65, 205–6.

32. On the impact of PSCs see Susanne Schmeid and Lisa Rimli, *The Impact of Private Military and Security Companies on the Local Population in Post-Conflict Countries. A Comparative Study for Afghanistan and Angola* (Bern: Swiss Peace, 2007) and Antonio Giustozzi, "The Privatizing of War and Security in Afghanistan: Future or Dead End?", *The Economics of Peace and Security Journal* 2, no. 1 (2007), 19–23. On issues of "friction" see Giustozzi, *Qur'an Kalashnikov and Laptop*, 163–4, 166, 190, 194, 198.

33. For a list with references see: http://en.wikipedia.org/wiki/Civilian_casualties_of_the_War_in_Afghanistan_(2001%E2%80%93present)#References.

34. Personal observation, Kunduz, 2003–4; personal communication with tribal elders, Gardez, May 2007.
35. War widows were given priority access to jobs in some NGOs and international organizations; episodes of harassment by Afghan men and particularly guards and police were reported.
36. The best known example is that of Christian convert Abdur Rahman, who in spring 2006 was helped to flee the country to avoid a death sentence for apostasy.

CHAPTER 4

1. Samuel P. Huntington, "The Clash of Civilizations?" *Foreign Affairs* 72, no. 3 (Summer 1993), 22–49.
2. Paul R. Brass, "Groups, Symbol Manipulation and Ethnic Identity Among the Muslims of South Asia," in David Taylor and Malcolm Yapp (eds), *Political Identity in South Asia* (London: Curzon Press, 1979), 60.
3. In his superb history of the *Jama'at-i-Islami* in Pakistan, Seyyed Vali Reza Nasr points out that the JI is "one of the oldest and most influential of the Islamic revivalist movements and the first of its kind to develop an Islamic ideology, a modern revolutionary reading of Islam, and an agenda for social action to realize its vision." Syeed Vali Reza Nasr, *The Vanguard of the Islamic Revolution: The Jama'at-i Islami of Pakistan* (Berkeley, CA: University of California Press, 1994), iv.
4. Syed Abu'l-ala-Maududi, "Islamic Law and Constitution," in Stephen Hay (ed.), *Sources of Indian Tradition, Volume Two: Modern India and Pakistan*, 2nd edition (New York: Columbia University Press, 1988), 408–11.
5. Ayesha Jalal, *Democracy and Authoritarianism in South Asia: A Comparative and Historical Perspective* (New York: Cambridge University Press, 1995), 238.
6. S.V.R. Nasr, *The Vanguard of the Islamic Revolution*, 122.
7. Ayesha Jalal, *Democracy and Authoritarianism in South Asia*, 222.
8. Christophe Jaffrelot, "Nationalism without a Nation: Pakistan Searching for its Identity," in Christophe Jaffrelot (ed.), *Pakistan: Nationalism Without a Nation* (London: Zed Books, 2002), 36.
9. *Ibid.*
10. S.V.R. Nasr, "The Rise of Sunni Militancy in Pakistan: The Changing Role of Islamism and Ulama in Society and Politics," *Modern Asian Studies* 34, no. 1 (February 2000), 139–80.
11. Khawar Mumtaz and Farida Shaheed, *Women of Pakistan: Two Steps Forward, One Step Back?* (Lahore, Pakistan: Vanguard Books, 1987).
12. Suroosh Irfani, "Pakistan's Sectarian Violence: Between the 'Arabist Shift' and Indo-Persian Culture", in Satu P. Limaye, Robert G. Wirsing and Mohan Malik (eds) *Religious Radicalism and Security in South Asia*, 154.
13. Stephen Philip Cohen, *The Idea of Pakistan* (Washington, D.C.: Brookings Institution Press, 2004), 173.
14. *Ibid.*, 169–70.
15. S.V.R. Nasr, "The Rise of Sunni Militancy in Pakistan", 157.
16. For a comprehensive history of *madrasahs* in Pakistan, see International Crisis Group, "Pakistan: Madrasas, Extremism and the Military", *Asia Report* no. 36, 29 July 2002.

17. Rasul Bakhsh Rais, "In the Shadow of the Past", in Craig Baxter (ed.), *Pakistan on the Brink: Politics, Economics and Society* (Lanham, MA: Lexington Books, 2004), 39–40.
18. Steve Coll, *Ghost Wars: The Secret History of the CIA, Afghanistan, and bin Laden, from the Soviet Invasion to September 10, 2001*, (New York: The Penguin Press, 2004); Husain Haqqani, *Pakistan: Between Mosque and Military* (Washington, D.C.: Carnegie Endowment for International Peace, 2005); Zahid Hussein, *Frontline Pakistan: The Struggle Within Militant Islam*, (London: I.B. Tauris, 2007).
19. Zahid Hussain, *Frontline Pakistan*, 2007, 132.
20. M. Ilyas Khan, "Ready to Rumble", *The Herald* (August 2004), 63.
21. Ahmed Rashid, "The Taliban: Exporting Extremism", *Foreign Affairs* (November/ December, 1999), 26.
22. Rais, 43.
23. Ahmed Rashid, "The Taliban: Exporting Extremism", 28.
24. Zahid Hussain, *Frontline Pakistan*, 190.
25. Rais, 3 "In the Shadow of the Past", 8.
26. *Ibid.*, 41–5.
27. Zulfiqar Ali, "For the Record," *The Herald* (July 2005), 55–6.
28. Pervez Musharraf, *In the Line of Fire: A Memoir* (New York: Simon and Schuster), 201–7.
29. Ashley J. Tellis, "US-Pakistan Relations: Assassination, Instability and the Future of US Policy". Prepared testimony to the House Committee on Foreign Affairs, Subcommittee on the Middle East and South Asia, 16 January 2008.
30. Samina Ahmed, "Extremist Madrasas, Ghost Schools, and US Aid to Pakistan: Are We Making the Grade of 9/11 Commission Report Card?" Testimony on Madrasas and US Aid to Pakistan before the US House of Representatives Subcommittee on National Security and Foreign Affairs, 9 May 2007.
31. Ahmed Rashid, "He's Welcome in Pakistan", *The Washington Post*, 26 February 2007.
32. Ayesha Siddiqa, "The Mystery that is Pakistan", *Newsline*, February 2007.
33. Stephen P. Cohen, *Catastrophe or Last Chance in Pakistan* (Washington, D.C.: The Brookings Institution, 5 November 2007), 2.
34. Ahmed Rashid, "Emergency for Pakistan—And the World", *Yale Global Online*, 11 December 2007, http://yaleglobal.yale.edu.
35. Hassan Abbas, "A Profile of Tehrik-i-Taliban Pakistan", *CTC Sentinel* Vol. 1, no. 2 (January 2008), 1.
36. Nicholas Schmidle, "Next-Gen Taliban", *The New York Times Magazine*, 6 January, 2008, 48–53.
37. The TNSM is banned by the Pakistani government. It resurfaced in 2006 under the leadership of Maulana Fazlullah, and in 2007 it took control of large areas of the Swat and Shangla districts of Malakand division in the northern part of the NWFP, where the Pakistan military is engaged in a massive counter-insurgency operation. For information on the TNSM and its operations in the Swat Valley, see Hassan Abbas, "The Black-Turbaned Brigade: The Rise of the TNSM in Pakistan", *Terrorism Monitor* 4, no. 23 (30 November 2006), http:www.jamestown.org; and Syed Adnan Ali Shah Bukhari, *Swat: A Dangerous Flashpoint in the Making*, Pakistan Security Research Unit (PSRU), University of Bradford, UK, 6 December 2007.

38. Hassan Abbas, "A Profile of Tehrik-i-Taliban Pakistan", 2.
39. Ahmed Rashid: remarks delivered at a panel discussion on "Insurgents and the Afghanistan-Pakistan Border". United States Institute of Peace, Washington, D.C., 6 December 2007.
40. Stephen P. Cohen, *Catastrophe or Last Chance for Pakistan*, 3.
41. Out of fifty-six suicide bombings in Pakistan in 2007, thirty-six targeted military personnel and installations, including two against the ISI, two against the army head-quarters in Rawalpindi, and one against the air force in Sargodha. Hassan Abbas, "A Profile of Tehrik-i-Taliban Pakistan", 3.
42. Ahmed Rashid, "Pakistan on the Edge," *The New York Review of Books*, 49, no. 15 (10 October 2002).
43. For analyses of the military-defence complex, see Ayesha Jalal, *The State of Martial Rule: The Origins of Pakistan's Political Economy of Defence* (Lahore, Pakistan: Van-guard Books, 1990); Stephen P. Cohen, *The Pakistan Army* (Karachi, Pakistan: Oxford University Press, 1992); and Ayesha Siddiqa-Agha, *Pakistan's Arms Procurement and Military Buildup, 1979–1999* (New York: Palgrave, 2001).
44. Zahid Hussain, *Frontline Pakistan*, 69.
45. Islamist parties in Pakistan are politically and ideologically distinct, they represent diverse socio-economic constituencies, and they differ over goals, strategies and tac-tics. Various sects in Islam are affiliated with one or another of the major parties: the *Jamiat-ul-Ulema-i-Islam* (JUI), for example, is based in the Deobandi sect, while the *Jamiat-ul-Ulema-i-Pakistan* (JUP) is associated with the Barelwi sect. For an excellent analysis of Islamist parties and organizations in Pakistan, see Mohammed Wasim, "Origins and Growth Patterns of Islamic Organizations in Pakistan", in Satu P. Limaye, Mohan Malik and Robert Wirsing (eds), *Religious Radicalism and Security in South Asia* (Honolulu, Hawaii: Asia-Pacific Center for Security Studies, 2004), 21.
46. Massoud Ansari, "Fight to the Finish", *Newsline*, July 2007.
47. The Lal Masjid clerics are said to have had close ties with the Taliban and al-Qaeda. The mosque complex is reported to have housed proscribed jihadi groups like *Jaish-e-Mohammed, Harkat-ul-Mujahideen* and *Harkat-e-Jihad-Islami*, whose members trained and fought in Afghanistan and Kashmir. Zahid Hussain, "The Battle for Paki-stan's Soul", *Newsline*, July 2007.
48. Steven Kull, "A New Lens on Pakistan", *World Public Opinion*, 24 January 2008, http://www.worldpublicopinion.org.
49. C. Christine Fair, Clay Ramsay and Steve Kull, "Pakistani Public Opinion on Democ-racy, Islamist Militancy, and Relations with the US", Working Paper, United States Institute of Peace (Washington, D.C.: United States Institute of Peace, January 2008).
50. *Ibid.*
51. United States Government Accountability Office, *Combating Terrorism in Pakistan*, April 2008.

CHAPTER 5

1. Giora Eliraz, *Islam in Indonesia* (Brighton: Sussex Academic Press, 2004), 17.

2. Interview with Din Syamsuddin, head of Muhammadiya and deputy chair of MUI, Jakarta, 19 July 2006.
3. Interview with Zuhairi Misrawi, (Nahdlatul Ulama) Indonesian Society for Pesantren and Community Development, Program Coordinator, Jakarta, 19 July 2006.
4. Interview with Din Syamsuddin, head of Muhammadiya and deputy chair of MUI, Jakarta, 19 July 2006.
5. Interview with Zuhairi Misrawi, (Nahdlatul Ulama) Indonesian Society for Pesantren and Community Development Program Coordinator, Jakarta, 19 July 2006.
6. *Ibid.*
7. Interview with Din Syamsuddin, head of Muhammadiya and deputy chair of MUI, Jakarta, 19 July 2006.
8. *Ibid.*
9. Interview with Zuhairi Misrawi, (Nahdlatul Ulama) Indonesian Society for Pesantren and Community Development, Program Coordinator, Jakarta, 19 July 2006.
10. *Ibid.*
11. Eliraz, *Islam in Indonesia*, 69.
12. Interview with Eva Kusuma Sundari, Member of Parliament PDI-P, Jakarta, 17 July 2006.
13. ICG, "Indonesia: Overcoming Murder and Chaos in Maluku", *Asia Report* no. 10 (December 2000), 4–5.
14. Kirsten E. Schulze, "Laskar Jihad and the Conflict in Ambon", *The Brown Journal of World Affairs*, IX, no. 1 (2002), 62–3.
15. Jacques Bertrand, *Nationalism and Ethnic Conflict in Indonesia* (Cambridge: Cambridge University Press, 2004), 117.
16. *Ibid.*, 118.
17. Schulze, "Laskar Jihad and the Conflict in Ambon", 62–3.
18. Interview with Ali Fauzi and Nasir Rahawarin, Muslim informal community leaders, Ambon, 20 December 2001.
19. For a detailed analysis of *Laskar Jihad*'s ideology see Noorhaidi, *Laskar Jihad: Islam, Militancy and the Quest for Identity in Post-New Order Indonesia*, (Utrecht: Utrecht University, 2005).
20. Interview with Yahyia Abdel Malik, *Laskar Jihad*, Jakarta, 17 April 2001.
21. Law on the Governance of Aceh (Jakarta 2006) article 125, paragraph 2.
22. *Ibid.*, article 126, paragraph 2.
23. Amendment to the by-law of Nanggroe Aceh Darussalam (Banda Aceh), article 1, paragraph 20, 16 February 2006.
24. *Ibid.*, paragraph 21.
25. Kirsten E. Schulze, *The Free Aceh Movement (GAM): Anatomy of a separatist organisation* (Washington: East-West Center, 2004).
26. Interview with Amni Ahmad Bin Marzuki, GAM, Banda Aceh, 24 June 2001.
27. Interview with Amni Ahmad Bin Marzuki, GAM, Banda Aceh, 7 April 2002.
28. *Ibid.*
29. Interview with Imam Suja, Muhammadiya Chairman for Aceh, Banda Aceh, 27 June 2001.
30. Interview with Malik Musa, Chairman of Muhammadiya Youth, Banda Aceh, 26 June 2001.

31. Interview with Alyasa Abubakar, Head of the Shariah Office, Banda Aceh, 12 April 2002.

32. Interview with Eva Kusuma Sundari, Member of Parliament PDI-P, Jakarta, 17 July 2006.

33. *Ibid.*

34. Interview with national parliamentarian, Prosperous Peace Party PDS, Jakarta 13 July 2006.

35. Interview with Eva Kusuma Sundari, Member of Parliament PDI-P, Jakarta, 17 July 2006.

36. Interview with national parliamentarian, Prosperous Peace Party PDS, Jakarta 13 July 2006.

37. Interview with Eva Kusuma Sundari, Member of Parliament PDI-P, Jakarta, 17 July 2006.

38. Interview with Abu Bakar Ba'asyir, alleged *emir* of Jemaah Islamiyya, Jakarta, 2 September 2003.

39. *Ibid.*

40. *Ibid.*

41. For a detailed discussion on the origins and structure of JI see International Crisis Group, "Al-Qaeda in Southeast Asia: The case of the 'Ngruki Network' in Indonesia", *Asia Briefing*, 20 (August 2002), and International Crisis Group, "Indonesia Backgrounder: How the Jemaah Islamiya Terrorist Network Operates", *Asia Report* 43 (December 2002).

42. For a detailed discussion of the split and the younger militants see International Crisis Group, "Terrorism in Indonesia: Noordin's Networks", *Asia Report* 114 (May 2006).

43. *Ibid.*

44. Interview with Abu Bakar Ba'asyir, alleged emir of Jemaah Islamiyya, Jakarta, 2 September 2003.

45. See International Crisis Group, "Jemaah Islamiya in Southeast Asia: Damaged but still Dangerous", *Asia Report* 63 (2003).

CHAPTER 6

1. Samuel P. Huntington *The Clash of Civilizations* (New York: Simon and Schuster, 1997), 27, 45, 56–78.

2. *Ibid.*, 137–8.

3. *Ibid.*, 253, 264.

4. Patricio N. Abinales, and Donna J. Amoroso, *State and Society in the Philippines* (Lanham: Rowman and Littlefield Publishers, 2005), 123–5.

5. Ben Reid, "Bush and the Philippines: Transnational class alliances, mutual opportunism and democratic retreat", in M. Beeson (ed.) *Bush and Asia: America's Evolving Relations with East Asia* (Melbourne: Palgrave, 2006), 145–61.

6. Abinales and Amoroso, 49–55, 69–70.

7. Tom McKenna, "Saints, scholars and the idealized past in Philippine Muslim Separatism", *The Pacific Review*, 15, no. 4 (2002), 544.

8. Abinales and Amoroso, *State and Society in the Philippines*, 123–5.

9. Reid, "Bush and the Philippines", 2006, 150–2; Yojiro Hayami, Agnes R. Quisum-
   bung, and Lourdes S. Adriano, *Towards an Alternative Land Reform Paradigm: A
   Philippine Perspective* (Quezon City: Ateneo de Manila Press, 1990), 42–4.
10. Reid 2006, 159–61.
11. Hayami et al., *Towards an Alternative Land Reform Paradigm*, 42–4.
12. Rene E. Ofreneo, *Capitalism in Philippine Agriculture* (Manila: Foundation for
    Nationalist Studies, 1980), 61–96.
13. S. Islam Syied, "Islamic Independence Movements in Patani of Thailand and Mind-
    anao of the Philippines", *Asian Survey*, 38, no. 5 (1998), 448–9.
14. Charles O. Frake, Abu Sayyaf, "Displays of Violence and the Proliferation of Con-
    tested Identities amongst Philippine Muslims", *American Anthropologist* 100, no. 1
    (1993), 47.
15. Marites D. Vitug, and G.M. Gloria, *Under the Crescent Moon: Rebellion in Mindanao*
    (Quezon City: Philippine Center for Social Affairs and Institute for Popular Democ-
    racy, 2000).
16. Vitug and Gloria, 2000.
17. Reid 2006, 153–6.
18. McKenna 2002, 540.
19. James C. Scott, *Weapons of the Weak: Everyday forms of peasant resistance* (Yale: Yale
    University Press, 1987).
20. Vitug and Gloria 2000, 113–16.
21. James Cotton "Southeast Asia After 9/11", *Terrorism and Political Violence* 15, no. 1
    (2003), 148–170.
22. United States Department of State Foreign Terrorist Organizations, www.state.gov/s/
    ct/rls/fs/37191.htm, (accessed 25 February 2007).
23. Vitug and Gloria 2000, 20–30.
24. See Stephen Rood, *Issue on Cordillera Autonomy: Conference Proceedings* (Baguio:
    Cordillera Studies Centre, 1987).
25. Abinales and Amoroso 2005, 109–13.
26. *Ibid.*, 113–29.
27. Vitug and Gloria 2000, 30–3.
28. Salah Jubair, *Bangsamoro: A nation under endless tyranny* (Kuala Lumpur: IQ Marin,
    1999), 248–50.
29. Octavio Dinapo, "A Last Extended Interview with Janjalani", *Philippine Daily Inquirer*,
    22 January 2006.
30. Z. Abuza, *Militant Islam in Southeast Asia, Crucible of Terror* (Boulder and London:
    Lynne Reinner Publishers, 2003), 97.
31. See International Crisis Group, "Southern Philippines backgrounder: Terrorism and
    the peace process" *ICG Asia report* 40 (2004). The ICG is headed by former Austral-
    ian Foreign minister Gareth Evans. Evans continued Australia's policy of being the
    only state in the world to *de jure* recognise Indonesia's sovereignty over the disputed
    territory, despite clear evidence of considerable atrocities being carried out by the
    Indonesian military. By 2008, however, the ICG conceded "US-backed security opera-
    tions in the southern Philippines...are also confusing counter-terrorism and counter-
    insurgency with dangerous implications for conflict in the region. ... it runs the risk of

pushing them into the arms of the broader insurgencies in Mindanao, the Moro Islamic Liberation Front (MILF) and Moro National Liberation Front (MNLF)" See ICG, "The Philippines: Counter-insurgency vs. Counter-terrorism in Mindanao" *Asia Report* no. 152 (14 May 2008).

32. Grace Cantal-Albasin, "MILF no longer on US list of terror groups: GMA," *Philippine Daily Inquirer*, 28 July 2002.
33. Abuza 2003, 90.
34. Reid 2006, 149.
35. *Ibid.*, 160–1.
36. Cynthia Balana, C. Avendana and J. Alipala, "IC Urges gov't, MNLF to Stop Fighting", *Philippine Daily Inquirer*, 17 April 2007.
37. Avelino Cruz, *Fourth Plenary Session—Setting National Security Priorities—Avelino Cruz Jr, Secretary of National Defence, the Philippines*, 5th Asia Security Summit, The Shangri-La Dialogue, Republic of Singapore, www.iiss.org (04 June 2006).

REGION II

1. I would like to thank Sakah Mahmoud and Terje Østebø for their comments to this introduction.
2. Ali A. Mazrui, "Religion and Political Culture in Africa", *Journal of The American Academy of Religion*, 53, no. 4 (1985), 820.
3. *Ibid.*
4. This agenda was in many ways more a dream than an agenda within the range of Egyptian capabilities. See Gerard Prunier in this book.
5. The Stockholm International Peace Research Institute, *Yearbook of World Armaments and Disarmaments* (Oxford: Oxford University Press, 2000).
6. Roy Love argues that the Rwandan genocide was connected with religion, because of the Catholic Church's role in the colonial period, where it participated in the defining process of what Hutu and Tutsi consisted of, and because of its non-action during the genocide. However, he admits that it was indirect. Non-action, although not laudable in this case, should not be confused with causing and promoting, if this is the case the whole world participated in causing the Rwandan genocide. See Roy Love, "Religion Ideology and Conflict in Africa", *Review of African Political Economy* 33, no. 110 (2006), 628.
7. Paul Anber, "Modernization and Political Disintegration: Nigeria and the Ibos", *The Journal of Modern African Studies* 5, no. 2 (1967), 167.
8. Jeffrey Haynes, "Islamic Militancy in Africa", *Third World Quarterly*, 26, no. 8 (2005), 1335; Millard Burr and Robert Collins, *Alms for Jihad*, (Cambridge: Cambridge University Press, 2006), 40.
9. Grant Ferrett, "Africans trust religious leaders", *BBC News*, 14 September 2005.
10. Timothy Carney, "The Sudan, Political Islam and Terrorism", in Robert I. Rothberg (ed.), *Battling terrorism in the Horn of Africa* (New York: The World Peace Foundation, 2005), 123.
11. Haynes 2005.
12. *Ibid.*, 133.

13. Dan Connell, "Eritrea, On a slow Fuse", in Robert I. Rothberg (ed.), *Battling Terrorism in the Horn of Africa* (New York: The World Peace Foundation, 2005), 64–91.

CHAPTER 7

1. Staff writer, "Miss World Nigeria boycott spreads", *BBC News*, 6 September 2002. http://news.bbc.co.uk/2/hi/africa/2240790.stm (accessed 3 October 2003).
2. The country was also prominently featured in an academic article by Princeton Lyman and J. Stephen Morrison, "The terrorist threat in Africa", *Foreign Affairs* 83, no. 1 (2004), and in a United States Institute of Peace (USIP) seminar on "Political Islam in Sub-Saharan Africa", *USIP Special Report* (2005).
3. See Sakah Saidu Mahmud, "Islamism in Nigeria", *African Studies Review*, 47, no. 2 (2004). Also see Ibrahim Gambari, "Islamic Revivalism in Nigeria: Home-grown or Externally Induced?" in John L. Esposito (ed.), *The Iranian Revolution: Its Global Impact*, (Miami: Florida International University Press, 1990).
4. In order to avoid any confusion it is important to clarify that the focus is on Northern Nigeria—where most of the conflicts have occurred.
5. See the introduction to this book for a discussion of the different approaches used by various scholars. Because of space constraints, a discussion of these theories will not feature in this chapter.
6. John Paden and Alan Feinstein, *African Revolutionary: The Life and Times of Nigeria's Aminu Kano* (Boulder and London: Lynne Rienner Publishers, 1987).
7. *Ibid.*
8. Paden 1973, 183.
9. Abubakar Gumi, *Where I Stand* (Ibadan: Spectrum Books, 1994), 105–10.
10. See Ahmadu Bello, *My Life* (Cambridge: Cambridge University Press, 1962), 217–18.
11. These include "the submission of the faithful to the authority of the Sufi sheikhs and the obligation to give them [sheikhs] donations (sadaqa)." For these and a full pro-gramme of the Izala see Roman Loimeier, *Islamic Reform and Political Change in Northern Nigeria* (Evanston: Northwestern University Press, 1997), 228–30. The entire book offers an excellent account of the Sufi brotherhoods and the Izala as well as the relationship between them.
12. Formally launched in 1978, the group's ideological foundation is based on the Saudi Wahhabi reformist and anti-Sufi interpretation of Islam. Sheikh Gumi was associated with Wahhabi and Saudi authorities since the 1950s. In fact, the Sufi brotherhoods used this affiliation in their counter-attack of Izala implying that it was a foreign agent. However, the focus of Izala was on the condition of practice of Islam by the brother-hoods, which Izala considered as "innovations" (*bida'a*) unacceptable to Islam.
13. Both mainstream Islamic groups and the governments (state and federal) refused to accept the movement as Islamic but rather as a criminal group. The leader was killed in a gun battle, thereby depriving the public from hearing from him about more of the movement's intentions.
14. Violent riots took place in Kano (1980), Bulunkutu in Borno State (1982), Gombe in Bauchi State, Yola in Gongola State and Kaduna (1984 and 1985). For various

accounts and explanations see Toyin Falola, *Violence in Nigeria: The Crisis of Religious Politics and Secular Ideologies* (Rochester: University of Rochester Press, 1998); Mervyn Hiskett, "The Maitatsine Riots in Kano: An Assessment", *Journal of Religion in Africa* 17, no. 3 (1984); Elizabeth Isichei, "The Maitatsine Risings in Nigeria: 1980–85", *Journal of Religion in Africa* 17, no. 3 (1987); and Paul M. Lubeck, "Islamic Protest under Semi-Industrial Capitalism: Yan Tatsine Explained", *Africa* 55, no. 4 (1985).

15. These include Cameroon (the leader's country of origin), Chad, Mali, Niger Republic and Burkina Faso many of whose people endure appalling living poor conditions.

16. The period also happened to be one of general economic decline and hardship for many Nigerians. For the economic interpretation, see Paul M. Lubeck, "Structural Determinants of Urban Islamic Protest in Northern Nigeria: A Note on Method, Mediation and Materialist Explanation", in William R. Roff (ed.), *Islam and the Political Economy of Meaning: Comparative Studies of Muslim Discourse*, (Berkeley: University of California Press, 1987). In his anti-materialist position, Marwa preached against modern technology and "modern conveniences such as radio, bicycles, [and] frowned upon money. Anyone who went to sleep at night in the possession of more than two naira (about twenty US cents) was considered an unbeliever," (Allan Christelow, "Religious Protest and Dissent in Northern Nigeria: From Mahdism to Quranic Integralism", *Journal of Institute of Muslim Minority Affairs* 6, no. 2 (1985), 376. As a fanatic or lunatic his anti-Islamic utterances include the rejection of the Sunnah of the Prophet, which is a major part of Shariah, and his claim to be the ****** of the Prophets.

17. Also, the government had ignored the warning signs two months earlier when some Muslims began to denounce the contest as a "parade of nudity". See staff writer, "Miss World Nigeria boycott spreads", *BBC News*, 6 September 2002. http://news.bbc.co.uk/2/hi/africa/2240790.stm (accessed 3 October, 2003).

18. Lydia Polgreen, "Nigeria Counts 100 Deaths over Danish Caricatures", *The New York Times*, 27 February 2006.

19. The report claimed that "the driver was reversing the truck when he accidentally ran into a religious study group and drove over the copy of a Qur'an that a student dropped as he was getting out of the way". See staff writer, "Nine die in Kano gang fights", *BBC News*, 18 December 2001. http://news.bbc.co.uk/hi/english/world/africa/newsid_1716000/1716891.stm.

20. The Muslim students allegedly laid in wait for the teacher after the examination where they fatally attacked her. A Muslim teacher who attempted to protect her was also severely beaten but not killed. See staff writer, "Religious fanatics render 10 months old baby motherless", *Daily Sun* (Lagos), 29 March 2007. http://odili.net/news/source/2007/mar/28/808.html (accessed 03/29/2007). These types of conflicts are often sudden, intense and passionate. The violence over the Miss World pageant and the Danish cartoons may have been the action of organized groups, since the tensions lasted days, long enough to mobilize the violent outbursts. The latter two episodes, however, seem to have been spontaneous rather than organized.

21. The reigning Emir at the time was Isah Muhamadu who was reported to have gone to the campus to reconcile the two groups but failed. For excellent accounts of the vari-

ous conflicts between the groups during the mid 1980s see Toyin Falola, *Violence in Nigeria* (University of Rochester Press, 1998); Matthew H. Kukah, *Religion, Politics and Power in Northern Nigeria* (Ibadan: Spectrum Books, 1993); and Karl Maier, *This House Has Fallen* (Ibadan, Spectrum Books, 2000).

22. The protests against Bonnke in Kano in 1980 were triggered by the earlier refusal of the government to give permission for a Muslim preacher to visit the predominantly Muslim city, while permission was granted to a Christian preacher.

23. The fact that most of the military leaders came from the region made the perception more painful and the activists more agitative.

24. In his study of the phenomenon, Y.B. Usman associated religious manipulation to religious conflicts. He regarded manipulation as a tool of elite exploitation of the masses. Yusuf Bala Usman, *The Manipulation of Religion in Nigeria: 1977–1987* (Kaduna: Vanguard Publishers, 1987).

25. R. Jeffrey Seul, "Ours is the Way of God," Journal of Peace Research 36 (5) 1999, 562.

26. Norimitsu Onishi, "Rising Muslim Power in Africa Causes Unrest in Nigeria," *The New York Times*, 1 November 2001.

27. The alleged Nigerian al-Qaeda operative is being "arraigned over a five-count charge of receiving money in foreign currencies from Talha and Na'deem (al-Qaeda operatives) of the Tabliqh Headquarters, Lahore, Pakistan, for recruiting and training of terrorists whose main objective was to attack the residences of Americans living in Nigeria." Other charges include sponsoring about twenty mujahedin fighters to "receive training on terrorism from an Algerian terrorist network known as Salafis Group," in Niger Republic. *Vanguard* (Lagos), Friday, 23 February 2007; and *The Guardian* (Lagos), Friday, 23 February 2007.

28. The Pew Global Attitudes Project reporting on "America's Image and US Foreign Policy" found that support for the US-led "war on terror" among Muslims in Nigeria fell from 60 per cent in 2003 to 49 per cent in 2006. 13 June 2006, http://pewglobal. org/reports/display.php?PageID=825. The same report has 89 per cent of Nigerian Christians with a favourable view of the US compared to 32 per cent of Nigerian Muslims.

29. The federal government recently got into a war of words by referring to the Shariah security outfit (*Hisba*) in Kano State as a terrorist gang, seeking to train "jihadists". But a case against the group was dismissed in court for lack of evidence and witnesses. For earlier case see staff writer "'Our Hisba Group is not a terror Gang,' says Kano State Governor, Mallam Ibrahim Shekarau", *The Punch* (Lagos), 18 August 2005. http:// odili.net/news/source/2005/aug/18/461.html (accessed 8/18/2005). Another report stated that the "Federal Government accuses Kano State government of seeking foreign sponsorship to train 'jihadists'", Tume Ahemba "Federal Government accuses Kano State government of seeking foreign sponsorship to train 'jihadists'", http:// naijanet.com/news/source/2006/feb/10/1002.html *Najanet* 10 February 2006.

30. In his autobiography, the powerful Premier of Northern Nigeria, the late Sir Ahmadu Bello, expressed a very sympathetic view of the British and their role in the region that would perhaps surprise most people. See Ahmadu Bello, *My Life* (Cambridge: Cambridge University Press, 1962), Chapter 18.

31. Christopher Clapham, *Africa and the International System: The Politics of State Survival* (Cambridge: Cambridge University Press, 1996), 126–7.
32. Thus even during the height of the Shariah debates, State governors and Emirs were appealing to Western powers to invest in their societies.
33. In fact, compared to the initial vigour and intensity, only Kano of all the twelve Shariah states retains a rhetorical commitment to Shariah. Shariah hardly makes the headlines in public discourse in the other eleven states.
34. Only in Kano and Zamfara states were there sporadic statements on Shariah and even there, the focus was on social development.

CHAPTER 8

1. The identity of several interviewees has been disguised for their own safety.
2. Staff writer, "Somalia, Battle for the Horn of Africa," *Der Spiegel Magazine*, 2 January 2007.
3. The Ogaden war lasting from the summer (it escalated slowly so an exact start date is hard to give) of 1977 to 9 March 1978. The war started when Somalia intervened in support of the Western Somali Liberation Front (WSLF) fight for the control of the Somali populated Ogaden region of Ethiopia.
4. Stig Jarle Hansen "Armageddon East Africa", *Command* (forthcoming).
5. Haggai Erlich, *The Struggle over Eritrea, 1962–1978* (Stanford: Hoover Institution, 1983), 22–3; Bereket H. Selassie, *Conflict and Intervention in the Horn of Africa* (London: Monthly Review Press, 1980), 64.
6. John Young, *Peasant Revolution in Ethiopia, the Tigray People's Liberation Front 1975–1991* (Cambridge: Cambridge University Press, 1997).
7. Stig Jarle Hansen, "Shariah courts holds sway in Mogadishu", *Foreign Report* 10 (2006).
8. Stig Jarle Hansen, "Enemies or allies?" NIBR working paper (forthcoming).
9. Danish Immigration Services, *Human Rights and Security in Central and Southern Somalia*, (København: Danish Immigration Services, 2004).
10. Stig Jarle Hansen, "Somalia provides a test case of counter-terrorist efforts", *Jane's Intelligence Review*, 16, no. 9 (2003).
11. Interview with Ali Mahdi, 2 March 2007.
12. Interview with anonymous court leader, x2, Mogadishu, 22 February 2007; interview with Sheik Ali Dheere on 26 February 2007. The two disagree over the exact date, x2 claims it was on the 19 March.
13. Andre Le Sage, *Stateless Justice in Somalia, Formal and Informal Rule of Law Initiatives* (Geneva: Centre for Human Dialogue, 2005), 42.
14. Yohannes Kassahun, *The Courts: Problems, Prospects and Role in Somalia's Emerging Regions* (Nairobi: European Commission Somalia Unit, 1997), 40.
15. Interview with anonymous x7 Mogadishu, 23 November 2006; interview with Ali Mahdi, Mogadishu, 1 April 2007.
16. The clan in question was the Agonyar, of the Harti, of the Abgal of the Hawiye.
17. In February 1999 several courts managed to appoint a common spokesperson, Sheik Hassan Adde, and deploy around 1,000 militiamen for the negotiations surrounding

the creation of a regional administration. The Ifka Halan court was central in the process. In April 1999, the Joint Islamic Councils (JIC) was formed, consisting of a few courts in Mogadishu only and mainly intended to handle the justice in the Bakara Market. Another attempt to organize the courts; the Shariah Implementation Council (SIC), also known as the Islamic Courts (IC), was created in 2000. However, there was a decline in the number of courts when the transitional government created in Arta in 2000 sought to include them in its governance structures, and the governing council of the courts was disbanded.

18. Interview with anonymous court qadi, 23 February 2007.
19. Staff writer, "Mogadishu Factions Meet to Narrow Gap", *Xinhua*, 25 February 1999, International Crisis Group, "Can the Somali Crisis be Contained?" *Africa Report* 116 (2006), 7–8.
20. Interview with anonymous female activist x 3, Mogadishu, 20 February 2007.
21. The survey only registered firms with over fifteen employees.
22. Interview with former Adane militia (anonymous) x 4, Mogadishu, 23 February 2007.
23. Interview with anonymous x 8, Mogadishu, 23 February 2007.
24. Interview with Hussein Aideed, Nairobi, 23 November 2004.
25. International Crisis Group "Can the Somali Crisis be Contained", *Africa Report*, 116 (2006), 7–8.
26. It can be argued that the *Shebab* failed to maintain discipline during the combat with the Ethiopian and governmental forces in December 2006. The *Shebab* was then largely expanded as unemployed youths were enrolled directly into its units; moreover it faced highly trained and disciplined Ethiopian units with artillery and air support. The comparative advantage of the *Shebab* fighters was quite strong when compared with the warlords' militias in the spring of 2006; during the fighting in December of that year the situation was less clear.
27. International Crisis Group, "Somalia's Islamist", *Africa Report* (2005), 100.
28. Two Oromo fighters: Mashru Hassan Hussein and Abdulla Tani Aden, who were captured by the Somali forces, later gave an interview claiming that they had been trained by a contingent of 270 Oromo fighters. There might have been other contingents. Staff writer, "Somalia: Arrested Foreign Fighters Admit They Helped Islamists", *Shabelle Media Network*, 9 January 2007.
29. At the time three suspected Arab fighters were paraded publicly by Ethiopia; a Somali jihadist video, never endorsed publicly by the courts, showed a small number of seemingly Arab fighters; eyewitnesses in Kismayo claimed to have seen Arab fighters disembark from ships in the harbour.
30. The radical wing of the SCIC created the foundation of the first pure jihadi group in Somalia, the Youth Islamic Movement, based on the old *Shebab* group, which so far has admitted responsibility for suicide attacks and road-side bombs, and posted suicide videos on web sites created by global jihadi organizations.
31. The claim of Sheik Fuad Mohamed Khalif, the head of the courts' educational department, before the fall of Mogadishu, was in many ways the foundation of much of the SCICs propaganda: "I want to warn you against the infidels...the infidels want to occupy our capital... infidels want to humiliate the Muslims... infidels want to remove

the hijab of our women, so you should join the [resistance], join till the last of you die." Mohammed Abdi Farah, "Somalia: Islamists vow to invite foreign Jihadists if the UN lifts the arms embargo", *SMN*, 28 November 2006.

32. Large scale Ethiopian use of artillery and tanks to fight the insurgency, an insurgency notably based in clearly clan defined areas, and more than 400,000 refugees fleeing Mogadishu as a result of this attack might precipitate further radicalization, but this has so far not happened.

CHAPTER 9

1. In the incident commonly referred to as the "Axumite Hijrah", early followers of prophet Muhammed fled from Mecca to Axum and received asylum from the Christian king there in 615, seven years before the establishment of the first *Ummah* in Medina. See Spencer Trimmingham, *Islam in Ethiopia* (London: Frank Cass, 1965), 44ff.

2. Haggai Erlich, *Ethiopia and the Middle East* (Boulder and London: Lynne Rienner Publishers, 1994), 31ff.

3. Hussein Ahmed, "Coexistence and/or Confrontation? Towards a Reappraisal of Christian-Muslim Encounter in Contemporary Ethiopia", *Journal of Religion in Africa*, 36, no. 1 (2006), 4.

4. John Markakis, *Ethiopia: Anatomy of a Traditional Polity* (Oxford: Clarendon Press, 1974), 251, 255.

5. For more details, see Hussein Ahmed, "Islam and Islamic Discourse in Ethiopia (1973–1993)", *Proceedings of the 12ᵗʰ International Conference of Ethiopian Studies* (Lawrenceville, NJ: Red Sea Press, 1994), 791; "Islamic Literature and Religious Revival in Ethiopia (1991–1994)", *Islam et sociétés au sud du Sahara*, 12 (1998), 97f.

6. For more details, see Tim Carmichael, "Contemporary Ethiopian Discourse on Islamic History: The Politics of Historical Representation", *Islam et sociétés au sud du Sahara* 10 (1996) and Terje Østebø, "Creating a new Identity: Ethiopian Muslims in a Contemporary Perspective", *Swedish Missiological Themes* 86, no. 3 (1998).

7. Hussein 1994, 794.

8. I am here applying the perspective of Stuart Hall seeing identification as a process of construction; as a process of "becoming". Stuart Hall, "Introduction: Who Needs Identity", in Stuart Hall (ed.), *Questions of Cultural Identity* (London: Sage Publications, 1996), 1–17.

9. The term commonly used in Ethiopia is *Wahhabi* Islam. Because its followers prefer to be called *Salafis*, I have chosen this term. Other terms used are *ahl al-Sunna* or *tawhid-*followers. *Tawhid* refers to the absolute oneness and singularity of Allah, something strongly emphasised in *Salafi* Islam.

10. Few studies have been made of the *Salafi* movement in Ethiopia. For some details on its developments in Harar, Arsi, Addis Ababa, Wollo and Bale see respectively; Patrick Desplat, "The Articulation of Religious Identities and their Boundaries in Ethiopia: Labelling Differences and Processes of Contextualization in Islam", *Journal of Religion in Africa*, 35, no. 4 (2005); Temam Haji-Adem, "Islam in Arsi, Southeast Ethiopia (c. 1840–1974)", (unpubl. MA thesis, Addis Ababa University, 2002); Bauer Oumer,

"The Development of Islamic Propagation (Da'wa) in Addis Ababa and its Surroundings (1936–2003)", (unpubl. MA thesis, Addis Ababa University, 2006); Jon Abbink, "Transformations of Islam and Communal Relations in Wallo, Ethiopia", forthcoming in Benjamin F. Soares and René Otayek (eds), *Islam and Muslim Politics in Africa* (Palgrave-Macmillan: New York, 2007); Terje Østebø, "The Power of Muslim Institutions in Consolidating Democracy: A Perspective from Bale", forthcoming in Kjetil Tronvoll (ed.), *Contested Power: Traditional Authorities and Elections in Ethiopia* (Oxford: James Currey, 2007).

11. *Jama'at al-Tabligh* is the world's largest Islamic missionary movement established by Sheikh Muhammed Iliyas in India in 1929.
12. Bauer 2006, 70f.
13. Bauer 2006, 79. See also Nega Aba Jebal, "The History of the Awaliyya School 1961–1986" (unpubl. BA-thesis Addis Ababa University, 1986).
14. See also Hussein 1998, 98f.
15. *Takfir wal Hijrah* emerged in Egypt in 1977, where its leader, Shukri Mustafa, advocated a rather radical interpretation of Islam, defying any Muslim except his own followers as *kafirs*. The movement has in Ethiopia held similar views. Shukri was later tried and executed by Egyptian authorities.
16. For more details, see David Commins, *The Wahhabi Mission and Saudi Arabia* (London: I.B. Tauris, 2006), 130f.
17. Ethiopia is today divided into nine regional states where its geographical boundaries are drawn according to ethnic boundaries.
18. For a survey of such incidents, see Hussein 2006.
19. Lit. "those who go out" or "outlaws". The *Kharijites* were originally a group supporting Ali in his struggle for the Caliphate. The group has been characterized as extremist, rejecting any form of authority. For more details, see *Encyclopedia of Islam (CD-rom edition)*, vol. IV (Leiden: Brill, 2003), 1074.
20. In both Arsi and Bale conflicts labelled as Christian-Muslim conflicts have occurred, yet closer investigations have shown that they in fact have been of an ethnic character, i.e. Oromo vs. Amhara.
21. Alem Zele-Alem, "Saudi Arabia's Wahhabism and the threat to Ethiopia's national security", www.dekialula.com, (accessed 15 February 2005). See also Hibret Selamu, "Proof of Wahhabi activities in Ethiopia," www.ethiomedia.com/newspress/proof_of_wahhabism_in_ethiopia, (accessed April 10, 2005); Johannes Sebahtu, "The emergence of radical Islam in Ethiopia," www.ethiomedia.com/commentary/radical_islam_in_ethiopia, (accessed December 15, 2004).
22. Gilles Kepel, *Jihad: The Trail of Political Islam* (London: I. B. Tauris, 2002), 45.
23. See David Westerlund, "Reaction and Action: Accounting for the Rise of Islamism," David Westerlund and Eva Evers Rosander (eds), *African Islam and Islam in Africa: Encounters between Sufis and Islamists* (London: Hurst, 1997), 313f.
24. In the aftermath of the national election in 2005, several representatives of civil society (NGOs and the media) were arrested.
25. EIASC was reorganised in 1995, where the election to the new council was closely monitored by the regime. Nowadays there is a criterion that the council's leadership has to be a member of the ruling party. For more details, see Jon Abbink, "An Histor-

ical-Anthropological Approach to Islam in Ethiopia: Issues of Identity and Politics",
Journal of African Cultural Studies 11, no. 2 (1998), 111; Østebø 2007.

CHAPTER 10

1. The expression "Sudan's multiple marginality" was first coined by Ali Mazrui.
2. The cultural landscape of Arab geographers saw Africa as divided into strips from north to south. First came "*an-Misr*" (Egypt) with "*al-Maghrib*" further on (the west, from Libya to Morocco) among civilized lands. South of those was "*as-Sahara*", the desert, followed southwards by "*as-Sahil*" (the shore) i.e. if the desert was seen as a metaphorical sea (of sand), then the strip where life reappeared was *as-Sahil*, the shore. Then south of that "*Sahil*" was "*al-beled as-Sudani*".
3. This made him of course a perfect "Ottoman". Under Muhammad Ali's rule the Sudan was to become a distant borderland of the Ottoman Empire.
4. In Sudanese Arabic tradition *al-Turkiyya*, "the time of the Turks", lasted from 1821 to 1885. Its connotation in Sudanese historiography is very negative.
5. The territory controlled by the "Turks" was at first much smaller than today's Sudan. Before Cairo's conquest there had been two states occupying a good chunk of today's Northern Sudan even if this occupation did not coincide with "Northern Sudan" as such.⁵ To the west was the Kayra Sultanate of Darfur which covered almost all of today's Darfur⁵ and by the late eighteenth century Kordofan as well⁵. And to the east was the Funj Sultanate of Sennar which extended from the Abyssinian plateau nearly to the Nile. By 1821 the two kingdoms were on the verge of touching since Sennar's westward expansion and Darfur's eastward one were both about to reach the NileValley.
6. This Quranic principle was not always adhered to, particularly when good-looking females were concerned.
7. In the moral geography of Islam the world is divided into *Dar al-Islam* (the world populated by those who are submitted [to God's Will]) and *Dar al-Kufr* (the world of unbelief) which is also seen as *Dar al-Harb* (the world of [legitimate] war).
8. The analogy could be extended to the so-called Congo Free State, to Eastern/Southern Angola and to Western Mozambique during the mid-to-late nineteenth century. The common "model" of all these territories was the primacy of commodity extraction, semi-private, semi-state military violence, an utter disregard for native ecology and human life and a marginal administrative relationship to the national centre of power. The American Far West was unique among these territories in that it included in its pattern population colonization and the genocide of the natives.
9. In popular Islamic eschatology the *Mahdi* is God's envoy at the end of times. He is supported by *Nabi Issa* (the Prophet Jesus) and fights *al-Dajjal* (the Antichrist). The *Mahdi* triumphs, there is a thousand years of peace and then the Last Judgment comes.
10. This intervention resulted in the defeat of a British expeditionary force in the Sudan and later in the siege of Khartoum and the death of the famous Victorian adventurer Charles Gordon.
11. On this see Giovanni Vantini, *Christianity in the Sudan* (Bologna: Editrice Missionaria Italiana, 1981).

12. On this see J. Spencer Trimingham: *Islam in the Sudan* (London: Frank Cass, 1949) and Ali S. Karrar, *The Sufi Brotherhoods in the Sudan* (London: Hurst, 1992).

13. There are of course exceptions to this rule. But they are rare and they often concern very special cases like the culturally mixed Fertit of Bahr-el-Ghazal, or isolated individuals who, for reasons of social marginality, have adhered to the Muslim Brotherhood.

14. The only "true" biological Arabs in the Sudan are the members of the Rashaida tribe, which migrated to the Sudan in the early nineteenth century to escape the turmoil of the Wahhabi wars in the Hijjaz. Paradoxically their "true Arab" biological status gives them no special place in the Sudanese social pecking order.

15. This is written in May 2007.

16. An amusing folk comment on this is the northern Sudanese saying "*kull al-habuba khadamat*" ("all the grandmothers were servants" i.e. black slaves). This is said in intimate circumstances to bring back to his senses somebody who tries to picture himself as better than others. The use of this saying by a foreigner is usually not appreciated.

17. Abd-el-Wahhab al-Effendi, *Turabi's Revolution* (London: Grey Seal Books, 1991).

18. Hence the term *Awlad al-Beled* (lit. "sons of the land") used by the Nile Valley Arabs to speak of themselves. The fact that this implicitly makes everybody else a kind of "non-native" is blandly denied.

19. In many ways this "Africanism" is just as fantasmatic as the "Arabism" of the *awlad al-Gharb*. Darfur is culturally mixed, its Arabs are not "real" Arabs and its "Africans" have been extensively arabized. But in a situation of economic and political competition for extremely scarce resources, everybody is falling back on fantasized "primeval identities" in order to legitimate political and military alliances.

20. The Arabic dialect used in the south (often called "Juba Arabic") is a Creole version of Arabic that nobody speaks as a first language except some very marginal groups of the Fertit.

21. The Anglo-Egyptian Condominium (1898–1956) was special only in that the overwhelming military force differential it had in relationship to its subjects allowed it to use that force sparingly and in that its commodity extraction policy was much more sophisticated than those of the regimes the Sudan was ruled by, either before or since. These two traits made the manifestations of its power milder, even if its principles of government were not basically different from its predecessors or successors.

22. This word, which simply means "the government", "the state", is loaded in the Sudan with massive extra-legal and extra-political connotations. *Hokum* brings to mind images of arbitrary force and violence rather than notions of administration and justice.

23. This was more true of the irregular Baggara militias know as *Murahleen*, who could freely pillage and traffic in slaves, than of the soldiers drafted in the regular army.

24. The reader might find the word "sold" a bit exaggerated and consider it polemical. It is not. Sadiq al-Mahdi, who was short of cash and wanted to win the elections after the overthrow of Nimeiry's dictatorship, literally sold the province for an amount of between $18 and $35 millions to Colonel Gaddafi. But then once the deal was done and Gaddafi started claiming his pound of flesh in the shape of military bases against Chad, Sadiq al-Mahdi desperately tried to wiggle out of it, indirectly unleashing a wave of extreme civil violence in Darfur.

25. This period (1986 to 2003) which is key to understanding the origins of the present conflict, has never been documented in depth. For further information see Gerard Prunier, *Darfur: The Ambiguous Genocide* (London: Hurst, 2005).
26. This does not deter ideologically-motivated superficial observers such as the French "philosopher" Bernard-Henry Lévy from writing that Islam is at the root of the conflict, which he reinterprets as an example of the struggle between "moderate Islam" (the SLM rebels) and "radical Islam" (the Khartoum government) [see Bernard-Henry Lévy: "Dangerous Thinking", *The Financial Times Week-End Supplement* 4 May 2007].
27. It is one of the most entrenched myths about the conflict that in Darfur "*the Arab tribes are killing the Africans*". This is not so. The *Janjaweed* irregulars are recruited among the minority Arab tribes of North Darfur (*abbala*) and among social misfits. The main Arab tribes such as the various Baggara groups from South Darfur have declined to transfer their earlier membership in the *Murahleen* into joining the *Janjaweed*.
28. Signed in January 2005, it is usually called "the Comprehensive Peace Agreement" or CPA, a misnomer if ever there was one.

REGION III

1. I would like to thank Åse Grødeland for the comments to this intro.
2. Conservative estimates suggest that some 13 million Muslims live within the borders of the EU. EUMC, *Muslims in the European Union, Discrimination and Islamophobia* (Brussels: EUMC, 2006), 8.
3. Moshe Gammer, *The Lone Wolf and the Bear. Three Centuries of Chechen Defiance of Russian Rule* (London, Hurst, 2006), 9.
4. Tim Judah, *The Serbs* (London, Yale University Press, 1997), 44.
5. The writings of Miroslav Hroch, Anthony Smith and John Hutchinson suggest that religion had a decisive role in the formation of modern nations. Miroslav Hroch acknowledged the need for linguistic or religious ties enabling a higher degree of social communication within the group than beyond it, in the formation of modern nations; Miroslav Hroch, "The Nature of the Nation", in John A. Hall (ed.), *The State of the Nation (Ernest Gellner and the Theory of Nationalism)* (Cambridge: Cambridge University Press. 1988), 93; Anthony Smith, *Theories of Nationalism*, (London: Duckworth, 1971), 245; John Hutchinson, *The Dynamics of Cultural Nationalism: The Gaelic Revival and the Creation of the Irish Nation State* (London, Allen and Unwin, 1987), 37.
6. See the chapter by Hughes in this book.

CHAPTER 11

1. This argument is developed further in the author's book-length study of the conflict. See James Hughes, *Chechnya: From Nationalism to Jihad* (Philadelphia: University of Pennsylvania Press, 2007).

2. For academic accounts see Valery Tishkov, *Ethnicity, Nationalism and Conflict in and After the Soviet Union: The Mind Aflame* (London: Sage, 1997); and John B. Dunlop, *Russia Confronts Chechnya: Roots of a Separatist Conflict* (Cambridge: Cambridge University Press, 1998). For journalistic accounts see Carlotta Gall and Thomas de Waal, *Chechnya: A Small Victorious War* (New York: New York University Press, 1998); and Anatol Lieven, *Chechnya: Tombstone of Russian Power*, (New Haven, Connecticut: Yale University Press, 1998.)

3. For Shamil's role as a leader of jihād see Anna Zelkina, "Jihād in the Name of God: Shaykh Shamil as the Religious Leader of the Caucasus", *Central Asian Survey* 21, no. 3 (2002). 249–64.

4. For the demonstration and spill over effects of anti-Soviet nationalist movements in this period see Mark Beissinger, *Nationalist Mobilization and the Collapse of the Soviet State* (Cambridge: Cambridge University Press, 2002).

5. See Zelimkhan Yandarbiev, *V preddverii nezavisimosti* (Grozny: Groznenskii rabochii, 1994), and Zelimkhan Yandarbiev, *Checheniia—bitva za sovobodu* (Lviv: Svoboda Narodiv, 1996). Yandarbiev was assassinated by Russian foreign intelligence service agents in Qatar in February 2004.

6. Yandarbiev (1994), 9, 5, 73–91, 113–22.

7. For the Islamist references see Yandarbiev (1996), 79, 145–6, 281–2, 435–6. The secular basis of Yandarbiev's thinking on national identity in the early 1990s is reflected in his articles "Kavkazskost'" (Caucasianness) (1990), and "Suti i aspekty natsional'nogo edinstva" (The essence and perspective of national unity) (June 1991) in Yandarbiev (1996), 387–418.

8. See Hughes 2007, 40–42.

9. Yandarbiev 1994, 27–30.

10. At the time no one analysed the declaration of sovereignty as being anything other than a secular nationalist document. See Timur Muzaev, *Chechenskii Respublika: Organy Vlasti i Politicheskie Sily* (Moscow: Panorama, 1995), 159–60; Tishkov 1997, 199–200.

11. The indigenous nationalist elites in the Baltic States generally framed, and continue to frame, their legal claim to independence partly on the basis of their "illegal" annexation by the USSR under the Molotov-Ribbentrop Pact. Thus, they were engaged in a "restoration" of sovereignty rather than a new assertion of it against the USSR. However, their moral claim for sovereignty is often grounded in the charge that the USSR perpetrated genocidal deportations against the Baltic peoples in the late 1940s and 1950s.

12. See Muzaev 1995, 68. For Dudayev's career see Dunlop 1998, 97–8, and Gall and de Waal 1998, 86–8.

13. See Alla Dudayeva, *Million pervyi* (Baku: Zeinalov and Synov'ia, 2002), 63–4.

14. Yandarbiev, 1994, 30–1; Gall and de Waal 1998, 88–9.

15. Tracey C. German, *Russia's Chechen War* (London: Routledge, 2003), 31.

16. According to Anatol Lieven, when he interviewed Gantemirov the latter exhibited an embarrassing lack of knowledge of what Islamism meant. See Lieven 1998, 364.

17. Muzaev 1995, 95–6, 130–1.

18. Chechen Electoral Commission data are reported in Dunlop 1998, 114.

19. Vice-President Aleksander Rutskoi, Yeltsin's main emissary to Dudayev, played a pivotal role in shaping the idiom on the Russian side.
20. Yandarbiev famously articulated his anathema toward the Russians in verse. For example, his poems included lines such as "unwashed you were, and unwashed you remain", and reference to Russia as a "Bitch". See Yandarbiev 1996, 443, 486.
21. For the decrees see *Izvestiia*, 5 November 1991, 2. For Dudayev's views on independence see Irina Dement'eva, "Odinokii volk pod lunoi", *Izvestiia*, 1 November 1991, 8.
22. Iury Bespalov, "Oruzhie sdali po prikazu moskvy", *Izvestiia*, 14 January 1995; Valery Yakov, "Svidetelia luchshe ubrat'", *Izvestiia*, 14 January 1995; Muzaev 1995, 28–9.
23. Muzaev 1995, 165–6.
24. Svante Cornell, *Small Nations and Great Powers: A Study of Ethnopolitical Conflict in the Caucasus* (London: Curzon, 2001), 215.
25. International Alert, *Chechnia: Report of an International Alert fact-finding mission, September 24th-October 3rd 1992*, (London: International Alert, 1992).
26. See Dzhokhar Dudaev, cited in German 2003, 59.
27. Interview with Dzhokhar Dudaev, Official Kremlin International News Broadcast, 12 August 1992.
28. Ekaterina Sorianskaya, "Families and Clans in Ingushetia and Chechnya: A Fieldwork Report", *Central Asian Survey* 24, no. 4 (2005): 453–67.
29. See Dzhokhar Dudaev, *K voprosu o gosudarstvenno-politicheskom ustroistve v chechenskoi respubliki* (Grozny: Groznenskii rabochii, 1993), 3–16.
    Chechnya had some major economic assets that offered potential for strong state development. The Baku-Novorossiisk pipeline, a major part of the Russian state pipeline network that carried significant volumes of oil from the Caspian, traversed Chechnya. Grozny was the site of Russia's largest oil refinery, and a major petrochemicals industry. There were numerous oil fields scattered across Chechnya, though they were relatively small by Russian standards. The main railway line linking Russia to Daghestan and Azerbaijan also passed through Chechnya. Consequently, an independent Chechnya was economically viable.
30. Tishkov 1999, 585–6.
31. Boris Yeltsin, *Midnight Diaries* (London: Weidenfeld and Nicolson, 2000), 54.
32. Aleksei Malashenko and Dmitrii Trenin, *Vremia Iuga: Rossiia v Chechne, Chechne v Rossii* (Moscow: Gendal'f, Carnegie Center Moscow, 2002), 73.
33. See Hughes 2007, 97–107.
34. See Yandarbiev 1996, 281.
35. See Hughes 2007, 13; Andrei Babitski, *Un Témoin Indésirable* (Paris: Robert Laffont, 2002), 42.
36. See his message c. 1995 to "Honorable Scholars of the Arabian Peninsula and Saudi Arabia in particular" in Bruce Lawrence (ed.) *Messages to the World. The Statements of Osama Bin Laden* (London: Verso, 2005), 17.
37. Khattab had earlier fought with Islamists during the civil war in Tajikstan. The biography of Khattab is much disputed. An "official" biography is provided by one of the main websites for the Islamists of the Chechen resistance: see http://www.kavkaz-center.com/eng/photo/amir_khattab/page1.shtml.
38. The most famous was the video of an attack against a Russian armoured column at Shatoi in April 1996.

CHAPTER 12

1. Berna Turam, "A bargain between the secular state and Turkish Islam: politics of ethnicity in Central Asia" *Nations and Nationalism* 10, no. 3, (2004), 358.

2. Nilufer Gole, "Authoritarian Secularism and Islamist Politics: The Case of Turkey", in Agustus Richard Norton (ed.) *Civil Society in the Middle East* (Leiden: E.J. Brill, 1996); Cengiz Candar, "Some Turkish Perspectives on the United States and American Policy Toward Turkey", 117–52 in Martin Abromowitz (ed.), *Turkey's Transformation and American Policy* (New York: The Century Foundation Press, 2000), Ahmet T. Kuru, "Passive and Assertive Secularism", *World Politics* 59, no. 4 (2007)

3. John H. Garvey, "Fundamentalism and American Law", in Martin Marty and Scott Appleby (eds), *Fundamentalism Project: Vol. 2, Fundamentalisms and society: reclaiming the sciences, the family, and education* (Chicago: University of Chicago Press, 1993), 38.

4. Gole 1996; John Keane, "Secularism?" *The Political Quarterly* 71, no. 1 (2000), 5–6.

5. Tanel Demirel, "The Turkish Military's Decision to Intervene: 12 September 1980", *Armed Forces and Societies* 29, no. 2 (2003), 243.

6. Ayse Kadioglu, *Cumhuriyet Iradesi Demokrasi Muhakemesi* (Istanbul: Metis, 1998).

7. Binnaz Toprak, "The Religious Right", in Albert Hourani, Philip S. Khoury and Mary C. Wilson (eds), *The Modern Middle East* (London: I.B. Tauris, 1993), 630–1.

8. Mesut Yegen, "The Turkish State Discourse and the Exclusion of Kurdish Identity", *Middle Eastern Studies* 32, no. 2 (1996).

9. Bernard Lewis, *The Emergence of Modern Turkey* (Oxford: Oxford University Press, 1968), 416; Hakan Yavuz, "Political Islam and the Welfare (Refah) Party in Turkey", *Comprative Politics* 30, no. 1 (1997), 63–4.

10. Haldun Gülalp "Modernization Policies and Islamist Politics in Turkey", in Sibel Bozdogan and Resat Kasaba (eds) *Rethinking Modernity and National Identity in Turkey* (Seattle and London: University of Washington Press, 1997), 52; Deniz Kandiyoti, "Gendering the Modern: On Missing Dimensions in the Study of Turkish Modernization", in Sibel Bozdogan and Resat Kasaba (eds), *Rethinking Modernity and National Identity in Turkey* (Seattle and London: University of Washington Press, 1997), 129.

11. Sami Zubaida, "Turkish Islam and National Identity", *Middle East Report* 26, no. 2 (1996), 71.

12. Serif Mardin, "Turkish Islamic Exceptionalism Yesterday and Today: Continuity, Rupture and Reconstruction in Operational Codes", *Turkish Studies* 6, no. 2 (2005); Howe 2000, 2; Omer Laciner, "JDP: 'Orta sinif'in sahneye cikisi", *Birikim* 149 (2001).

13. Levent Koker, *Modernlesme, Demokrasi ve Kemalizm* (Istanbul: Iletisim, 1990).

14. Koker 1990; Mahmood Monshipouri, *Democratization, Liberalization and Human Rights in the Third World* (London: Lynne Rienner, 1995), 20.

15. Gülalp 1997.

16. Toprak 1993, 628.

17. Hakan Yavuz, "Political Islam and the Welfare Refah Party in Turkey", *Comparative Politics* 30, no. 1 (1997), 66–7.

18. Nilufer Gole, "Secularism and Islamism in Turkey: The Making of Elites and Counter-Elites", *Middle East Journal*, 51, no. 1 (1997) 53–7; Menderes Cinar and Aysegul Kadioglu, "An Islamic Critique of Modernity in Turkey: Politics of difference backwards", *Orient* 40, no. 1 (1999), 61–9.

19. Anat Lapidot, "Islamic Activism in Turkey since the 1980 Military Takeover", 62–74, in Bruce Maddy-Weitzman and Efraim Inbar (eds), *Religious Radicalism in the Greater Middle East* (London: Frank Cass, 1996), 67–70.

20. Yavuz 1997, 73, italics added.

21. Metin Karabasoglu, "Projenin iflasi", *Birikim* 131, (2000), 45–7.

22. See Andrew Purvis, "Turkey's Great Divide", *Time* 170, no. 3 (23 July 2007), 22–6.

23. Göle 1997.

24. Hakan M. Yavuz, "Turkey's Fault Lines and the Crisis of Kemalism", *Current History* 99, no. 633 (2000a); Hakan M. Yavuz, "Cleansing Islam from the Public Sphere and the February 28 Process", *Journal of International Affairs* 54, no. 1 (2000b).

25. Nilufer Gole, "Islam in Public: New Visibilities and New Imagineries", *Public Culture* 14, no. 1 (2002), 182.

26. Candar 2000.

27. Dietrich Jung and Wolfango Piccoli, "The Turkish-Israeli Alignment: Paranoia or Pragmatism?" *Security Dialogue* 31, no. 1 (2000), 93.

28. John Gorvett, "What Happens Next?" *The Middle East* (May 2004), 16–17; Staff writer, *Newsweek*, 11 October 2004, 38–42; R. Quinn Mecham, "From the ashes of virtue a promise of light: the transformation of political Islam in Turkey", *Third World Quarterly* 25, no. 2 (2004), 339–45; Erhan Dogan, "The Historical and Discursive Roots of the Justice and Development Party's EU Stance", *Turkish Studies* 6, no. 3 (2005), 421–37.

29. Rusen Cakir, *Ayet ve Slogan: Turkiye'de Islami Olusumlar* (Metis: Istanbul, 1990); Rusen Cakir, *Ne Seriat Ne Demokrasi* (Istanbul: Metis, 1994); Omer Laciner, "DP, ANAP ve Sonunda JDP", *Birikim* (2002), 163–4; Yavuz 1997; Heper 1997; Metin Heper and Sule Toktas, "Islam, Modernity and Democracy in Contemporary Turkey: The Case of Recep Tayyip Erdogan", *The Muslim World* 93, no. 2 (2003); Yildiz 2003; Soli Ozel, "After the Tsunami", *Journal of Democracy* 14, no. 2 (2003); Ziya Onis and E. Fuat Keyman, "A New Path Emerges: Turkey at the Polls", *Journal of Democracy* 14, no. 2 (2003); Mecham 2004; Dogan 2005.

30. Ozel 2003, 83–5; Onis and Keyman 2003, 97.

31. Suleyman Sozen and Ian Shaw, "Turkey and the European Union: Modernizing a Traditional State", *Social policy and Administration* 37, no. 2 (2003), 61; Ozel 2003, 86; Onis and Keyman 2003.

32. Gulalp 1997; Caglar Keyder, "Whither the Project of Modernity? Turkey in the 1990s", pp. 37–51, in Sibel Bozdogan and Resat Kasaba (eds) *Rethinking Modernity and National Identity in Turkey* (Seattle and London: University of Washington Press, 1997), 46–8; Onis 1997; Dietrich Jung and Wolfango Piccoli, *Turkey at the Crossroads: Ottoman Legacies and a Greater Middle East* (London: Zed Books, 2001), 119; Hakan Yavuz, *Islamic Political Identity in Turkey* (Oxford: Oxford University Press, 2003), 15.

33. Ozel 2003, 84–6.

34. Ahmet Insel, "Olaganlasan demokrasi ve modern muhafazakarlik", *Birikim* 163/4 (2002); Menderes Cinar, "Secimlerin ardindan: Siyaset Yeniden", *Birikim* 163/4 (2002); Tanil Bora, "2002 Secimleri ve Siyasi Guzergah Problemleri", *Birikim* 163/4 (2002); Volkan Yarasir and Tarik Akgun, *Tanri, devlet ve medeniyet: Siyasal Islam ve JDP* (Istanbul: Akyuz, 2002); Ozel 2003; Yavuz 2003;

35. Onis and Keyman 2003.

36. Laciner 2002, 13.

37. Alfred Stepan and Graeme B. Robertson, "Arab, Not Muslim, Exceptionalism", *Journal of Democracy* 15, no. 4 (2004), 143.

38. Fatih Altayli, "Vicik vicik olmak istiyoruz", *Hurriyet*, 28 December 2004. Retrieved (31 January 2005) from http://www.hurriyetim.com.tr/archive_articledisplay/0,, authorid~9@sid~9@nvid~516210,00.asp.

39. Vural Savas, *Irtica ve Boluculuge Karsi Militan Demokrasi* (Ankara: Bilgi, 2001), 263–74.

40. Savas 2001, 443.

41. Dogan 2005.

42. Mecham 2004, 340.

43. Laciner 2001, 4–5.

44. Onis and Keyman 2003.

45. Graham E Fuller, *The Future of Political Islam* (New York: Palgrave Macmillan, 2003), 2.

46. Fuller 2003, 2.

47. Staff writer, *Radikal*, 11 January 2004.

48. Yalcin Akdogan, *Muhafazkar Demokrasi* (Ankara: AK Parti Yayinlari, 2003); Nuray Mert, "Muhafazakarlik, fundamentalizm degildir", *Karizma* 5, no. 17 (2004); Ahmet Turan Alkan, "Turkiye'nin Muhafazakarlari Liberaldir" *Karizma* 5, no. 17 (2004), 50–2.

49. Andrew Mango, "A Move to the South Atlantic?" *Middle Eastern Studies* 1, no. 2 (2002); Jenkins 2003.

50. Stephen Kinzer, "The Quite Revolution", *Insight Turkey* 6, no. 1 (2004), 15.

51. *The AK Party Program* (Istanbul, 2005).

52. Interviews with the party officials in Istanbul and Kayseri April, August 2004.

53. *The AK Party Program* (2005); Dogan 2005, 421–37.

54. Sandra Lavanex and Emek M. Ucarer, "The External Dimension of Europeanization: The Case of Immigration Policies", *Cooperation and Conflict* 39, no. 4 (2004), 421.

55. Menderes Cinar, "Secimler vasitasiyla AKP uzerine", *Birikim* 180 (2004), 31–2.

56. Barry Buzan and Thomas Diez, "The European Union and Turkey", *Survival* 41, no. 1 (1999); Ziya Onis, "Domestic Politics, International Norms and Challenges to the State: Turkey-EU Relations in the Post-Helsinki Era", *Turkish Studies* 4, no. 1 (2003).

57. See the speech by PM Erdogan, *Hurriyet*, 3 September 2005.

58. Omer Laciner, "Turks Militarizmi I-II", in Ahmet Insel and Ali Bayramoglu (eds), *Bir Zumre Bir Parti Turkiye'de Ordu* (Istanbul: Birikim, 2004), 20–2; staff writer, *Hurriyet*, 3 September 2005.

59. Kinzer 2004, 11.

60. Helena Smith, "Turkey rebuffs French demands ahead of EU talks", *The Guardian*, 5 August 2005, 17.

61. Umit Cizre, "Introduction", in Umit Cizre (ed.) *Secular and Islamic Politics in Turkey: The making of the Justice and Development Party* (London: Routledge, 2007), 2.

62. Hakan Yavuz (ed.), *The Emergence of a New Turkey* (Utah: The University of Utah Press, 2006).

63. Henry J. Barkey and Yasemin Congar, "Deciphering Turkey's Election: The Making of a Revolution", *World Policy Journal* 24, no. 3 (2007), 64.

64. Umit Cizre, "Demythologyzing The National Security Concept: The Case of Turkey", *Middle East Journal* (2003); for the details of a recent military intervention into domestic politics in the name of secularism see, *Hurriyet*, 28 April 2007.

65. Tanil Bora, *Turk Saginin Uc Hali* (Istanbul: Birikim, 1998), 82.

66. Feroz Ahmad, *The Making of Modern Turkey* (London: Routledge, 1993), 213.

67. Tuncay Kardas, "Security Governmentality in Turkey", unpublished PhD thesis, University of Wales, Aberystwyth 2006, 101–137; Sencer Ayata, "Changes in Domestic Politics and the Foreign Policy Orientaions of the AK Party", in Lnore G. Martin and Dimitris Keridis (eds), *The Future of Turkish Foreign Policy* (Cambridge: The MIT Press, 2004), 244–8.

68. Ben Lombardi, "Turkey-The Return of the Reluctant Generals?" *Political Science Quarterly* 112, no. 2, 213.

69. *TRT-INT News*, 5 November 2002.

70. Interview with Prof. Metin Heper, *Zaman*, 12 August 2004, 3.

71. Cizre 2003, 226; Cizre 2007, 145–54; Jenkins 2003, 66.

72. Tanel Demirel, "Soldiers and Civilians: The Dilemma of Turkish Democracy", *Middle Eastern Studies* 40, no. 1 (2004); Jenkins 2001; Yavuz 2000a, 36.

73. Jenkins 2001, 33–5.

74. Cizre 2003, 216.

75. Gurgen *Radikal*, 09 January 2003.

76. Mustafa Balbay, *Cumhuriyet*, 13 January 2003; Cumhuriyet is the representative of the state secularism in the media. Its political power and influence spring from its ideological linkage not its level of circulation.

77. Abbas Guclu, "Nasil Bir YOK Yasasi", *Milliyet*, 15 September 2003, 10.

78. Staff writer, *Cumhuriyet*, 15 September 2003, 3.

79. Umit Cizre-Sakallioglu, "The Anatomy of Turkish Military Autonomy", *Comparative Politics*, 29, no. 4 (1997), 155–65.

80. Staff writer, *Radikal*, 15 September 2003, 7.

81. Barkey and Congar 2007, 64.

82. *Ibid.*

83. *Ibid.*

84. Mortan Abramowitz and Henry J. Barkey, "Turkey's Judicial Coup D'etat", *Newsweek*, 14 April 2008.

85. Saban Kardas, "The Turkish Constitutional Court and Civil Liberties: Question of Ideology and Accountability", *SETA Policy Brief*, no. 16 (June 2008), 1.

86. Staff writer, *Taraf*, 7 June 2008, 1.

87. Cizre 2007, 141–2.

88. Kardas 2006.

89. Fatih Altayli, "Askerden geceyarisi alosuna: Sizinleyiz", *Hurriyet*, 21 December 2004. Retrieved (31 January 2005) from http://www.hurriyetim.com.tr/archive_articledisplay/ 0,,authorid~9@sid~9@nvid~513136,00.asp.

90. Ian Manners, "Normative Power Europe: A Contradiction in Terms?" *Journal of Common Market Studies* 40, no. 2 (2002).

91. Frank Schimmelfennig, Stefan Engert and Heiko Knobel, "Cost, Commitment and Compliance: The Impact of EU Democratic Conditionality on Latvia, Slovakia and Turkey", *Journal of Common Market Studies* 41, no. 3 (2003).

92. Sevgi Drorian, "Turkey: State, Society and Security in Troubled Times", paper presented at the 29th BISA Annual Conference, University of Warwick (22 December 2004); Pinar Bilgin, "Turkey's changing security discourses: The challenge of globalisation", *European Journal of Political Research* 44, no. 1 (2005).

93. Jenkins 2003.

94. Ergun Ozbudun, *Contemporary Turkish Politics: Challenges to Democratic Consolidation* (Boulder, Colorado: Lynne Reinner, 2000), 2.

95. Cizre 2003, 225; Umit Cizre, "Problem of democratic governance of civil-military relations in Turkey and the European Union enlargement zone", *European Journal of Political Research* 43 (2004), 108.

96. Menderes Cinar, "The Justice and Development Party and the Kemalist establishment", in Umit Cizre (ed.), *Secular and Islamic Politics in Turkey: The making of the Justice and Development Party* (London: Routledge, 2007), 122.

97. Saban Kardas, "Turkey under the JDP: Between Transformation of 'Islamism' and Democratic Consolidation", *Critique: Critical Middle Eastern Studies* 17, no. 2, 175–87.

98. Rusen Cakir and Fehmi Calmuk, *Recep Tayyip Erdogan: Bir Donusum Oykusu* (Istanbul: Siyahbeyaz, 2001), 101.

99. Staff writer, *The Middle East*, May 2004, 17.

100. Umit Cizre, "The Justice and Development Party and the military", in Umit Cizre (ed.) *Secular and Islamic Politics in Turkey: The making of the Justice and Development Party* (London: Routledge, 2007), 134.

101. See the cover story of *Time* magazine, "Turkey's Dilemma", 23 July 2007; Kalypso Nicolaidis, "Turkey is European...For Europe's Sake", pp. 1–9 in in Ioannis N. Grigoriadis (ed.), *Turkey and the European Union: From Association to Accession?* (Ministry of Foreign Affairs, the Netherlands, January 2004). Retrieved (26 August 2005) from http://users.ox.ac.uk/~ssfc0041/turkey_european.pdf.

102. Onis and Keyman 2003, 125–46; Burhanettin Duran, "Islamist Redefinition(s) of European and Islamic Identities in Turkey", 125–46, in Mehmet Ugur and Nergis Canefe (eds), *Turkey and European Integration: Accession Prospects and Issues* (London: Routledge, 2004).

103. Interviews with party officials, August 2004, Istanbul.

104. Dogan 2005, 421–37; Burhanettin Duran, "JDP and Foreign Policy as an Agent of Transformation", in Hakan Yavuz (ed.), *The Emergence of a New Turkey* (Utah: The University of Utah Press, 2006), 281–305.

105. *The AK Party Program*, 2005; Duran, 2006.

CHAPTER 13

1. Samuel P. Huntington, *The Clash of Civilizations And the Remaking of World Order* (London: Simon and Schuster, 1996, 261.
2. John Fine, *The Bosnian Church: A New Interpretation* (New York, 1975.)
3. In Dubrovnik *Osman* by Ivan Gundulić (1638), in Croatia *Smail Aga's Death* by Ivan Mažuranić (1846), in Montenegro *The Mountain Wreath* by Petar Petrović Njegoš (1847).
4. It is important to underline that Huntington sees the clash of civilizations as a product of modernity, not primordial cleavages: refer to the introduction of this book.
5. The writings of Miroslav Hroch, Anthony Smith and John Hutchinson suggest that religion had a decisive role in the formation of modern nations. Miroslav Hroch acknowledged the need for linguistic or religious ties enabling a higher degree of social communication within the group than beyond it, in the formation of modern nations. Miroslav Hroch, "The nature of the Nation", in John A. Hall (ed.), *The State of the Nation (Ernest Gellner and the Theory of Nationalism)* (Cambridge: Cambridge University Press. 1988), 93; Anthony Smith, *Theories of Nationalism* (London: Duckworth, 1971), 245; John Hutchinson, *The Dynamics of Cultural Nationalism: The Gaelic Revival and the Creation of the Irish Nation State* (London, Allen and Unwin, 1987), 37.
6. John V.A. Fine, "The Various Faiths in the History of Bosnia: Middle Ages to the Present", in Shatzmiller 2002, 15.
7. Dušan Bataković. *The Kosovo Chronicles* (Belgrade: Plato, 1992).
8. Norman Cigar, *Genocide in Bosnia: The Policy of 'Ethnic Cleansing'* (Austin, TX: Texas A&M University Press, 1995), 24–30.
9. Bringa, "Islam and the Quest for Identity in Post-Communist Bosnia-Herzegovina", in Shatzmiller 2002, 26.
10. Gilles Kepel, *Jihad: The Trail of Political Islam* (London: I.B. Tauris, 2004), 243.
11. *Ibid.*, 250.

CHAPTER 14

1. I would like to thank Frank Peter for his comments on an early draft of this chapter.
2. María Jesús Viguera, "Al-Andalus como interferencia" in Monserrat Abumalham (ed.), *Comunidades islámicas en Europa* (Madrid: Trotta, 1995), 61–70.
3. On the history of Spanish nationalism and identity, see Eduardo Manzano Moreno and Juan Sisinio Pérez Garzón, "A difficult nation?", *History and Memory*, 14, no. 1–2 (2002), 259–86.
4. José Álvarez-Junco, "The formation of Spanish identity and its adaptation to the age of nations", *History and Memory* 14, no. 1–2 (2002), 13–36.
5. See Fernando Amerigo Cuervo-Arango, "Breve apunte histórico de la relación Estado-confesiones religiosas en España", *Comunidades islámicas en Europa*, ed. Monserrat Abumalham (Madrid: Trotta, 1995), 161–2.
6. *Ibid.*, 163.
7. See Iván Jiménez-Aybar, *El Islam en España: Aspectos institucionales de su estatuto jurídico* (Pamplona: Navarra Gráfica Ediciones, 2004), 68.

8. On this subject see María Soledad Carrasco Urgoiti, *El moro retador y el moro amigo: Estudios sobre fiestas y comedias de moros y cristianos* (Granada: Universidad, 1996).

9. On the uses of the past in Spanish colonialism, see Ignacio Tofiño-Quesada, "Spanish Orientalism: Uses of the Past in Spain's Colonization in Africa", *Comparative Studies of South Asia, Africa and the Middle East* 23, no. 1–2 (2003), 141–8.

10. On the negative view of the "moro" in leftist discourse, see María Rosa de Madariaga, *Los moros que trajo Franco. La intervención de tropas coloniales en la guerra civil* (Barcelona: Martínez Roca, 2002), 365–80. The texts compiled by de Madariaga show how the enemy was depicted with a more xenophobic and even racist discourse, which at the same time is also linked to the religious affiliation of the North African troops as the "secular enemy of Christianity".

11. María Rosa de Madariaga 2002, 348.

12. See for instance Abdennur Prado, *El islam en democracia* (Córdoba: Junta Islámica, 2006).

13. In 1989, and following the rule imposed by the state of having only one representative body for all Muslim associations, the first umbrella organization, the Federación Española de Entidades Religiosas Islámicas (Spanish Federation of Religious Entities, FEERI), was created. Two years later, the Muslim Association of Spain split form FEERI to create the Unión de Comunidades Islámicas de España (Union of Islamic Communities of Spain, UCIDE) as a result of the internal dissension. The division blocked the dialogue with the state, which lead to the establishment of the Islamic Commission of Spain in April 1992, only a few days before the signature of the agreement.

14. This is the case for political actors, as shown by Gunther Dietz, "Frontier hybridization or culture clash? Transnational migrant communities and sub-national identity politics in Andalusia, Spain", *Journal of Ethnic and Migration Studies* 30, no. 6 (2004), 1087–112; and also for Muslim local leaders in general, as revealed by Gema Martín Muñoz et al., *Moroccans in Spain* (Madrid: Fundación Repsol, 2003), 114–19.

15. Dietz 2004, 1087–112; Ricard Zapata-Barrero, "The Muslim community and Spanish tradition: Maurophobia as a fact, and impartiality as a desideratum", in Tariq Modood, Ricard Zapata-Barrero and Anna Tryandafyllidou (eds), *Multiculturalism, Muslims and Citizenship: A European Approach* (London: Routledge, 2005), 151.

16. See for instance: César Vidal, *España frente al Islam: de Mahomad a Ben Laden* (Madrid: La Esfera de los Libros, 2004) and Gustavo de Arístegui, *La yihad en España: la obsesión por recuperar al-Andalus* (Madrid: La Esfera de los Libros, 2005).

17. Staff writer, "El Gobierno carece de un registro de imanes y de mezquitas para controlar a los islamistas. El Ministerio de Justicia confirma que fieles y 'Gobiernos extranjeros' financian los templos", *El País*, 5 June 2004.

18. Mohammed Chaib, the first Muslim deputy in the Parliament of Catalonia since 2003, is an expert on immigration and Muslim issues. Mohammed Chaib, *Ètica per una Convivència: Pensar la immigració. L'Íslam a casa nostra* (Barcelona: L'Esfera dels llibres, 2005), 176.

19. For the public debate provoked by this announcement see: Elena Arigita, "Representing Islam in Spain: Muslim Identities and the Contestation of Leadership", *The Muslim World* 96, no. 4 (October 2006), 571–5.

20. See for instance Javier Jordán, Fernando M. Mañas and Humberto Trujillo, "Perfil sociocomportamental y estructura organizativa de la militancia yihadista en España. Análisis de las redes de Abu Dahdah y del 11-M", *Inteligencia y Seguridad. Revista de Análisis y Prospectiva* n° 1 (December 2006), 79–111.

21. According to the last Census of 01/01/2005 (see www.ine.es), Morocco is the country that provides the largest number of immigrants at 511,294. Other Muslim countries with a large number of immigrants lag far behind: Algeria (42,278), Pakistan (31,913) and Senegal (29,608).

22. In May 2004, only two months after the attacks in Madrid, initial contacts were made to establish common strategies in the fight against terrorism. The Minister of Justice who was leading the official visit declared that this meeting with the Minister of Religious Affairs had had the aim of "deepening and increasing our understanding of the Islamic community of Spain". See *El País*, 20 May 2004.

23. See Victor Pérez-Díaz, Berta Álvarez-Miranda and Carmen González-Enríquez, *España ante la inmigración* (Barcelona: La Caixa, 2001), 119.

24. See Martín Muñoz, 'Percepciones sobre la inmigración de origen musulmán', *Congreso Mundial Movimientos Humanos e Inmigración* (2004), available at http://www.iemed.org/mhicongress/dialegs/tots/papers/gemamartin.pdf (Accessed 10 June 2006).

25. See http://www.mae.es/NR/rdonlyres/1DCF2FB3-262F-4618-8B83-7A86A1E 56676/0/Alianzaingles.pdf (accessed 20 June 2006). While the concept of Alliance of Civilizations has resulted in various initiatives at different levels, it needs to be noted that documents by the High Level Group in the UN seem to dismiss the civilizational perspective and focus primarily on political, economic, and social explanations and recommendations.

26. On this polarization see Hisham D. Aidi, "The interference of al-Andalus: Spain, Islam and the West", *Social Text* 87/24.2 (2006), 80ff.

27. This speech was widely commented in Spain few days later and very much criticized, mostly because of the lack of historical accuracy. See the editorial "El teatro del horror", *El País*, 23 September 2004.

28. See Zapata Barrero 2005, 142.

REGION IV

1. Samuel P. Huntington, *The Clash of Civilizations* (New York: Simon and Schuster: 1996), 199–206.

2. IPPR, *Britain's Migrants* (London: IPPR, 2007), 14; Kristin Henriksen, *fakta om 18 invandrergrupper i Norge* (Oslo: Statistisk Sentralbyrå (SSB), 2007), 30.

3. Hanna Rogan, *Jihadism online—a study of how al-Qaeda and radical Islamist groups use the Internet for terrorist purposes*, (Oslo: Forsvarets Forskningsinstitutt (FFI), 2006), 11.

CHAPTER 15

1. Munira Mirza (ed.), *Living Apart Together, British Muslims and the Paradox of Multiculturalism*, (London: Policy Exchange, 2007), 6.

2. An expression used in the Arab press (*al-Hayaat, al-Sharq al-Awsat*) by the end of the 1990s. Londonistan is a neologism coined to refer to the presence of radical Islamists in London.

3. Some of the followers of Abu Qatada and the Supporters of Shariah have remained in Britain. Others left for the Iraqi, Chechen or Afghan fronts, or settled in Pakistan or in Saudi Arabia to further their knowledge of Islamic studies and live their lives in a society which corresponds to their religious ideals.

4. According to the Policy Exchange Report, 7 per cent of British Muslims declare they have sympathies with the ideas of al-Qaeda. Among this group, 17 per cent are between the age of 16 and 24.

5. This group is now known as the Followers of Ahl al-Sunna wal Jamaa. It was founded in November 2005 by Sulaiman Keeler, Omar Brooks and Anjem Choudary. After Omar Bakri's exile to Lebanon in August 2005 the spiritual sons of this Islamic preacher followed his Salafist Jihadist doctrine.

6. They are referred to as British Muslims by scholars as well as by the British authorities. Even the representatives of British Islam identify themselves as British Muslims. See Philip Lewis, *Islamic Britain: Religion, Politics and Identity among British Muslims* (London: I.B. Tauris, 2002). Since 2003 many Islamist cells have been dismantled, involving Muslims from Indo-Pakistani and Afro-Caribbean origins.

7. These are immigrants who settled in Britain in the 1990s. They are mainly Muslims from the Balkans, the Caucasus or Arabs from the Maghreb countries or from Egypt. These immigrants had fled their home countries for political reasons and aim to continue their struggle against their regimes from Great Britain. They also consider the to be responsible for the political situation in their respective countries.

8. Adam Lusher, Jasper Copping, "Islamic charity linked to car bomb suspect", *Daily Telegraph*, 8 July 2007.

9. Staff writer, "Failed transatlantic bomb plot was ready to go in days", *The Times*, 10 October 2006.

10. See Ameli Saied Reza, *Globalization and British Muslim Identity* (London: Saied Reza, 2002).

11. This is due to the fact that their focus is on the Arab world and more importantly because their objective is essentially to inform and not to mobilize or recruit supporters in Britain. They act as opposition groups in exile.

12. A case in point is the site *Azzam Brigades* which no longer exists but was a pioneer in broadcasting information about the jihadist fronts in Bosnia and Chechnya. See also sites such as *al-Ansar* or *al-Qalaa*.

13. The *Barelwi* are the followers of a traditional school founded by Ahmed Reza Khan (1856–1921) in India. It has its roots in an older Sufi sect, *Al-Quadiryia*, founded in twelfth-century Iraq. Reza Khan spread the mystic practices of Sufi Islam and the cult of saints (*pir* in Urdu). The *Deobandi* is a group of *ulama* from the Hanafi School (one of the four schools of Sunnism), founded in 1865 in the town of Deoband, north of Delhi. Basically reformist, this group is opposed to all the traditional practices of Sufi Islam. The *Jama' at I-Islami* movement is a Pakistani political group founded in 1941 by Abû l-'Ala' Mawdoudi (1903–1979). The *Tablighis* are the disciples of *Jamaiya at-Tabligh*—association for preaching—a transnational association founded in India

by Mawlana Illyas. It aims at regenerating and converting the whole society into Islam and this is through preaching purely Islamic values without any apparent political intentions. See Dominique Thomas, *Londonistan: Le Jihad au Coeur de l'Europe* (Paris: Michalon, 2005).

14. Gilles Kepel, *A L'Ouest d'Allah* (Paris: Seuil, 1994), 131–2.

15. Examples of adjustments are: planning separate spheres for men and women to practice sport; allowing people to have a break for prayer times; promoting the creation of Islamic financial institutions such as Islamic banks or charities.

16. Among these measures we can refer to the involvement of Britain in the Iraqi War or the question of the *niqab*, a veil that covers the face entirely. It is true that many British citizens contested these measures, but their arguments were not the same as those held by the British Muslims.

17. Some of the British Muslims who adhered to radical groups such as Supporters of Shariah (SOS) or *Hizb ut-Tahrir* have often expressed their dissatisfaction with and difference from the official representatives of Islam in Britain, namely the Muslim Council of Britain, the United Kingdom Islamic Mission, and The Islamic Foundation. Their views are published in reviews such as *Al-Jihaad, Al-Khilafah* (www.alkhilafah.info) and in forums such as the forum of *Ahl al-Sunna wal-Jamaa* followers, www.muntadaa-aswj.net (accessed 20 April 2007).

18. See associations such as "Stop Islamophobia" which is highly active among university students, Islamic Human Rights Commission (www.ihrc.org.uk) or www.islamophobia.watch.com. The early results of the enquiry made by Policy Exchange analysis, Munira Mirza (ed.), *op. cit.*, shows that 58 per cent of young British Muslims consider Western society arrogant when it comes to Islam. This said, 84 per cent of the persons polled confirm being treated fairly by the authorities. See *Daily Telegraph*, 29 January 2007; actually the theme of Islamophobia is a recurrent subject in the discourse and forum of radical movements. For instance, the followers of *Ahl us-Sunna wal-Jamaa* have organized many conferences on the subject since 2006. They accuse the British government of xenophobia and Islamophobia.

19. By traditional we mean a traditional Islam practised by local and community groups which are often influenced by some tribal, regional, or syncretic practices.

CHAPTER 16

1. Samuel P. Huntington, "The Clash of Civilizations?", *Foreign Affairs* 72, no. 3 (1993).

2. Although the notion of "perverse modernization" is meant in a derogatory sense, it is not at all related to any moral judgement. It underscores the fact that its bearers are not "traditional" people and it pinpoints the fact that they are modernized in a way that absolutizes violence and promotes death as the only alternative to the "devilish" western society.

3. Patricia Tourancheau, "Bensaïd et Belkacem comparaisent à partir d'aujourd'hui à Paris", *Libération*, 1 October 2002.

4. Farhad Khosrokhavar, *L'islam dans les prisons* (Paris: Balland, 2004).

5. Emmanuelle Santelli, *La mobilité sociale dans l'immigration, itineraries de réussite des enfants d'origine algérienne* (Presses Universitaries de Mirail, Toulouse, 2001). See

equally Catherine Withold de Wenden and Rémy Leveau, *La Beurgeoisie* (Paris, Éditions du CNRS, 2001).

6. For the French and English cases see James A. Beckford, Danièle Joly and Fahrad Khosrokhavar, *Muslims in Prison, Challenge And Change In Britain and France* (Basingstoke, Hampshire: Palgrave Macmillan Publishers, 2006).

7. See Georges Felouzis, Françoise Liot, Joële Perroton, *L'Apartheid Scolaire, Enquête sur la segregation ethnique dans les colleges* (Paris: Seuil 2005).

8. Staff writer, "Notes d'actualité n° 51", Centre Français de Recherche sur le Renseignement, http://www.cf2r.org/fr/actualite/dans_presse.php?t=o, (accessed 15 June 2007).

9. Khaled Kelkal's interview with Dietmar Loch "Moi, Khaled Kelkal", *Le Monde*, 7 October 1995.

10. Among them some young Frenchman of North African origin who died fighting American forces in Iraq. Redouane Al Hakim, a 19-year old, was killed in Fallujah on 17 July of 2004; Tarek Ouinis and Karim (Abou Salman) died on 17 September, Abdel Halim Badjoudj, 19 years old, died on 20 October also in a suicide attack in Fallujah.

11. Staff writer "22 French Muslim citizens fighting in Iraq, seven being killed and two imprisoned", *AFP Report*, 23 November 2005.

12. Benedict Anderson, *Imagined Communities: Reflections on the Origin and Spread of Nationalism*, rev. ed. (London: Verso, 1991).

CHAPTER 17

1. The writers wish to give warm thanks to Professor Ottar Brox, Dr Lars Gule, Kari Vogt, and Göran Larsson for their valuable comments to this chapter.

2. Ministeriet for Flygtninge, Invandrere og Integration *Testversion af Indfødtsretsprøve* (København: Ministeriet for Flygtninge, Invandrere og Integration, 2007); Rita Kumar, "Det norske stedet sett med nye øyne", speech given during the Norwegian Planmøte, 21 September 2006, Oslo; Anders Johnson, *Inte bara valloner* (Stockholm: AB Timbro, 1997), 46.

3. Utlendingsdirektoratet Tall og Fakta 2007, Oslo 2007; Utlendingssærvice, 'Hovedtall på Asylområdet', http://www.nyidanmark.dk/resources.ashx/Resources/Statistik/statistik/2006/seneste_tal_udlaendingeomraadet_da.xls (accessed 27 July 2007); Åke Nilson, 'Dagens invandrare—hustrur och barn', *VälfärdsBulletinen* 4, 2.

4. There are approximately 200,000 Muslims in Denmark (2 per cent of the population) and approximately 115 registered mosques. In Sweden there are 250–400,000 Muslims approximately 1.8–4.4 per cent of Sweden's population of 9 million. Norway hosts approximately 140,000 Muslims, this out of a population of 4.6 million. Migrasjonsverket, "Uppheoldstilstand", http://www.migrationsverket.se/; Oddbjørn, Leirvik, Islam i Norge, http://folk.uio.no/leirvik/tekster/IslamiNorge.html#tendensar, (accessed 27 May 2007); The Norwegian figures are sum of the categories "First generation immigrants" and "Persons born in Norway with two foreign born parents". Statistisk Sentalbyrå, "Population 1st January 2006 and 2007 and changes in 2006, by immigrant category and country background", *Population statistics. Immigrant population, 1 January*

2007, http://www.ssb.no/english/subjects/02/01/10/innvbef_en (accessed 13 June 2007); Lene Kühle, *Mosques in Denmark: Islam and Muslim Places of Worship* (Copenhagen: Univers, 2006), 65.

5. *Ibid.*, 11.
6. Göran, Larsson "Muslims in the EU: Cities Report, Sweden" *EU Monitoring and Advocacy Programme* 2007, http://www.eumap.org/topics/minority/reports/eumuslims/background_reports (accessed June 16 2007).
7. In addition to these there are 900–1000 converts. Statistic sentalbyrå, 2006.
8. Lena Schroder, *Integration vägen till utveckling och tillväxt*, (Stockholm: Integrasjonverket, 2006).
9. TNS Gallup, Holdninger *til integrasjon og internasjonale konflikter blant muslimer i Norge og den norske befolkningen generelt* (Bergen: TV2 2006).
10. TNS Gallup, 2006.
11. Kristin Henriksen, *Fakta om 18 innvandrergrupper i Norge*, (Oslo: Statistisk Sentralbyrå, 2007), 30; Anna Gärdqvist, "Stora utbildningsskillnader mellan invandrargrupper", *Välfärd* 4 (2006), 1.
12. Lena Schroder, *Integration vägen till utveckling och tillväxt* (Stockholm: integrasjonverket, 2006); Kristin Henriksen, *Fakta om 18 innvandrergrupper i Norge* (Oslo: Statistisk Sentralbyrå, 2007), 30 Ministeriet for flykninge, innvandring og integrasjon, 2006, 68.
13. Staff writer "2500 danskere er konverteret til islam", *Ekstra bladet*, 4 June 2006 http://ekstrabladet.dk/nyheder/samfund/article201711.ece (accessed 15 May 2007).
14. Anna Reimann, "Legoland is burning", *der Spiegel*, 10 February 2006.
15. Helge Øgrim "Will print the sensitive Mohammed Cartoons", *Dagbladet*, 10 January 2006, http://www.dagbladet.no/kultur/2006/01/10/454375.html (accessed 15 May 2007).
16. Tor Arne Andreassen "De norske skuddene i Afghanistan", *Aftenposten*, 10 June 2006 http://www.aftenposten.no/amagasinet/article1347208.ece (accessed 29 May 2007).
17. Interviews with Muslim leaders by Jørgen Johansen in Delhi, Jakarta, Ramallah and Gothenburg (December 2006).
18. Staff Writer "Eksporttabet etter Muhammedkrisen er vokset", Aarhus School of Business, University of Aarhus, http://www.asb.dk/about/news/archive/2007/muhammed_krise.aspx (accessed 20 August 2007).
19. A suicide bomber in a car filled with 25 kg TNT detonated the bomb outside the embassy, six people were killed and more than twenty injured. Al-Qaeda claimed to be behind the attack and threatened to continue the terrorist campaign if the Danish did not apologize. The next day a truck with 1,000 kg of TNT was stopped outside Islamabad.
20. Knut J. Meland, "Muslimer viser Muhammed karikatur", *Nettavisen*, 17 August 2007.
21. Josef el Mahdi, "Reinfeldt och fredsagenterna parerade Vilks-krisen briljant", *SvD*, 7 October 2007.
22. *Ibid.*
23. Malene Grøndal and Torben R. Rasmussen, Kristine Sinclair, *Hizb ut-Tahrir i Denmark: Farlig Fundamentalisme eller Uskyldigt Ungdomsoprør?* (Aarhus: Aarhus University Press, 2003), 16.

24. Michael T. Jensen "Jihad in Denmark, An overview and analysis of jihadi activity in Denmark 1990–2006", *Danish Institute for International Studies, Working Paper no. 2006/35* (2006), 15–23.

25. Gilles Kepel, *Jihad: The Trail of Political Islam* (London, New York: I.B. Tauris, 2002), 303.

26. Peter Ernstved Rasmussen, Anni Kristensen, Thomas Andrew, Christina Wildfang Nissen, "Terrormistænkte varetægtsfængslet" *Jyllandsposten*, 4 September 2007.

27. "Syv Års Fengsel i Terrorsag", *Denmark's Radio*, www.dr.dk/Nyheder/Inland/kriminalitet/2007/02/15/153729.html (accessed May 15 2007).

28. Kenneth Lund, Aalsmeer, Holland, Morten Skjoldager, "Tiltalte i Vollsmose havde bombemål i Danmark", *Politiken*, 10 April 2007, http://politiken.dk/indland/article280860.ece.

29. The former one of al-Qaeda's European leaders, the latter sentenced for participation in the 9/11 attacks: staff writer "Dom I sagen anklagermyndigheden mod Said Mansour", *Københavns Byret*, 11 April 2007.

30. *Ibid.*, 54.

31. Ansar al Sunnah, "Ansar al Sunnah Sweden", http://mypetjawa.mu.nu/archives/jaish_ansar_al_sunnah_sweden_website.htm (accessed 14 June 2007).

32. Gilles Kepel, *Jihad: The Trail of Political Islam* (London: I.B. Tauris and Co, 2002), 303.

33. Anders Sundelin, "Pojkrumsterroristerna", *Fokus* 2 Juni 2006.

34. Staff writer, "Tre Terrormistenkte Pågrepet i Sverge", *ABC Nyheter*, 8 February 2008.

35. Hamade Kassem "Ni kommer få det största straffet" *Expressen* 1 January 2007, http://www.expressen.se/1.231454 (accessed June 15 2007); an early terrorist case conserned a secular group. Abu Nidal set up a cell here with an arms cache in a forest near Arlanda international airport in 1988.

36. The gun that fired the shots was a .44 calibre, an Abilene or a Dan Wesson according to the investigation. Fortunately the publisher recovered. The material from the investigation is still classified; Odd Isungsett, *Attentatet*, (Trondheim: Tiden Norsk Forlag A/S, 2000), 68.

37. Michael Isikoff and Mark Hosenball, "Hitting the pocketbook", *Newsweek Internet* (nd) http://www.msnbc.msn.com/id/16192655/site/newsweek/page/3/ (accessed 1 August 2007).

38. *Ibid.*

39. Morten Øverby, "Osama bin Laden er en god Muslim", *VG*, 6 June 2005.

40. Staff writer, "Terrorsporet som smuldret bort", *VG*, 5 October 2002, 4.

41. Johan Hultgren, "Tiltales for terror og drapsforsøk", *Dagbladet*, 15 May 2007, 8–9.

42. Johan Hultgren, Tore Bergsaker, Per Arne Solend, "Her er hele terrorsamtalen", *Dagbladet*, 30 September 2007, 6–7.

43. The views of a Norwegian veteran politician, Kåre Willoch, were frequently referred to in the media.

44. Interview with X1, Member of the Shebab support committee in Norway, Oslo, January 2008. (This support committee was joined during the spring of 2008 with other committees supporting other insurgency groups in Somalia, under one umbrella.)

CHAPTER 18

1. The higher figure often cited by American Muslim leaders comes from an analysis by Ilyas Ba-Yunus and Kassim Kone based on an extrapolation of counts of mosques and Islamic institution membership lists. They concluded that the Muslim population was just under 6 million and probably more, which would make it equivalent to the Jewish population. See Ilyas Ba-Yunus and Kassim Kone, "Muslim Americans: A Demographic Report", in Project MAPS, *Muslims' Place in the American Public Square* (Georgetown: Center for Christian-Muslim Understanding, Georgetown University, 2001). The lower figure comes from the most recent and systematic national survey, conducted by the Pew Research Center, "Muslim Americans: Middle Class and Mostly Mainstream", 22 May 2007. Its estimate of under 3 million American Muslims also tracked an earlier assessment by Tom W. Smith, Director of the General Social Survey at the University of Chicago, drawing upon various national survey results. See Tom W. Smith, "The Muslim Population of the United States: The Methodology of Estimates", *Public Opinion Quarterly*, Vol. 66, (2002), 404–17.

2. Project MAPS, *Muslims' Place in the American Public Square* (Georgetown: Center for Christian-Muslim Understanding, Georgetown University, 2001).

3. A Pew Research Center survey, "Muslim Americans: Middle Class and Mostly Mainstream", 22 May 2007, found them on a par with average Americans, while the Project MAPS survey found significantly higher educational and income levels for American Muslims.

4. Project MAPS, *Muslims' Place in the American Public Square.*

5. Steven Emerson, *American Jihad: The Terrorists Living Among Us* (New York: The Free Press, 2002), Appendix C.

6. Emerson, *American Jihad*, 197–203.

7. Audrey Hudson, "CAIR Membership falls 90% since 9/11", The *Washington Times*, National Weekly Edition, 18 June 2007.

8. 43rd Annual Convention of the Islamic Society of North America, Chicago, 1–4 September 2006.

9. Sarah Childress, "Islam: Ingrid Mattson: Raised Catholic, this Muslim Professor is Bringing the Moderate Viewpoint to the World", *Newsweek*, 25 December 2006—1 January 2007 issue.

10. Project MAPS, *American Muslim Poll 2004: Shifting Political Winds and Fallout from 9/11, Afghanistan, and Iraq*, (Georgetown: Center for Muslim-Christian Understanding, Georgetown University, 2004).

11. Project MAPS, *American Muslim Poll 2004.*

12. Ahmed Younis, National Director of the Muslim Political Affairs Council, described how the American Muslim Political Coordinating Council, consisting of several of the major American groups, endorsed Bush because the candidate came out against secret evidence. Younis, who felt that this was not enough to warrant an endorsement, described the 2000 initiative as a "fiasco". Interview with Ahmed Younis, 14 June 2006, Washington DC.

13. Project MAPS, *American Muslim Poll 2004.*

14. *Ibid.*

15. Interview with Ahmed Younis, National Director, Muslim Political Affairs Council, 14 June 2006.

16. Muslim American Society 'Press Release', 10 November 2006.

17. Ihsan Bagby, "The Mosque and the American Public Square", in *Muslims' Place in the American Public Square*, 325.

18. Project MAPS, *American Muslim Poll, 2004*.

19. See for example: Peter Lüchau, "Report on Surveys of Religion in Europe and the United States", Working Paper History of Religions Section, University of Copenhagen 2004; *Stanley R. Sloan*, "How Does Religion Affect Relations between America and Europe" *Eurofuture*, Winter 2005.

20. Pew Research Center, 'Muslim Americans', 30.

21. Interview at the Islamic Society of North America conference, Chicago, 1 September 2006.

22. As quoted by Spencer Ackerman, "Why American Muslims Haven't Turned to Terrorism," *The New Republic*, 12 December 2005.

23. Interview with Radwan Masmoudi at the Islamic Society of North America Conference, 1 September 2006.

24. Abdulaziz Sachedina, *The Islamic Roots of Democratic Pluralism* (New York: Oxford University Press, 2001); Maher Hathout, with Uzma Jamil, Gasser Hathout, and Nayyer Ali, *In Pursuit of Justice: The Jurisprudence of Human Rights in Islam* (Los Angeles, CA: Muslim Public Affairs Council, 2006); Abdullahi Ahmed An-Na'im, *Toward an Islamic Reformation: Civil Liberties, Human Rights and International Law* (Syracuse, NY: Syracuse University Press, 1990); Khaled M. Abou El Fadl, *Islam and the Challenge of Democracy* (Princeton, NJ: Princeton University Press, 2004).

25. Imam Feisel Abdul Rauf, *What's Right With Islam is What's Right With America* (San Francisco: HarperCollins, 2005).

26. Taha Jabir al-Alwani, 'Toward a Fiqh for Minorities: Some Reflections', in *Muslims' Place in the American Public Square*.

27. Karen Leonard, "American Muslim Politics: Discourses and Practices," *Ethnicities*, 3, no. 2 (2003), 147–81.

28. Paul Weller, 'Fethulla Gulen, Turkey, and the European Union', paper presented at the Second Annual Conference on Islam in the Contemporary World: The Fethulla Gulen Movement in Thought and Practice, University of Oklahoma, November 3–5, 2006. Weller takes the term *dar ul-hizmet* from Muslim scholar Ihsan Yilmaz.

29. In *Mecca and Main Street*, chapter 6, Geneive Abdo profiles young Muslim women who make the case for greater roles in their mosques and institutions. An excellent summary of diverse women's voices is by Yvonne Yazbeck Haddad, Jane I. Smith, and Kathleen M. Moore, *Muslim Women in America: The Challenge of Islamic Identity Today* (New York: Oxford University Press, 2006). Other reform voices include Riffat Hassan, a feminist whose prolific work is summarized by Haddad et al.; and Irshad Manji, *The Trouble with Islam: A Muslim's Call for Reform in Her Faith* (New York: St Martin's Press, 2003).

30. Pew Research Center, 'Muslim Americans', p. 26.

31. The way American Muslims became more religious, but also independent, is described by Geneive Abdo, *Mecca and Main Street: Muslim Life After 9/11* (New York: Oxford University Press, 2006).

32. Karen Leonard, 'American Muslim Politics: Discourses and Practices'.
33. I illustrate this with respect to Sudan in *Freeing God's Children: The Unlikely Alliance for Global Human Rights* (Lanham, MD: Rowman and Littlefield Press, 2005), chapter 7.
34. Neil MacFarquhar, "Muslim Chairty Sues Treasury Dept. and Seeks Dismissal of Charges of Terrorism," *The New York Times*, 12 December 2006.
35. E.A. Torriero, "They're 100% American, and pro-Hezbollah: US Scrutiny in Dearborn," *Chicago Tribune*, 27 July 2006.
36. Mary Beth Sheridan, "Conflicting Views of Justice: US Muslims Face Hardball Tactics in an Era of Threats," *The Washington Post Weekly Edition*, 11–17 September 2006.
37. Spencer Ackerman, 'Why American Muslims Haven't Turned to Terrorism'.
38. A number of the critics of Muslim leaders are listed by John L. Esposito, "Moderate Muslims: A Mainstream of Modernists, Islamists, Conservatives, and Traditionalists," *American Journal of Islamic Studies* 2, no. 3 (2005): 11–20.
39. www.DanielPipes.org. (accessed 1 May 2007).
40. Daniel Pipes and Sharon Chadha, "CAIR: Islamists Fooling the Establishment," *Middle East Quarterly*, Spring 2006.
41. Steven Emerson, *American Jihad*, 12–18.
42. Khaled Abou El Fadl, as quoted by Karen Leonard, 'American Muslim Politics: Discourses and Practices', *Ethnicities*, Volume 3, number 2, 2003, p. 156.
43. Stephen Schwartz, *The Two Faces of Islam* (New York: Doubleday, 2002); Robert Baer, *Sleeping with the Devil* (New York: Crown Publishers, 2003); Caryle Murphy, "The Salafi Conundrum," *The Washington Post Weekly Edition*, 11 September 2006.
44. James Woolsey and Nina Shea, Center for Religious Freedom, Freedom House, "Saudi Publications on Hate Ideology Fill American Mosques" (New York: Freedom House, 2005).
45. M.A. Muqtedar Khan, "Living on Borderlines", in *Muslims' Place in the American Public Square*. See also "Putting the American in 'American Muslim'", *The New York Times*, 7 September 2003.
46. Interview with Nihad Awad and a female college student, both at the ISNA convention, September 2006.
47. Sulayman S. Nyang, *Islam in the United States of America*.
48. As quoted by Yvonne Yazbeck Haddad, "The Dynamics of Islamic Identity in North America", in *Muslims on the Americanization Path?*, edited by Yvonne Yazbeck Haddad and John L. Esposito (New York: Oxford University Press, 2000).
49. Interview with Ahmed Younis, 14 June 2006, Washington, DC.
50. M.A. Muqtedar Khan, *American Muslims: Bridging Faith and Freedom* (Beltsville, MD: Amana Publications, 2002), 3–4.
51. Maher Hathout, with Uzma Jamil, Gasser Hathout, and Nayyer Ali, *In Pursuit of Justice: The Jurisprudence of Human Rights in Islam*.
52. Karen Leonard, "American Muslim Politics", 168.
53. In addition to *Islam and the Challenge of Democracy*, the many books by Khaled M. Abou El Fadl include *The Great Theft: Wrestling Islam from the Extremists* (2005); *Speaking in God's Name: Islamic Law, Authority, and Women* (Oxford: Oneworld, 2001).

365

54. Reza Aslan, *No God but God: The Origins and Future of Islam* (New York, Random House, 2005).

55. Abdullah Ahmed An-Na'im, *Toward an Islamic Reformation: Civil Liberties, Human Rights, and International Law* (Syracuse, NY: Syracuse University Press, 1993).

56. Hamza Yusuf is a scholar whose popular lectures are recorded on numerous CDs. One of them is titled "Nine Hundred Years: Reviving the Sprit of Andalusia," Alhambra Productions, 2005.

57. Imam Zaid Shakir, *Scattered Pictures: Reflections of an American Muslim* (Hayward, CA: Zaytuna Institute, 2005).

58. Fiqh Council of North America, fatwa issued 28 July 2005.

59. Pew Forum on Religion and Public Life, "Will Views Toward Muslims and Islam Follow Historical Trends?" March 2006 (www.pewforum.org).

60. Ann Coulter, "This is War," *National Review Online*, 13 September 2001 (www.nationalreview.com).

61. Kevin R. den Dulk, "Evangelical Elites and Faith-Based Foreign Affairs," *The Review of Faith and International Affairs*, Spring 2006.

62. Laurie Goodstein, "Seeing Islam as Evil' Faith, Evangelicals Seek Converts," *The New York Times*, 27 May 2003.

63. Akbar Ahmed, professor at American University in Washington DC is author of *Islam Under Siege*. He elaborated to me how isolated incendiary comments by American religious leaders become magnified and are taken by foreign Muslims as representative of the broader American community.

64. Pew Research Center, "Muslim Americans," pp. 8, 51, 54.

65. Most examples come from Daniel Pipes, "Converts to Terrorism", *New York Sun*, 6 December 2006. On the "Portland Seven" see Ben Jacklet and Janine Robben, "Hawash Regrets 'Worst Decision'", *Portland Tribune*, 10 February 2004. On the Ohio group see Jerry Seper, "Ohio Arrests Tied to Charity Accused of Aiding Hamas", *The Washington Times National Weekly Edition*, 27 February-5 March 2006.

66. Staff Writer, "Cleric Bakri barred from Britain", *BBC News Website* 12 August 2005, http://news.bbc.co.uk/2/hi/uk_news/4144792.stm, (accessed 26 June 2007).

67. Staff Writer, "Radical Islamics in New York City Desecrate an American Flag", *Videoplayer.es* 18 October 2006, http://www.videoplayer.es/video/radical-islamics-in-newyork-city-desecrate-an-american-flag/7OYOvcZBEyY/ (accessed 26 June 2007).

68. Daniel Pipes, "No American Muslim Terrorists?" *FrontPageMagazine.com*, 12 December 2005. Citing a finding that 86 per cent of the 212 terrorist attacks against the west since 1993 have come from Muslim immigrants (with the remainder largely from Muslim converts), he extrapolates from his figure of thirty converts who engaged in terror-related activities to arrive at the figure of 175 immigrant terrorists.

69. Harvey Kushner with Bard Davis, *Holy War on the Home Front: the Secret Islamic Terror Network in the United States* (New York: Sentinel, 2004); Steven Emerson, *American Jihad: The Terrorists Living Among Us* (New York: The Free Press, 2003).

70. The case of Taheri-Azar is recounted by Daniel Pipes, "Sudden Jihad Syndrome," Frontpagemag.com, 14 March, 2006. "Sudden Jihad Syndrome" is a term coined by Pipes to describe how a few individual Muslims, angered by Islamic grievances, have committed acts of seeming random violence. Adam Gadahn's odyssey from troubled

youth to al-Qaeda spokesman was recounted by Brian Ross, "American Al Qaeda Unmasked," ABC News, 9 November 2004.

71. Spencer Ackerman, "Why American Muslims Haven't Turned to Terrorism," *The New Republic*, 12 December 2005.

72. Testimony of Charles E. Allen, Assistant Secretary for Intelligence and Analysis and Chief Intelligence Officer, Department of Homeland Security, before the US Senate Committee on Homeland Security and Government Affairs, hearing titled "The Threat of Islamic Radicalization to the Homeland," Washington DC, 14 March 2007.

73. Joseph L. Lieberman, Opening Statement before the Committee on Homeland Security and Governmental Affairs, hearing titled "The Threat of Islamic Radicalism to the Homeland," United States Senate, Washington, D.C., 14 March 2007.

74. Maher Hathout, presentation at the ISNA convention, September 2006.

75. Interview with Ahmed Younis, 14 June 2006.

76. Ahmed Younis Interview, 14 June 2006.

77. The 2004 figure of 38 per cent is from Project MAPS, sponsored by Georgetown University, "American Muslim Poll 2004," conducted by Zogby International; the 2006 figure of 55 per cent is from a poll conducted by the Council on American-Islamic Relations, as summarized by Julia Dunn, "Muslims in US are Mostly Democrats," *The Washington Times*, National Weekly Edition, 30 October, 2006.

78. Muslim Public Affairs Council, "MPAC Report: Religion and Identity of MusUSlim American Youth Post-London Attacks," conducted at the ISNA convention, September 2005 (www.mpac.org;; accessed 1 May 2007).

79. Daniel Pipes and Sharon Chadha, "CAIR: Islamists Fooling the Establishment," *Middle East Quarterly*, 2006. The spokesman was Ibrahim Hooper.

80. M.A. Muqtedar, "Putting the American in 'American Muslim,'" *The New York Times*, 7 September 2003.

81. The Muslim American Society reports on Sabri Ben Khala, who was found not guilty after an arduous process that involved incarceration by Saudi officials, aggressive FBI investigations, and repeated interrogation. "MAS Calls for Support and Justice for Brother Sabri Ben Khala", news release, 17 April 2007, www.masnet.org.

82. Karen Leonard, American Muslim Politics, 152.

83. "Desert Islam," which suggests disdain for urban and cosmopolitan civilization, is how some critics depict the influence of Wahhabi teaching.

84. This ranking comes from Charity Navigator, the nation's largest charity evaluator, as reported by Islamic Relief USA on 22 February 2007, www.irw.org.

CHAPTER 19

1. From the treatise by the Syrian Salafist resident in the United Kingdom, Abu Baseer al-Tartousi: (الصّراع بين الحضارات حقّ واقع أم ادعاء كاذب) ("*The Clash between Civilizations, a Self-Evident Truth or a Misleading Claim?*"). *Abu Baseer Tartousi* 2004. http://www. tawhed.ws/a?i=4, (accessed 22 August 2007). Al-Tartousi details the motives for the clash: that Islamic civilization is based on the doctrine of *tawhid* ("oneness", the exclusivity of God), and is based on faith in the Prophets; that the non-Muslims bear hatred

for God's true faith; and that they fear what they know to be the truth. A good English language treatment of these issues is provided by the Hizb al-Tahrir's publication: Anon. 'The Inevitability of the "Clash of Civilization"', *Al-Khilafah Publications*, 2002, http://www.e-prism.org/images/clashofcivilization.pdf, (accessed 21 August 2007).

2. An analysis of "*Foreign Policy in Islam*" was published by the Al-Muhajiroun group, but in fact occupies itself mostly with the internal relationships of the subjects and with the rights of Dhimmis (non-Muslims) within this state. Shaykh Faris al-Zahrani's: العلاقات الدولية في الاسلام ("*International Relations in Islam*"), *Islamic Centre for Studies and Research (al-Qaeda)* http://www.tawhed.ws/a?i=9, (accessed August 22 2007) occupies itself with asserting the exclusivity of Islamic concerns; see also Abd al-Qadim Zallum, الأموال في دولة الخلافة (*Finance in the Caliphal State*), (Beirut: Dar al-Umma, 2004).

3. This is the theme of al-Suri's fascinating studies on the failed jihads in Syria and Algeria; Abu Mus'ab al Suri, 'ملاحظات حول التجربة الجهادية في سوريا' ("*Observations on the Jihadi Experience in Syria*") in الثورة الإسلامية الجهادية في سوريا ("*The Islamic Jihadi Revolution in Syria*"), http://www.tawhed.ws/a?i=78, (accessed 22 August 2007). Among other numerous works on the subject, see Abu Baseer al-Tartousi: أسباب فشل بعض الحركات الجهادية في عملية التغيير ("*Reasons for the Failure of Some Jihadist Movements in Transformation Operations*") *Abu Baseer Tartousi*, 2002, http://www.abubaseer.bizland.com/articles.htm, (accessed 22 August 2007); عندما ينزل البلاء بالمجاهدين ("*When Trials befall the Mujahedin*") *Abu Baseer Tartousi*. 2004, http://www.abubaseer.bizland.com/articles.htm, (accessed 22 August 2007), and 'هؤلاء أخافهم على الجهاد والمجاهدين' ("*These things I fear for the Jihad and the Mujahedin*"). *Abu Baseer Tartousi*, 2004, http://www.abubaseer.bizland.com/articles.htm, (accessed August 22 2007).

4. Abu Bakr Naji, Idarat al-Tawahhush "The Management of Barbarism—the most dangerous period the Nation will pass through", *Center for Islamic Studies and Research*, http://www.tawhed.ws/a?i=416, (accessed August 21 2007), 12. See Stephen Ulph, "New book lays out al-Qaeda's military strategy", *Terrorism Focus* 2, no. 6, (2005).

5. Wiktorowicz points out that Reformist Islamists refer to the medieval Salafi scholar Ibn Qayyim al-Jawziyya and his four levels of forbidding evil. According to al-Jawziyya there are four possible consequences of any action: 1) the evil is replaced with something good; 2) the evil is diminished without ending completely; 3) the evil is replaced by an equivalent evil; and 4) the evil is replaced by an even greater evil. The first two are considered religiously acceptable, the third involves *ijtihād* (the exercise of independent judgment), and the fourth is forbidden. Quintan Wiktorowicz, "The New Global Threat—Transnational Salafis and Jihad", *Middle East Policy* 8 no. 4, (2001).

6. Ali Hasan al-Halabi, a former student of Shaykh Muhammad al-Bani. Wiktorowicz, *ibid.*

7. According to J. Stemmann, "Mosques are losing their importance in the radicalization process that leads Salafis to become terrorists, whereas religious courses in private homes, visits by itinerant radical recruiters, and Internet are all gaining importance in the radicalization and recruitment process." Juan Stemmann, "Middle East Salafism's Influence and the Radicalization of Muslim Communities in Europe," *The Middle East Review of International Affairs* 10, no. 3 (2006).

8. "These Salafi scholars play a critical but not widely observed role in the global jihadi movement. Ideology is often overlooked and is considered separate from the strategic

and operational aspects of Islamist militancy. Yet, the scholars behind the jihadi movement set the framework for debates and provide direction that is by and large adhered to, or is at the least a determining factor in the planning of attacks." Chris Heffelfinger, "The Ideological Voices of the Jihadi Movement", *Terrorism Monitor*, 4, no. 24 (2006).

9. The debate is well covered in the monograph by Reuven Paz, "Islamic Legitimacy for the London Bombings", *PRISM Occasional Paper* 3, no. 4 (2005).

10. Al-Maqdisi's argument in his works, 'وقفات مع ثمرات الجهاد' ("*Deliberations on the Fruits of Jihad*") *Minbar al-Tawhīd wal-Jihad*, (June 2004 http://www.tawhed.ws/r?i=2785), مناصرة ومناصحة لابي مصعب الزرقاوي, (accessed August 21 2007) ("*Support and Advice to Abu Mus'ab al-Zarqawi*") *Minbar al-Tawhīd wal-Jihad*, 2004, (http://www.tawhed. ws/r?i=2979), (accessed 21 August 2007) was that the jihad was being "dwarfized" through rash excesses and that suicide bombings were only acceptable in extreme and exceptional circumstances, not to be carried out in an uncontrolled fashion "due to a misguided understanding of the rules of warfare".

11. An entire literary genre is appearing on this subject, cf. Abd al-Muhsin al-'Abbād, "With Which Intellect and Religions Can Suicide Bombings and Destruction Be Considered Jihaad?", *Salafipublications.com*, (Accessed 24 August 2005), and Abu Baseer al-Tartousi's محاذير العمليات الاستشهادية أو الانتحارية ("*The Perils of Martyrdom or Suicide Operations*") *Abu Baseer Tartousi* 24 August, 2005., http://www.abubaseer. bizland.com/, (accessed 22 August 2007).

12. Husayn Bin Mahmud, نحن جهال اغرار ("*We Are Ignorant Deviants*") *At-Tibyan Publications*, 2003. (http://ia310930.us.archive.org/1/ite...t-Deviants.pdf) (accessed 21 August 2007). Abu Muhammad Yusuf bin Salih Al-Uyyayri, في جواز قتل الأسارى هداية الحيارى *Center for Islamic Studies and Research*, http://www.tawhed.ws/r?i=799, (accessed 22 August 2007). Anon: أقوال العلماء في قتل السفراء ("*Voices of the Scholars on the Killing of Ambassadors*") *Prism 2005*, (www.e-prism.org) (accessed 20 July 2005). Dr. Umar Ghani Sa'ud al-Ani, القول المبين في مفهوم التترس وأحكامه في الدين, ("*The Explanatory Words on the Concept of Tatarrus and its Verdicts in Faith*") (http://www. islamacademy.net/Index.aspx?function=Itemandid=2532andlang=AR) (accessed 21 August 2007).

13. Anon: تساؤلات وشبهات حول المجاهدين وعملياتهم ("Questions and Uncertainties Concerning the Mujahedin and their Operations"), *A Group of Those Strongly Attached to the Mujāhidīn (al-Qā'idūn)* http://www.tawhed.ws/c?i=56, (last accessed 21 August 2007). An earlier work of this nature, أباطيل وأسمار ("Prattle and Idle Talk") by Abu Abdallah al-Sa'di appears to have been superseded by this encyclopaedia. Abu Abdallah al-Sa'di, أباطيل وأسمار ("Prattle and Idle Talk") *Sawt al-Jihad*, http://www.tawhed. ws/c?i=128, (accessed 22 August 2007).

14. *Questions and Uncertainties, Taqdīm*.

15. Sawt al-Jihād "Mu'askar al-Battār", *Mu'askar al-Battār* I, no. 3 (unknown). The *Mu'askar* featured heavily the work of Shaykh Yusuf al-Uyyayri (killed in June 2003) on physical training, the former Egyptian military officer Sayf al-Adel on security and communications, and the one-time head of the Peninsular Al-Qaeda organization, Abd al-Aziz al-Muqrin (killed in June 2004) on military tactics and guerrilla warfare. Over its 22-volume history it published a full sample of military and ideological preparation, much of which would have formed part of the curriculum in Afghanistan.

16. The inauguration of the *Sawt al-Khilāfa* ("Voice of the Caliphate") broadcasts from Iraq in September 2005 was a milestone in this development.

17. Cf. the March 2005 call from the *Katibat al-Jihad al-I'lami* (Information Jihad Battalion) in Iraq for contributors to the "Design Squadron", the "Language Squadron" and the "Publication Squadron". An exhaustive report on the size and sophistication of the Iraq insurgency Internet propaganda effort has been authored by Daniel Kimmage, and Kathleen Ridolfo, "Iraqi Insurgent Media, the War of Images and Ideas", *Radio Free Europe/Radio Liberty*, 26 June 2007.

18. The most impressive being the Anon. موسوعة الاعداد ("*Encyclopedia of Preparation*"). *Unknown*, http://www.geocities.com/i3dad_jihad4/, (Last accessed 25 August 2007) which gives the introductory text and the structure, but the constituent URLs are now blocked. It is unique in its form, since the contents list on weaponry, guerrilla warfare, training and tactics—which is itself extensive—is a construction of myriad URLs leading to further pages—with further URLs leading the researcher to ever more precise information. The work is constantly updated.

19. According to Forbes and Shwery, "a small, exclusive group of Arabic-language websites now forms the core of this virtual community. These forums serve as the point of interaction for active members and passive supporters worldwide." Their analysis using the traffic-tracking website www.alexa.com, running this tool against the URLs of the primary websites of the Electronic Jihad, provided a breakdown of their traffic which indicated that the bulk of visits to jihadi websites came from the Middle East and North Africa, rather than the diaspora communities of Europe or the Persian Gulf states (which were previously assumed to be the epicentres). Rebecca Givner-Forbes, and Clay Shwery, "Mapping the Electronic Jihad: an Outline of the Virtual Jihadi Community", *RSIS Commentaries*, 33 (2007). The "citation analysis" method undertaken by West Point Academy's Combating Terrorism Center established that the primary modern authorities for jihad ideology remain Sayyid Qutb, Muhammad al-Maqdisi, Abdullah Azzam, Abd al-Qadir bin Abd al-Aziz and Yusuf al-Uyyayri, all of them Arabic language authors from the Middle East. William McCants, and Jarret Brachman, *Militant Ideology Atlas*, (West Point: Combating Terrorism Center, 2006)

20. Mitchell Silber and Arvin Bhatt, *Radicalization in the West: The Homegrown Threat*, (New York: NYPD Intelligence Division, 2007). The significant value of this analysis is that it studies examples of self-radicalization from a number of arenas across the globe, each of which shows signs of this consistent pattern to the radicalization process.

21. Examples are: Bin Abd al-Aziz, Abd al-Qadir, *The Criticism of Democracy and the Illustration of its Reality*, from الجامع في طلب العلم الشريف, *unknown*, http://www.tawhed.ws/a?i=6, (accessed 21 August 2007) and Abu Osama: "The Plague of the West; the Western Civilisation Laid Bare" *Islambase Publications*, http://downloads.islambase.co.uk/books/PlagueWest.pdf, (accessed 21 August 2007). On the second issue, see primarily: Abu Muhammad al Maqdisi, الشرعية الدولية ومناقضتها للشريعة الاسلامية ("International Law and its Contradiction to Islamic Law") *Minbar al-Tawhid wal-Jihad* October 2002, http://www.tawhed.ws/r?i=48, (accessed 21 August 2007).

22. Silber and Bhatt, 2007, 35.

23. The classic works include:

Abu Muhammad al-Maqdisi, ملة إبراهيم ودعوة الأنبياء والمرسلين وأساليب الطغاة في تمييعها وصرف الدعاة عنها ("Abraham's People"—The Call of the Prophets and Messengers, and How the Tyrants Dilute it and Steer the Call Away from it) *Minbar al-Tawhid wal-Jihad*. http://www.tawhed.ws/r?i=1, (accessed 21 August 2007); Abdallah ibn Yusuf Azzam, في الجهاد آداب واحكام ("*On Jihad, its Culture and Legal Verdicts*"), *Jihad Publications*, 1987. http://www.tawhed.ws/r?i=1601, (accessed 21 August 2007).

Abdallah ibn Yusuf Azzam, إتحاف العباد بفضائل الجهاد ("*The Gift to the Worshippers on the Virtues of Jihad*"), *Minbar al-Tawhid wal-Jihad*, http://www.tawhed.ws/a?i=77, (accessed August 21 2007); Abdallah ibn Yusuf Azzam, الحق بالقافلة ("*Join the Caravan*"), *Minbar al-Tawhid wal-Jihad*, April 1987, http://www.tawhed.ws/r?i=1600, (accessed 21 August 2007).

24. For example Abu Khubayb and Abu Zubayr: "The Slandered Jihad (Refutation of Jihad Asghar)", *The Path to Paradise*, http://thepathtoparadise.com, (accessed August 21 2007).

25. See Hamud al-Shu'aybi: حكم الجهاد واستئذان الوالدين فيه ("Verdict on Jihad and Seeking Parental Permission"), *Minbar al-Tawhid wal-Jihad*, August 2001, http://www.tawhed.ws/r?i=822, (accessed 22 August 2007).

26. This class of offensive jihad is implied in: Anon. "The Inevitability of the Clash of Civilisation", *Al-Khilafah Publications*, May 2002, http://www.e-prism.org/images/clashofcivilisation.pdf, (accessed 21 August 2007).

27. Anon.: رسالة في الحكم الاصلي في دماء واموال واعراض الكفار ("Essay Regarding the Basic Rule of the Blood, Wealth and Honour of the Disbelievers"), *Tibyan Publications*, August 2004 http://ia310930.us.archive.org/1/ite...sbelievers.pdf (accessed 21 August 2007).

28. This psychological focus is true of even the more strategic works by jihadists. 'Abd al-Qadir bin Abd al-Aziz: "On Equipping for Jihad in Almighty God's Path", *Da'wat al-Tawhid Series*, no. 3. http://www.tawhed.ws/a?i=6, (accessed 21 August 2007).

29. Even one of the most strategically focused works, such as Abu Mus'ab al-Suri's دعوة المقاومة الاسلامية العالمية ("*Call for Global Islamic Resistance*"), devotes sizeable chunks of its 1600 pages to matters bound up closely with the minutiae of Islamic law. In fact, virtually half of the Second Part of the work focuses on character and behaviour, right down to whether the true mujahid should swear at animals; al-Suri, Da'wa, *Unknown*, 2004.

30. Cf. the comments of a UK intelligence official: "It's like the old game of Space Invaders ... when you clear one screen another simply appears to take its place" Rosie Cowan and Richard Norton-Taylor "Britain now No 1 al-Qaeda target—anti-terror chiefs" *The Guardian*, 19 October 2006.

31. A. Ripley, Time Magazine, July 16, 2007: p.23.

32. AIVD, *Violent Jihad in the Netherlands, Current trends in the Islamist terrorist threat*, (Amsterdam: Ministry of the Interior and Kingdom Relations of the Netherlands, 2006), 49.

33. That is "6,000 and counting", according to Loh Chee Kong, "New worry: Homemade extremists" speech at the 6th International Institute of Strategic Studies' Asia Security Conference, Singapore, 2 June 2007.

371

34. "With the aggressive proliferation of the jihadi-Salafi ideology online, it is nearly impossible for someone to avoid this extreme interpretation of Islam." Silber and Bhatt, 2007.

35. The enthusiasm with which the Internet has been co-opted into the service of the jihad can be judged by the quality and quantity of materials in circulation. A number of sites have specialised in hosting entire libraries of doctrinal and ideological materials related to jihad, such as http://tawhed.ws, the site most frequently used by al-Qaeda to host their literature.

36. More precisely—the 'association' of a partner to God.

37. Abu Anas, "Multi-cultural Society or Racist Society?" *Islambase Publications*, http://www.hizb-ut-tahrir.org, (accessed 25 August 2005).

38. The conception of interfaith dialogue as an extension of perennial enmity against Islam is the theme of an entire chapter in the *Hizb al-Tahrir* online publication Anon. "Dangerous Concepts to Attack Islam and Consolidate the Western Culture" *Al-Khilafah Publications*, 2001 http://www.hizb-ut-tahrir.org/index.php/EN/books/, (accessed 21 August 2007). Al-Suri is also explicit on this point. In Chapter 4 of his work *Call for Global Islamic Resistance*, al-Suri divides up the Crusades, not according to the traditional European historical tradition, but into three broader phases: the First Crusades (1090–1291); the Second Crusades (1798–1970) focusing on "the ideological invasion with its consequences for the political domain"; and the Third Crusades (1990-) encapsulated in the "new world order" In this phase al-Suri highlights how America is "co-opting the professional Islamic sector in the 'Battle of Ideas' to distort the faith and snuff out resistance and the jihad. [America does this] by means of distorted collaborationist *fatwas* made under what is termed the fight against terrorism and extremism, and ... under various guises such as 'justice', 'moderation' 'cooperation' and 'dialogue with the other'". See Abu Musʿab al-Suri, دعوة المقاومة الاسلامية العالمية ("*Call for Global Islamic Resistance*"), Unknown, (2004), 897.

39. Shaykh Abdalazīz al-Jarbū. الإعلام بوجوب الهجرة من دار الكفر إلى دار الإسلام ("*The Announcement of the Obligation to Emigrate from the Land of Disbelief to the Land of Islām*") *Minbar al-Tawhīd wal-Jihad*, 2001, http://www.tawhed.ws/r?i=529, (accessed 22 August 2007). Al-Jarbūʿ cites a succinct definition of the obligation by Shaykh Hamad ibn ʿAtīq: "And what is intended (by display of the religion) is the clear demonstration by continuous hostility and hatred towards the one who does not single out His Lord, so whoever fulfils this with knowledge and action, and clearly demonstrates this until the people of his land are aware of this from him, then emigration (*Hijrah*) is not an obligation upon him from whatever land he is in." The *āyah* adduced is: "*Verily, we are free from you and whatever you worship besides Allāh, we have rejected you, and there has emerged between us and you, hostility and hatred for ever, until you believe in Allāh Alone.*" [*Qur'ān*, LX, 4].

40. This explains the confusion suffered by the media on the use of the term "tyrant" to refer to western leaders. The term originally denoted a pre-Islamic idol, and by extension any object or individual that prevents mankind from doing good. In jihadist literature it is commonly used to denote heads of state of Muslim countries that are not governed by Shariah law.

41. The ruling in the German case was subsequently overturned and the judge removed from the case in March 2007. The Canadian Shariah court began work in 1991 when the province of Ontario authorized the use of Shariah law in civil arbitrations, if both parties consented. In 2003 it applied to the government for arbitration status so that their verdict could not be challenged in a Canadian court, but in 2006 the Canadian government passed another law repealing that law of 1991.

42. Shaykh Marzouq Salem Al-Ghamdi at Al-Rahmah mosque in Mecca. Shaykh Marzouq Salem al-Ghamdi, "Contemporary Islamist Ideology Authorizing Genocidal Murder", *MEMRI, Special Report* 25 (2004).

43. "The notion of an Arabic language sanctified by the fact that God had chosen it as the vehicle by which to address humankind was too powerful. Henceforth, correct usage of the grammatical and lexical rules of Arabic is sufficient to ensure the permanent validity of the meanings. Hence the 'linguistic' introductions to works of *usūl al-fiqh*"; Mohammed Arkoun, *Islam: To Reform or To Subvert?* (London: Saqi Books, 2006), 161.

44. Shaykh Abu Baseer al-Tartousi, احذر ثقافة المهزومين ("*Beware of the Culture of the Defeated*") *Abu Baseer Tartousi*, 2000, http://www.abubaseer.bizland.com/, (accessed 22 August 2007).

45. The success of this compartmentalization can be judged from the significant number of technicians of one form or another in the leadership ranks of Islamist movements—engineers, medics, even lawyers of Western jurisprudence. These are practitioners, not innovators. That is, people who have accumulated technical rather than conceptual knowledge in an easily compartmentalised form.

46. 'Abu Anas' "Multi-Cultural Society or Racist Society", *Islambase Publications*, http://www.hizb-ut-tahrir.org, (accessed 25 August 2005).

47. Sheikh Taha Jabir al-Alwani, cited in Eric Brown, "After the Ramadan Affair: New Trends in Islamism in the West" in Hillel Fradkin, Husain Haqqani, and Eric Brown (eds), *Current Trends in Islamist Ideology II*, (Washington: Hudson Institute, 2005), 26.

48. A distinguished victim of this veto on progress was the Sudanese scholar Mahmud Muhammad Taha who was executed in 1985 on charges amounting to those of heresy. His work *The Second Message of Islam* sets out to delineate those aspects of the Qur'ānic text that were specific to the time and place of the Revelation, and those that are of universal application. His argument is that texts such as *Sūrat al-Māʾida* (V, 3): "Today I have perfected your religion for you" and *Sūrat al-Nahl* (XVI, 44): "And We have revealed to you the Reminder so that you may explain to mankind that which has been sent down to them" should not be understood as the end of the process, but rather the beginning: "The Qur'ān can never be finally and conclusively explained. Islam, too, can never be concluded. Progress in it is eternal." Mahmud Muhammad Taha. *The Second Message of Islam*, (New York: Syracuse University Press, 1996), 146–7.

49. Abd al-Qadim Zallum, الديمقراطية نظام كفر يحرم أخذها أو تطبيقها أو الدعوة إليها ("*Democracy is a Kufr System, which it is Forbidden to Adopt, Apply or Promote*") *Hizb al-Tahrir Publications*, 1990, http://www.hizb-ut-tahrir.org/index.php/AR/books, (accessed 22 August 2007), 22.

50. Anon, *Dangerous Concepts to Attack Islam and Consolidate the Western Culture* Al-Khilafah Publications, 1997, 7.

51. This allows for even the most extremist preacher to square the circle of calling for the destruction of the Western system, at the same time as acquiescing in abiding in this system, under its rules.

52. Tartousi, *Beware of the Culture of the Defeated*, 2000.

53. Originally a term referring to Iranian dualists persisting after the Islamic conquests, the term *zindīq* was later used to denote those who opposed the revealed law, or who "personalised" their religion by following allegorical readings of the holy text. Later the term denoted skeptics who applied a critical eye to revelation or tradition, hence: libertines or atheists. Abu Baseer al-Tartousi, in his قوافل زنادقة العصر ("*The Train of Modern Day Zindiqs*") applies the term to modern Muslim and Islamist thinkers such as Hassan Al-Banna, Hassan al-Turabi and Dr Muhammad Sayyid al-Tantawi (Sheikh of Al-Azhar University), for their opposition to the jihadists' literal readings. Abu Baseer al-Tartousi, *Abu Baseer Tartousi*, 2006, قوافل زنادقة العصر, http://www.abubaseer.bizland.com/articles.htm, (accessed 22 August 2007).

54. Tartousi, *Beware of the Culture of the Defeated*, 2000.

55. Steven Stalinsky, "Sheikh Yousef Al-Qaradhawi in London to Establish 'The International Council of Muslim Clerics'" *MEMRI Special Report* no. 30 (2004).

56. Yusuf al-Qaradawi: "Apostasy, Major and Minor, Section on 'Hidden Apostasy'", *Islam Online*, 13 April 2006, www.islamonline.net/English/contemporary/2006/04/article01c.shtml, (accessed 22 August 2007).

57. It is interesting to see how jihadi Salafist thinkers continue to employ the language of hostilities even in the context of Muslims living peaceably in western states. In the work *Essay Regarding the Basic Rule of the Blood, Wealth and Honour of the Disbelievers*, Anon.: رسالة في الحكم الاصلي في دماء واموال واعراض الكفار ("Essay Regarding the Basic Rule of the Blood, Wealth and Honour of the Disbelievers"), *Tibyan Publications*, August 2004, http://ia310930.us.archive.org/1/ite...sbelievers.pdf, (accessed 21 August 2007), constant reference is made to the Muslim abiding peacefully in enemy territory on the basis that there has been a *mutual* exchange of security (*amān*) agreements.

58. An interesting evaluation of the problems of citizenship of Muslim minorities in a liberal state is the work by Andrew March, "Liberal Citizenship and the Search for an Overlapping Consensus: The Case of Muslim Minorities", *Philosophy and Public Affairs*, 34. No. 4 (2006).

59. "Some trends on the ground would suggest that ideological supremacy in the definition of Western Islam is likely to remain a difficult religious obligation for the mainstream Islamists to fulfill. Surely, the West has emerged not simply as a 'Land of *Dawa*' but a land in fact of many Islamic calls." Brown, 2005.

60. al-Suri, 2004, 1160–4.

CONCLUSION

1. Huntington 1996, 64.

2. *Ibid.*, 256; in one of his articles Huntington refers to Gurr who explicitly refutes the "Clash" hypothesis. However, it seems Gurr neglected to define wars that had religious

cleavages as "clash" wars. Ted R. Gurr "People Against States: Ethnopolitical Conflict and the World System", *International Studies Quarterly* 38, no. 3 (1994). See also Ted R. Gurr, *Ethnic Conflict in World Politics* (San Francisco, 1994).

3. Huntington 1996, 64.
4. Gilles Kepel, *The Revenge of God: The Resurgence of Islam, Christianity and Judaism in the modern world* (University Park: Pennsylvania State University Press, 1994), 2.
5. Ibid, 647–9.

See for example, Paul Collier and Anke Hoeffler, "Greed and Grievance in Civil War", *Oxford Economic Papers* 56, no. 11 (2004);.or Tanja Ellingsen, "Towards a revival of religion and religious clashes", *Terrorism and Political Violence* 17, no. 3 (2005), 318.

7. *Ibid.*
8. Haynes 1994; Huntington 1996.

Contributors

Stig Jarle Hansen has a PhD from Aberystwyth, University of Wales, and has specialised in Islamic philosophy as well as political Islam in Somalia. He has been used as an advisor by several governments and has appeared frequently in the media. He is currently a senior researcher at the NIBR Institute in Oslo, Norway.

Atle Mesøy has a Masters degree in International Relations from Aberystwyth, University of Wales. He has been working as a senior analyst for Protocol, contributing to and editing their journal *Strategic Insights*. His field of research is Political Islam. He is currently working on a research project in Africa.

Tuncay Kardas has a PhD from Aberystwyth, University of Wales. He is Assistant Professor of International Relations at Sakarya University in Turkey. He has specialized in International Politics and security studies. His research interests lie in the politics of security and social theory

Andrew Rigby is the author of several books on issues concerning the Israeli/Palestine conflict, including *Living the Intifada*. He is a professor at the Centre for Peace and Reconciliation Studies, Coventry University.

Jørgen Johansen has worked in the Middle East for years and lectured at several universities worldwide. He has published extensively on conflicts and nonviolence.

Hicham Bou Nassif was an assistant professor of international law at the Lebanese University in Beirut, Lebanon, before joining the Phd program at Indiana University, United States. He has studied the Lebanese conflict for most of his life, focusing on the sectarian dynamics of Lebanon and the Middle East.

Antonio Giustozzi, currently based at London School of Economics, works on the security dimension of failed states and states in a critical situation. He also researches the political aspects of insurgency and warlordism and states' response. Recent additions to his fields of study are ethnopolitics and the study of administration-building in recovering states. In recent years, he has mainly been working in and on Afghanistan.

Kavita Khory's scholarship and teaching traverse the fields of international relations and comparative politics. Informed by a variety of disciplinary perspectives, Professor Khory's work ranges from analyzing political violence in South Asia to exploring forms and patterns of migration in global politics and questions of political identity and citizenship in multicultural societies. She has written about nationalism and ethnic conflict in Pakistan, insurgency movement and regional security challenges in South Asia, and the domestic and foreign policy implications of the US war on terror for Pakistan. She has been involved in a number of curricular initiatives at Mount Holyoke, including serving as co-director of a project funded by the Hewett Foundation for promoting the case method across the curriculum.

Kirsten E. Schulze, currently based at the London School of Economics, has worked extensively on political and militant Islam in Indonesia. She has published on the role of Laskar Jihad in the Ambon conflict as well as Indonesia's deradicalisation efforts. She has also published extensively on the ethno-nationalist conflict in Aceh, including her book and questions of political identity and citizenship in multicultural societies.

Ben Reid is a specialist in Philippine and Southeast Asian politics and political economy. His acclaimed book *Philippine Left: Political Crisis and Social Change*, examines the changes that have taken place in Philippine insurgency movements. He is currently lecturing at the University of Bath, United Kingdom.

Sakah Saidu Mahmud is associate professor of political science at Transylvania University in Lexington, Kentucky where he teaches comparative politics of the developing world. His publications include a book *State, Class and Underdevelopment in Nigeria and Early Meji Japan* (Macmillan, and

St. Martin's Press, 1996) and a specialized monograph *Can the Nigerian Democracy Succeed?* (1998) for the Stoke Phelps Foundation, New York. His publications have appeared in Africa Today, Human Rights Quarterly and African Studies Review.

Terje Østebø has been specialising in the role of Islam in Ethiopian society. He is the author of the acclaimed *A history of Islam and inter-religious relations in Bale, Ethiopia* and has conducted intensive field studies on the topic. His PhD submitted at the University of Stockholm, Sweden, specialises in the role of Salafism in Ethiopia. He is currently associate professor at NLA school of religion, education and international studies, Bergen, Norway.

Gérard Prunier is a researcher at the CNRS in Paris and director of the French Centre for Ethiopian Studies in Addis Ababa, he is the author of several acclaimed books including *The Rwanda Crisis: History of a Genocide*, and *Darfur: The Ambiguous Genocide*.

James Hughes is head of the Conflict Studies programme in the Department of Government at the London School of Economics. His research spans the policy responses of democracies and authoritarian states to political violence and terrorism. His geographical focus is Russia; the Balkans; the Caucasus; Northern Ireland; Iraq. His most recent book is *Chechnya: From Nationalism to Jihad* (University of Pennsylvania Press, 2007).

Svein Mønnesland is a professor of Slavic studies at the University of Oslo, Norway. His speciality is former Yugoslavia, language, culture and history. He has been frequently used by the Norwegian press as an expert commentator on Balkan-related issues, he has also lectured for the Norwegian Department of Defence as well as for the Norwegian Ministry of Foreign Affairs, as well as published several books.

Elena Arigita graduated in Arabic and Islamic studies from the University of Granada and pursued further study in Cairo, Egypt, where she also taught Spanish at the University of Cairo and Al-Azhar Islamic University (1995–1999). Her PhD thesis focused on institutional Islam in modern-day Egypt. From 2004–2006 she was a postdoctoral fellow at the Institute for the Study of Islam in the Modern World (ISIM) in Leiden, Netherlands. She is a member of a research group on Contemporary Arab Studies at the University of Granada, and is currently a senior researcher at Casa-IEAM in Cordoba.

Dominique Thomas is a specialist in Islamic movements at the École des Hautes Études en Sciences Sociales, France. He has been the author of acclaimed books as *Londonistan: Le Djihad au Coeur de l'Europe* and *Le Londonistan: la voix du Djihad*.

Farhad Khosrokhavar has been professor at the École des Hautes Études en Sciences Sociales, France, since 1998. He has published extensively on Iran and Islam in Europe: *Suicide Bombers: The New Martyrs of Allah* (Pluto Press, London, 2005); *Muslims in Prison*, with James Beckford and Danièle Joly (Palgrave Publishers, London, 2006); *Inside Jihadism: Understanding Jihadi Movements Worldwide* (The Yale Cultural Sociology Series) by 2008.

Allen Hertzke is Presidential Professor of political science at the University of Oklahoma. He is author of several books, including *Freeing God's Children, The Unlikely Alliance for Global Human Rights*; and co-author of *Religion and Politics in America*. Hertzke is a frequent news commentator; he has been featured in *The New York Times, Washington Post, Wall Street Journal, Weekly Standard, L.A. Times, National Review, BBC World Service, PBS, National Public Radio*, and *Swedish Radio*.

Stephen Ulph is Senior Fellow at the Jamestown Foundation and specializes in the literature of Islamist radicalism on the Internet. He is the founder editor of Jamestown's *Terrorism Focus* and of both *Islamic Affairs Analyst* and *Terrorism & Security Monitor* for Jane's Information Group, and lectures widely on the 'radicalization curriculum' and on counter-ideology.

Index